Yale Studies in Political Science, 25

Modern Social Politics in Britain and Sweden

From Relief to Income Maintenance

Hugh Heclo

New Haven and London, Yale University Press

Designed by John O.C. McCrillis
and set in Baskerville type.
Printed in the United States of America by
Thomson–Shore, Inc.
Dexter, Michigan

Published in Great Britain, Europe, and Africa by
Yale University Press, Ltd., London.
Distributed in Latin America by Kaiman & Polon,
Inc., New York City; in India by UBS Publishers'
Distributors Pvt., Ltd., Delhi;
in Japan by John Weatherhill, Inc., Tokyo.

For

Richard and Kay Titmuss

"...we learned that in quiet places
reason abounds, that in quiet people
there is vision and purpose..."

Contents

Preface

At the time this research began, in 1967, policy studies appeared a largely untended field of political science, and comparative policy studies seemed in a positively virginal state. Since then, at least four new periodicals (*Policy Sciences, Policy Studies Journal, Journal of Social Policy,* and *European Journal*) on the subject have materialized; policy study groups have grown up in the American Political Science Association and European Consortium for Political Research; policy sessions have been completed or threatened at conferences of the Committee on Political Sociology, Social Science Research Council, International Political Science Association, Ford Foundation, and other groups in a moveable feast from the United States to Canada, the West Indies, Western Europe, Eastern Europe—even Scotland. Such are academic fashions that the virgin is now threatened less with neglect and more with abuse.

When research addresses the real world, there are at least four ways in which it can fail: (1) it may ask the wrong questions, (2) it may seek answers in the wrong way, (3) the real world may withhold the answer, (4) the answer may be wrongly perceived and interpreted. Each danger is of course fatal, but the first—asking the wrong question—seems the most disastrous of the foursome. Faulty interpretation or incompletely revealed truths about the real world may not necessarily preclude advances in technique; even poor methodology can be forgiven if good questions stimulate others to search out better ways of finding important answers. But poor questions waste everyone's time from start to finish; moreover, poor questions, rather than stimulating more insightful work, only tend to bore and exasperate people into thinking less. The methodology of this study is less than clinical (although the idea of starting with a simple question and organizing results into answers to discern larger patterns has been given the imposing title of "guided retroduction").* Its interpretations are certainly open to argument, although the body of evidence has been presented as impartially as possible to facilitate other interpretations. If nothing else, however, I have tried to pose an interesting question.

*N. R. Hanson, *Patterns of Discovery* (Cambridge: Cambridge University Press, 1958).

The aim of this volume is to compare social policy making in Britain and Sweden and to assess the effect of democratic politics on the development of income maintenance policies during the last century. Although I shall be concerned with the contemporary history of the welfare state, this is far from a historians' history book. Economic doctrine is an essential part of the story, but, as my economist friends are quick to remind me, this is not an economic study. Students of sociology and social administration will recognize the issues of social change and descriptions of policy content, but this discussion is for me only the means to another end. That end is political understanding. For too long students of politics have been apologetic about approaching substantive public policy. My purpose in rummaging through recent and long forgotten struggles in the welfare state is to appreciate better the political process and its relationship to the collective social choices embedded in public policy. In doing so, I hope that something will also have been said to interest historians, economists, sociologists, and students of social administration.

Ideally the data for this study would have consisted of a vast collection of case studies, each case covering a major policy decision and employing a unified analytic framework. Such a collection unfortunately does not exist and could only be created by a large team of co-ordinated researchers working over many years. Perhaps that day will come in comparative policy analysis, but there is already a body of good, if less than ideal, monographic data upon which secondary analysis can build. One of the more crippling misconceptions in recent social science has been the presumption that original research consists solely in original data gathering. The result is a scholarly premium on writing new accounts and a dearth of cumulative studies trying to knit together what has already been learned. In particular areas dealt with here—the development of Swedish unemployment insurance and British superannuation—there is little existing research, so original data have been compiled and presented in the text.

In other areas I have built upon the excellent work of scholars interested in particular policies and periods. My first obligation is to those who so generously aided my research in this way: Bentley Gilbert, Pat Thane Williams, José Chambers Harris, Allen Murie, Bertil Ohman, Åke Elmér, Joseph Board, and Charles Hanser. All allowed me to read and discuss their unpublished manuscripts with them; all were more patient than a poorly informed outsider deserved. Others of my creditors have been involved in making as well as writing about policy; fortunately they were also willing to talk about policy, and I have profited greatly from my discussions in both nations with Ernst Michanek, Pierre Vinde, Jan Nasenius, Per Holmberg, D. N. Chester, Richard Dale, Brian Abel-Smith, and Sir John Walley. Many others in political parties, interest groups, and civil services were kind enough to devote time to answering my questions on contemporary policy developments, but they must remain anonymous. I hope the results here will seem a fair, if not always favorable, return on their investment. F. Scott Fitzgerald said that there are always some kisses which nature does not intend, and I am doubly grateful that one by-product of this research has been the formation of many friendships among members of my "data base." Far from contaminating the objectivity of my analysis, these relations have helped provide the openness to serious, often vehement argument which good friendships and good research require.

Data should be worth thinking about for at least as long as they have taken to gather. Many have helped me do so by reading and commenting on parts of the manuscript and/or its logic: Robert Dahl, James Fesler, Robert Lane, Charles E. Lindblom, Theodore Marmor, Martin Rein, Gaston Rimlinger, and Stein Rokkan. In particular my thanks go to three mentors who succored manuscript drafts and author in good times and bad. Joseph LaPalombara stirred an interest in realistic comparative research despite a host of arid graduate school requirements; Aaron Wildavsky showed the joys of tight analysis, crisp expression and, later, coauthorship; Richard Rose, during a dark winter in Manchester, performed perhaps the most surprising feat by first making political science seem as interesting as politics.

Above all there is my debt to Richard Titmuss, who taught by example the moral basis of a commitment to welfare.

There is much injustice in relegating my mother and my wife Beverley to an expression of gratitude for technical assistance, but both provided one of the most demanding and rare of professional services—expert secretarial aid—without pay. Cecilia Dohrmann worked through portions of the final version on an underpaid basis. I am also grateful to the Foreign Area Fellowship Program and Danforth Foundation for funds supporting full and part-time work on this research. All Swedish quotations in the text are my translations from the original, a sufficient explanation for any awkwardness of expression in these passages. Swedish linguists be warned.

Finally, I thank my former New Haven and Washington colleagues and in particular William Bacchus, who fulfilled the promise of his family name. If not always inspiration, there was at least commiseration. That is not a small thing among scribblers, who must bear the same relation to their creations as Burns's fieldmouse to its home:

> That wee bit heap o' leaves an' stibble,
> Has cost thee monie a weary nibble;
> Now thou's turned out, for a' thy trouble . . .
> To thole the winter's sleety dribble.

30 Old Queen Street
London
August 1972

Hugh Heclo

1 Politics and Social Policy

One of the things most astonishing to posterity about our own times will be not how much we understood but how much we took for granted. We revel in every new excuse to label our times revolutionary; ours is the atomic/permissive/electronic/affluent/space age. Attention centers on the glittering pageant and dramatic incident, rather than on the elusive processes that evoke the incidents. Revolutions must be visible, palpable, and immediate, although it is the annual change of only one percent that can produce some of the greatest transformations. Paradoxically, a glib preoccupation with the "revolutionary" has tended to reduce our sensitivity to change itself.

For anyone interested in the human terms of politics, perhaps the must fundamental change that is taken for granted is the growth of modern social policy. Occurring within the span of three or four human generations, it entails a transformation that writers of the 1930s and '40s were accustomed to call "a new phase in man's history."[1] Almost the only time our great grandfather came in direct contact with the state was when he posted a letter or encountered a policeman. No passport or code number identified him as a citizen and virtually all of what he earned he disposed of as he saw fit. Although the government might try to protect him from several infectious diseases, the ideal citizen was the independent citizen paying his own way and needing no public help, Positive state social policy was reserved largely for that distinct and small residue who did not pay their own way and fell upon the poor rates. Such public relief went not to the poor but to paupers, a group who paid for the support of the community by being stigmatized and set apart as something less than full citizens. The vast majority, however, could live and hardly notice the state.

Today, in most industrialized nations, the citizen finds much of what he earns disposed of by the state. A great deal of this money goes to provide for his future before any question arises of his personal inability to help himself. If he is ill or becomes injured, if he grows old or is

1. H. L. Beales, *The Making of Social Policy*, p. 3; an earlier appreciation of the phenomena under way is in Ernest Barker, *The Development of Administration, Conscription, Taxation, Social Services, and Education.*

1

unable to find a job, if his mate bears children or dies, if he seeks housing or education, some explicit or implicit involvement with a state social policy is almost unavoidable. The citizen so involved will be regarded not as an outcast but as part of the vast majority and often as exercising a right of his citizenship. Of course almost every activity of national governments has grown in the last hundred years. But while the rate of total government spending in industrialized nations has grown perhaps 80 to 90 times in real terms during this period, the rate of spending on social policy has probably mushroomed by 5,000 to 6,000 times. If one could imagine the thousands of laws, the millions of written pages, the hundreds of millions of discussions from cabinet tables to kitchen tables—in short all the actions and reactions that have intervened in the last century to bring about this transformation, then perhaps the words *pageant* and *revolution* are not overly dramatic.

When such changes in social provision by government are identified, they have usually acquired the collective label *welfare state,* a term again suggesting a dramatic upheaval somehow spontaneously created after World War II and outside historical time. In this study, I prefer to use the term *social policy* to designate state interventions designed to affect the free play of market forces in the interests of citizens' welfare. This welfare objective can take a number of forms, three of the most prominent being investment (e.g. education), consumption (public assistance payments), and compensation (industrial injuries). But whatever form it takes, the distinguishing mark of social policy seems to be its character as a unilateral transfer, in contrast to the bilateral exchange of a market.[2] The changes of the last century represent the expansion of state transfer programs from the narrow and disqualifying relief of the poor law to a vast range of transfers by right, including pensions, health care, unemployment insurance, housing subsidies, education benefits, and many others.

How, politically, has this transformation to modern social policy come about?

From Politics to Policy

The substance of the last century's revolution in social policy has been largely the province of sociologists. Understandably, their interpretations have stressed social rather than political relationships.

2. Elaborations on the meanings of social policy and the welfare state are in T. H. Marshall, "The Welfare State: A Sociological Interpretation" and "Value Problems of Welfare-Capitalism"; and Richard Titmuss, *Commitment to Welfare.*

What are the forms of collective provision and how have these changed, under what social conditions have policies been created, and what is their effect on family and community life—these are the kinds of issues typically considered in tracing the development of the nineteenth-century poor law into contemporary social policies.

This study will approach the same phenomena from a more political perspective by asking how political forces have influenced the advent and extension of modern social policy. Rather than trying to discover a comprehensive theory of social causation or the ultimate sources of modern social policy, I shall look at proximate sources and causes. How have issues of social policy arisen; where have the substantive ideas about what to do come from; what is the process by which they have been politically accepted and changed through time—in short, how have governments come to do the specific things they do? The discussion does not emphasize political factors because of any belief in an either/or separation between political and social agents. Quite the opposite. The major premise behind this study is that politics is inextricably rooted in society. My aim in concentrating on political factors is to appreciate better the ways in which the politics of public policy serves as the handmaiden of social adaptation. The political contribution to making and changing collective arrangements of social policy can be called social politics.

Although expressed at a high level of philosophical and normative abstraction, a concern with public policy has for centuries been at the heart of Western political thought. Reflections on how men should govern and be governed have addressed policy on the broadest scale, that is, policies for making policies. Only with the twentieth-century ascendance of behavioral over normative approaches has public policy receded somewhat from the center of political studies. Comte once traced the advance of the "positive spirit" through successive applications of the objective method—from mathematics to physics to chemistry to biology, and finally to sociology, the study of man himself. A fanciful person might perceive a similar progression of self-consciousness in behavioral studies of the state—from elections and parties to interest groups to institutional behavior, and most recently to public policy itself. Whatever the sequence, it does seem true that the systematic, behavioral study of the state's own activities as distinctive phenomena in society is just awakening.[3]

3. Some of this ferment in policy studies is discussed in Heclo, "Review Article: Policy Analysis." Auguste Comte's schema is set out in *A Discourse on the Positive Spirit*.

Unfortunately, the term *policy* has become so fashionable that it may now becloud more than it reveals. As used here, policy will designate a course of action or inaction pursued under the authority of government. It is employed as a concept at the middle-range level of analysis, larger than a decision (for example, increase benefits this year, extend coverage to women) and smaller than a social movement (for example, womens' rights, working-class mobilization). A policy may or may not be made up of a series of decisions; it may or may not contribute to a social movement.

Similarly, it is useful to distinguish a policy from a program. Programs are those specifically enacted pieces of legislation and regulation that are administered by government officials. While a policy may be expressed through programs, it seems unduly constricting to exclude from the meaning of policy courses of state action without programmatic backing. A policy can consist of what is not as well as what is being done or, as Winston Churchill once described British defense policy, courses of inaction where governments are "decided only to be undecided, resolved to be irresolute, adamant for drift, all powerful for impotence." One may find, for example, that there is no pension provision through state programs but that a public policy is consistently expressed through the free hand given to private pension companies.

Is policy more than an intended course of action? While the term is often used in everyday speech as if it were synonymous with intellectual resolve, we will find it useful to assume that a statement of purpose does not itself constitute the sum of a policy. The purpose of a policy maker is certainly one of the factors creating policy, but the purpose may or may not coincide with the policy itself. For example, the main purpose of the men who designed the 1834 British poor law undoubtedly was to reorganize the treatment of the poor in a scientific way that would benefit all concerned; the policy as it existed was something viciously different. The term *outputs* has occasionally been used to distinguish the intended policy result from unintended, often broader, effects (outcomes).

The point of distinguishing policies from programs, decisions, social movements, and intentions is to suggest that policy is not a self-evident, independent behavior fact. Policy acquires meaning because an observer perceives and interprets a course of action amid the confusions of a complex world. Policy exists by interrogating rather than by intuiting political phenomena.

Policy analysis can, of course, serve a variety of purposes. It is customary to label studies as being concerned with policy making or content or impact. Historically, most academic emphasis (in the postwar United States at least) has been on the process of making policy, while reformers have called for greater attention to content; studies of policy effects have usually run a poor third. There can be some question whether these distinctions have caused more mischief than anything else in policy studies, and this book eschews any once-and-for-all choice among the three orientations. In a study of this broad scope, a complete separation would be misleading for one important reason: the content of a policy can itself be a crucial independent factor in producing effects on the policy-making process. E. E. Schattschneider, in his early and still immensely readable study, *Politics, Pressures, and the Tariff,* put the point succinctly: "New policies create new politics" (p. 288). As we shall see throughout our discussion, even the most innovative creations are decisively shaped by the content of previous policy.

There is another reason we cannot realistically hope to deal with process in isolation. Explaining the making of policy assumes we have a good idea of what is being made. But in fact, political studies have tended to ignore the substantive policy developments that call for an explanation. It would be naïve in the extreme to begin by assuming that social policies express simply the inexorable historical advance of equity, equality, or social justice ideals. We cannot, for example, refer to a nation's pension or unemployment policy and expect the important issues to be readily intelligible. A good deal of this study must, therefore, be devoted to a basic descriptive mapping of policy contents and the contours of change.

The same comments apply with even greater force to using the policy process to explain not only contents but also impacts. Political party bargaining, interest-group pressure, administrative politics, and so on are of little intrinsic interest to most people and understandably so. It would require a remarkably stunted aesthetic sense to study politics, even the politics of social policy, for its own sake. The only ultimately satisfying answer I know to the infuriating and invaluable question "so what?" is that such matters affect people's lives. Yet for almost any policy one cares to choose, there is little systematic evidence of impact—on clients or anything else. No one can be certain, for example, that the typical individual who falls ill, becomes unemployed, or in any other way is deprived of his working power receives very much more today in humane social care than he did 300 years ago through village and agrarian family life. What has demonstrably changed is the organization of much social provision into immense national programs. It is on this organizational change and on the impact of policy on subsequent state action that my attention will be focused. Lacking any reliable evidence, I can discuss the vital human impact of national social policy only insofar as it has given rise to dissatisfactions expressed in the policy process. But it is better to face up to the "so what" question at the beginning than to meet it unexpectedly at the end.

Limited knowledge about changes in policy contents and consequences has not prevented writers from debating the nature of the political forces behind the changes. Four major interpretations have been advanced at one time or another, and each explanation can alert us to possibly important relationships in the historical record.

The most pervasive tradition identifies the electoral process and party competition as central to policy formation in democratic states.[4] Few suggest that elections permit citizens to participate directly in policy formulation; rather, writers such as Schumpeter and Lipset have argued that elections allow indirect popular guidance through choice among competitors for public office. Those in office are thus held accountable for what they have done, and those both in and out of office can seek the favor of electors on the basis of what they promise to do. Using the analogy of the reactions of business firms to consumer preferences, Anthony Downs has posited the most direct relationship: electoral competitors formulate policies in order to win elections, rather than win elections in order to formulate policies. Others have suggested that the primary manifestation of electoral accountability is more indirect and stems largely from the policy makers' expectations of the likely responses of voters.

The democratic influence of elections and parties has usually been considered particularly important in the development of modern social

4. Although emphasis and claims differ, a range of views based on this interpretation can be found in A. V. Dicey, *Law and Public Opinion in England*; E. F. M. Durbin, *The Politics of Democratic Socialism*; Robert A. Dahl, *A Preface to Democratic Theory*; Robert A. Dahl and Charles E. Lindblom, *Politics, Economics, and Welfare*; Patrick Rooke, *The Growth of the Social Services*; S. M. Lipset, *Political Man*; Joseph Schumpeter, *Capitalism, Socialism, and Democracy*; Anthony Downs, *An Economic Theory of Democracy*. V. O. Key identified policy preferences as important for marginal shifts in usual party loyalty in the U.S. but did not trace these effects to resulting policies. V. O. Key, *The Responsible Electorate*.

policies, because these policies are thought to be of most direct interest to electoral "consumers." The extension of democratic political forms is said to have provided greater popular control of leaders, who responded over the years with the broader welfare policies the electorate wanted. Certainly this interpretation has permeated every debate on wider popular participation, having been shared both by conservatives who feared and by socialists who relished the results of more democratic competition. If this view is correct, we may expect that the existence of an extended suffrage, organized mass parties, and parliamentary government should be associated with a more generous social policy—with, for example, more risks covered, easier benefit conditions, more responsive increases in rates, and so on.

A second interpretation has emphasized interest-group power as the decisive force behind the development of policy.[5] While some have stressed the importance of popular agitation groups to achieve specific reforms, others have considered institutionalized interests such as labor and business groups to be increasingly important in policy making. Concepts of indirect popular control have shaded into group theory through an interpretation of policy changes as a defensive accommodation by power holders to threats posed by groups of non-power holders. However broadly *group* may be defined, the common theme is that conflicts, bargains, and accommodations among the various interested groups are seen to play the crucial part in shaping final policies. If this is the case, the observer may be able to identify the stands taken by individual groups and find evidence that their voices have been particularly important in influencing government actions.

Except under the most inclusive group theory, administrative officials and state organizations are usually considered a distinctive source of public policy. A third interpretation of policy making has placed greatest emphasis on the internal workings of government itself.[6] Evaluations range from the everyday compromises of bureaucratic politics to more far-reaching claims to see tacit state/interest-group conspiracies or a new administrative elite. Careful historical research

5. A summary of the extensive interest group literature is in Harry Eckstein and David Apter, *Comparative Politics*. Recent interpretations in this vein are Theodore Lowi, *The End of Liberalism*: J. W. Peltason and J. M. Burns, *Functions and Policies of American Government*; and on social policy in particular, Frances Piven and Richard Cloward, *Regulating the Poor*.

6. See, for example, Piet Thoenas, *The Elite in the Welfare State*; Emmette Redford, *Democracy and the Administrative State*; and Oliver McDonagh, *A Pattern of Government Growth, 1800–1860: The Passenger Acts and Their Enforcement*.

has suggested the self-reinforcing nature of administrative involvement in early social policies, as pragmatic responses to industrial problems lead to official demands for more effective enforcement, wider regulation, and greater administrative discretion. Taking this interpretation, one may expect to find an increasing role in the formulation of social policy being played by relevant officials, co-opted experts, investigatory bodies, and bureaucratic entrepreneurs.

Finally, some have argued that political forces as such are distinctly secondary to socioeconomic changes in creating modern welfare policies. The amount of economic resources, extent of industrialization, and attendant social disruptions of family and community life are sometimes seen as the main factors behind the creation of national policy responses in any country. Early analyses of aggregate relationships between socioeconomic and political variables on the one hand and policy outputs on the other seemed to suggest few independent political effects among the states in the United States; later correlation research has tended to reestablish the importance of political differences when the timing and redistributive nature of policy (rather than absolute expenditure levels alone) are taken into account. One of the rare international comparisons has demonstrated little consistent difference (education being the major exception) in expenditure output between capitalist and communist nations along a large number of policy dimensions.[7]

These four interpretations are not mutually exclusive and do not by any means exhaust possible explanations for the growth of modern social policy. Moreover, all four factors may be mixed, and conceivably the mixture will vary both with different policies and with different stages of the same policy. Each does, however, set out what has been a major line of inquiry, and the importance of each is not intuitively obvious. Did unemployment insurance, for example, develop from counterbidding among parties for working-class votes, from union or socialist pressure, from enlightened administrators, or from a random mixture of actors depending on the stage of economic development? Since social science findings tend to sound self-evident in retrospect,

7. Frederick Pryor, *Public Expenditure in Capitalist and Communist Nations*. Good reviews of the literature trying to relate political variables to policy outputs are John Fenton and Donald Chamberlayne, "The Literature Dealing with the Relationships between Political Processes, Socio-economic Conditions, and Public Politics in the American States"; Brian Fry and Richard Winters, "The Politics of Redistribution"; and Walter Dean Burnham, "Some Relationships between Electoral Politics and Policy Outputs in the United States."

it is as well to begin by noting that all of these interpretations are plausible but difficult to integrate with each other.

Two features stand out in most attempts to assess the political bases of social policy. First is the tendency to consider the role of political factors in isolation rather than in interaction through time. Analysis typically involves listing the important "who's" of policy making—parties, voters, interest-group representatives, administrators, or, more abstractly, socioeconomic development. Attempts to knit the factors together have usually taken the form of disputing whether policy is an expression of elitism or pluralism, of control by a coherent few or of multicentered adjustment among a great many.

This study begins from the premise that social policy is not like a shoe or a loaf of bread; it is too complex to be explained simply as the predicate of some "maker." We should seek to examine not only who has contributed to social policy but how their contributions have been related. We should inquire not only how things work but how, if at all, the working of things has changed through time. How do policy choices occur without anyone deliberately making them? Do elitism and pluralism coexist in social policy making and, if so, how do they fit together? Is there evidence that policy has been increasingly derived from state/interest-group collaboration, from internal processes of institutionalized parties, from organizing client groups?

A second feature of most political interpretations is to consider the role of politics in policy making as almost exclusively a question of power. Insofar as politics is concerned, policy is said to change because of changes in the relations of power.[8] State social policy alters as power shifts among participants, who then institute their conceptions of narrower or broader interests. Yet unless power is so broadly conceived as to explain everything—in which case it accounts for nothing—it is not intuitively obvious that social policy has developed solely or largely as an outgrowth of power. Whether important policy changes are traceable to the arrival of interest groups in or at the fringes of office, to the play of power among administrators, to party responses to newly enfranchised voters, and so on are empirical questions. And where changes in the exercise or location of power do seem important spurs to action, can we infer the substance of what is done from identity of the power holders? If not, how has policy content been derived politically?

8. See, for example, Vernon Van Dyke, "Process and Policy as Focal Concepts," in *Political Science and Public Policy*, ed. Austin Ranney, pp. 31ff.

In trying to bring evidence to bear on these questions, we can begin to reassess not only the power orientation but the way in which public policy links politics and society.

Tracking the Intractable

Answers to questions such as the ones I have raised are not only far from obvious; they also yield but little to analysis in the aggregate. There are, however, a few regularities. The invention and diffusion of social programs does not appear to be a random phenomenon. If one charts the diffusion of state income-maintenance programs that cover major sources of income insecurity (occupational accident, sickness and maternity, old age and invalidism, unemployment, large family size), at least three things become clear (see Figure 1).

First, these forms of social provision have spread internationally; adoption of a program in one country has been followed by adoption in other countries. Second, the different forms have been associated internally; adoption of one program has usually been followed in the

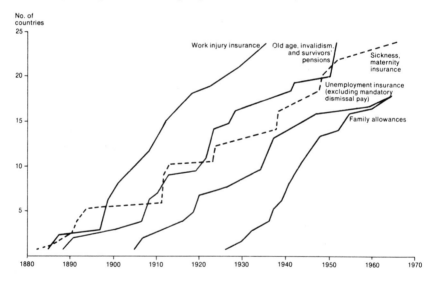

Figure 1. The Diffusion of Income Maintenance Programs

Source: Based on Gordon, *Study of Potential Changes in Employee Benefits*, Vol. 2, Figure 16, p. 45. The 24 nations are: Australia, Austria, Belgium, Brazil, Canada, Chile, People's Republic of China, Denmark, France, West Germany, Great Britain, India, Iran, Israel, Italy, Japan, Mexico, Netherlands, New Zealand, South Africa, Sweden, USSR, UAR, and USA.

same country by adoption of the other programs. Finally, despite what is declared to be an accelerating rate of diffusion in technological innovation, the rate of diffusion in these social innovations appears to have changed little in the last century. Between 50 and 80 years is the likely diffusion time for all such programs. Clearly there seems to be more at work than isolated "makers" of policy and idiosyncratic power relations. Yet aggregate analysis of even the simple dates of statutory enactment raises more questions than it answers. In several programs, authoritarian Imperial Germany leads the United States despite the latter's older male suffrage and mass party competition; late economic developers such as Scandinavia lead the first industrial nation, Great Britain. A nation like Germany may lead in some programs (for example, workmen's compensation) and lag in others (for example, family allowances).

General policy relationships become even murkier when we look at more complex and informative characteristics than dates of first enactment. Many writers have tried, for example, to relate absolute expenditures, rates of benefit increase, and other broad policy features to levels of economic development.[9] Some have concluded that social security spending (as a share of national income) rises with economic development; others have found evidence of just the opposite; still others have observed that vaguer, noneconomic factors, such as history and geography, account for up to four-fifths of the international differences in the proportion of national wealth going to social security programs. Overall patterns often seem to depend on the particular programs in question; certain benefits, such as state sickness payments or basic old age pensions, appear to be relatively higher (in relation to national average earnings) in developing than in developed nations. Social expenditure commitments seem on the average to be determined primarily by the age of the program, but other studies have shown this relation to hold in some areas of social policy and not in others.

The adequacy of basic state pensions (in relation to consumer ex-

9. These and succeeding findings are contained in Koji Taira and Peter Kilby, "Differences in Social Security Development in Selected Countries"; Paul Fisher, "Minimum Old Age Pensions"; Franco Reviglio, "The Social Security Sector and Its Financing in Developing Countries"; Felix Paukert, "Social Security and Income Redistribution: A Comparative Study"; Henry Aaron, "Social Security: International Comparisons," in *Studies in the Economics of Income Maintenance*, ed. Otto Eckstein; and Joseph Pechman, Henry Aaron, and Michael Taussig, *Social Security: Perspectives for Reform;* Guy Peters, Economic and Political Effects on the Development of Social Expenditures in France, Sweden and the United Kingdom," *Midwest Journal of Political Science,* 16 (1972).

penditures, assistance benefits, or poverty standards) demonstrates little clear pattern at all between the dozen or so countries for which data exist. Ranking nations by ratios of social security expenditures to total current government spending shows a third of the developed nations placing higher than the most developed nation, the United States; use of general tax revenue (as opposed to separate employer-employee contributions) to pay for social security varies as much among developed as between developed and undeveloped countries. The degree of financing by special earmarked taxes seems important for the magnitude of some programs, but not perhaps for others. Few if any of these variations clearly differentiate groups of capitalist and socialist nations. Moreover, all of these findings seriously oversimplify policy by considering largely gross expenditure levels and formal rather than operational provisions of the law.

In short, a few overall policy relationships are apparent, but the variations within any group of nations are likely to be at least as interesting as variations between groups. Policy patterns do not flow straightforwardly from analysis of general correlations among aggregated variables. The policy process seems too delicate for that. Understanding how, or whether, politics has affected the advent of modern social policy seems to depend less on statistically unearthing and more on inductively building up generalizations from detailed if somewhat less tidy accounts. This study tries to look not at isolated, timeless factors in many settings but at strands of development in a few settings.

But where and how to find the evidence? There is not a single decision dealt with in this book that could not alone have occupied at least a year's study of just how and why it occurred. Even if there were the resources to approach such finality, however, common sense would require that the investigation be limited to what seems sufficient to arrive at reasonably probable answers to the question posed; in any event, no one would care to read 200 pages on the amendment of the 1922 Pension Act. Settling on a level of analysis requires choices about the scope of policies to be covered, the number of countries, and the period to study.

In its broadest terms, the welfare state is identical to the first half of Aristotle's dichotomy of states into just governments that rule in the interest of all and despotic governments that rule in the interest of the rulers.[10] Our policy terrain must be more limited. Of the many social

10. *Politics*, Book III, Chap. 6.

policies in existence, this study will concentrate upon what are known as *income maintenance policies,* that is, state actions with the object of providing alternate income when normal private sources have been permanently or temporarily interrupted. The heart of the last century's revolution in social policy is the change from punitive and disqualifying poor law approaches to a new conception of guaranteed social rights of citizenship. Throughout this period it is the question of cash payments for income loss that has infolded the basic change from public aid as a matter of sufferance to public aid as a matter of right.

Among the many income maintenance policies, I will focus attention upon three of the most important. Unemployment insurance is now one of the smaller income maintenance programs, but the issues it has raised have been pivotal to the last century's social politics. As we shall see, much of the history of the poor law and the shaping of modern social policy have revolved around what to do about the "able-bodied" poor who do not work. Almost by accident, unemployment insurance became involved in this central controversy and, more than any other income program, determined the nature and timing of modern welfare legislation.[11] A second policy area, which counterbalances the small physical scale of unemployment insurance programs, is old-age pensions. In the sheer number of citizens aided and amount of money spent, old age pensions have become the largest single social undertaking for most national governments in the West. The development of these basic state pensions will constitute the second leg of this study. Finally, I turn to a more recent area of social policy growth—state superannuation. Although in some ways an extension of old age pensions, plans for earnings-related occupational insurance are also, as we shall see, a far-reaching departure from many traditional social policy assumptions. These three topics—pensions, superannuation, and unemployment insurance—are not all of income maintenance policy, nor is income maintenance policy by any means all of social policy. They are selected as strategic rather than representative. It will always be appropriate to recall that our generalizations are derived from what is only a portion of a very complex body of social provision in modern society.

By their nature, the questions asked require more than a case study of one or two contemporary decisions. To study the advent of any

11. A general appreciation is in Asa Briggs, "The Welfare State in Historical Perspective," and T. H. Marshall, *Class, Citizenship, and Social Development.*

part of modern social policy is to confront a complex series of changes over a fairly long period of time. The most relevant period for pensions and unemployment insurance extends back 90 years to the 1880s; superannuation is largely a post-World War II phenomenon. If we are to appreciate the cumulative effect of politics on social policy and substantive feedbacks from inherited policy itself, we must be willing to dig in these long historical records and not stop at momentary cuts in time.

Similarly, a study of policy in only one country would provide little basis at all for generalization. National social policies have usually been treated as *sui generis,* and perhaps there is good reason to do so. The point is that we cannot readily judge in the abstract whether doing so is justified. Identifying the probable effect of any given factor, such as party competition, depends heavily on observing its operation in at least two contexts. Even if one agrees that every national experience is unique, that uniqueness becomes fully perceptible only in relation to other nations. Ideally, all major countries, or at least a somewhat representative selection of countries, would be included in such a study, but given the vast amount of historical information on any one policy in any one country, two may be the maximum feasible number for any one researcher. Even then the account may seem superficial to each nation's professional historians. The aim, however, is not to rewrite history but to reanalyze the history that has been written and to do so with an eye to more general political/policy relationships in comparative sites. Thus, I have sought to find two countries that, if not necessarily representative, were at least strategic in understanding social politics; each country should be intrinsically important in the development of modern social policy, and each should be amenable to comparative analysis.

In any account of twentieth-century social policy, Great Britain and Sweden must command special prominence. Each nation falls among the first innovators in what became a worldwide diffusion of social programs (see Figure 1, p. 10). Sweden, with the world's first national pension program for all citizens, and Britain, with the world's first national unemployment insurance program, have for years been at the forefront of social policy changes and have often served as models to other nations. Since the 1930s, when Sweden stood out as an oasis of good sense, it has held a popular reputation as a home of the most advanced social policy. The so-called "Beveridge Report," issued from the depths of the Second World War, gave Britain a uniquely prominent position as the home of (the label it coined itself) the welfare state.[12] It would be difficult to find two nations of greater intrinsic importance to the history of social policy. While conclusions reached for Britain and Sweden may not necessarily be representative or applicable elsewhere, we may be sure that any general theory that does not account for the experiences of these two nations is likely to be inadequate.

Britain and Sweden are also well suited to comparative analysis. On the one hand, differences are not so great as to smother the points of comparison. Each is a north European nation with a relatively homogeneous population of common racial and cultural characteristics. Unlike Germany, each has a continuous territorial integrity and has maintained its national independence throughout the modern era. Each also has among the most reliable statistical records in the world. On the other hand, there are important contrasts between Britain and Sweden that lend themselves to our comparative interests. Britain stands as the first industrial nation, Sweden among the last in Europe. In political terms, substantial differences arose in timing the introduction of democratic elections, parliamentary government, and mass parties. By the outbreak of World War I, Britain had a long history of electoral politics and parliamentary government, while predemocratic Sweden lagged in both. Within a broader international perspective, Sweden is often seen as closely related to Bismarckian influences, with social policy serving as an antisocialist tool of nineteenth-century, mildly anticapitalist conservatives. British experience, along with that of related Commonwealth nations, is often interpreted as an accommodation of classic liberalism to the politically felt needs of the workers. The validity of such shorthand expressions for extremely complex series of events is of course an empirical question. Therefore while neither Britain nor Sweden is a "pure" case of anything, there are suggestive contrasts and useful similarities that promise to make comparisons worthwhile.

---

12. William Beveridge, *Social Insurance and Allied Services*. On Sweden's leadership, see Marquis Childs, *Sweden: The Middle Way*; Wilfrid Fleisher, *Sweden: The Welfare State*; and Donald Hancock, *Sweden: The Politics of Post-Industrial Change*. Britain's pathbreaking role is described in V. George, *Social Security: Beveridge and After*; Maurice Bruce, *The Coming of the Welfare State*; and G. Hoshino, "Britain's Debate on Universal or Selective Social Services: Lessons for America." A general overview is in Guy Perrin's, "50 Years of Social Security."

The following chapter begins to draw these comparisons by identifying what seem to be the most relevant points of difference and similarity in the economic, social, and political development of the two nations. Special attention must be given to the particular poor-law background out of which each nation's contemporary social policy grew; in 1880 as now, the policy question was usually not "where do we go?" but "where do we go from here?" Chapters 3, 4, and 5 contain detailed comparative analyses of the development of unemployment insurance, pensions, and superannuation, respectively. How, we ask, have parties, elections, interest groups, and administrators interacted within the context of economic development to produce each nation's respective pattern of social policy growth? Where have the substantive policy ideas come from, and how have they been expressed politically? By what forces have these ideas been transformed into authoritative public policy, and what political processes have effected the adaptation of these courses of action through time? To the extent that we can begin answering these questions, we shall have learned something about the nature of social politics.

In the final chapter I return to broader questions about the policy process, summarizing the evidence on how political forces have shaped modern social policy, assessing the relation of elitism to pluralism, and recasting the traditional power orientation in policy studies. Throughout this and other sections, the nature of the data and questions is such that the analysis must necessarily be interpretive; it will not provide definitive answers or conclusive evidence on causation. The opposite of being definitive is not, however, to be arbitrary. While it is no doubt unrealistic to expect clear-cut proofs, it is nevertheless possible to produce reasons and adduce evidence for thinking that some relationships are more likely than others. My assessments will be based on interpreting the plausibilities of imperfect evidence rather than on proving laws from a large number of cases. We deal in that difficult but perhaps rewarding middle zone—between the large questions with no determinate answers and the small questions of tiresome and often insignificant conclusiveness. As usual, the challenge is to find a balance between being irrefutable and being worth refuting.

2 The Context of Social Policy

Public policies never exist in a vacuum. To begin by immediately comparing the course of social policy in Britain and Sweden would not only obscure many of the extremely important conditioning factors for such policy but also ignore something of which the zealous comparativist needs constantly to remind himself: countries are not interchangeable pieces. Britain is not Sweden. Each nation is planted within its own historical stream, and while the analyst may discern common patterns of movement and current, similar declivities and obstacles, the Thames is still the Thames and not the Ume. Whatever commonalities stand out do so precisely because they are imbedded within their particular national idioms of historical expression. This chapter attempts to give some sense of this likeness amid diversities by comparing the economic, social, and political settings of modern social policy in Britain and Sweden.

In both nations, economic forces have shaped the raw materials with which social policy has had to work. Modern social policy has built upon an unprecedented foundation of improved economic standards, a foundation which, however, carried within itself an intensified form of economic vulnerability. Earlier industrial and urban changes in Britain greatly increased the challenges to policy there as compared to the more agrarian Sweden. These challenges acquired substantive meaning through the differing political structures of each nation. Strong central administration and poorly developed parliamentary institutions in Sweden appeared more resistant to the swings of opinion against poor relief, while an active legislature and vigorous sense of local autonomy in Britain facilitated harsh overreactions in both national and local doctrines of poor law deterrence. Partly because of these factors, Sweden at a later period had the advantage of a more flexible, less doctrinaire policy inheritance.

One of the most important but most often neglected aspects of this policy environment is inherited policy itself. Generals are only one type of policy maker forever correcting the mistakes of the last war. Every innovator with a bright idea staggers forward with and against a vast deadweight of accumulated practices and ways of thinking. In an intractable world, the correction of known evils can easily seem more prudent than the problematic venturing for unknown goods. The final section of this chapter considers the social policy inheritance from which the twentieth century departed. Although poor law history in each nation has usually been treated as a unique development, I will emphasize the considerable extent to which the policy records are comparable.

Before considering economic and political factors, it is worth pausing to note the physical contexts of policy. One can identify a political entity called "Great Britain" existing for over 250 years and a "Sweden" for over 400 years. Apart from the Irish division and the several centimeters by which Britain subsides into the sea each century, the two nations have had the good fortune among European states to remain territorially intact in modern history. Moreover, for purposes of contact with the European mainland, Sweden can be regarded throughout most of its history as almost as much an island as Britain. A northern location and the nature of premodern transportation made Swedish peninsularity little different in effect from British insularity. Thus, while both Britain and Sweden lie less than 50 miles from the mainland, this has usually been sufficient to isolate each nation from the continental movement of armies and peoples. The inhabitants of both nations became seafolk, attacking others and defending themselves from the water more often than relying on large land-based armies. As we shall see, the exceptional continental engagements that did occur brought politically important changes to each country.

Topographically, the cycle of advancing and retreating ice ages sculpted countries of schematically similar appearance. In the north lies a mountainous and inhospitable region which gradually subsides southward into a central area of hill and valley. Farther south, broad, gentle plains reflect the millennia of erosion. In all of these regards, however, nature acted upon a somewhat larger scale in Sweden than in Britain. If Scotland and the Highlands are extensive, Lapland and Norrbotten seem illimitable; if Pennine streams sufficed to power the early Lancashire mills, the vast cataracts of Norrland can now power almost the entire Swedish nation; the Kansan may recognize the farmland of Northamptonshire, but in Skåne he will feel truly at home.

This difference of size is a central factor to bear in mind in any comparison between the two countries. Relative to Britain, Sweden is a large land but a small nation. In land area Sweden is about twice the size of Britain, but its population is only one-seventh, or approximately the same as the Greater London area. We know too that this population differential between the two nations has remained the same for at least the past 200 years and probably longer. But the fact that the Swedish population has remained little larger than London's does not mean that Swedish policy making has necessarily been made easier. In the sense of administrative economies of scale, Britain has had the advantage. Administrative headaches with the small Scandinavian population have only been increased by its dispersion, with eighteen Swedes per square kilometer compared to 228 Britons in 1969. These physical conditions are, of course, only the most palpable points of comparison. For a fuller appreciation of the context of modern social policy we turn to the socioeconomic changes which prepared the way.

Economic Growth and Social Change

Little understanding of the policy environment can be gained simply by labeling Britain and Sweden as economically developed nations. The term *developed* suggests a terminal state of some kind, whereas both nations are very much in midpassage. While it may be self-flattering to see our own times as a culmination, a historical perspective on social policy yields no beginnings or ends, only middles. Moreover, developed is simply a code word concealing far more about the past than it reveals. Twentieth-century policies against want started from a foundation of affluence unique in human history. But while Britain was the first industrial nation, Sweden was one of the last in Europe. Here we can only outline some of the human aspects of development most relevant to social policy.

One of the most important conditioning factors of modern social policy occurred simultaneously in both nations: a sustained increase in population during the last two and one-half centuries. Although it is one of those revolutions that we readily take for granted, such sustained population growth is without precedent in recorded history; without this revolution, four out of five of the present inhabitants in Britain and Sweden would not exist today. Booms in human reproduction had occurred before in Britain and Sweden, particularly in the thirteenth and sixteenth centuries. Always, however, the good times had led to bad, and a resurgent death rate had grimly followed apace. Now, in the last two centuries, the death rate in Britain and Sweden continued to fall, ushering in the modern era of population growth. Whether, like the nineteenth-century Swedish writer Tegner, one ascribes the sustained growth to "peace, vaccine, and potatoes" or to other causes is outside the scope of the present study, but the social implications of this change should not be ignored.

The primary reason for a fall in death rate was a decline in infant mortality. It meant, for example, the elimination of the eighteenth-century conditions in Sweden and Britain under which every fifth child might die before the age of one year. Rather than producing large numbers of children with the hope of salvaging some adults, the family could gradually begin to produce only the final number wanted and be fairly sure of their survival. Human reproduction became imbued with an element of stability it had never known before. One can only speculate on the bundle of psychological effects attending these changes. Life must certainly have come to seem less capricious and more subject to rational human control; expectations could be built and plans laid with a greater certainty than ever before. Hard times there might be, but no longer would fortuitous famines, plagues, and epi-demics devastate vast sections of the population. A kind of primary "social security" was being developed in demography with no one deliberately planning it. One graphic illustration of this stabilizing tendency is found in Heckscher's famous time series for Sweden (see Figure 2). With the smoothing of these extreme fluctuations, a

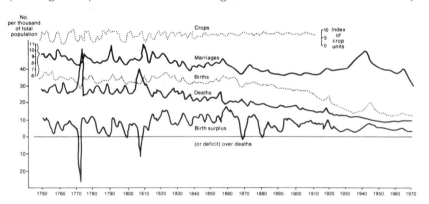

Figure 2. Population and Crop Movements in Sweden, 1750-1970

Sources: Based on Eli Heckscher, *Economic History of Sweden,* Chart 2, p. 134; and *Statistiska Årsbok för Sverige, 1972* (Stockholm: Statistiska Centralbyrån, 1972), Table 40, p. 72.

basic security was introduced into human life, a security that the twentieth century, while more worried about man's interventions, continues to take for granted from nature.

Population growth has also entailed socially important changes in the age structure of each nation. The proportion of the population above and below certain ages (usually 14 and 64) is often referred to as the dependency ratio. Contrary to the usual assumptions, however, evidence from both Britain and Sweden indicates that the dependency ratio has been smaller during this century than during earlier times (see table). Productive age groups have had a relatively lighter

Dependency Ratios in Britain and Sweden, 1750–1971
(percentage of total population)

Date	0–14 years		65 or older	
	Britain	Sweden	Britain	Sweden
1750	...	33.2	...	6.2
1800	...	32.3	...	5.7
1851	35.0	33.0	4.6	4.8
1871	36.0	34.0	4.7	5.4
1891	35.0	33.3	4.7	7.7
1911	30.6	32.0	5.2	8.4
1931	23.8	25.0	7.4	9.2
1951	22.1	23.0	11.0	10.2
1971	24.2	20.8	12.9	14.1

Sources: Data for Britain are calculated from *Abstract of British Historical Statistics*, Table 4; for Sweden from *Historisk Statistik för Sverige*, Table A. 16.

burden (itself a misleading term) of dependents to support in the twentieth century than in the previous two centuries. With the more recent decline in birth rates and adult mortality, what has occurred is a general aging of each nation's population during the last hundred years. During most of the nineteenth century, less than 6 percent of Sweden's and 5 percent of Britain's populations were 65 or older; by 1951 this proportion had risen to 10 percent and 11 percent respectively and is still rising.

To speak of population growth is of course to use a shorthand term for complex patterns of change. Despite its basic simultaneity, modern population growth in Britain and Sweden was distributed in vitally different ways. Population increases occurred within, as well as affecting, each nation's inherited social structure and thus acquired a different content in each case. British population grew within a framework of relatively high urbanization and contemporaneous with the industrialization process. In Sweden population grew within a nonurban context and prior to any large expansion in industrial production; the Swedish manufacturing that did exist was very much decentralized. Thus while the social pressure of population growth was felt in each country, in Britain it was felt relatively more in urban, industrial areas and in Sweden more in the agricultural sector.

Urbanization statistics in the two nations are not exactly comparable, but rough orders of magnitude can be identified. It seems safe to say that the Swedish rural proportion has been at least double that of the British for the last several centuries. In 1800, about 10 percent of all Swedes lived in towns with over 5,000 inhabitants; in 1801 the proportion in Britain in such towns was 25 percent. By 1851, the proportion of the population in Britain's principal towns (that is, generally those with over 10,000 population) was 26 percent compared to Sweden's 10 percent in such cities.[1] Thus in both countries, population and urban agglomerations were clearly increasing, but the relatively higher British urbanization remained persistent.

The consequences of these differing patterns are by now almost oral tradition in each nation. Population growth within Britain's more urban context brought a host of new and complex problems. One need not enter into the debate as to whether the ordinary person was made better or worse off by modern economic development in order to appreciate that an entirely unprecedented range of social problems was being created—from the morals of young factory workers to blackened skies and lungs. But it is also clear that Britain was spared the extreme hardships, more familiar in history, of a mushrooming population within a rural framework and the agrarian poverty which resulted. It was, of course, industrialization itself that shaped these events, and before looking at further social ramifications we should examine more closely the differences in the manner of the two nations' emergence from agrarian to industrial societies.

Reverend Malthus used Sweden as a major illustration to English-

---

1. Phyllis Deane and W. A. Cole, *British Economic Growth, 1688–1959*, p. 11; *Abstract of British Historical Statistics*, pp. 20, 24; *Historisk statistik för Sverige*, p. 16 and table A. 12. Cairncross puts Britain's rural population in 1841 at 39 percent; by 1911 this had fallen to 19 percent. In Sweden, at the same dates, the proportions of population in what were classified as rural areas were 90 percent and 70 percent respectively. A. K. Cairncross, *Home and Foreign Investment, 1870–1913*, pp. 64, 83; *Historisk statistik för Sverige*, tables, A. 3 and A. 14.

men of his cautionary tale on population growth. What he did not point out was that by the time he wrote (1798), Britain had already largely avoided the dangers of a population explosion within an agrarian context. Economic development in both Britain and Sweden entailed a fundamental transformation from agricultural to industrial production; the major difference between the nations lay in timing. The Swedish transformation was both later—occurring roughly 70 to 90 years after the British—and faster—telescoping almost two centuries of British-type change into less than a hundred years. An appreciation of these differences may be gained by examining the altering distribution of national product between manufacturing and agricultural sectors, as in Figure 3. The transformation in each country represented

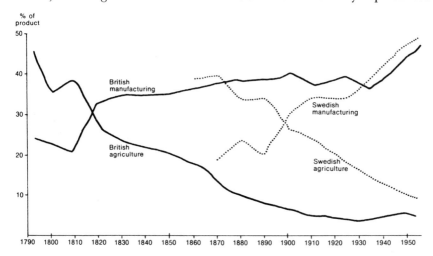

Figure 3. Economic Composition of British National Income and Swedish Gross Domestic Product, 1790-1950

Sources: Deane and Cole, *British Economic Growth,* Tables 35, 37, 40, 41; and Johansson, *Gross Domestic Product of Sweden and Its Components,* Table 55. My illustrations represent only the general magnitudes and should not be taken to indicate exact yearly figures.

far more than a reversal from agricultural to industrial prominence; it was a change from agricultural prominence to industrial hegemony. With manufacturing at or near the 50 percent level in each country, Britain and Sweden have now become more dependent on this sector than they were upon agriculture at the onset of the era of modern economic growth. By the same token, agriculture has been reduced to a position of insignificance unmatched by manufacturing at the onset.

Britain thus entered the twentieth century and the era of modern social policy as an already industrialized nation, while Sweden was in the midst of changing from an agrarian society. In saying this, one should not overlook the similar foundation of agricultural surplus upon which each nation built. By the middle of the nineteenth century, Sweden like Britain had substantially solved the fundamental problem of providing increased food supplies to keep pace with its unprecedented population growth. The vital difference was the social implications of the ways in which each nation achieved this increased food production. In Britain the means was a movement off the land and a substantial decrease in small holdings; in Sweden the change was essentially to smaller, consolidated holdings of resident-cultivators.[2] Sweden increased agricultural output by parceling out the recently consolidated peasant farms, but the race between people and land subdivision was foredoomed.

Far more than for Britain, the social consequence of population growth for agrarian Sweden was steadily mounting rural poverty during the nineteenth century. The landless groups—a rural proletariat of cottagers and paupers—exhibited by far the fastest relative population growth, rising from one-quarter of all peasants in 1751 to one-half in 1815. During the nineteenth century, even the cottagers, a landless but settled group, became proportionately less important while paupers, crofters, and a new class of landless, paid-in-kind labor grew in prominence. These changes carried through their logic into international population movements. British emigration figures are fragmentary but one can doubt if anything in the British experience compared with the exodus of Swedish population in the last half of the nineteenth century. From 1860 to 1908, Sweden suffered a net population loss through migration of 973,965, a number equal to 60 percent of the increase in population during these years or one-fifth of the total 1910 population. As usual, the most affecting facts of social history—human suffering, sorrow, and privation—cannot be measured.

In the longer run, Sweden's later industrialization did carry some natural advantages. While Swedish agricultural productivity has

---

2. Of course there were instances of English-type landlord reform. The first landlord in Sweden to carry out such massive consolidations and reforms was in fact an emigrant from Britain, Rutger Maclean, who had gained experience with enclosures there before moving to Sweden. This tendency reached its height in the flat southern farmlands of the Skåna plains, not unlike those of southern England. Oscar Bjurling, "The Baron's Revolution."

generally lagged behind British, its industrial productivity has historically exceeded Britain's; and with its less rigid industrial inheritance
Sweden has pushed ahead during the last century. If economic growth
means a sustained increase in product per capita (or worker), then
Sweden in the last hundred years has been the world's leader, un-
equaled in any long period by any country for which data are available.[3] Figure 4 depicts the overall economic growth rates in Britain
and Sweden. Statistics on national product in the two countries are
not exactly comparable, but they are adequate to give an idea of the
general magnitude and pacing of change in each country's economy.

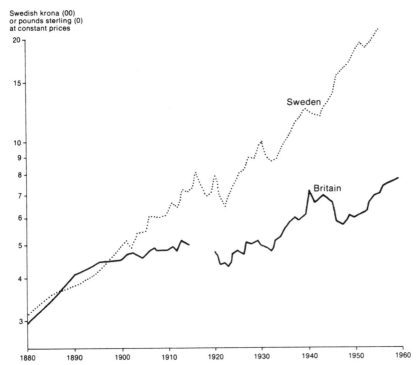

Swedish krona (00)
or pounds sterling (0)
at constant prices

Figure 4. British National Income and Swedish Gross Domestic Product per Capita in
Constant (1913) Prices, 1880-1960

Sources: Deane and Cole, *British Economic Growth,* Table 90; and Johansson, *Gross
Domestic Product of Sweden and Its Components,* Table 60.

3. Simon Kuznets, *Modern Economic Growth,* p. 64, table 2.5. The Swedish average growth
in GDP has been 28 percent per decade; one exception to the above generalization is the
U.S.S.R. for the period 1928–58. Considering the travail suffered in Russia to achieve its
growth, the Swedish record appears even more outstanding.

Since 1895, the Swedish growth rate has clearly and consistently been superior to the British rate. The great Swedish lead was established after 1895 and continued to increase for most of the next 60 years.

Such differences should not, however, overshadow the more fundamental similarities. Certainly the general directions of economic change have been substantially the same in each country. This roughly simultaneous occurrence of good and bad times in each country (which would show up more clearly if Figure 4 were on a current rather than constant price basis) reflects the fact that for at least the last hundred years Britain and Sweden have been part of an international economic system, sharing together its common successes and reversals. These economic fluctuations appear to be largely independent of many major political decisions. During this period Sweden has avoided the two total and several colonial wars that Britain has fought, but it has not escaped the essentially tandem economic movement.

A far more crucial similarity underlies both nations' figures. Historically, economic growth has not muted welfare issues, as some contemporary growth advocates forget. Quite the opposite. The era of activist social policy springs from precisely the period of unprecedented economic growth. Translated into social and human terms, these changes in productivity and economic growth have meant profoundly altered ways of life, a phenomonon easy to suggest but difficult to prove. The first social surveys are less than a hundred years old, and the life of the great mass of the people in previous centuries is a shadowy realm ignored by most contemporary histories and accounts. But to treat the development of twentieth-century policy without appreciating the affluent foundation upon which it built is simpleminded in the extreme. Modern economic growth appears to have brought with it a sustained improvement in mass living standards which is historically unique. To take one possible forerunner, the fifteenth century seems to have been a period of some prosperity in both Britain and Sweden. The scanty record of food budgets shows agricultural servants in Sweden obtaining as many calories as the average Swedish citizen in 1912; a study of building wage rates and consumption prices in Britain shows real wages doubling between 1350 and 1420.[4] But the prosperity of the fifteenth century had followed the devastation by plague in the four-

4. E. H. Phelps Brown and S. V. Hopkins, "Seven Centuries of Builders' Wage Rates"; Eli Heckscher, *Bidrag till Sveriges ekonomiska och sociala historia under och efter världskriget.*

teenth century and was followed itself by the return of severe hardship in the sixteenth century. A century after their fifteenth-century peaks, caloric intake had fallen again by one-third and building wage rates had been halved in real terms, regaining the fifteenth-century level only in 1880.

The record of economic growth in Britain and Sweden since the eighteenth century is of course only part of an overall technical and economic explosion. Two writers have gone so far as to suggest that since the last Ice Age only the Neolithic Revolution of ten millennia ago is on a scale comparable to the transformation experienced in the last 200 years.[5] Perhaps it would be prudent to avoid claiming too much vis-à-vis the Stone Age until the accounts are in on the twentieth century. What is certain is that with the shift to industrial processes and rising productivity, vastly increased populations have been provided not only with employment but also with substantially higher real wages for that employment. In the last century, real wages have risen about four times in Britain and six and one-half times in Sweden. The fact that these rates, an annual 1.5 percent and 1.9 percent respectively, seem modest to contemporary eyes only illustrates how far our modern perspective has been conditioned by this momentum of growth. Our spiraling expectations are themselves a function of the capacity of this economic upheaval to sustain itself, to create a growth that feeds on growth, to improve techniques for improving techniques, to produce a pie that grows as it is consumed. In effect, the masses of new people that so worried Malthus gave employment to each other, as the extra income generated by the activity of each provided the market for the output of all. Figure 5 shows one attempt to estimate this unprecedented change in real wages in Britain and Sweden.

The rise in British and Swedish real wages, particularly in the period before the First World War, seems to have been decisive in lifting the mass of workers' households above outright destitution. In 1860, one-quarter of the British population was probably insufficiently nourished, even when the lower standard of 3,000 calories per man each day is accepted, while about the same proportion managed to attain 3,500. During the next 20 years, the general standard of living seems to have improved, so that most were above the minimum standard and even

5. E. H. Phelps Brown and Margaret Brown, *A Century of Pay*, p. 25. The following discussion of real wages is based on this work. An account of Swedish developments is in Arthur Montgomery, *Industrialismens Genombrott*.

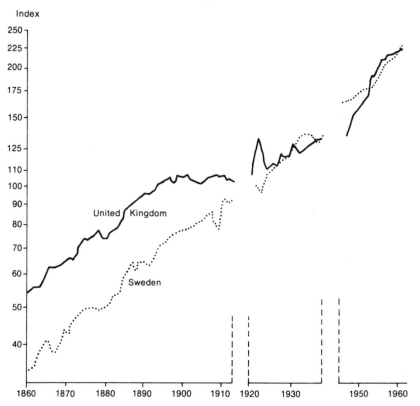

Figure 5. Indexes of Wage Earnings in Composite Units of Consumables (United
Kingdom in 1890-99 = 100)

Source: Based on Phelps Brown and Brown, *A Century of Pay,* Figure 1B.

the lowest tenth was not much below the 3,500 standard. In general
it was the rise in real wages during this 20-year period, 1860–80, that
eliminated outright hunger from the household of the wage-earner—
providing these wages were not interrupted. The comparable period of
rise in real wages in Sweden was approximately 20 years later, from
1880–1900, or about the same time that the rush of emigration began
to dry up.[6] In both countries, economic growth was the device for reducing in a very general way the most abject and severe mass poverty.

6. Sweden's later economic development, as well as higher productivity and economic
growth, is reflected in this figure. In 1905, Swedish workers worked longer hours for real wages
one-fifth lower than the British standard. By the 1960s, it was the British worker who was
putting in substantially longer time for a smaller basket of goods. Phelps Brown and Brown,
A Century of Pay, pp. 55, 206, 278, and table 31.

If the achievement seems modest to modern eyes, it was nevertheless a fundamental break with the sorry record of previous centuries.

A new human vulnerability was, however, created by these economic changes. In Gregory King's estimate of population in England and Wales in 1685, only one-third of the families had a wage-earner as breadwinner; in the 1911 census, six out of seven in the occupied British population were working for salaries or wages.[7] The elimination of destitution through higher real wages depended in part upon a person's becoming a wage-earner. But equally important, it depended on having these wages without serious interruption. Providing for oneself and one's family increasingly came to depend upon what one could buy from a variety of other increasingly specialized producers; this in turn rested on the money income obtained from the sale of labor. More and more, the individual's *social* security depended upon *economic* security which, in turn, depended upon *income* security.

This concatenation of vulnerability stemmed not only from wage dependence. The primary locus of social support, the family, was also changing. From its former centrality in virtually every sphere of human activity, the family in industrial and factory society increasingly became a refueling and refreshment station, the place where one repaired from work rather than the work unit itself. If industrialization fragmented the family as a labor unit, the gradual extension of public schooling and mass entertainment had a similar effect on the family as an earning unit and leisure unit. Family cohesion, a function of common activities, loosened with the dispersal of these activities. From an extended group of all ages and many children, the Swedish and British family in the modern era has tended to contract into a nuclear group composed of two parents with one to three children. In this way the individual member of the family also became economically more vulnerable by becoming dependent upon fewer earners and thus more likely to find himself alone in a wage-earning society. During the twentieth century these tendencies have intensified; in both Britain and Sweden for almost any periods in which data are available, the evidence shows a decreasing family size. Modern social policy in Britain and Sweden thus built upon a vast base of primary social security and improved real economic standards. At the same time, the concomitant conditions of this improvement left the individual more susceptible to setbacks in these higher standards should any loss or interruption in

7. Cited in Deane and Cole, *British Economic Growth*, p. 251.

income-earning power occur. One way of looking at the following three chapters is as an exploration of how two societies are learning—through politics—to create policies to deal with this new vulnerability among the unemployed and elderly.

A number of other social aspects relevant to the policy environment are less directly related to economic growth. Cross-national comparisons of social cleavages are full of difficulties, but several major points stand out. Compared to most other nations in the world, Sweden and Britain are distinguished by their social homogeneity. Racial differences have been insignificant throughout each nation's modern history and ethnic subcultures (always excepting the Irish) have not been sufficiently large to affect seriously the political process during the last several centuries. The Finnish community in Sweden has been less than .5 percent of the population and the Lapps less than .2 percent. The Welsh in Britain have been about 5 percent and the Scots 10 percent of the total population, and in each case the vital conflicts surrounding the amalgamation of each group were settled by the middle of the eighteenth century. In both nations the major questions of religious affiliation were also settled early. During the 1600s, the national monarchs of Britain and Sweden broke with the Catholic church, took most of the substantial church lands and property, and established national Protestant churches. Today, 95 percent of Swedes belong to the state Lutheran church, with which every Swede is enrolled unless making a specific declaration to the contrary. In Britain about three-fourths of those with religious affiliation belong to the Church of England, and another 6 percent and 4 percent belong to the Churches of Scotland and Wales respectively. Not only was the uniform cultural identity of each nation established from an early date but, as noted in the next section, the crises of national political identity were also settled before the modern era. In terms of cultural, racial, and religious affiliation, there is probably greater social uniformity in Britain and Sweden than almost any other two nations in the world.

Socioeconomic divisions are another matter. Anyone who has lived in each country has experienced these divisions, from the class distinctions among British pubs to the Swedish telephone directories (which until recently listed surnames in strict occupational order, from professional to manual.) While such status differences are often the most vivid phenomena, they are also the most difficult to document. The data available allow no detailed statistical comparison of the development of British and Swedish social structures. In Britain especially, the quality of occupational statistics is deplorable, so much so that one writer after a lengthy survey concludes that one "can do no more than admit the inadequacy of our knowledge of the changing social structure of England and Wales."[8] The differing pace of industrialization of course entailed the far earlier emergence of an industrial working class in Britain than Sweden. While the British working class in the mid-nineteenth century was attaining a position of numerical and social, if not political, power, Sweden remained one of the most agrarian nations in Europe. The growth of the Swedish industrial working class became particularly noticeable only during the last quarter of the nineteenth century. Between 1855 and 1900 the proportion of nonagricultural workers doubled to one-third of the employed Swedish population and by 1930 had risen to 45 percent, or approximately the same level as Britain in 1901.

Discussions of persisting status differences are a fertile field of partisan conflict in both Britain and Sweden. In both countries writers can easily concentrate upon how much or how little social equality has been achieved, and persuasive cases are often made in each direction. Here we can only work from the most reasonable tentative conclusions concerning such social divisions. It seems clear that compared to a century ago the *scope* and the *range* of social differences have narrowed. By this we mean that such differences seem to be less important in all aspects of any one individual's life (scope), and that the extremes of such differences seem to have narrowed in any one aspect of all individuals' lives (range). The British and Swedish worker of 1870 was distinguishable as a worker in virtually everything he did. The worker of the 1970s seems less sharply differentiated—from the time schedule of his day to what he consumes, how he moves about, or the appearance he presents to the world. In Sweden, for example, the title *herr*, originally limited to knights and then to the four estates, is now used for all social levels; the British title *esquire*, which once served to designate gentry immediately below knighthood, is now accepted in the correspondence of all male commoners. At the same time the extreme qualitative differences in particular areas of life, such as the legal standing or education of pauper and lord, no longer play a large part in either nation's social climate.

Nevertheless, differences do remain and are a clear part of social life in each nation. The income maintenance policies in our analysis have developed in a context of persisting ambiguity and tension be-

8. David C. Marsh, *The Changing Social Structure of England and Wales*, 1871–1961, p. 207.

tween the claims of individual equity and social equality. Unemployment insurance, pensions, and superannuation have themselves contributed to the ongoing social compromise between the divisions and
ties among citizens. Changes in the distribution of educational opportunity can be taken as one illustration of the social equality that
has been achieved and the inequality that remains. Compulsory, free,
elementary education began in Sweden in 1842 and generally covered
six years for all youths. Beginning in the mid-1930s this was gradually
raised to seven years and after long deliberation to nine years in 1962.
In this 120 year interval, elementary education therefore became both
a privilege of all individuals and a more extended part of each individual's life. At the end of the 1860s, approximately 400 students
took higher education examinations; an average of one in ten boys
from middle-class families attained the higher education level, compared to one in 300 from workers' or farmers' families (and these
usually from the largest farms). By 1963 the number of those taking
higher education examinations had grown 50 times to 19,000. By this
time one in three from middle-class families attained this level compared to one in fifteen of those from farmers' and workers' families.[9]
Educational chances had thus improved both within and between
social groups. The thirtyfold difference of 1860 in educational recruitment between middle and working class had been reduced to
fivefold, but the difference clearly remained.

Britain's democratization of education started later and seems to
have gone less far. Provision of elementary educational facilities for
all began in the 1870s but not until the twentieth century did free
elementary compulsory education come fully into being. By 1938
still only 38 percent of all 14-year olds were in full-time education.
By the end of the 1950s, when some 42 percent of Swedish youths
between 15 and 20 were in full-time education, only about 20 percent
of British youths between 15 and 18 were, although this was an increase
over earlier rates of attendance. From 1 percent of the relevant age
group going to universities in 1900, the figure had risen to 5 percent
by the early 1960s. In 1958–59, 4.6 percent of the relevant age group
entered higher education in Britain compared to 7 percent in Sweden.
The proportions have increased since then, but in neither country do

9. Sten Carlsson, "Folkhemspolitiken," p. 114, summarizes these changes. Within groups,
variations were even greater, e.g., 80 percent from academic families and 1 percent from
mining and timber workers' families entered institutions of higher education.

as many as one in ten children go on to higher education, and the class bias in recruitment has remained strong.[10]

Education is of course only one indicator of the ameliorated but persistent social divisions in both Britain and Sweden. What poor data there are suggest that perceptions of social class divisions remain strong in each nation, with a greater sense of working class self-identification in Sweden than in Britain; but as sociologists have found, there is little chance of understanding such distinctions between the two developed nations without considering the purposive actions, or more generally the social policy making, of each.[11] The Epilogue concludes with the contemporary rediscovery of persisting social inequality and the recent revival of social politics in each nation. For the moment we can turn to a second important facet of the policy environment and examine the political tools with which each nation has equipped itself for dealing with social policy.

POLITICAL DEVELOPMENT

Britain and Sweden are, of course, what are termed Western democracies, and each has often been considered as something of a model of modern democratic government. This section does not necessarily quarrel with this designation but rather tries to draw distinctions between the two nations' politics. In particular we will be looking at the emergence of parliamentary power, universal suffrage, political parties, and other institutions often said to be instrumental in realizing popular demands for activist social policies.

Perhaps the most important background factor to democratic development lay in what did not happen rather than what did. For a variety of reasons, both Britain and Sweden were able to avoid the oppressive medieval feudalism which played such an important part in many continental nations. It is symptomatic of this nonevent that most British and Swedish studies in political history have focused on how royal power came to be restricted and held reponsible; in international perspective, however, it is the limitation of nobles' power over the common people that seems far more distinctive. The greatest

---

10. *Report of Central Advisory Council for Education (Crowther)*, 1959. Erik Höök, *Den Offentliga Sektorns Expansion*, chap. 6. *Report of Committee on Higher Education (Robbins)*, pp. 44, 45. A. M. Carr-Saunders and D. C. Jones, *Survey of Social Structure: England and Wales*, chap. 11.

11. Richard Scase, "Industrial Man: A Reassessment with English and Swedish Data," p. 217.

threats of feudal supremacy occurred in each nation with the political and economic pressures created by major European land campaigns, sixteenth-century wars in the case of Sweden and thirteenth-century wars in the case of Britain. In each nation, these threats were removed when the leading royal opponent defeated the monarch but then embarked upon a national rather than feudal career. A broader, if oversimplified, summary is that both Britain and Sweden followed the path of "bourgeois soical revolution" in arriving at the modern era. The change from agrarian to modern society was achieved without the acquisition of overwhelming power against peasants and workers by monarchy, landed aristocracy, bourgeoisie, or any of these in combination.[12]

The emergence of parliaments was itself an expression of the mixture rather than predominance of power among social groups. Both Britain and Sweden have had among the longest experience with parliamentary institutions of any nations in the world, beginning roughly from the fourteenth century in Britain and fifteenth century in Sweden. But there is also a significant difference between the nations. Through all of the shifts of power between crown and parliament, the important fact for present purposes is that by the nineteenth century Britain had emerged with a far stronger parliamentary system of government than Sweden. Power in Britain, but not in Sweden, rested decisively with the legislature and a cabinet of legislators. While the British monarch in the eighteenth century gradually lost power to the parliamentary party managers, the Swedish monarchy reacted strongly against what had become a virtually full-blown parliamentary regime in the mid-eighteenth century (the so-called Era of Liberty). Sweden's subsequent period of moderate absolutism after 1772 led to an unsuccessful war against Napoleon and ended with another military coup. The 1809 constitution, which is still in force, sought to establish a system of countervailing powers which would prevent dominance by either king or parliament (*Riksdag*). Yet, despite the formal checks of the Swedish constitution, royal power remained predominant. Ministers were appointed personally and usually singly by the king; in no case did they resign as a whole council of ministers; and the financial power of appropriation was scarcely ever used by the Riksdag against the king. Thus while cabinet government based upon a strong parliamentary system came to prevail in Britain, Swedish national government

12. Barrington Moore, Jr., *The Social Origins of Dictatorship and Democracy*.

remained largely in the hands of the king and his aristocratic and civil service advisers throughout most of the nineteenth century.

In 1866, parliamentary forms were somewhat altered in Sweden when the four estates were finally replaced with a bicameral parliament of very restricted franchise. During the last half of the nineteenth century there was a gradual but by no means continuous tendency for Swedish ministries to gain some independence from the crown, to become less dependent on the bureaucracy, and to develop stronger ties with parliament. After the reforms of 1866, parliamentary initiative was somewhat strengthened, not least by the fact that it now met annually rather than every three to five years and could speak with a greater unity than in the days of four separate chambers of estates. However, it would also be easy to overestimate the departures introduced in 1866. The constitutional change essentially brought parliamentary forms into closer correspondence with the prevailing distribution of propertied privilege rather than creating any democratization of power. The continuity of conservative forces from the four estates to the bicameral parliament was far more noticeable than any changes; ten years elapsed before the first farmer entered the First Chamber and twelve years before the first manual worker was elected to the Second Chamber.[13] Disagreement between the conservative First Chamber and more popularly representative Second Chamber still limited any great increase in parliamentary power, and even E. G. Böström, the first nineteenth-century chief minister (1891–1900) never to have been a civil servant of the crown, and under whom the closest ties between ministry and parliament grew, had no sympathy for parliamentary government. At a time when politicians in Britain were jockeying for parliamentary majorities to form new governments, the Swedish ministries in fact as well as in form continued to remain in power at the pleasure of the crown rather than parliament. Sweden finally established a system of cabinet government responsible to parliament in 1914 when, in a dispute over rearmament, the nineteenth-century separation of powers fully gave way to a modern system of predominant legislative and cabinet power.

The other major step toward parliamentary government in Sweden entailed limiting the independent power of the First (or upper) Cham-

13. In Sweden, the popularly elected chamber is referred to as the Second Chamber (*Andra Kammar*), and the upper chamber, indirectly elected, is referred to as the First Chamber (*Första Kammar*).

ber. The 1866 reforms had created an upper chamber indirectly elected by local councils, with property and income qualifications so high that only an estimated 6,100 persons in the entire country were eligible for election in the 1870s. The First Chamber remained clearly dominated by the highest civil servants and upper classes until the reform of 1909 substantially reduced the property and income tests for voting in elections to the electoral councils. In 1918 and 1921 the electorate was largely democratized and the old fortyfold scale of voting completely abolished. Thus the independent power of the upper chamber was altered not so much by limiting its powers of action, as in the British House of Lords, but by limiting the distinctiveness of its constituency through the creation of substantially the same electorate as for the Second (or lower) Chamber. From 1921 onward, the distribution of party power in the Second Chamber was roughly reflected in the First.[14]

The tendency for Sweden to lag behind Britain in the development of

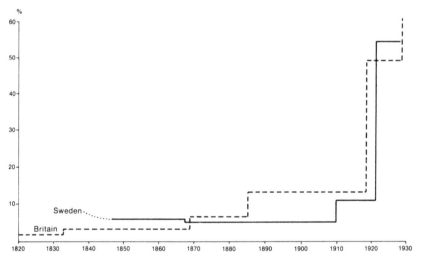

Figure 6. Approximate Percentage of Population Entitled to Vote, Britain and Sweden, 1820-1930

Sources: Figures are taken from estimates in Smellie, *A Hundred Years of English Government,* Appendix 3; Butler and Freeman, *British Political Facts, 1900-1960,* p. 129. The Swedish figure for 1845 is an estimate calculated from G. Heckscher, *Nagra drag ur representationsfrågans sociala bakgrund;* other Swedish data are from Verney, *Parliamentary Reform in Sweden, 1866-1921,* pp. 179, 213.

14. A discussion of these changes is in Lar Sköld and Arne Halvarson, "Riksdagens sociala summansättning under hundra år," pp. 410 ff. The upper chamber became so redundant that it was eventually abolished in 1973.

parliamentary government was paralleled by its late extensions in the franchise. Figure 6 gives an approximation of the changing percentages of the total population qualified to vote as a result of suffrage extensions. The 1866 Swedish reform actually reduced the size of the electorate, while in 1885 Britain enfranchised some 12.5 percent of the total popu-lation. By the time Sweden experienced its first virtually universal male suffrage in the 1911 election, for what was only just becoming a parlia-mentary government, Britain had held eight general elections over 26 years with such an extended suffrage and had enjoyed, if that is the correct term, parliamentary government for almost a century and a half. The 25 years (1885–1911) mark the period of greatest difference in British and Swedish democratic institutions as well as the crucial formative era for the social policies included in this study. For both nations, by far the greatest extensions in the voting rolls occurred after the First World War, and in each case the elections of the 1920s were the first with the potentiality to reveal the policy effects of universal suf-frage. What policy differences, if any, have resulted from these de-mocratic reforms is a question for later chapters.

Since 1909, one persisting structural difference in electoral politics in the two nations has been the existence of proportional representation in Sweden and single-member plurality elections in Britain. One can scarcely argue that proportional representation (PR) has created a multiparty system in Sweden. As Figure 7 suggests, what PR has done is to moderate the amplified shifts in parliamentary seats produced by plurality elections. Between 1929 and 1931, for example, the British Labor party's electoral share fell from 37 to 32 percent, while its share of parliamentary seats fell from 47 to only 8 percent; in Sweden, the Social Democratic vote between 1924 and 1928 dropped from 41 to 37 percent, but its percentage of parliamentary seats (in the Second Chamber) fell only from 45 to 39 percent.

If proportional representation prevented such periodic devastation of parliamentary parties, it also lacked the distorting effects which pro-duced frequent parliamentary majorities. Of the eighteen elections in Britain between 1900 and 1970, in only three has a party, always the Conservative, received a popular majority; in the nineteen Swedish general elections since 1911, only two times has a party, always the Social Democratic, received a popular majority. Yet these same elec-tions have produced twelve clear parliamentary majorities in Britain and only two in Sweden. During the period before the Social Democrats

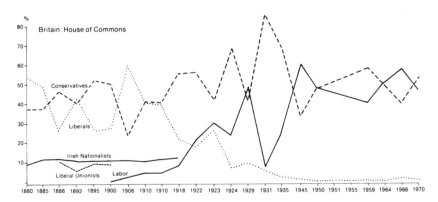

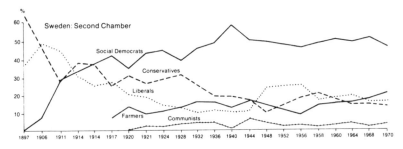

Figure 7. Distribution of Party Strengths in Parliament, Britain and Sweden, 1880-1970

Sources: Butler and Freeman, *British Political Facts,* and *Statistiska Årsbok* for each election year.

established their predominance, this could and did lead to a series of instable minority governments (nine between 1913 and 1932) but except for this period, it cannot be argued that PR has produced instable government in Sweden. Consistently achieving over 40 percent of the popular vote since 1932, Social Democrats have been able to form majority coalitions with the Farmers' party and thereby established the most long-lived party government in the western world. As Figure 8 makes clear, it is possible to speak of a two-party system in Britain only during the last 40 years; Sweden throughout this century has had a multiparty array of four major parties, but one which has justifiably been called a working multiparty system.[15]

Differences in the adoption of parliamentary government and extension of popular suffrage were reflected in the relatively late develop-

15. See Dankwart Rustow, "Scandinavia: Working Multiparty Systems," in *Modern Political Parties*, ed. Sigmund Neumann.

ment of Swedish political parties. Contemporary British and Swedish parties may be traced back to the parliamentary factions that had developed centuries earlier during struggles surrounding royal power. In Britain the extension of party factions to electoral organizations had been given a strong stimulus with the requirement of the 1832 Reform Act that all voters had to be registered, and the electoral reforms of 1866 and 1885 added further incentive for party organizations to penetrate into the mass of the electorate. By 1880, both Conservative and Liberal parties had their own national associations of constituency organizations to develop reasonably coherent partisan clashes in the elections.

But the revival of royal power in Sweden after 1775 destroyed the incipient Swedish parties and throughout most of the nineteenth century government responsibility in Sweden resided with the conservative royalist-bureaucratic oligarchy rather than with parliamentary factions. The reform of 1866 in Sweden also provided only a limited stimulus to party organization. The elementary state of Swedish parties was well illustrated in 1880; the Rural party, which was the one semi-coherent parliamentary faction and the force responsible for the failure of many of the weak, bureaucratic ministries since 1867, was asked and refused to form a government. The first national electoral organization was formed in 1889 by the Social Democratic party; seven years later that party finally became committed to the electoral, parliamentary road to power when Hjalmar Branting, with Liberal cooperation, was elected the first Social Democrat in the Riksdag. Only in 1902 were the factions of the Liberal party able to come together in a national electoral organization (*Frisinnade Landsföreningen*), with Karl Staaf and David Bergström raising money from 2,000 subscribers to support candidates sympathetic to suffrage reform. In 1904 the conservative groups in the Riksdag responded with their own unified electoral organization (*Allmänna valmansförbundet*). Following their election victory in September 1905, Staaf and his Liberal supporters formed the first ministry in Swedish history with a clear party coloring.

Beyond the fact that organized, electorally competitive parties in Britain preceded those in Sweden by at least a generation, it is important to note that the Swedish Labor party developed in a more favorable chronological context than its British counterpart. Founded in 1900, the British Labor party appeared well after the major contours of that nation's democratic politics had taken shape. While the young

Labor groups in Britain could be and were looked upon with a certain disdain by the well-established Liberal party, Swedish Labor and Swedish Liberalism in a sense came of age at the same time and gained a common legitimation in their struggle for the establishment of a democratic political system. Both parties could unite in the 1890s to fight for suffrage extensions, both were outsiders against the entrenched conservative system, both could and did achieve a working political relationship when at last the Liberals came to power. What was perhaps even more important, the mass of working class voters in Sweden had not had the chance to become attached to existing bourgeois parties before the establishment of the Social Democratic al-

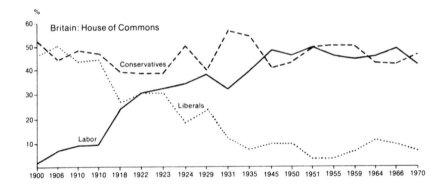

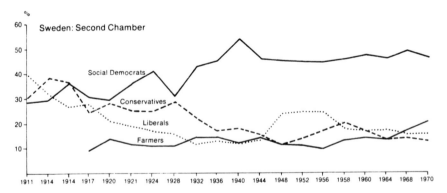

Figure 8. Distribution of Popular Vote by Party, Britain and Sweden, 1900-1970

Sources: Butler and Freeman, *British Political Facts,* and *Statistiska Årsbok* for each election year.

ternative.[16] Despite Sweden's later economic development and relatively smaller industrial working class, the Social Democrats before the First World War were already obtaining 30 percent of the popular vote, while the British Labor party had never received more than 8 percent. Contemporary studies have shown the importance of inherited party identifications, and it is reasonable to assume that the same factor was a powerful force in retarding the electoral growth of the British Labor party compared to the Swedish Social Democratic party. Moreover, the unique Swedish committee process, inherited from decades of civil service experience, tended to ensure that once parliamentary representation was achieved, even socialist members would necessarily be recruited into the practicalformulation of social policy.

If the development of parliamentary government, a democratic electorate, and a modern party system were somewhat later in Sweden than in Britain, the Swedes clearly led in the creation of a modern civil service. As early as 1634, under Gustavus Adolphus II and the exigencies of 30 years of continental war, Sweden laid the outlines of a well-ordered civil service. Largely at the hands of Adolphus's commanding chancellor, Axel Oxenstierna, a centralized body of administrators was created as a corps of impartial professionals who were accountable to their political heads. Five central boards were established in Stockholm, with regional administrative units (*Län*) each under a centrally appointed governor (*Landshövding*). Despite the various advances and retreats in royal power, this basic framework remained unchanged. In 1840, a departmental system was initiated with each political minister having his own department of state, but the central administrative boards remained intact. To this day the Swedish central government retains the division between the small departments (usually less than 100 employees, including office and janitorial staff) designed to develop policy and the fairly independent boards handling the bulk of general administrative business.[17]

16. The use of the word *bourgeois* in this book follows the general Swedish usage, simply to distinguish Conservative, Liberal, and Farmer parties from the ostensibly socialist parties, and it implies no other judgments.

17. A. B. Carlsson, *Den Svenska Centralförvaltningen, 1521–1809*. Recent conditions are discussed in Bjorn Molin and Mansson Strömberg, *Offentlig förvaltning*. The distinction between policy and administration is of course rarely clear. As one illustration of the unique position of the administrative boards, their civil servants are accountable, not to political heads as in Britain, but to the criminal law structure; the civil servant in a department is not legally responsible. A discussion of contemporary practice can be found in Pierre Vinde's valuable book, *Hur Sverige Styres*.

In comparison, a centrally organized and professional civil service could scarcely be said to exist in Britain even 200 years after Oxenstierna's reforms. Only after the mid-nineteenth century, and drawing heavily upon experiments with a European-type centralized administration in India, did a modern civil service become established in Britain. Parliamentary demands for economy and less political corruption had begun in 1815 following the experiences of the Napoleonic Wars; by 1900, with the reforms completed, the "economized" civil service had grown from the 25,000 of 1815 to 116,000. This later development and the fact that the civil service was founded amid criticism against the political corruption of administration probably forestalled any possibility that British civil servants might openly take part in policy making or parliamentary proceedings, let alone become members of the legislature. With the much longer traditions of administrative integrity and the later development of political parties, Swedish administrators were viewed as natural participants in the policy process and have generally formed an important part of the Riksdag's membership. These differences in sequencing meant that the era of modern social policy began in Sweden with administrators in an accepted policy-making role and political parties as newcomers; in Britain the newcomer was the civil service profession among well-established parties. The relative cloistering of British and open participation of Swedish civil servants has continued to the present day—as is evident from surveying the affiliations of writers on any public question in the two countries.

The influence of this administrative tradition in Sweden can be traced in an additional and very important difference between the two nations' political institutions: the committee system. Ever since there have been governments there have probably been committees, but in few countries have they reached the luxuriance of Sweden's. Historically, one important type has been the joint standing committees (*utskott*) of the Riksdag, bodies established by law in the Constitution of 1809 as a means to coordinate the deliberations of the four estates. After 1866 the *utskotts* became composed of members from each of the two chambers. These committees have often served as agencies of policy intelligence and have always had a free hand to amend but never to pigeonhole all bills sent to them. In eras of minority governments, particularly earlier in this century, the *utskotts* have been extremely influential, often exceeding the power of the cabinet itself.

Needless to say, at a time when the birth-pangs of standing committees are just beginning to be felt in the British Parliament, nothing in Britain has approached the position of this Swedish parliamentary tool. It is even more doubtful if anything in Britain can compare with the political role played by Swedish ad hoc investigatory commissions,[18] of which there have been over 4,000 since 1855. There is the ever present danger of comparing incommensurables, and immediate confusion can arise on whether the Swedish *utredning*'s counterpart in Britain is the royal commission or the departmental committee. The leading student of Swedish commissions makes his comparisons with the former while the leading student of British investigations uses the latter. Still, whether one counts British departmental committees, royal commissions, or both together, it is clear that the institutionalized Swedish investigative bodies find no match in Britain, either in terms of numbers or significance in the normal political process.[19] For over 150 years—and drawing upon a tradition extending back to the early civil service of the medieval period—the typical procedure before the submission of any government proposal in Sweden has been the appointment of an investigating commission to study the subject and make its recommendations. Throughout most of the nineteenth century these investigations seem to have been initiated by the crown and made up largely of civil servants, although the gradually increasing role of legislature and outside organizations was evident by the end of the century. The development of parliamentary government and a democratic party system greatly increased the role of the Riksdag in initiating and providing members for such commissions; since the mid-1950s, the civil service may again have developed into a more preeminent force. But throughout all of these variations, the *utredning* itself has remained a central factor in Swedish policy making. Collecting and analyzing facts, thrashing out the diverging views of various groups, the commissions have constituted a vital preliminary stage in the formulation of almost all government proposals.

18. Technically, these investigatory bodies (*utredning*) are also called committees (*kommittee*) in Sweden, but I will use the word *commission* to distinguish them from the joint standing committees of the Riksdag. Their deliberations and reports appear in the government series *Statens Offentliga Utredningar* (SOU), an invaluable source of documentation on Swedish life.

19. Hans Meijer's *Kommitteväsendets Utveckling 1905–1954* is a pathbreaking study of Swedish commissions. For Britain, see Charles J. Hanser, *Guide to Decision: The British Commissions*; his later work, "Investigatory Commissions, An International View"; and R. E. Wraith and G. B. Lamb, *Public Inquiries as an Instrument of Government*.

In Britain, the royal commission is traceable to the Domesday survey (1081–86) and has traditionally played a more prestigious and independent intelligence role than in Sweden. The high water mark of royal commissions came in the nineteenth century, when many major items of Victorian reform stemmed from their recommendations. At the same time, legislative select committees flourished and expressed the central position of Parliament. Such select committees were the most common method of British inquiry in the nineteenth century and their use closely paralleled the changes in parliamentary power. After 1660 the select committees of Parliament became the chief form of organized policy analysis in British national government. Between 1801 and 1851 the average annual number of royal commissions expanded over five times (to almost nine new commissions a year), and similar increases occurred in select committees, with over 500 reporting in the same 50-year period. By the mid-nineteenth century, the *annual* product of parliamentary papers in terms of number, size, and circulation was greater than the product of all of the centuries before 1800 put together. For the most part, this unprecedented increase in governmental investigation was a function of the increasing problems being thrust upon the state by a rapidly changing society. A study of their work shows that the original impetus behind the early establishment of most new investigations was the intention to relieve industry and labor from restrictions inherited from a preindustrial society; the result however was a vast increase in government operations. The paradox of unprecedented growth in state investigation in the era popularly recognized as the heyday of laissez-faire deserves emphasis, for the expansion of these government intelligence functions was determined less by a self-conscious philosophy of government and more by the practical analytic needs of policy makers, or as one historian put it, "because lawmaking of a character so new and comprehensive required a closer examination of complex facts than busy ministers could give."[20]

The later nineteenth century, however, witnessed a clear decline in British royal commissions and select committees, until by the 1930s there was less use of these outside investigative bodies than there had

---

20. G. M. Trevelyan, *British History in the Nineteenth Century, 1782–1901*, p. 242. This mushrooming of political intelligence was but a part of that period's emphasis on what has been called "rational and purposive control, based upon measuring, counting, and observing." Sir Llewellyn Woodward, *The Age of Reform, 1815–1870*, p. 39.

been 120 years earlier. In a sense, the unprecedented growth of royal commissions and select committees in the nineteenth century had been a compensation for the administrative impoverishment of the national government in an era of industrial revolution; a major feature distinguishing the British from the Swedish investigations in the nineteenth century had always been the limited part played by government administrators in Britain. The decline in the British investigatory organs after the mid-nineteenth century was almost exactly counterposed by the growth of the civil service, not only in numbers but particularly in terms of diverse and expert personnel. Organized efforts at policy intelligence and investigation generally withdrew into an anonymous civil service, a tendency given further impetus by the First World War.

Throughout the period of modern social policy, there is no mistaking the general difference between British and Swedish practice: the inclusion of groups outside the civil service has remained an occasional, usually haphazard, event in Britain rather than a routinized political procedure; non-civil service groups have typically been treated as parties to be consulted rather than as participants integrated into the formulative policy deliberations. At the same time, British royal commissions have become an infrequently used tool for submitting major controversial issues to ostensibly impartial, outside experts—the last royal commissions to deal with social security, for example, being the 1930 Commission on Unemployment Insurance and 1938 Commission on Workmen's Compensation. The "blue ribbon" status of British royal commissions is itself one indication of their exceptional rather than normal part in the policy process. British public inquiries have become mechanisms devoted almost exclusively to resolving conflict and gathering information on problems of day-to-day administration, not major policy making. The Swedish investigatory commission on the other hand remains an everyday phenomenon where the "partiality" of all participants is assumed in an attempt to balance the views of various groups; on major issues, it will include representatives of the civil service, the four political parties, and affected interest groups.[21] The involvement of legislators, which has been found in about

21. In rare cases a British type of impartial commission has been used, e.g. in the 1963 investigation of the handling by the government of a case of espionage by a top-ranking Swedish military officer, Stig Wennerström. In the interwar period some attempt was made in Britain to use "conferences" of interested parties to arrive at agreement on major issues; examples are the 1914 conference on Irish home rule, 1919 on industry, 1926 on imperial policy, and 1931–33 on Indian government. These conferences were rarely successful.

one-half of all Swedish commissions in this century and in the majority of investigations of major questions, remains quite exceptional in Britain. British advocates of including MPs in policy investigations have typically emphasized the educational value to the MPs, not the value to the commission. Reliance on extra-civil service inquiry is still likely to be regarded by informed British opinion as a sign of weakness in the normal governmental process.

While a snapshot view of contemporary social policy could cursorily label both Britain and Sweden as parliamentary democracies, studying developmental tendencies illuminates potentially important political differences in the policy environment. The formative period for pensions, unemployment insurance, and other income maintenance policies characteristic of the welfare state was roughly the 40 years preceding World War I. During most of this time British politics was characterized by far more coherent political parties, a long-established parliamentary system, almost universal male suffrage, and a relatively weak administrative machine; Swedish politics contained far fewer democratic elements and depended more heavily on a bureaucratic-aristocratic government integrated with a strong system of collaborative investigatory commissions.

There is no self-evident answer as to what effect these political differences had on social policy. For that, the only alternative is to examine the detailed evidence on individual policies. But before doing so we must turn to a third aspect of the policy environment which set the stage for modern social policy: the inheritance from past policy itself.

The Policy Inheritance

The men who charted the first departures into modern social policy were not amnesiacs. The substance of their policies was not a simple by-product dictated by economic, social, and political preconditions; a record of rising personal income or developing parliamentary government provides very little guidance on what practical measures to take against cycles of unemployment or poverty among the aged. Of course reasonable men have always tried to pick their way through complexity and uncertainty by looking at what has been done in the past. In modern social policy, however, the tie with the past was more profound. Here, perhaps to an exceptional degree, what reformers hoped for was a function of what they were reacting against. With varying degrees of deliberateness, all were reacting against a background of inherited techniques, forms, and presumptions collectively known as the poor law. To begin understanding the substance of what they did, we must turn to what had already been done.

At the period when this study begins, the poor law was the only form of state provision for those in need. The core of this policy was to present the needy with an unpleasant trade-off: public aid in cash and in kind would be provided near a subsistence minimum, but in return for this the recipient had to suffer social stigma through the loss of personal dignity and citizenship rights. The aided citizen had to become a subcitizen, a pauper.

There were important differences between Britain and Sweden in the rigidity and organization of this doctrine and thus in policy inheritances. At the same time broad, common trends characterized the sequence of each nation's early social policy. The three generally comparable phases in this development were the delivery of charity-oriented relief through the church, its overshadowing by state control and prohibitions, and finally deliberate poor law attempts at social engineering in accord with the "laws" of political economy. What follows is only a sketch in the broadest possible strokes, but even this can help us appreciate the differences and similarities in each nation's inherited policy record,[22] as well as bring out several important points about social policy making that may be as relevant today as in the premodern era.

Reflecting its common Western European heritage, early social policy in both Britain and Sweden was centered in the institution of the Church. The Church's importance lay not only in its religious tenets but in its social reality as a geographic unit of believers living in the local parish. Relief of "God's poor" was a parish function and Christian duty throughout the medieval period, with part of the tithe (often grain) reserved for needs of the parish poor and distributed by a parish official. In Christian doctrine, poverty could be considered a virtue and begging an accepted means of livelihood. Most important,

---

22. General accounts of early Swedish social policy are Karl Höjer, *Svensk Socialpolitick Historia*; Arthur Montgomery, *Svensk Socialpolitick under 1800–talet,*; K. Hansson-Preusler, "Den Kommunala fattigvården i arbete" and, for changes after 1871, Walter Korpi, *Fattigdom i välfärden*. My discussion of poor law history in England draws heavily on Sidney and Beatrice Webb's *English Local Government: English Poor Law History*, vols. 1 and 2, and W. E. Tate, *The Parish Chest; A Study of the Records of Parochial Administration in England*. A recent and most readable account is Brian Inglis's *Poverty and the Industrial Revolution*.

the emphasis of such Church relief was always upon the giver rather than the recipient. The word *alms* was itself derived from the Greek word for pity, and charity was a moral imperative believed to play a vital part in building up a credit of heavenly rewards and dispensations.

A vital change occurred with the Reformation and establishment of state churches in Britain and Sweden during the sixteenth century. With the supplantation of the Catholic Church, the state for the first time assumed ultimate responsibility for the care of the poor. Any immediate changes in the treatment of the poor were probably small, and parishes as local administrative units survived for 400 years in each country. But in principle and in the long term, the change from religious duty to state authority was crucial. State responsibility meant a fundamental alteration in the previous religious perspective, despite the politics and corrupt dispensations which had crept into religion's appeal to charitable virtues. If the Church was concerned primarily with virtues of the giver, the state was most concerned with maintaining social order. Primary emphasis in the new Swedish and British regulations for poor relief—regulations first promulgated under authority of the sixteenth-century national monarchs—was placed upon controlling the widespread begging and vagrancy, particularly that of the able-bodied. Each national government first attempted to prohibit begging and, when this proved impractical, began to institute a system of issuing begging permits.

At the heart of these changes was far more than an abstract theory of church-state relations; throughout Europe the period was one of intense social upheaval. Under the impact of a rapid growth in freer markets and wage labor, Church charity was clearly becoming outpaced by the problem of the poor. Even before the Reformation, the religious system was demonstrating its incapacities, as unrestricted charity without regard to the recipients seemed to many to encourage the growing hordes of beggars. One major concern of Reformation intellectuals was precisely this need for a new, more controlled, secular approach to the entire question of poor relief. It is perhaps not too much of an exaggeration to say that a key motivating force behind the Protestant ethic and its emphasis on duty, work, and self-support was a reaction against the indiscriminate charity of previous Church social policy. Henceforth, poverty could be considered a disgrace and sign of reluctance to work; attention would focus on aiding only those who were "deserving."

The most important point here is to recognize the essentially international character of these attempts at developing secular alternatives in social policy. The period 1490–1530 saw a vast upsurge of such reformist zeal in the European market for social policy ideas. Poor relief reform became a major topic of leading thinkers across the continent—thinkers such as John Major (1516) in Paris, Martin Luther (1520) in Germany, Ulrich Zwingli (1524) in Zurich. Luther, in his *Appeal to the Christian Nobility*, called on the nobles to abolish begging and provide assistance to the needy, while Thomas More's *Utopia* (1516) gave a humanitarian view of the problem and criticized the increasing resort to repression. Nor were Protestants the only participants in this policy discussion. In 1526 the Catholic humanist Juan Luis Vives of Burges produced a tract on poor relief and the need for complete civil government responsibility which became a European best seller. In particular, the system adopted in Ypres in the 1520s was widely publicized and copied throughout Europe. By prohibiting begging, organizing private charity, and establishing private citizens as overseers and prefects to determine needs and distribute relief, the massive vagrancy problem in this depressed medieval town was cut dramatically. What Ashley said of English policy applies as well to Swedish policy:

> The English legislation beginning in 1536 and leading to "the poor law of Elizabeth" was but the English phase of a general European movement of reform. . . . It was not called for by anything peculiar to England, either in its economic development or in its ecclesiastical history. . . . English statesmen, at every step of their action in this matter, moved in an atmosphere of European discussion.[23]

The first major acts of the Reformation and the immediate period thereafter stamped the character of national poor law policy in both Britain and Sweden for the next 300 years. It was a policy based largely upon repressive measures against begging and vagrancy, exhortations for local parish support, and some attempt to distinguish between those unable to work—who were tolerated and supported with a variety of local techniques—and the able-bodied, who were constrained by the

23. Sir William J. Ashley, *An Introduction to English Economic History and Theory*, Part 2, p. 350. A good description of early Swedish acts can be found in the *Fattigvårdskommittee betänkande angående fattigvården i riket*, 1837.

established medieval prohibitions against mobility. One should not, however, confuse the essentially international scope of policy deliberations with effective policy as implemented. Rarely has the gap between promise and performance been greater. Formally, policy was being developed by British and Swedish national monarchies within an atmosphere of European discussion involving a small, learned elite. In practice, policy was heavily dependent on dispersed local elites—the gentry and provincial groups with the administrative resources to implement poor relief. Whatever national law was enacted could usually be but poorly enforced and was often no more than an expression of intent. The key local units in both nations remained the parishes (headed by justices, vicar, and several churchwardens) and overseers of the poor, local householders serving annual unpaid terms.

Amid the local variations, certain important differences grew up between the two nations, flowing at least in part from the differences in political development mentioned earlier. The more centralized administration in Sweden allowed somewhat more coherent controls, as in 1638 when all governors (*landshövding*) were instructed to "urge" parishes not to issue further begging passes but "to support their own poor until they do die." As in Britain, regulations in Sweden (1686) laid down the parishes' duty to provide almshouses (*fattigstugor*) for the poor, but the obligation was measurably strengthened by specific instructions for governors to see to it that parishes did indeed build and maintain such dwellings. In Britain, initial attempts at centralization were stopped more abruptly. The vital contribution of the Elizabethan poor law to social policy had been to establish the supremacy of secular powers in poor relief; with justices of the peace exercising general supervisory control, overseers and churchwardens were appointed to be responsible for providing for the destitute and were empowered to institute compulsory poor rates. Between 1590 and 1640 the centralizing tendency reached its climax with the emergence of national Commissioners for the Poor, largely privy councillors who served irrespective of changes in monarch and reviewed poor law information from all parts of the country. In effect, the Civil War decapitated not only Charles I but also this evolving central administration; the trunk, in the form of local justices of the peace and parish officers, was left intact to function with supreme power until Britain's 1832 reforms.

In both Britain and Sweden a few enlightened localities at various times sought to establish specialized institutions for categories of the poor, such as the aged, sick, young, and criminal. In Britain the economic and administrative resources were particularly inadequate for drawing these distinctions, and the institutions invariably reverted to the traditional mixed poorhouse which forced all varieties of the poor together. Nowhere was the importance of Swedish central administration better demonstrated than in hospital care. Late in the 1600s, the first county medical officer was appointed under authority of the national administration and during the next century their numbers grew considerably. In the mid-1700s, the first county hospital was established and by the beginning of the 1800s there existed, as there did not in Britain, a fairly clear institutional separation between poor relief and treatment of the ill.

Against this ramshackle and motley base of secular poor relief in Britain and Sweden occurred the next great challenge to traditional medieval policy—the unprecedented population growth of the eighteenth century; the resulting demand for policy responses has continued until the present day. In both nations, the increasing pressure of population growth on poor relief is evident from around the middle of the 1700s, and in both nations the typical reaction was to make more intensive use of existing poor law techniques.

The problems of rapid population growth were not so dramatically apparent in the more thinly populated and rural Sweden. With the subdivision of lands into smaller consolidated lots and persistent predominance of the agricultural sector, much of the poor relief problem could be disguised in a multitude of subsistence farms and rural underemployment. But even in this setting traditional Swedish social policy could not remain entirely unchanged, again under prodding of national bureaucrats. In 1763 a central government decree stipulated that every parish was to be responsible for its poor and to tax its members at a yearly rate for the support of children's homes and hospitals. Local objections altered the plan so as to allow each locality the right to decide methods of financing, but the decree of 1763 did firmly fix local responsibility for the first time and has been rightly looked upon as the first national social assistance law (*fattigvårdsförordning*) in Sweden. During the latter half of the 1700s, a tendency also developed in some Swedish parishes to transform small almshouses into larger poorhouses similar to those in the more populous areas of Britain. But despite these accommodations of traditional policy to population growth and economic change, the customary forms of poor relief remained predominant in agrarian Sweden. One of the oldest, begging, also remained one of the most common, and even in the 1830s the Swedish poor law investigators were unable to make accurate estimates of poor relief costs in many parishes because of the widespread reliance on mendicancy.

Developments in Britain took a different turn from those in Sweden, particularly with regard to workhouse institutions. To some extent this was due to the different socioeconomic preconditions; in both countries the workhouse was typically an urban phenomenon, and, given Sweden's late economic development, the workhouse movement there was unlikely to go nearly as far as in the more urban Britain. A related and important reason for Britain's preoccupation with workhouses lay in the policy inheritance itself and the political power of local economizing interests. The workhouse as a technique of social policy was a learned device borrowed from emerging industrial forms by local, not national, leaders in order to deal with their new secular responsibility for the poor. During the last half of the seventeenth century, and drawing inspiration from a number of other municipal experiments in Europe, attempts had been made in many British towns to set the poor to profitable employment, attempts usually made by reformers with commercial and manufacturing backgrounds. Basically, the plan was to provide raw materials and employ the poor in primitive factories which, by increasing national wealth, would not only be good mercantilism but would also enable the poor to be self-supporting. In all of these municipal workhouses the founders' original intention ultimately failed: the workhouses were not profitable enterprises analogous to private business. But two unintended by-products of the system led to dramatically reduced poor relief costs in a Bristol experiment and encouraged other towns to copy the workhouse technique. In the first place, one municipal workhouse meant economies of scale compared to the various parish units. Far more important was the fact that by means of the workhouse movement British policy makers in the first half of the 1700s accidentally discovered the infamous workhouse test: offering a place in the public factory could be considered a way of distinguishing between those who were and those who were not in real need. Even if the workhouse did not turn out products that increased national wealth, assigning the poor to it had a stigmatizing effect and cut down significantly the number of requests for poor relief. And since secular relief had brought with it compulsory government taxation, cost reduction was a key issue to the local ratepayers. Throughout the country, municipal poor law reformers in the eighteenth century succeeded in drastically reducing such costs using workhouses solely as semi-penal deterrents with no pretension of productive employment.

Willingness to accept miserable conditions as the test of destitution could be effective against layabouts, but it condemned to misery those truly in need. The Webbs estimated that by the last quarter of the eighteenth century, the British workhouse had become almost exclusively the home of the infirm, disabled, sick, and young, or what were then called the "impotent poor." At the same time, contracting out had become a common way of avoiding direct parish administration and was subject to its own particular abuses. A fixed sum payment to contractors could result in the most inhumane cost-cutting techniques, while per capita payments led to the tolerance of promiscuity and drunkenness in order to attract clients.

Well before the democratic era or even the threatening example of the French Revolution, policy was being adapted to correct some of the perceived failings of past policy. The major figures in the call for new policy reforms were local magistrates, men of letters, or, more generically, the English gentry, which traditionally had supervised the parish poor relief system. During the 1760s, a continuing blast of humanitarian criticism from press, pulpit, and county seats of the squirearchy left little doubt about the misery engendered by workhouses and particularly by the contracting-out system used in smaller parishes. One parliamentary investigation in 1767 showed no less than 93 percent of parish pauper infants dying before the age of three. In 1782, after 20 years of agitation, the viewpoint of the country gentlemen legislators finally prevailed in national legislation. Against the indiscriminate institutionalization in workhouses, the local policy makers were encouraged to undertake a more selective and systematic use of the earlier idea (which workhouses in turn had been reacting against) of outdoor relief. By the end of the eighteenth century, poor law policy was for all practical purposes concentrated in the discretionary authority of local magistrates to provide cash allowances.

An old policy idea in new circumstances can easily become something novel, and this now occurred in British social policy. With the agrarian revolution under way, the problem was not simply population growth and rural indigence but a growing core of landless agricultural laborers inherently surplus to the economy and impoverished in an era of high prices. The concrete response was evolved through a wide-ranging and uncoordinated series of policy adjustments by local officials, as simultaneously in the mid-1790s a number of magistrates in the south (where the agricultural laborer problem was most severe) began to experiment with more systematic forms of outdoor relief for the able-bodied poor. The fundamental difficulty lay in the conflict between, on the one hand, an unwillingness or inability to raise wages sufficiently in an inflationary, worker-surplus agriculture and, on the other hand, the fears and compassion which prevented magistrates from allowing mass destitution through inadequate work and pay. The specific policy technique was hit upon at a meeting of Berkshire justices at the Pelican Inn in Speenhamland on May 6, 1795. After discussing and rejecting the idea of fixing minimum wages, the magistrates agreed on a comprehensive table of relief rates for the parishes. The new rates, based on the price of bread and family size, would supplement inadequate wages to bring workers' incomes up to a level sufficient to provide physical subsistence.[24] This crude but automatic cost-of-living adjustment and ease with which the tables could be used elsewhere provided an elegant new relief technique, and the Speenhamland system became ever more widely adopted, extending to most areas of the country. In a more sophisticated form, the justices had returned to the "indiscriminate" outdoor relief prevalent before the workhouse movement had become fashionable at the beginning of the eighteenth century.

The Speenhamland system remained the predominant expression of British social policy throughout the Napoleonic Wars and until 1815. There can be little doubt that the cost of poor relief rose dramatically in the 20 years after 1795, but most recent economic research shows this to have been a general phenomenon in counties both with and without the Speenhamland system. What higher costs did exist in Speenhamland counties seem attributable more to the economic limitations of traditional wheat-growing areas than to any administrative arrangements of relief.

24. The table assumed that a man requires a minimum of three loaves of bread per week and dependents one and a quarter to one and a half loaves per week. Thus poor relief would be raised 3 pence to a man for every 1 penny by which the price of a loaf rose above one shilling, with adjustments for the number of dependents. At the beginning of 1795, Buckinghamshire magistrates had ordered married men's wages supplemented up to a minimum of 6 shillings per week, and Hampshire justices had acted similarly.

As usual in politics, the vital factor was not what actually happened but what men believed to be happening. Reliance on outdoor relief for the able-bodied came to be accepted as the cause of mounting relief costs, and the greater development of representative political institutions in Britain vis-à-vis Sweden helped ensure greater scope for effective protests by ratepayers against these costs. Complaints were widespread in the British Parliament and focused on the rate in aid of wages and indiscriminate poor relief. The impact of this "popular" representation was heightened through rudimentary but influential investigations by parliamentary committees; gradually their reports and severe strictures against outdoor relief helped lead many poor law vestries to abandon the Speenhamland system.[25] The existing poor relief methods were condemned as not only profligate and burdensome to ratepayers but also as disadvantageous to the worker, since it was said to pay employers to keep wages low and thus leave the parish to bear the burden of raising income to a subsistence level. While all investigations roundly condemned supposedly ruinous Speenhamland relief, no constructive remedies were offered by Parliament and Tory ministries refused to interfere with the local magistracy. In most parishes abandonment of the magistrates' scale meant reversion to discretionary allowances at the hands of parish overseers.

With this background, it is perhaps easier to see why the policy inheritance and thus the nineteenth-century point of departure for modern social policy differed somewhat in Britain and Sweden. Swedish policy had contained isolated examples of wage supplementation but no counterpart to the extensive British Speenhamland system. In 1834 British policy reacted with a vengeance against outdoor relief scales. Once again the creation of a positive policy alternative stemmed from local experimentation. From the beginning of the 1820s, poor law reforms in Nottinghamshire under George Nicholls had attracted increasing attention throughout the country. In essence, the "new" approach aimed at reorganizing relief into a more systematic use of the deterrent workhouses of a century earlier. With a flood of pamphlets and Nicholls's evangelizing zeal, the decade prior to 1834 witnessed a number of local reforms along these more restrictive lines. Although

---

25. J. D. Marshall, *The Old Poor Law, 1795–1834,* provides a valuable summary of these developments and a review of the literature. The conflicting pressures of excessive demands and penurious reactions were summed up in one parish overseer's record book: "William Owens. Wants everything. Allowed nothing." Quoted in Tate, *The Parish Chest,* p. 235.

later arguments for the workhouse approach were to emphasize various advantages, including the moral benefits to the poor themselves, there can be little doubt that the original and sustaining force behind the reform movement lay in the familiar desire of local civic leaders to cut relief costs.[26] Far from being a by-product of the 1832 enfranchisement of the emerging middle class, the substance of the 1834 poor law reform was largely a reconfirmation of the deterrent workhouse idea rediscovered and spread locally in the previous decade. The relevant investigation was begun before members of the newly reformed parliament took their seats.

What marked 1834 policy as novel was the tighter and more deliberate intellectual and administrative framework for the workhouse idea. Like most major reforms in the nineteenth century, the 1834 act followed a "scientific" royal commission investigation. The commission investigation was an unprecedentedly detailed study of existing poor relief conditions, with commissioners traveling throughout Britain to gather information. In their analysis, however, the investigators had clearly begun with a conviction that outdoor relief to those able to work was ruining the nation, and their instructions were framed to elicit evidence to support this conclusion. Instructions to the roving commissioners had been written personally by Nassau Senior, Britain's leading political economist, and it was the tight theoretical structure of political economy that provided the systematic, intellectual underpinnings to the investigation. Following from the principles of political economy, the commission's two major recommendations were clear and simple: "all relief to able-bodied persons or their families otherwise than in a well-regulated workhouse shall be declared unlawful" (the workhouse test), and the able-bodied workman's "situation, as a whole, shall not be made really or apparently so eligible as the situation of the independent laborer of the lowest class" (the principle of less eligibility). In essence, the commission's substantive recommendations formalized the evolving workhouse practice, found in many parishes, which in turn were drawing upon eighteenth-century precedents.

26. Nicholls was from an old Cornish family and prospered through family connections in shipping. In 1821, he became overseer of the poor in Southwall, a town of 3,000 inhabitants, and was largely responsible for economies in relief in this agricultural area. By his own account, from the first, "we contemplated the workhouse as little more than an instrument of economy, calculated to lessen the parish expenditure by a reduction of the poor rates." Concern with the "moral condition" of the poor came later. Sir George Nicholls, *A History of the English Poor Law*, p. xiii.

Equally important, this coherent policy doctrine was now to be embodied in a national administrative structure. Establishment of "well-regulated" workhouses was not to be left to the play of traditional local forces but assured by creating local unions of parishes, new organizations administered by locally elected guardians and supervised by a central government board. Although the common inclination was to blame outdoor relief for the ills of the country, the Speenhamland system, like the earlier workhouse experiments, seems to have deteriorated largely because of the lack of administrative resources in the amateur magistracy. It was in terms of *administrative* form rather than policy content that the 1834 poor law gave expression to utilitarianism. Compulsory central direction was now to be vested in a national board of three Poor Law Commissioners, experts meeting in private who would construct a new structure of social policy administration and do so without consent of localities or parliamentary ratification. In all essentials this new administrative plan followed the model for a Ministry of Indigence Relief formulated by Jeremy Bentham in his *Constitutional Code*. Bentham's disciples became the driving figures in a struggle to end medieval parochialism and establish a central administration in social policy. With the new complexity of social problems and premium upon research and administrative planning, it was largely their practical administrative talents rather than their political theories which brought Benthamites to positions of power. It is essential to realize that the workhouse test was primarily a way of reducing information demands upon the limited administrative resources: "Thus the parish officer, being furnished with an unerring test of the necessity of applicants, is relieved from his painful and difficult responsibility."[27]

The new doctrine was preached widely by enlightened reformers, and while opposed by much of the press and some representatives of growing industrial towns, the investigation's recommendations were overwhelmingly accepted in Parliament. The Poor Law Reform Act adopted in 1834 was not a party issue but commanded support among a majority of both Whigs and Tories in the reformed Parliament. Although political difficulties and compromise were to blur the ap-

27. This and preceding quotations from the commission are taken from the *Report of an Inquiry into the Administration and Practical Operation of the Poor Laws* (1834), reprinted in *Social Welfare in Transition*, ed. Roy Lubove; the administrative justification for the proposed policy content is set out most clearly in pp. 58 ff.

plication of the 1834 principles, the basic expression of British policy for the rest of the nineteenth century remained deterrent workhouses under national administrative supervision. In substance, it was a policy derived from the mixture of reaction against past policy experiences and administrative precepts of some of the period's brightest intellectual talent. Before discussing the alterations that occurred during subsequent implementation, it is useful to pause and compare this policy inheritance with developments in Sweden.

The passage of the 1834 reform represented the final overthrow of the magistracy's power in British poor relief and the beginning of central administration based on a nationally formulated social policy. Unlike the Swedish experience, British central administration from the beginning was thereby deliberately tied to a specific policy doctrine. In Sweden, as we have seen, the nineteenth century brought with it a steadily mounting problem of rural proletarianization. But partly because of greater administrative centralization, partly because of differing economic contexts, Swedish social policy did not swing between the British extremes of outdoor relief and workhouse deterrence.

During the first part of the nineteenth century there were sporadic Swedish attempts to strengthen medieval regulations on mobility of the poor and the penalties against vagrancy. During the Napoleonic Wars, some attempt was made to use forced workhouses to deal more systematically with vagrancy, but by the 1820s it was clear that the number of persons was too large and that means were lacking to build sufficient institutions. In 1819, pressures on those prisons and workhouses that did exist led the national government to revise the medieval policy and order that only criminals and beggars who were public nuisances should be sent to such institutions. Several years later the regulation that unemployed vagrants could be forced into military service was dropped, and vagrancy for its own sake ceased to entail punishment. National government policy was gradually and belatedly adjusting itself to the emergence of an independent labor force.

The central government's actions aroused widespread complaint, particularly from the Riksdag and local commune representatives. No equivalent to the British magistracy's allowance scales existed in Sweden, but complaints could still be made against the abandonment of the old regulations and what were perceived as liberalizations in poor relief by the central government. As in Britain, the return of economic depression and higher relief costs in the 1830s brought vehement local appeals for poor law reform, so much so that the government was forced to retreat somewhat; in 1833, at the insistence of Riksdag and local representatives, the national government issued new regulations sharpening certain penalties against the general category of the unemployed. Even then central government organs generally objected that hardships and complications would result, given the changing nature of the working class, and through special regulations sought to mellow the more severe penalties. Although the 1833 law attempted to distinguish between "depraved" and normal vagrancy, the familiar consequences developed: a vast influx of unemployed farm workers into whatever institutions existed and mixture of these with hardcore criminals. In 1834–35, the Riksdag also tried to extend migration restrictions beyond Stockholm, to limit landless labor and persons with underaged children from moving out of their own parishes, and to make employers financially liable for any relief costs of employees whom they brought into a new area.

As in Britain, the government responded to these pressures by establishing a top level investigatory commission in 1837, the first comprehensive national investigation of poor relief in Sweden. Commission inquiries revealed vast national variation in the provision for poor relief. In general, the more populous the area, the more organized secular poor relief was undertaken, from the poorhouses and workhouses in the southern urban areas to a total lack of public poor relief in the thinly populated north. Unlike its British counterpart, however, the 1837 commission contained a strong contingent of government civil servants and was particularly sensitive to actual administrative problems attendant upon any possible poor law reforms. The regulations against vagrancy were considered unenforceable; the commission explicitly recognized that it was a practical impossibility to distinguish between the vagrant and the ordinary unemployed of an evolving economy. The most widely discussed solution was to import from Britain the workhouse test. Again, however, the commission concluded that administrative difficulties connected with this course outweighed any possible advantages; institutional care played a secondary role in most localities and was unknown in many. Even supporters of the workhouse idea came to doubt that a sufficient number of such institutions could be built or effectively administered. In large part, the British model was also rejected because of what can only be called the more objective investigatory process in Sweden. The Swedish commission's thorough study of poor relief statistics gave little support to the often heard complaints that overly indulgent poor relief was leading to the pauperization of workers and burdening society. As the commission concluded, "Neither costs nor poorhouse inmate numbers seem to have risen to any height by which worries need be aroused."[28] In the end, the major policy alteration to result from the investigation was a strengthening of previous restrictions against the migration of bad welfare risks and of the employers' financial liability should migrating employees require poor relief. As a means of fighting against ignorance, a factor that was seen as a major cause of poverty, the commission recommended a comprehensive program of public elementary education.

Comparison of the ferment for poor relief reform in Britain and Sweden during the 1830s shows many of the same arguments used for reform but substantially dissimilar results. The economic and social contexts were, of course, different in each country, with Swedish practice coming closest to British in the few urban areas which existed. Also, the policy inheritance in Sweden contained no equivalent to the Speenhamland system that had led to a strong counterreaction in Britain. Finally, the Swedish policy process was more decisively influenced by professional central administration and investigation and more immune from the economizing pressures of parliamentary representatives and local interests.

Yet there is one important commonality between the two nations. In comparison with previous national policy, the nineteenth-century deliberations on poor relief in both countries exhibited a uniquely developed attention to questions of social relations, what one author has called "the discovery of society."[29] It was with regard to questions of poor relief and pauperism that the political community first became concerned with understanding and manipulating social conditions by means of deliberate political policy. During this period of supposedly

28. *Fattigvårdskommittee betänkande,* pp. 23 ff.

29. Karl Polanyi, *The Great Transformation,* p. 33. This societal viewpoint remained central to the poor law, as reflected in the defense given it by James Davy, Chief Inspector for the Poor Law Division, in testimony to the 1906–09 Royal Commission on the Poor Law: "according to my view, what you have to consider is not this or that pauper, but the general good of the whole community; and the general good of the whole community is, I submit, that every obstacle should be put in the way of a man settling down into the status of a pauper— for pauper he is, whether he is disenfranchised or whether he is not." *Report of the Royal Commission on the Poor Law,* 1909, appendix vol. 1, minutes of evidence, question 3219.

laissez faire government, a shift becomes perceptible from the medieval policy of largely negative state prohibitions to new attempts at deliberate social engineering. In Britain, it is precisely because of this self-conscious aim to structure incentives for the good of society that the 1834 reformers and their successors were able to accept the admitted hardships that the workhouse test and less eligibility principle entailed. The nineteenth-century British poor law was a manifestation of the period's most enlightened principles of Malthusian social science and political economy, a heroic attempt at social planning in the broadest sense. In Sweden, the far-reaching but more prudent scope of this planning was well expressed in the 1837 investigation's criticism of early and imprudent marriages as a cause of higher poor relief costs. Proposals for forbidding marriage of persons under 25 or those without sufficient means were seriously discussed but rejected, with the astute administrative observation that any such regulations would only increase illegitimacy and add further to the relief burden; eventually, faith was put in that great surrogate for more detailed planning, education, to solve the problem.

Developments after the 1830s in Britain and Sweden brought some accommodations to practical administrative difficulties but little fundamental change in poor law policy. Particularly in Britain the hopes of 1834 quickly proved to be administrative nonsense. Faced with local protests, Poor Law Commissioners never fully implemented the supposed prohibition of outdoor relief to the able-bodied. The original 1834 reform had also intended separate institutional care apart from the workhouse for the young, sick, and old, but in practice there were simply not sufficient administrative resources to provide such specialized care. The general mixed workhouse unintentionally became the typical manifestation of British social policy during the remainder of the nineteenth century. Localist resentment against the unbridled powers of the Poor Law Commissioners and a series of scandals on workhouse conditions also led Parliament to abolish the commissioners' independent power. In 1845 the commission was made into a Poor Law Board with one political head who sat in Parliament, and in 1871, under the pressure for tighter control of relief costs, the board was absorbed into the newly created Local Government Board. Likewise, stringency in the application of poor law doctrine fluctuated. At times local autonomy increased and central administrators tended to rely on painstaking adherence to formal procedures; after the commercial depression of

1866–67 and an accompanying increase in poor relief, central officials launched a vigorous attack against almost all outdoor relief—thus going further than even the 1834 report, which had recommended the workhouse test only for the able-bodied and their families.

Throughout these fluctuations, the consideration of British policy at the national level fell largely to permanent officers of the Poor Law Board. This was not, as in Sweden, simply an influential national administration but an administration specifically established to implement the particular principles of 1834. Swedish poverty was certainly no less severe than British, but without the doctrinaire approach of the 1834 British act and its administrative institutionalization, policy was somewhat more adaptive to variable conditions. After the 1830s, Swedish poor relief policy exhibited its usual central-local balance, bred by a fine regard for administrative feasibility. As in the past, the central administration found itself continuously attacked by a parliament and local interests favoring more restrictive measures. Difficulties multiplied in operating restrictions on migration, with the government intervening against extreme local interpretations of the regulations. Despite a storm of parliamentary protest, in 1853 the central government finally fixed residency in the commune where the applicant was or ought to be census-registered; the duty was now laid clearly upon the communes to provide care and support to those poor unable to work. Communes unable to meet their relief obligations could apply to the county authorities for financial support. A right of appeal was also established for applicants who had been denied poor relief by the local communes. These reforms brought no revolutionary change but did bring more efficient organization and a more effective tax base into poor relief policy.

As in Britain, Swedish policy fluctuated between concerns for adequacy and economic restrictiveness. The same international economic crisis experienced in Britain in the 1860s brought Swedish poor relief expenditure to its highest level of the century and again fomented the familiar demands for poor law reform. As in Britain, the result in 1871 was a turn to more restrictive poor law policies. In particular, criticism was vigorously expressed in the new "reformed" Riksdag and directed against the obligatory nature of central regulations by which applicants could enjoin communes to distribute poor relief. The major policy consequence of the 1866 reform strengthening representative institutions of Swedish government was a revived restrictiveness in social policy in keeping with the interests of those more effectively represented. A general statute of 1871 was initiated by the Riksdag and reduced obligatory poor relief to a minimum, covering only orphans and the insane and otherwise allowing the localities to give relief as they thought necessary. The statute also abolished the right of appeal unless it could be shown that the commune had acted contrary to legal procedure. The most effective force opposing and mellowing this reaction remained Sweden's national administrators.[30]

At approximately this point—the last quarter of the nineteenth century—lay the origins of modern cash provision for old age and unemployment in Britain and Sweden. Any thorough history would have to detail a large number of continuing changes made within the poor law system, changes that depended greatly upon the philanthropic reformers and essayists who worked to make relief regulations less severe. But further alterations in the poor law (such as excusing the sick from the workhouse test and making educational provision for pauper youths) will not be dealt with here, for the major changes in modern social policy now occurred *outside* the poor law in areas such as old age pensions and unemployment insurance. Neither Britain nor Sweden started from a tabula rasa; deep marks were left by the change to secular poor relief and its emphasis on costs, domestic order, the quality of recipient rather than giver and, ultimately, social planning. In Britain, the marks of the poor law went particularly deep. Strong local autonomy, a powerful legislature representative of propertied interests, and lack of effective central administration were important political factors, not only in facilitating a restrictive relief policy but in fostering a vacillation between extremes of indulgence and a particularly doctrinaire system of deterrence.

The preceding sketch of the context of modern social policy begins to flesh out one major theme: the considerable impact of policy inheritances upon the substance of policy making. Well before the contemporary era of democratic participation, party competition, and interest group organization, social policy was not a static or unresponsive set of decrees but a moving, reacting social process. The reaction was not only to socioeconomic change in the abstract but also to previous policy itself. In general, policy was one beat behind the rhythm of events, forever remedying the defects perceived to be emerging from

30. These conflicts are more fully discussed in Hàgan Berggren and Göran Nilsson, *Liberal Socialpolitik, 1853–1884.*

the previous policy change. Speenhamland reacted against workhouse abuses but sought to preserve patriarchal support for the agricultural worker's subsistence just as his labor was increasingly becoming a commodity in the money relationships of a national market; nineteenth-century poor law reforms were designed to remedy a supposedly misused relief system among agricultural workers but did so at a time when industrial workers were beginning to predominate and were abandoning the old agrarian society for new forms of wage dependence and social vulnerability. The one thing as sure as continuing challenges to social policy is the mistiming of responses.

Nations, like individuals, rarely start equal. Differences in industrialization's timing, democratic structures, and policy inheritances created different backgrounds for twentieth-century changes in British and Swedish social policy. Yet despite these differences, both nations began to consider the same policy departures almost simultaneously at the end of the nineteenth century. To begin understanding this paradox and the substance of the resulting social policies, we must turn in the following chapters to far more detailed accounts. How is it that these modern states have come to aid those unable to find work or too old to work?

3 Support for the Unemployed

Unemployment was not the first area of need to be attacked by modern social policy, but it was perhaps the most strategic. For four centuries, the driving concern behind most major changes in poor law policy had been the problem of the "able-bodied poor." Undoubtedly a key reason for this policy attention to the able-bodied over all other needy groups lay in the state's concern with poor relief as a tool of social order; it was not the sick or infirm who burned hayricks and broke shop windows.

By the end of the nineteenth century, British policy had reacted with what was ostensibly the prohibition of all outdoor relief to the able-bodied and acceptance of a place in the workhouse as the test of need. In practice, local conditions remained quite variable, and particularly in urban industrial areas the able-bodied poor could expect meager outdoor relief, possibly in exchange for some task of physical labor. In Sweden restrictions on labor mobility were common, and while the government formally required communes to provide work for the able-bodied poor, local provision was again variable and particularly restrictive after 1871. Thus at the end of the nineteenth century the poor law in Britain and Sweden was being increasingly strained by that troublesome category of the poor who were neither infirm nor working. In both countries, poor relief, with its accompanying disgrace and opprobrium, remained the only major avenue open to the unemployed citizen seeking state aid.

Seventy years later, state insurance against unemployment is a universally accepted part of most workers' lives. A study of policy making in the intervening period does show the forces of power and conflict at work but it also shows something more. The generation and development of unemployment insurance well illustrate the variegated, indeliberate, often halting process of social learning through politics. Initiation of British and Swedish unemployment insurance was scarcely the direct result of political party turnover, electoral competition, or interest group pressure. The technique of insuring against unemployment was invented by private and municipal experimentation throughout Europe. On a national basis, the idea was developed and pushed by what were essentially liberal reformers in and at the fringes of the civil service, men seeking a way around the outmoded poor law in an era when cyclical unemployment was a recurring fact of economic life. Introduction of the world's first national program in Britain was a result of several remarkable personal efforts, while the substance of the plan was almost entirely an administrative creation. By virtue of such learning, Sweden, despite its relatively later economic and democratic development, found unemployment insurance an item on its policy agenda at the same time Britain did.

Before turning to detailed accounts of unemployment insurance, we should recognize the distinctive theoretical sophistication of its policy environment. What could and could not be learned in policy was significantly shaped by the fact that the unemployed, as the ablebodied workless became known late in the nineteenth century, were the subject of a well-developed intellectual framework. Classical economic theory was the most powerful analytic tool available and guided British and Swedish policy makers until well into the twentieth century, when its employment doctrine was superseded by Keynesian economics. Policy making, like unemployment insurance, has been bound up with the content of economic doctrine, a fact reflected in Keynes's comment that "practical men, who believe themselves to be quite exempt from intellectual influences, are usually the slaves of some defunct economist."[1] Unemployment insurance policy was embedded in more general economic approaches to the question of unemployment itself.

A basic precondition for development of unemployment policies outside the poor law was the perception of unemployment as a distinctive problem. Throughout most of the nineteenth century, however, unemployment was viewed by the best minds as an accidental phenomenon resulting from minor frictions in economic relations and occasional bad harvests. The heart of the analysis of unemployment lay in political economy and Say's Law (first presented in 1803), which suggested that production generated its own demand. Since there could never be insufficient demand or excessive production, the question of unemployment could be largely dismissed from serious discussion. According to this doctrine, the only possible cause of extensive unemploy-

1. J. M. Keynes, *The General Theory of Employment, Interest, and Money*, p. 383.

ment in society was the setting of wages at too high a level. Since in a state of equilibrium wages corresponded to the marginal product of labor, a rise of wages beyond this level necessarily meant that a part of the labor force could not be employed. Any proposal for major public expenditure to combat unemployment ran up against the same entrenched tenets of a fixed wage and capital sum in society; increased public expenditure would only result in a corresponding reduction in private investment, employment, and capital formation. Money spent on relief payments to the unemployed was at best an expedient dispensation granted by political economy to meet social emergencies outside the bounds of sound economic doctrine. Orthodox economic thinking thus undergirded the traditional viewpoint of the poor law: worklessness as a basis of need resulted from personal failings and not from any impersonal working of poorly adjusted economic aggregates. This economic-social theory could provide a potent and at the time unanswerable analysis to show that individual hardships, while perhaps unfortunate, ultimately contributed to the good of the entire society by maintaining incentives for market adjustments.

In the 80 years before the Second World War, trade cycles brought rising unemployment in some four years out of every eight. These recurring crises could neither be denied nor easily accommodated in classic economics. Modifications in well-established economic doctrines were necessary but this did not alter the assumptions of wage flexibility, Say's Law, or concentration on micro-theory and long-run, static equilibriums. The first systematic empirical studies of trade fluctuations began in the last decades of the nineteenth century. In the works of Swedes Knut Wicksell and Gustav Cassell and British neoclassical economists led by Alfred Marshall, economic theory became accommodated to the reality of trade cycles. Unemployment received new attention as economists now held that significant short-term economic fluctuations in production and employment could occur—largely it was believed through "loss of confidence" and speculative purchases. Equally short-term government measures aimed at facilitating economic adaptations could be of assistance, but at best these would be palliatives; "Before the Great Depression, no government in the world officially accepted responsibility for maintaining a high and stable level of employment"[2] The most politically explosive of these palliatives

2. Robert A. Gordon, *The Goal of Full Employment*, p. 43. For a review of the views of British economists, see K. Hancock, "Unemployment and the Economists in the 1920s"; the leading

was unemployment insurance. Its advent represented one strategic step toward modern social policy.

POLICY INITIATION

Insurance against unemployment is a technique of social organization. Like any piece of technology it had to be invented and diffused, both to other parts of society and to other nations.

Unemployment insurance originated through the uncoordinated responses of diverse workers' associations to the needs of their members. By the nineteenth century, contemporary industrial society had added a new dimension to the traditional type of unemployment; not just poor seasons and harvests but financial adjustments and poor markets for industrial goods could now leave the worker and his family without adequate support. The response of many groups of better-off workmen was to do collectively and more systematically what prudent individual workers had always done—to set aside a part of income for use in bad times. In doing so, the early unions were also serving their own interests by denying in practice a central premise of traditional economic theory: union unemployment benefits were designed not only to relieve distress but to deter the unemployed from undermining wage levels. The first such formal unemployment fund in Britain was created by the foundrymen's union in 1831. Within ten years the number of funds had increased sixfold and, by 1908, 2.4 million workers, largely the higher skilled and paid, were in unions with out-of-work benefits. In Sweden the later industrialization and tardy union growth were reflected in a later and less extensive development of such private collective efforts. The first unemployment fund began with the typographers' union in 1884 and by 1908 there were still only 79,000 union members (largely metalworkers) covered, or approximately 4 percent of the Swedish labor force compared to Britain's roughly 13 percent.[3]

The development of state-supported unemployment insurance in Britain and Sweden must be understood in an international context of

---

Swedish views on unemployment have been well set out in Bertil Öhman's unpublished dissertation, "Arbetslöshet i Svenska historia." For general discussions, see Mark Blaug, *Economic Theory in Retrospect*, and T. W. Hutchinson, *Review of Economic Doctrines, 1870–1929.*

3. Statistics for the two nations are taken from Cd. 5703, 1911; C. 7182, 1893; Andra Kammar tillfälliga utskott, no. 1, *Utlåtande* no. 25 (1909), p. 25; and SOU 59 (1922), p. 52 and table IV. There were of course a number of earlier, informal benefits to the unemployed. "Tramp benefits" for travel originated with journeymen in the Middle Ages and only gradually gave way to stationary benefits, as local depressions merged into national trade depressions.

communication and policy discussion. In the mid-1800s, continental exiles, such as Mazzini, had provided one spur to the development of workingmen's organizations and the idea of contributory subscriptions to private workers' funds. The first shifts toward public involvement, however, occurred in localities where there were few preexisting trade union efforts to supersede. The first *publicly* organized action on unemployment insurance took place in the small cantons of Switzerland. In the 1880s, Germany's experiments with social insurance for industrial injuries and old age had made state insurance a fashionable intellectual topic throughout Europe. The European economic depression in the first half of the 1890s encouraged several economists toward the notion of modeling a similar state insurance against unemployment. Gradually in the next ten years, municipal unemployment insurance schemes began sprouting throughout Western Europe. It was during this time that the initial policy techniques and alternatives were evolved.

In 1892, under the leadership of the economist Valsiljeff, Bern made the first attempt at public unemployment insurance with a voluntary commune insurance fund for those who could expect to be unemployed in the winter. A similar rise of unemployment in building and textiles in St. Gallen led to a decision by the canton council to adopt the world's first compulsory unemployment insurance scheme. By canton referendum in 1894 it was agreed to institute graduated contributions and benefits according to three income categories, along with a town grant, for a provisional two-year period. But local democracy could also be inimical to the extension of social policy. After the second year, with unemployment above the expected 10 percent level and a far larger proportion of contributors than expected belonging to the lowest income class, the fund had a deficit of 5,550 francs. A referendum in the same year ended the expriment, largely it seems because of the resentment of better-off workers at having to contribute to the benefits of others. The experience of St. Gallen was disseminated among policy makers and acted as a strong damper on proposals for any obligatory unemployment insurance in other communes. After a number of years of discussion such a scheme was defeated by referendum in Basle in 1900, and again the opposing votes of the better-off workers themselves seem to have been decisive.[4] In Zurich a similar fate had met a similar proposal in 1898.

4. The defeat was unexpected, since the proposal had the backing of officials from all parties. Of 16,098 entitled to vote, 6,577 voted, with 5,488 against the proposal. My account

Positive as well as negative lessons were being learned and disseminated. In Belgium, where the union movement was relatively old and well-established, a new variant was advanced. Experiences of the Swiss cantons had discouraged the idea of compulsory state insurance, but the city of Ghent began experimenting with the use of public funds to subsidize existing union unemployment insurance plans. In August 1901 the first grants by the Ghent commune were made to unions, as well as to a "thrift fund" for unorganized workers. Although the voluntary fund for the unorganized quickly fell into disuse, results were judged to be so favorable for union members that within six years most major communes in Belgium had adopted similar programs. The "Ghent system" soon spread to France, covering by 1907 a majority of the major municipalities. By the end of the decade, Ghent-type schemes could also be found in Milan, Amsterdam, Strasbourg, and a number of other European cities. In 1904, the Norwegian national government adopted a plan based upon the Ghent model but provided for joint national and commune contributions to union unemployment insurance funds. In Denmark, where unions were especially strong, a similar plan came into effect in August 1907. It was within this international policy environment and shared body of experience that Swedish and British policy discussions of unemployment insurance began.

Sweden

Swedish initiatives on unemployment insurance depended on a handful of liberal reformers and civil servants who were reacting to the emerging cycle of unemployment. Both drew heavily on foreign experiences to devise a poor law alternative.

By the 1890s unemployment remained a problem of poor relief administered in various ways by diverse commune poor relief authorities. Deteriorating economic conditions of the 1880s quickly turned into depression and caused an unprecedented intensification of unemployment in the early 1890s. This was particularly true in the few Swedish urban centers. Under this pressure the administrative governor of the Stockholm area established in 1894 the first Swedish investigation of unemployment. Leading the committee was the progressive government administrator, Count Hugo Hamilton, a reform-minded aristocrat

---

of Swiss developments is drawn from *Promemoria angående Arbetslöshetsförsäkring* and Oskari Auteri, *Arbetslöshetsförsäkringen i utlandet.*

whose humanitarian social views earned him the nickname, "the red baron." Although investigation was restricted to the haphazard system of work relief in Stockholm and other major cities, it did mark the first Swedish study of unemployment insurance and carefully reviewed the schemes of Bern and St. Gallen. The committee concluded that the topic was too new and that no definite recommendations could yet be made. In 1895, the fashion of municipal unemployment insurance spread to the towns of Norrköping and Göteborg, but the voluntary plans quickly fell under the disapproval of large employers. With the return of good economic conditions later in the decade, interest in the unemployment question again subsided.

Initiation of sustained policy discussion on Swedish unemployment insurance suggests the importance of international influences and of the small circle of Liberal reformers in Sweden. The first political initiative for unemployment insurance occurred in 1900 with a motion in the parliamentary Second Chamber by Eduard Wavrinsky. Wavrinsky was a Liberal member sitting for Stockholm, the director of a large private insurance company, and an outstanding leader of the Scandinavian temperance movement. Wavrinsky argued that, with the breakdown of traditional patriarchal relations between employer and worker, the latter was left isolated and vulnerable and that "society must intervene in order to lessen these perils." The motion strongly bears the mark of Wavrinsky's foreign experiences and quotes extensively from his observations at German conferences in 1897 and 1898 on the well-developed employment exchanges in that country.[5] The motion emphasized the need for an investigation to establish such exchanges in Sweden, but also called for a separate investigation of insurance against involuntary unemployment. In both 1900 and 1901 Wavrinsky's motion was narrowly defeated in the Second Chamber, with Liberals and a number of urban Conservatives in favor and most rural members voting against.

The first forceful collective pressure for unemployment insurance came from liberal poor law reformers in the Central Association for Social Work (*Centralförbundet för Socialt Arbete*) under the leadership of

---

5. Andra Kammar motion 152, February 14, 1900. The motion was defeated 66–63 in 1900 and 98–86 in 1901. Although beginning as a Liberal reformer, Wavrinsky gradually moved left and joined the Social Democrats in 1911, sitting in the First Chamber from 1912 to 1924.

the noted reformer G. H. von Koch.[6] The association was concerned mainly with reforms to bring greater order into the haphazard poor law system and held its first National Congress on Poor Relief in 1906. At this conference a motion introduced by the executive was unanimously passed, petitioning the king for an investigation of public measures to promote unemployment insurance. Poor relief, argued these reformers, should be distinguished from unemployment aid. Whether unemployment insurance was arranged through public institutions or support for union funds, its primary aim was "to stimulate the worker's own self-help activity." Undoubtedly the main factor concentrating attention on the specific technique of unemployment insurance was implementation of the Norwegian program two months earlier; as the congress's motion pointed out, "Norway as well as Denmark has now passed us in this matter of unemployment insurance."[7]

Except among these self-conscious reformers, interest in unemployment policy followed the trade cycle, and in the year after the congress on poor relief economic events again triggered a more immediate interest in unemployment. From the autumn of 1907, the first major international economic crisis of the century began to be felt in Sweden; unemployment rose and remained at unusually high levels for the following three years. Only now did political parties become involved in the unemployment insurance issue, and under the same economic stimulus the Swedish legislature began its first extensive discussion of unemployment. After a gap of seven years, Wavrinsky again introduced a motion calling for a full-scale investigation of unemployment and its insurance. Wavrinsky had been influenced by his attendance at the 1906 congress to give pride of place to unemployment insurance over employment exchanges and included the congress's petition as a supple-

6. Holding a number of minor administrative posts in the state agricultural services, von Koch was strongly moved by the poor living conditions of rural workers and in 1897–98 traveled in England to study reformist movements, particularly cooperatives, and child care. Upon returning to Sweden, he decided to devote himself full-time to studying and publicizing questions of social reform, founding the CSA in 1903. In 1904, von Koch was sought out by the state's chief medical officer, who made a personal grant of 20,000 krona to the Association for the Study of Poor Law Reform. As a result the association set up a special Poor Relief Committee in 1905, which organized the 1906 conference. Somewhat more reform-minded than the British Charity Organization Society, the association united major philanthropists, social workers, poor law administrators, and some Liberal politicians to fight for modernization and professionalization of the poor law and greater organization of private charity. Most of its demands were realized in the 1918 poor law reform law. Among its many publications, see especially *Reformslinjer för svensk fattigvård lagstifting*.

7. *Berättelse ofver förhandlingarna vid kongressen för fattigvård* October 4–6, 1906, pp. 230 ff.

ment to his motion. Although not recommending any specific form of unemployment insurance, the motion argued that such public provision would reduce poor law penalties on those who were necessitous through no fault of their own.

In 1908, 1909, and 1910 Wavrinsky reintroduced his motion and aroused a succession of minor partisan clashes among the nascent Swedish parties. Yet these early debates of the emerging parliamentary democracy produced no direct results on unemployment insurance. In 1908 many of the disorganized Liberals and the small band of thirteen Social Democrats voted with Wavrinsky but Conservatives and Rural party members easily defeated the motion in the recently democratized lower chamber.

Although party strengths had not significantly altered, the motion passed the lower chamber in each of the two succeeding years. Citing the experience of Norway, Denmark, and Belgium, Wavrinsky amended his motion in 1909 and 1910 to recommend the Ghent system of union subsidy, and in return the Social Democrats acted as cosponsors. More important in securing passage was the fact that Liberals were now effectively organized in opposition to the Conservative government and under the leadership of Karl Staaf swung their 107 votes to carry the motion in the lower chamber. In both 1909 and 1910, however, the entrenched Conservative power of the upper chamber easily defeated the proposal.

No unified perception of policy objectives lay behind these party stances. While the Social Democratic party favored attacking unemployment's effects through government relief work, it became mildly favorable to Ghent-type insurance as an aid to unionization. Liberals gradually came to support unemployment insurance, not only as a means to further the poor law reformers' favorite "self-help" aims, but as a political point to be scored off the Conservative government. More subtly, state contributions to union insurance funds would be "an important force bringing the workers' movement in closer touch with central state organs in such a way that can only be advantageous." The modern term is engineered co-optation. Staunch Conservatives, on the other hand, cared little for such subtleties, citing instead the fillip unemployment insurance would give to the unions and thus to the closely associated Social Democratic party. In the summer of 1909 there occurred the first and last general strike in Swedish history, a flirtation with radicalism which ended quickly and ignominiously for the union movement. If anything, the general strike further hardened Conservative opinion against unemployment insurance. In rejecting the 1910 motion, the upper chamber emphasized the danger that unemployment insurance would "be used to support worker's wage demands," both by supporting strikers and "by deterring potential strikebreakers."[8]

These party clashes of the still emerging parliamentary system produced neither the investigation nor legislation Wavrinsky had called for. But they did help usher in more subtle and pervasive adaptations. Parties might be fulfilling the textbook function of articulating competitive demands, but probably the articulators were affected more than the demand. Parliamentary power and party control changed little compared to the changing perspective on unemployment itself. Continually recurring depressions were coming to be perceived to mean that worklessness was not necessarily a sign of personal failing. As the lower chamber standing committee pointed out in 1909, "unemployment insurance begins from the premise that, since workers are chronically exposed time after time to unemployment, they must take steps to make themselves economically prepared to go through these difficult crises, which cannot be prevented."[9]

At the same time, the Liberal party was gradually absorbing the concept of insuring against unemployment. There appears to have been nothing deliberate in this. The party leadership never made a comprehensive analysis of the merits and substance of such insurance, nor did the party make any significant effort to capitalize electorally or even publicly on its support for the issue. The unemployment insurance being talked about by internationally aware reformers reverberated in political discussions and gradually appeared to be a "natural" alternative for any reform-minded party.

In the 1911 general election campaign, the Liberals' attention to social insurance was concentrated on old age and disability, but buried in its list of recommendations was unemployment insurance. This was the first Swedish party election program ever to mention the issue, but the proposal can scarcely be said to have played any significant part in

8. Första Kammar tillfälliga utskott, no. 1, *Utlåtande* no. 24 (1910), p. 7. For earlier years, see Andra Kammar, motion 32 and debate, March 28, 1908; Andra Kammar, motion 193 and debate, May 5, 1909; Första Kammarens tillfälliga utskott, no. 1, *Utlåtande* no. 26 (1909), p. 9; and Andra Kammar tillfälliga utskott, no. 1, *Utlåtande* no. 5 (1909), p. 24; Andra Kammar, motion 185 and debate, April 20, 1910.

9. Andra Kammar tillfälliga utskott, no. 1, *Utlåtande* no. 25 (1909), p. 4.

the election. Election results gave the Liberals a chance to form their second government and the party's leader, Karl Staaf, undertook the prime ministership with a personal desire to carry forward reform work. As he said, "A little Lloyd George politics is what we need in the present hour." Less than a month after taking office, the Liberal cabinet on November 17, 1911, approved establishment of an administrative investigation on the unemployment insurance question. In doing so the cabinet cited the growing information acquired through unemployment statistics, Wavrinsky's Riksdag and Poor Relief Congress proposals, and the rapid development of such schemes abroad.[10]

The Liberal leader may have sought to emulate Lloyd George's politics, but the substance of any policy proposal depended on the groundwork already laid by the closely knit Swedish civil service. Even parliamentary proposals called only for the government to establish an investigatory commission on unemployment insurance—an analysis essentially by administrators.

The Swedish civil service had needed no such invitation to begin studying unemployment insurance. Four years before the Liberals' 1911 election victory, Board of Trade administrators had initiated the first serious Swedish study of the question. Like the reformers of the Poor Relief Congress, civil servants were aware of the subject and its topicality, particularly in Norway and Denmark. In 1906–7 and before the 1907 depression, an administrative analysis was carried out by a bright young economist-civil servant at the board, Gunnar Huss. Unlike Britain, Sweden had no national organ comparable to the Local Government Board and its institutionalized poor law principles. The flexible perspective and administrative freedom from poor law dogma were well expressed in the opening paragraph of the Swedish report:

> Those who have worked diligently and willingly, but because of insufficient demand for their working power are subjected to need, ought to be provided security another way than through general poor relief or private charity. . . . It is unjustifiable that inability for self-support, the cause of which lies not in the individual himself but in social relationships, should result in the reduction of citizen rights which poor relief entails.[11]

10. *Statsråd protokolle över civil ärenden,* October-November 1911, Riksarkivet. The preceding quotations from Staaf are taken from Leif Kihlberg, *Karl Staaf,* 2:272.

11. *Promemoria angående Arbetsloshetsförsäkring.*

This was not the random musing of an isolated civil servant. Huss was in fact one agent giving expression to a new economic approach and one of that select corps of young civil servants recruited to the Board of Trade during the first investigations of unemployment, 1906–10. During these years the labor statistics section of the board was headed by a typically forceful Swedish civil servant, Henning Elmqvist, who brought into his section three young economists, Huss, Gösta Bagge, and Otto Järte.[12] All had been university friends and all were, to varying degrees, students of the famous neoclassical economist Gustav Cassel. Together they were to dominate the substance of unemployment policy for the next generation.

Cassel's extremely influential book, *Socialpolitic,* had appeared in 1902 and presented a devastating critique of classic economic assumptions, particularly those of labor market mobility. Unemployment was a recurrent social problem, not an individual accident, and Cassel urged measures to mitigate seasonal and cyclical unemployment. Cassel's influence can be directly traced in Huss's emphasis on the social responsibility for unemployment and need for transitional assistance.[13] His 1907 report observed, however, that the one experiment in Switzerland with obligatory insurance had failed and that "even in Germany, experts have not found it possible to add unemployment insurance to existing obligatory schemes." The Ghent system had more promising results but, as the civil servant candidly pointed out, a major drawback was the close ties of most unions to the Social Democratic party; another major drawback was its ability to help only that minority of workers belonging to unions. The report cautiously concluded that it would be wisest to await the results of Norwegian and Danish experiments.

The administrative role advanced a step further with the unemployment of 1907–09. It was a Conservative government under the prodding of its civil minister, the 1890s reformer Hugo Hamilton, which commissioned Huss to prepare a report on unemployment in Sweden and commune measures being taken against it. Within a month Huss had reported back that no adequate unemployment statistics existed on which to base policy. Several days after this report and

12. Ivar Anderson, *Otto Järte-En Man för sig.* In 1908 Elmquist became official head of the Board of Trade and in 1912 the first permanent secretary of the newly created Social Board.

13. Cassel's influence can be seen in greater detail in Huss's later work, "Arbetslöshets och arbetslöshetsförsäkring," which again withholds judgment on unemployment insurance.

again under prodding from Minister Hamilton, the Conservative cabinet agreed to order all *lan* boards to carry out the first national unemployment count in Swedish history as well as to speed up already programmed public works and encourage farmers and other employers to begin new projects. The results yielded few new private jobs, and communes provided extra work for only about 4,000. State operations did not expand but at least they were not scaled down during the winter as strictly microeconomic calculations would have dictated.[14] It was a mild form of countercyclical policy consistent with Cassels's teaching and the advice emanating from the Board of Trade administrators. A similar unemployment count was conducted in January 1910, and in February 1911 the cabinet accepted an administrative plan for a regular enumeration of the unemployed in the labor statistics section of the Board of Trade, a task taken over the following year by the new Social Board. The significance of this new procedure lay not in any particular figures but in the establishment of a permanent technique for social monitoring, an additional information input readily intelligible and acceptable to any participant in the policy-making process.

When unemployment insurance was next looked at in 1911 by the new Liberal government, the expert appointed to conduct the investigation was Otto Järte, by now an actuary in the Board of Trade. Social Democrats greeted Järte's appointment enthusiastically as one of the new government's first initiatives in social policy and particularly welcomed the assignment of "our Party comrade Järte." Järte was then a promising young Social Democratic writer, but, more important, he was also absorbing the economic doctrine prevalent at the board. Whatever unemployment insurance plans might be drawn up would be the work of Järte and his civil service colleagues.

Järte carried his investigation to Denmark, Germany, and France in 1912 and to Belgium and England in 1913. From what records exist it seems very likely that the government, with Social Democratic support, was prepared to introduce an unemployment insurance scheme along the lines of the Ghent system, although the employers' organizations

---

14. The results of the count showed 20,106 unemployed on January 12, 1909, of whom 91 percent were unemployed because of the "lack of jobs" rather than sickness, strikes, personal, or other reasons. The unemployment count showed a comparably measured 14,412 unemployed for January 31, 1910. On the government action that resulted, see Andra Kammar, April 1, 1909, no. 1, p. 6.

were resisting because of encouragement it would give to union membership. At the cabinet meeting January 14, 1914, the Liberal civil minister reported that he hoped to present an unemployment insurance measure in the current parliament, and in accordance with his suggestion the government budget was amended the same day to include an extra 300,000 krona for this purpose.[15]

The administration's plan became the victim not of interest groups, parties, or elections but of largely fortuitous events. The Liberal government fell in the spring of 1914 on the entirely unrelated question of defense. Järte extended his travels to Germany, published a book strongly favorable to the German war effort, and was shortly expelled from the Social Democratic party. But Järte continued to rise as a civil servant under Conservative governments, becoming secretary and member of the important social insurance investigation during World War I and later a member of the Unemployment Commission. For the moment, however, the impetus behind Sweden's first efforts at unemployment insurance had been lost. Järte's 1915 report on the issue to the new Conservative government was quietly forgotten amid the exigencies of avoiding participation in a world war.

Britain

British discussion of unemployment insurance seems to have remained fairly immune from continental influences in the last decade of the nineteenth century. The question was completely ignored by the Commission on Labor, which reported in 1894, as well as by the Select Committee on Distress through Unemployment in 1895–96. But as in Sweden, the initial development of unemployment insurance was largely the work of Liberal reformers and civil servants reacting against a background of recurrent trade cycles and the fashion of German social insurance.

The first extensive public discussion of unemployment insurance in Britain was triggered by the depression of 1907. In July of that year William Beveridge, then leader-writer for the *Morning Post*, observed that an unemployment insurance scheme could be established and administered through a system of public labor exchanges. From this proposal flowed events that would result four years later in the world's first national unemployment insurance program. But as usual the sub-

15. *Statsråd protokoll*, January–February 1914; see also Andra Kammar interpellation, March 4, 1921, no. 19, p. 7; and debate, March 2, 1929, no. 15, p. 20.

stance of policy making was not a product of abstract analysis isolated from previous courses of action. Beveridge was reacting against a series of discredited measures that Britain had already tried.

There had, of course, been numerous attempts to aid the unemployed by local charity, the most prominent example being the special national relief funds revived during every major crisis; rarely however did subscriptions to aid the British unemployed exceed 5 percent of those raised for foreign charity funds.[16] The first official recognition of a non-poor law approach to the unemployed occurred in March 1886 when, apparently in response to the Trafalgar Square riots, Local Government Board President Joseph Chamberlain issued a new circular to local authorities encouraging them to set up work projects for relief of the unemployed. Those given such work were not to be stigmatized as paupers but would be paid at a lower rate than unskilled workers in private employment—as classic economic doctrine required. The attempt to rely on ad hoc work relief and private charity culminated with the Unemployed Workman Act of 1905. After massive demonstrations by the unemployed and dangers of domestic violence in the depression of 1903-4, the Conservative government had created a plan for London and extended it (against Local Government Board opposition) to other cities in 1905. This program provided for a joint metropolitan committee to examine unemployed relief applications and to separate respectable workmen temporarily unemployed from "ordinary paupers." For the former, it was hoped that relief work and several rural labor colonies would be provided, although no Exchequer grant was involved and major reliance was placed on private charity.

It was in reaction against this inherited policy that the British impetus for labor exchanges and unemployment insurance developed. Young William Beveridge had served as a member of the Joint Metropolitan Committee for London and in early 1907 reported that after two winters' operation of the plan, "the attitude of nearly all those engaged in its administration may fairly be described as one of growing hopelessness." Beveridge had left Oxford only a few years earlier, inspired by the words of Eduard Caird; in response to Charles Booth's study of London poverty, Caird had urged his students to "discover why, with so much wealth in Britain, there continues to be so much poverty and how

16. Computed from J. C. Harris, "British Unemployment Policy, 1870-1911," table VI. For my discussion of early British unemployment policy, I am greatly indebted to Mrs Harris's account.

poverty can be cured."[17] Beveridge soon became a subwarden of the Toynbee settlement house and with the revival of unemployment in 1903–4 was assigned administration of the canon's new Mansion House Relief Fund. From this point on, the young Beveridge's chief interest became unemployment and not settlement house work. In the process of personally selecting, interviewing, and organizing relief work for 467 unemployed, Beveridge gained first-hand knowledge of the nature of unemployment. Unlike any previous social workers, he also made it a point to re-interview the unemployed after they left relief work, and from this practical policy experience emerged the ideas Beveridge set out in the first essentially empirical study of unemployment.[18]

The perceived failure of this work relief and charity approach led Beveridge to search for other alternatives to the poor law. A nominal Liberal, Beveridge was not the first to propose labor exchanges in Britain; he was, however, the first and most forceful British advocate of a national system of employment exchanges as an everyday government service. As a member of the Employment Exchange Committee of the London joint committee, he had already participated in organizing exchanges in the metropolitan area. During 1907 and 1908, through a cloud of articles in the *Morning Post* and *Economic Journal*, before the British Association and elsewhere, Beveridge argued the case for exchanges and succeeded in interesting the Fabian reformers Beatrice and Sidney Webb in the idea.

More important, Beveridge was also the first to see the intimate and necessary connection between labor exchanges and unemployment insurance; he correctly perceived both the essentially *administrative* justification which had created the harshness of the poor law and the way to alleviate this. Writing in the *Morning Post* in July 1907, Beveridge praised the unemployment benefits paid by unions as "a great system of insurance," one which had worked precisely because unions had their own informal labor exchange service: "The state is forced into the costly and degrading harshness of the Poor Law simply because it has no control or supervision of the labor market. . . . It must rely always on the assumption that the applicant for help could find work if he looked for it because it is never in the position to satisfy itself that there is no work

---

17. The preceding quotations are taken from William Beveridge's "Labor Exchanges and the Unemployed," pp. 4 ff., and from his autobiography, *Power and Influence*, p. 9.
18. *Unemployment: A Problem of Industry.*

for him." By making registration at an employment exchange—rather than acceptance of the workhouse and disgrace of pauperism—the test of willingness to work, Beveridge believed he had circumvented an essential dilemma of the old poor law, and he was correct.

At the same time, Beveridge's reflections on the current discussion of noncontributory old age pensions played an important part in bringing him to the idea of contributory insurance. In his first column for the *Morning Post*, February 16, 1906, he had dismissed contributory social insurance on the German pattern, as had all British investigating committees, with the standard view that it would require an "un-British" amount of regulation of the individual. Beveridge, however, studied the German experiment more closely during the next year and concluded that the contributory insurance principle could not only reduce costs; it could also eliminate reliance on means tests. Insurance contributions, compulsory if necessary, could serve as the entitlement to benefit and thus obviate any test of means. A trip to Germany and first-hand inspection of German social insurance and labor exchanges in the summer of 1907 confirmed Beveridge in his ideas. By the end of 1907, with exchanges as the device for validating true unemployment and insurance as the device for establishing entitlement to benefit, Beveridge had the outlines of what was to be the world's first national unemployment insurance. Conceptually, the grip of the poor law had been broken.

Injecting the new approach into the policy process was accomplished more by persuading than replacing powerholders. The vital access to seats of power for Beveridge and his ideas was provided by Sidney and Beatrice Webb. By this time the Webbs were in effect a private research foundation and socialist pressure group, financially independent and devoting themselves full-time to policy analysis, research, and decorous lobbying. They accepted Beveridge's arguments on the need for employment exchanges and made a point of arranging small dinners to introduce Beveridge to important politicians. Among these introductions were several long interviews with George Hamilton, chairman of the Royal Commission on the Poor Law, and arrangements were made for Beveridge to present extensive evidence to the commission on the need for exchanges and unemployment insurance. But by far the most important introduction arranged by the Webbs was that to Winston Churchill. Through Churchill's personal efforts, both administrative resources and the Liberal party were eventually mobilized on the issue and Beveridge's ideas turned into concrete policy.

Up to this time and despite popular pressures, the Liberal party policy on unemployment had been little more than studied vagueness. Whenever assailed by the unemployed the party leader, in his words, "did not know what the mischief to say." The current Tory proposal for tariff protection to cure unemployment was, of course, strenuously attacked, but even during their victorious 1905 election campaign (that is, the election prior to drafting unemployment insurance plans) the Liberals had no definite proposals of their own. In the campaign the party leader "found that much mischief was being done by the notion that we had little or nothing to say about the unemployed. So I risked one foot upon that ice, but was very guarded and only spoke of inquiry and experiment."[19]

Elections and popular pressure suggested the need to say something but not what to say. In reconstructing the Liberal government following Campbell-Bannerman's illness and resignation, Prime Minister Asquith gave new prominence to several of the brightest young leaders of the party. It was these few individuals who imported the ideas to wrench the party from its previous apathy. Lloyd George was appointed chancellor and, following his successful tenure as undersecretary at the Colonial Office, Winston Churchill was given his first ministerial post as president of the Board of Trade. From this time dates the two men's partnership in radical Liberal reform, radical in the sense of moving beyond long-discussed reforms such as school meals and old age pensions. Unemployment insurance was definitely in this unknown territory for the Liberal party and Britain. It would be impossible here to separate how much of this reforming zeal arose from concerns for personal advancement, party advantage, or national interest; quite likely the three factors were not clearly separated in either politician's mind.

As early as March 1908, the young Churchill had announced his own personal conviction of the need for a strong Liberal program of social reform—with unemployment as the central focus. By no means

19. Letter from Campbell-Bannerman to Asquith, December 1, 1905, quoted in Bentley Gilbert, "Winston Churchill versus the Webbs: The Origins of British Unemployment Insurance," p. 850.

was this view easily accepted in the Liberal cabinet. Chief among the stand-patters was John Burns, now as always under the influence of his poor law officials at the Local Government Board. From the summer of 1908 unemployment was clearly on the rise, and Churchill warned the cabinet in August that winter would bring unusually severe unemployment. A minor cabinet crisis on the issue occurred in October 1908. "JB said nothing was the matter and nothing could be done. WSC arose and said something must be done and it was a burning question."[20] In the end, the cabinet agreed with Churchill but could offer no guidance on what to do about the problem.

Both Churchill and Beveridge had clearly been influenced by their association with the Webbs, particularly with regard to the latter's conception of social reform to achieve a "national minimum." But once having introduced Churchill to the usefulness of labor exchanges and to Beveridge, the Webbs were of little further influence and at least mildly opposed to unemployment insurance as it was developed by the Liberals. In later consultations at the Board of Trade, the Webbs's only suggestion to be accepted was the idea of limiting benefit duration in terms of a ratio to contribution-weeks (developed by Beveridge into the "1 in 5 rule," i.e., one week of benefit for every five weeks of contribution). Rather than supporting unemployment insurance, the Webbs favored compulsory labor exchanges and more effort to "reform" the habits and conduct of the unemployed.[21] The orthodox reformers of the Left had helped arouse interest and had propagandized on the labor problem, but they played little direct part in formulating the new policy departure into unemployment insurance.

Formulation of this departure began in earnest in July 1908, when Churchill as the new minister in charge invited Beveridge to join him as an assistant at the Board of Trade. As Beveridge later said, "In effect, Mr. Churchill asked Llewellyn Smith [former head of the Labor Department in the Board and since 1907 permanent secretary of the Board of Trade as a whole] and me as his apprentice, to try our hands at preparing a practical scheme of unemployment insurance."[22] But

20. L. C. Masterman, *C. F. G. Masterman*, p. 110. Burns's tenure at the Local Government Board is briefly discussed in Roy Macleod, *Treasury Control and Social Administration*, pp. 48 ff.

21. Sidney Webb, "Unemployment Insurance Criticisms," December 12, 1908, cited in Bentley Gilbert, *The Evolution of National Insurance in Great Britain*, and *Minority Report of the Royal Commission on the Poor Laws*.

22. Beveridge, *Power and Influence*, p. 83. My discussion of Llewellyn Smith is drawn from

it would be a mistake to assign exclusive importance to Churchill's personality and Beveridge's bright idea in the founding of unemployment insurance. In many ways, they were pushing against an open door at the Board of Trade and building upon the board's administrative innovations of the last fifteen years. As in Sweden, the Board of Trade had become a center inside government promoting the search for reliable labor statistics and mobilizing expert analysis on the unemployment problem. Just as Henning Elmqvist had used his official position as head of the new Swedish labor statistics section, so Llewellyn Smith also presided over the foundation of a similar section in the British Board of Trade to bring new intelligence inputs into the formulation of unemployment policy. Smith too had been inspired by his university associations (in his case Oxford of the 1880s) and the climate of committed social reform aimed at ameliorating working class distress. Smith had participated in the first empirical survey of social conditions in modern times, Charles Booth's *Life and Labour of the People of London* (1889 and 1891), and like Beveridge had been tempered by settlement house work in the east end of London. In short the British, like the Swedish, Board of Trade was activated by representatives from a new generation of civil servants eager and able to provide the data and analysis necessary for major policy innovations. It was in this context that Churchill, without official cabinet sanction or Liberal party endorsement of the idea, allowed his officials in the fall of 1908 to begin considering unemployment insurance. In all essentials, the plan finally adopted in Britain in 1911—and the first state-run program of insurance against unemployment in the world—was the proposal drawn up by Beveridge and Smith at the Board of Trade. With this plan, Churchill and the Board completely circumvented the Local Government Board, repository of poor law orthodoxy and formerly the only public authority concerned with cash aid to the citizen.

As for the interest groups, it was a question of the government department lobbying to persuade them rather than vice versa. With trade union funds already in existence the position of unions was most crucial, and a vigorous campaign was undertaken to obtain union agreement. Beveridge brought in as labor adviser to the Board of Trade his friend from the London Employment Exchanges Committee and leader of the Amalgamated Society of Engineers, Isaac Mitchell.

---

evidence in Robert Davidson, "Llewellyn Smith and the Labour Department," in *Studies in the Growth of Nineteenth-Century Government*, ed. Gillian Sutherland, pp. 227 ff.

Mitchell in turn assured full discussion with other union leaders and helped win labor support. The civil service planners were careful to accommodate details of the new state scheme to unions' existing insurance programs. It was also with Board of Trade encouragement that a committee of trade union leaders visited Germany in November 1908, in order to assess the effect of social insurance on labor organizations in that country. At year's end the committee reported back as expected to the government that Germany's social insurance "had in no way exercised an injurious effect upon the Trade Unions of the country."[23] For the moment at least the government department had succeeded in educating the union movement to the idea of state contributory unemployment insurance.

There would be no point in chronicling here the detailed analysis by which Beveridge and Smith framed their actual scheme. Development of the plan owed little to foreign programs; those working models used were the trade union unemployment insurance schemes and their requirements of signing-in for vacancies and waiting periods for benefits. By and large, however, the plan was produced by the intertwined contributions of Llewellyn Smith and Beveridge and owed little to examples in the private sector or elsewhere. By early in December 1908 Churchill's two civil service experts had drawn up the basic outline of what was to be the 1911 policy: tripartite contributions by employers, workers, and state; contributions recorded on a worker's insurance card; a week's waiting period before the virtually flat-rate (that is, uniform) benefits began; maximum periods of benefit in any one year; and administration and registration through a new network of state labor exchanges. These and other substantive issues were decided largely on the basis of the civil servants' anticipations of administrative difficulties and likely public reactions. The expectation of administrative problems in this unexplored field persuaded Beveridge and Smith to limit coverage in the first instance to a small, experimental section of the work force. The three trades chosen were shipbuilding, engineering, and building and works construction—trades where unemployment was

---

23. The committee was dominated by David Shackleton, Labor MP from Lancashire and chairman of the TUC. In September 1909 Shackleton was able, despite the strong opposition of Keir Hardie, to obtain a TUC resolution favoring unemployment insurance (*The Times*, September 8, 1909). At the previous year's TUC congress, the union movement had passed a resolution favoring government grants to unions paying out-of-work benefits. Shackleton left Parliament and became Senior Labor Adviser to the Home Office when Churchill moved there and in 1916 became permanent secretary at the newly created Ministry of Labor.

serious but largely seasonal or cyclical in character—an estimated three million workers in all.

Both the Webbs and the Trades Union Congress (TUC) favored the Ghent system of state subsidy to union insurance funds. Now inside the civil service, Beveridge was able to advance a strong contrary view in the interest of unorganized workers. His unprecedented empirical research had shown the immense unemployment among nonunion members of the labor force. Merely subsidizing existing insurance efforts, Beveridge argued, would have no impact on the unskilled or casual workers who, as his studies had shown, made up the bulk of the unemployed. Moreover Churchill was personally eager that contributors should include both workers and employers, arguing before the cabinet in November 1908 that "unemployment is primarily a question for employers . . . their responsibility is undoubted, their cooperation indispensable."[24] Llewellyn Smith pointed out that this would necessarily preclude the Ghent system, inasmuch as employers would object to contributing to any such union subsidy. Thus from the autumn of 1908 the Board of Trade excluded the approach which was the conventional favorite of continental labor movements and reformers.

With very little discussion, flat rates were chosen over variable benefits. Any graduation by need was thought to be an unacceptable inquisition into the worker's affairs and far too reminiscent of the poor law. Graduation by income (what was the German and later Swedish social insurance principle of compensation for income loss) was rejected as unnecessary since higher-paid workers could obtain additional insurance through unions. Besides, one uniform benefit rate put a minimum of strain on the still meager administrative resources of Whitehall.

The most portentous aspect of the civil servants' plan was the use of general state revenue to pay a portion of benefit costs. Central government funds had never been used for such purposes; even poor law relief was financed through local rates. The justification for this path-breaking use of state revenue was expressed best by young Churchill and sprang not from a political theory or doctrine of government but from the logic of the plan and interests of the groups involved: assuming that unorganized workers were to be included, provision of a state contribution prevented the more regularly employed workman from having to bear the extra cost of bringing along his high-unemployment-

24. Cab. 37/96, 159; cited in Gilbert, *Evolution of National Insurance in Great Britain.*

risk brethren in the same public insurance program. Although scarcely discussed, the state grant was an implicit subsidy for including those thought least able to pay and not simply a pooling of risks among groups of workmen. Continuing consultations before and after introduction of the bill showed that the main concern of workers' organizations lay precisely in avoiding the costs of any such common pool with poor-risk workmen. Thus the September 1909 TUC meeting had expressed demands for state assumption of a higher proportion of insurance costs, and in March 1910 the TUC parliamentary committee pressed the Board of Trade to leave all nonunion workers outside the plan. The British government's unprecedented involvement in the unemployment insurance business grew not because the interest groups (that is, unions) were weak but precisely because already strong unions refused to shoulder the welfare risks of all workers.

Significantly, the major disagreement within the Board of Trade and later within the government as a whole arose on the eligibility for benefit of those who lost jobs through personal failings. Resolution of this disagreement epitomized the meaning of the new direction being adopted in social policy. Throughout the poor law's history, the one persistent theme was an effort to discriminate in relief between the "deserving" and the "undeserving" poor. Smith likewise argued to his political chief Churchill that, not on moral but administrative grounds, those who lost employment through their own misconduct should be ineligible for unemployment insurance benefits; misconduct was an individual not a group hazard and thus incalculable and uninsurable. Churchill responded with an argument which well expressed the emerging new perspective on the unemployed. The person who had paid his contributions should be entitled to his benefit; malingering ought to be protected against by the automatic operation of impersonal insurance rules and not through personal inquiry by those dubiously qualified to define misconduct. The contrast with both the poor law and the Webbs—who objected to Churchill's and Lloyd George's insurance proposals precisely because "the state gets nothing for its money in the way of conduct"—could not have been greater. As Churchill put it:

> We seek to substitute for the pressure of the forces of nature operating by chance on individuals, the pressure of the laws of insurance, operating through averages with modifying and miti-

> gating effects in individual cases. . . . Chance and average
> spring from the same family. . . . As there is no proportion
> between personal failings and the penalties exacted, . . . more
> will be gained by an increase of ability to fight than will be lost
> through an abatement of the extreme consequences of defeat.

The syntax was Macaulay's and insurability of unemployment risks unproven, but the essence of Churchill's argument was pure twentieth-century social policy: the unchecked insecurities produced by the market were a debilitating not constructive force, a social not individual failing, a public not private responsibility. It was from this perspective that Churchill in the spring of 1909 vigorously pushed a hesitant Liberal cabinet into approving unemployment insurance. John Burns argued the Local Government Board view that there was insufficient protection against malingering. The only major alteration to be made by the cabinet against Churchill's wishes was to exclude from benefit for the first six weeks those who were discharged for misconduct or quit without just cause.[25]

Unemployment insurance was ready for submission to Parliament by the summer of 1909 but suffered several unrelated delays. The 1909 budget furor created one delay but also allowed the plan for establishing national labor exchanges, introduced as separate legislation, to be passed with little comment that summer. Succeeding party warfare over House of Lords reform and the two 1910 general elections occurred with the Liberals making almost no mention of their forthcoming unemployment insurance proposal. Further delay occurred in 1910 when Lloyd George generated intense departmental and personal rivalry by attempting to amalgamate the Board of Trade's unemployment insurance with his own health insurance plan. It was finally agreed merely to introduce the two plans as two parts of one national insurance act while keeping the schemes administratively distinct. The usual infighting with the Treasury reduced the scheme's cost to the state from £1.5 million to £1.1 million. In all essentials, however, it was the Churchill-Smith-Beveridge proposal that the government presented to Parliament in 1911.

25. Within the first two years 50,000 claims were disallowed for these reasons, but as eventually defined the regulation rarely denied payments to workmen regardless of their habits of life. Cd. 6965, 1913, p. 31. Churchill's philosophical position is set out and the above quotation appears in a letter to Llewellyn Smith, June 6, 1909, quoted in Gilbert, "Winston Churchill versus the Webbs," p. 856.

Parliamentary consideration of the government's plan was perfunctory and added nothing of substance. The unemployment insurance bill was laid before Parliament May 4, 1911, and passed its second reading the following May 29. All of the major substantive amendments were sponsored by the Board of Trade. The three basic principles remained largely ignored in parliamentary deliberations. At no time were the merits or demerits of *insurance* as an appropriate means of aid to the unemployed discussed. Apart from the Webbs outside Parliament and several extreme Conservatives within, the principle of *compulsory* insurance was not objected to. Nor was the propriety of a *state contribution* from general taxation seriously questioned.[26] Unemployment insurance easily passed the House of Commons third reading on December 6, the House of Lords on December 15, and received the royal assent December 16, 1911. With this began the world's first compulsory national unemployment insurance—as well as the first direct entry of British social policy into the life of the ordinary able-bodied workman.

In and out of Parliament, the British Left had played no direct part in this fundamental extension of modern social policy. Within Parliament, many Labor speakers continued to press for a higher state contribution to unemployment insurance, but the socialist party was in fact split on the issue. Party Chairman Ramsay MacDonald suggested job training as a condition of benefit but voted for the bill because it would "compel us to face problems that we should not have [faced] otherwise." Lansbury and Philip Snowden on the other hand voted against passage, calling the bill a shallow and false remedy—in contrast to a truly curative socialist approach.[27] The labor movement could scarcely be said to have had a clear position on the question of

26. This lack of partisanship on unemployment insurance was at least partly due to the intense heat generated by the health insurance portion of the plan. Where direct interests were affected, as in the case of trade unions, the long advance consultation process had smoothed these difficulties. Compared to the outstanding 6.1 million friendly society and insurance company policies against sickness, there were but 1.4 million "policies" against unemployment. See *Parliamentary Debates* (Commons) May 4, 25, 29, 1911, for isolated laissez-faire views. At the request of Conservative leader Bonar Law, Conservatives Worthington-Evans and Joynson-Hicks withdrew a wrecking amendment to make the plan voluntary. *Parliamentary Debates* (Commons), November 2, 1911.

27. *Parliamentary Debates* (Commons), December 6, 1911. Through their National Committee for the Prevention of Destitution, the Webbs protested against such expenditures, which did nothing to cure unemployment, and reiterated proposals of the Minority Royal Commission Report. Beatrice Webb, *Our Partnership*, p. 473. A general review of the sterility of Labor party ideas for practical reform at this time is in Arthur Marwick's, "The Labor Party and the Welfare State in Britain, 1900–1948."

unemployment or its insurance. During the period in which unemployment insurance was being prepared in the Board of Trade, the young
Labor party in Parliament had pressed its case for "work or maintenance" with three right-to-work bills; no specific proposals were
offered on how this might be achieved, short of an automatic solution
through socialism. On social security, Labor's demands were limited
to the abolition of the poor law and transference of its services to local
authorities.

Although chairman of his party, MacDonald was not able to carry
the bulk of party members with him in support of unemployment
insurance. Critics, led by Snowden, took the battle to the 1912 Labor
Party Conference, where a resolution attacking many aspects of the
government act and implicitly MacDonald's stand was approved by
a vote of 241–39. At its 1913 conference, the party called for repeal of
the health insurance portion of the 1911 act, its reestablishment on a
noncontributory basis, and rather offhandedly instructed the parliamentary Labor party to adopt the same approach on unemployment insurance. Although the Board of Trade's early consultations
with TUC leaders had prevented any crystallized opposition to the
initial adoption of unemployment insurance, the seeds were already
sown for Labor's opposition to the contributory basis of unemployment insurance in the interwar period.

INSURANCE VERSUS RELIEF

During the interwar period existing and proposed unemployment
insurance policies became heavily strained by persistently high unemployment in both Britain and Sweden. Common membership in
an international economic market led to a common pattern of unemployment in the two nations: sharp rises during postwar recession
in the early 1920s, a reduced but persistently troublesome residue of
unemployment during the remainder of the 1920s, and a burst, followed
by a gradual reduction, of joblessness during the depression of the
1930s (see Figure 9). Lingering unemployment of the 1920s, often
treated as a peculiarly British malady, was scarcely larger there than
in Sweden.[28]

28. From 1923 to 1929, unemployment was 11.3 percent and 11.0 percent among organized
Swedish workers and British insured, respectively. William Beveridge, *Full Employment in a
Free Society*, tables 1, 22; *Statistisk Årsbok*, 1914; and I. Svennilson, *Growth and Stagnation in
The European Economy*, table 3.

In Britain between the wars, unemployment insurance became a thinly disguised form of cash relief capable of precipitating major government crisis. For most of this period in Sweden, it remained a Socialist proposal with which to berate conservative governments of the day. This difference appears little related to differing electoral results, party competition, or government turnover in the two countries. British experience shows the Conservative party to have been at least as responsible as Labor for those dilutions of insurance principles that actually took place. British policy was responding not to elections but to an indirect popular control expressed through party leaders' anticipations of civil disorder should no such relief be given.

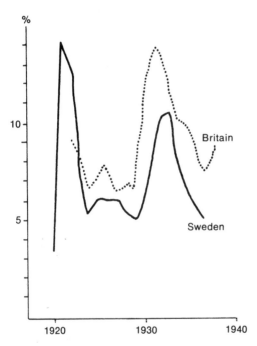

Figure 9. Unemployment as a Percentage of Nonagricultural Labor Force, Britain and
Sweden, 1920-1940

Source: Based on Phelps Brown and Brown, *A Century of Pay,* Figure 34.

Once again, however, public pressures gave little guidance about what to do substantively. Probably the most important factor behind differences in British and Swedish policy was the preexisting policy structure itself. Britain's early enactment and Sweden's fortuitous delay on unemployment insurance bequeathed different policy materials to each country. Only Britain had an ongoing unemployment insurance program to be extended; Sweden relied on amendments to its already developed "work approach."

Regardless of these differences, however, the dominant fact is that in both countries unemployment insurance was at the forefront of interwar debate on social policy. In all of the discussions leading up to its adoption in Britain and its largely fortuitous abandonment in Sweden, unemployment insurance had been looked upon as a limited technique for improving labor market organization. It was hoped that pooling risks would help workers avoid the disgrace of falling upon poor relief; it was not generally confused with cash relief itself. With the economic dislocations following the First World War, unemployment insurance in both countries became much more than this—it became a symbol of the commitment to relieve the plight of the unemployed. The preoccupation with unemployment insurance was also a symbol of parties' and governments' inability to break the conceptual hold of classic economics and offer a realistic program to deal with unemployment itself. British and Swedish leaders of all political colors were, in fact, tacitly united in subscribing to the prevailing economic dogma to deal with joblessness. Insurance against unemployment dominated attention because policy makers could think of nothing better to do. Eventually, the British Labor party was broken between the pressure for extending unemployment insurance as relief and an economic orthodoxy that precluded effective government action against unemployment itself. Leaders of the Swedish Social Democrats learned the value of the new Keynesian approach far more quickly and in doing so developed viable employment policies that went a long way in assuring their continued rule. Only as political administrators assimilated this new intellectual perspective did unemployment insurance recede into the political background as a tool of economic adaptation rather than general social provision.

Sweden

Although Sweden remained a noncombatant, wartime adjustments accentuated the role of civil servants in unemployment policy. Conservative successors to the Liberal Staaf government shared prevalent expectations that the European war would mean massive unemployment. With this fear in mind the government established an Unemployment Commission on August 10, 1914. Intended as an advisory "crisis commission" closely tied to and staffed by civil servants from the Social Board, the commission quickly began carving out its own policy preserve. In this emergency atmosphere, any idea of unemployment insurance was considered to be out of the question. The commission argued, however, that the wartime origin of unemployment dictated a presumption of state responsibility to help prevent those newly unemployed from falling upon poor relief. In accord with the commission's request, a special state grant of five million krona was made to support commune relief to the unemployed—the first direct national expenditure on the unemployed in Sweden.[29]

After the first several months of dislocation, the immediate wartime unemployment crisis quickly faded, but the Unemployment Commission continued to develop policy. From the beginning the administrators based their plans on the "work approach" (*arbetlinie*)—a notion that help to the unemployed in the form of work was morally and economically superior to other alternatives. Continuing their intimate relationship from the previous decade and Board of Trade, civil servants Järte and Huss were the most active members behind commission policy and, with F. H. Pegelow and poor law reformer von Koch, formed a quadrumvirate of orthodoxy emphasizing neoclassic economic theory and relief work rather than cash support. The officials' perspective was well summed up by former Social Democrat Järte, who replied to party leader Branting's invitation to rejoin the party, "I am no longer a socialist. I have learned the liberal national economics of Cassel and Heckscher."[30] In the spring of 1916 the commission began the first national work relief programs and expanded this activity during the following two years, always careful to pay below-market wages.

Only these likeminded administrators manifested a sustained interest in unemployment policy. In the meantime, with wartime and immediate postwar employment generally at record levels, all parties, cabinets, and interest groups were content with a desultory complacency on unemployment and its insurance. Wartime governments were not prepared to push the inherited Liberal plans for sickness and unem-

29. Proposition nr. 279, 1914. SOU 9 (1929), gives a history of these early developments. A more detailed analysis with emphasis on the 1920s is G. H. Nordström, *Svensk arbetslöshetspolitik, 1914–1933*.

30. Quoted in Ivar Anderson, *Otto Järte—En man för sig*, p. 169.

ployment insurance, preferring instead to establish another investigation. This new ten-member commission was headed by Anders Lindstedt, the experienced civil servant and social insurance expert who, as
we shall see, was a decisive force behind the creation of the first Swedish
pensions. The commission decided on technical grounds to deal first
with sickness insurance, not reporting on sickness until 1919, on disability benefit in January 1921, and finally unemployment insurance
in December 1922.[31] Thus was lost the opportunity for beginning
unemployment insurance contributions on the strong financial base
that years of high wartime employment would have provided.

By the end of World War I, unemployment insurance and employment policies were also topics of distinctly secondary importance to
Social Democrats. Swedish Socialists felt the "left wind" which blew
through Europe at the war's end and in 1918–20 put forward as radical
a program as they ever have before or since. Socialization and industrial
democracy became the key issues in the 1920 election; no party gave
serious attention to unemployment. The unusually apocalyptic approach of Social Democrats was also encouraged by the final establishment of electoral democracy at the war's end. Socialists attached high
hopes to the popular power expressed in democratic reforms. Once
representative democracy with universal suffrage came into operation,
the struggle for socialism would overtake disputes on ameliorative,
piecemeal reforms.[32]

These hopes were dashed; universal suffrage and proportional
representation brought not socialism but a series of indecisive minority
governments. Under the pressure of events, the issue quickly became
not socialism but the mundane question of what practical policy steps
could be taken against unemployment. This issue was brought home
most strongly to the unions' own unemployment insurance funds. By
1920 unemployment had begun to skyrocket, climbing from 5 percent
of union membership early in the year to 25 percent by year's end and
did not again fall below 10 percent until late in the 1930s. The story of
unemployment insurance in the 1920s was one of continuing and fruitless pressure by labor and the Social Democratic party against intran-

31. In June 1919 the civil minister had supplied the technical reasons for dealing with
sickness and accidents first and added that the government had an 11 million krona surplus
in the budget with which "society stands quite well-armed even against higher unemployment." Andra Kammar debate, June 3, 1919.
32. See especially Ernst Wigforss "Demokratiska problem."

sigent administrators, bourgeois parties, and employers' representatives, a fate that the new "democratic" political forms did not alter.

The postwar economic collapse brought administrative influence, in the form of the Unemployment Commission and *arbetlinie*, into unprecedented prominence. With the immense rise in unemployment at the end of 1920, Sweden's Unemployment Commission did not lapse as intended but was reorganized and strengthened with a chancellery organization equivalent to that in regular government departments. At the suggestion of the commission, the government in June 1921 created a state relief organization for the north (*Norrlands statsarbeten*) and followed in October with another for the south to arrange public relief work for the unemployed. Prior to this time, communes had been largely independent in operating work relief schemes; the commission now set out to correct some of the resulting local abuses. During the next three years the Unemployment Commission gradually took over most administration of relief work, setting the work, conditions, and wage rates. Policy of the commission was in fact quite independent. The commission possessed an "authority with bourgeois Riksdag opinion which allowed it to practice a freedom of activity completely unique in Swedish administrative practice."[33] Within the commission liberal economic doctrines were dominant and continued to give practical expression to the prevailing theoretical approach to unemployment.

The labor movement had little to offer in response except humanitarian criticisms of commission policy and proposals for unemployment insurance. From 1921 to 1930, in and out of Parliament, the Social Democratic party and union organizations pressed for introduction of state subsidies and encouragement to union unemployment insurance. The Socialist party's domestic program for the 1926 general election, for example, was issued in a booklet entitled "Unemployment Insurance"; while not advocating abolition of all relief work, the manifesto argued that unemployment insurance provided a more comprehensive solution, at least in the short term. This electoral appeal did not prevent a substantial defeat for the party in the following general election. Even the left wing of the movement advocated little more than abolition of the Unemployment Commission and obligatory state unemployment

33. Gustaf H. Nordström, *Svensk arbetslöshetspolitik, 1914–1933*, p. 40; see also SOU 32 (1936), 98, and SOU 39 (1948), 105ff. Elmer has described the commission as the most despised Swedish institution of the century. *Från fattigsverige till välfardsstaten*, p. 57.

insurance sufficient for full support of workers and their families.[34]

Conservative, Liberal, and Agrarian parties, economists and employers' groups were all united in rejecting the Socialist proposals; their argument was that no type of unemployment insurance true to its name would help the existing mass unemployment. Such unemployment could be combated only with conventional economic weapons: economy, retrenchment, and lower production costs—particularly wages. Shifts in party government did not alter this impasse. Europe's first Socialist government fell in 1923 before it acted on unemployment insurance. The Social Democrats returned to power as a minority government in the autumn of 1924 with the view that a Social Democratic government would be of use to the workers "just by sitting." As Branting told the king, "Provision of effective relief measures for the increasing number of workless was in the opinion of the Party reason enough for taking office." Unable to obtain Liberal support, the Socialist party again dropped its plans for Ghent-type unemployment insurance and instituted yet another investigation on the subject. Appropriately enough, in both 1923 and 1924 the Socialist governments fell as a result of conflict with the repository of orthodox economic doctrine, the Unemployment Commission. As one Socialist leader recalled, "The Commission represented the bourgeois majority . . . against which the government had no power and had to be satisfied with expressing its lack of confidence."[35]

The investigatory process elaborated the fundamental differences at stake. On December 30, 1922, the wartime Lindstedt commission finally reported, recommending labor exchanges as the most important measure against unemployment. All commission members recognized

34. *Arbetsloshetsförsäkring.* This party document cited left-wing pressures which were expressed in unanimous resolutions at the Göteberg and Stockholm National Conferences of the Unemployed: "the working class must unite and fight for unemployment insurance. . . . No compromise on this demand can be accepted." There were many Communist motions advocating that the state and employers pay the full cost of insurance; see Andra Kammar motions 129, 1928; 54, 1929; 119, 1930. Representative proposals for unemployment insurance by the Social Democratic party and LO were Första Kammar motion 123; Andra Kammar motion 276, 1924; Riksdag debate, April 14, 1924; Första Kammar motion 108, 1929, and debate, March 2, 1929; and LO, *Verksamhetsberättelse*, 1921, 1922. Pressure on union funds was such that, at the 1922 congress, the foundry workers moved that unions cease their unemployment support and demand state insurance. Congress rejected the motion in favor of state contributions to union funds.

35. Quotations are taken from Ernst Wigforss, *Minnen*, 2: 241, and Gunnar Gerdner, *Parlamentarismens Kris i Sverige vid 1920-Talets Början*, pp. 350, 460.

that only obligatory unemployment insurance could assure sufficient coverage to all workers but argued on traditional economic grounds that in the current depression costs would be prohibitive. The alternative suggested was state contributions for up to one-half union unemployment fund expenses, a plan covering one-quarter as many (200,000) workers but costing only one-sixth as much (3 million krona) as obligatory state insurance. The civil service and Liberal commission members found insurance a means of "help for self-help" but could endorse the commission plan "only with hesitation," suggesting delay until economic recovery had occurred. Socialist commission members urged abolishing the maximum state contribution limit and immediate enactment. The employers' representative and Conservative party representative completely rejected the proposal as a subsidy to unions and abandonment of the state's customary "neutrality" between employers and workers.[36]

The deadlock on Swedish unemployment insurance, compared with its rapid contemporary expansion in Britain, showed in essence that it was easier to distort an existing insurance program into relief than to create a new insurance program expressly for that purpose. This was at least partly because policy makers in general and civil servants in particular were observing and learning from experiences elsewhere. Subsequent investigations in 1928 and 1931 cited British evidence to show that demands for the extension of insurance to relief were likely to accompany any unemployment insurance program and to endanger the national economy; therefore no action should be taken on the question.[37]

The deadlock on unemployment insurance was due not simply to a clash of political or economic interests but to a pervasive economic doctrine that no amount of expert investigations and compromises could circumvent. Attention and conflict focused on unemployment insurance because no one could think of anything better to do than

---

36. Socialförsäkringskommitten, SOU 59 (1922), 56, 100–101, 104. For the importance of this "neutrality" idea, especially in the 1920s, see Sven-Ola Lindeberg, *Nödhjälp och samhällsneutraletet.*

37. SOU 9 (1929), 144. "We cannot close our eyes to the tendency especially in England, with pressure on the issue, to allow guarantees and limits to fall until all too many of the insured go over to simple relief without a protest from their side." For similar arguments and the reactions at the beginning of the depression, see Första Kammar motions 133, 1931; 188, 1932; debates, May 13, 1931; February 17, 1932; and Andra Kammar debate, May 16, 1931.

alleviate symptoms of mass unemployment. This was well illustrated by the blue ribbon investigation established by the Social Democratic government in 1926. Led by respected economist Eli Heckscher, the Liberal, Conservative, and Agrarian parties' representatives repudiated any idea of using unemployment insurance to deal with the jobless. The fundamental objections stemmed from the view that such state intervention in the labor market would only aggravate unemployment. A lengthy appendix written by Heckscher set out the authoritative economic arguments behind the current approach to unemployment and was widely quoted. There was, it said, no general lack of work opportunities, only a lack at excessively high wage levels. A state policy such as unemployment insurance would lead to "false" wage levels above the equilibrium point and thus actually create unemployment—besides contradicting the desired neutrality of the state between labor market parties. Poor relief was a generally valid form of aid applicable to the unemployed, and relief work at below market wages was beneficial, particularly if it helped to reduce general wage levels. The four opponents of unemployment insurance concluded that state aid to the unemployed should be based upon need, with unemployed persons treated like any other necessitous citizens.

Labor members of the investigation were led by Herman Lindqvist, venerable chairman of the LO (Landsorganisationen, the Swedish national federation of unions roughly equivalent to Britain's Trades Union Congress) but could not dispute the majority's analysis of unemployment. Observing that unemployment was a natural accompaniment of industrialization and that no essential change in its extent could be expected, the Socialists urged redistributing its burden through employers' contributions to unemployment insurance. The argument for wage-level adjustments to combat unemployment was accepted as true in the long run but of only "theoretical interest" for immediate aid to the unemployed. Any need-tested benefit was rejected, but the labor members could do little more than urge adoption of unemployment insurance and strengthened labor exchanges to meet the problem.

Although unemployment was the most politically contentious issue of the 1920s, there thus prevailed an extensive theoretical unanimity on unemployment policy itself. Social Democrats might consider much of this policy's operation "hard and morally disturbing" but they, like other political groups, accepted the doctrines of classical economics and the need for at least a small dose of wage reduction in order to cure unemployment.[38] Those alternatives the party did offer were almost exclusively in terms of a more humane social policy to relieve its hardships rather than an economic policy to prevent or reduce unemployment. In this situation, unemployment insurance seemed the obvious palliative, subject neither to the disgrace of the poor law nor the harsh regulations and patchy coverage of relief work.

The practical political breakthrough from traditional economic doctrines in Sweden was primarily the work of a Social Democratic politician, Ernst Wigforss. Keynesian economics was not the "working class economics" that some Socialist intellectuals had been calling for, but it did offer Wigforss the tools for redefining the terms of economic and social policy debate. By training a linguist rather than an economist, Wigforss was part of that bright young generation of politicians that included Per Alban Hansson and Gustav Möller and rapidly rose to leadership in the party following the death of Hjalmar Branting in 1924.

As early as 1924 Wigforss had questioned the inherent necessity of wage reductions to combat unemployment, but it was only in the late 1920s that he elaborated his analysis into a substantial program. Wigforss followed British debates on unemployment very closely and most current research concludes that this British influence was decisive.[39] He was particularly impressed by Keynes's and the British Liberal party's 1928 proposals (presented in the book *Britain's Industrial Future*), and made a point of citing Keynes's reflationary writings to support his arguments. Wigforss was in fact among the first in the world to use Keynesian economics as the basis for a practical political policy.

In 1928, eight years before Keynes formally published *The General Theory*, Wigforss began a strong counterattack on the classic economic approach to unemployment policy in Sweden, arguing that the heart of the difficulty was underconsumption rather than excessive wages. In the new view of countercyclical public expenditure, the palliative of

38. Leif Lewin, *Planhushållningsdebatten*, p. 51. The Socialist politicians' main reaction was to demand that other sectors of the economy bear the burden as well as workers receiving lower wages. See, for example, Branting's comments that "there are also many profits . . . which may be pruned under current conditions." Andra Kammar debate, March 15, 1921. Social Democrats tended to vacillate between accepting the wage theory when in office and rejecting it when in opposition. Lewin, *Planhushållningsdebatten*, pp. 55 ff.

39. The major studies of this influence are K. G. Landgren, *Den Nya Ekonomien i Sverige: Keynes, Wigforss och Ohlin, 1927–1939;* Leif Lewin, *Planhushållningsdebatten;* and Bertil Öhman, "Arbetslöshet i Svenska historia." Wigforss's position is most clearly set out in "Spararen slösaren, och den arbetslose"; "Arbetslöner, kristid, och kapitalbildning"; and "Professor Cassel och socialismen."

unemployment insurance receded from center stage. Rather than simply a more dignified form of cash relief, unemployment benefit was both good social policy and good economic policy as one way of stabilizing the worker's purchasing power. But unemployment insurance was also distinctly secondary to the full employment, Keynesian approach itself. In retrospect, the extent to which unemployment insurance had overridden full employment in the Social Democrats' policy proposals was clearly astonishing to Wigforss—if not shameful.[40]

Wigforss succeeded in convincing his close colleagues in the party leadership of the validity of Keynesian economics. At the hands of Hansson, Wigforss, and Möller, a new party program on unemployment was formulated and pressed for the first time in the 1930 Riksdag debates and commune elections. The new appeal argued that the entire approach of the previous decade was based on the false assumption that unemployment was a temporary phenomenon requiring only ad hoc measures. The party called for abolition of the Unemployment Commission, rejection of the entire work relief system and its replacement by an extensive program of productive public work paying normal wages. Clearly the Social Democratic policy cannot be considered an improvisation created by the depression, for the first shock of that economic crisis did not hit Swedish employment until 1931. When the depression did strike, the Social Democrats were the only party with a clearly mapped out and operational policy.

Through the leadership of Hansson, Möller, and Wigforss, the positive policy to meet the economic crisis and upon which to fight the 1932 general election campaign was accepted almost unanimously by the party executive. At the 1932 party congress, this action program ran up against rank and file socialist opinion, which called for a program based on orthodox socialism and the final crisis of capitalism. In response the party leadership argued that now—finally—the party had achieved a specific program linking its philosophy of justice and freedom with practical measures, rather than relying on the vague hope that nationalization would somehow, someday, solve unemployment. Wigforss's rebuttal speech to the Congress well expressed the deficiencies of past party appeals and the meaning of the intellectual leap contained in the new.

It is not clear that this present crisis will resolve itself in a catas-

40. *Minnen*, 2: 286.

trophe. I belong to those who have a very high regard for capi-
talistic society's resilience. . . . Rather than catastrophe, it may
lead to long, drawn out unemployment. . . . That we in this
situation are forced to say "as long as there isn't a catastrophe
we have no action program"—this is the party's weakness. . . .
What is lacking in our Social Democratic party, as well as in a
large number of foreign labor parties, is the belief in our own
power, and that is due to a large extent to a feeling that we do
not know what we ought to do.[41]

The congress overwhelmingly approved the executive's program.
Largely through Wigforss and his observations on the British experience, the party and in the long run Swedish society itself had acquired
a new conception of what ought to be done.

The response of bourgeois parties to the advancing depression was
to reaffirm traditional economic principles, as well as to emphasize
the political dangers of a permanent increase in state hegemony
entailed in the Socialists' "crisis policy" (as it now became known).
Unemployment insurance was only one of many proposals rejected
because of the idea that in the current depressed economic conditions,
public spending had to be held to a minimum.[42] The nonsocialist
politicians' arguments repeated those of the National Economic Union,
where respected economists such as Cassel, Heckscher, and Bagge
argued that public works would be difficult to implement, increase
state power, and, above all, merely take purchasing power from elsewhere in the community.

The Social Democrats fought the 1932 general election largely in
terms of their positive employment policy and deemphasized unemployment insurance. The results of that election gave the Socialists a
victory, although not a parliamentary majority and only a little more
than their popular percentage achieved in 1924 when they had no
positive program to offer. An account of the detailed maneuverings
and negotiations by which Social Democrats established a working
parliamentary majority would be out of place here. Suffice it to say
that an agreement (the so-called *kohandel*, or cattle-trade agreement)
was reached by which the Socialists supported economic concessions to

---

41. Social Democratic Congress, *Protokolle*, 1932. A brief survey of the relevant developments in the party is in Berndt Angman, *Socialist Theory or Welfare-State Reality*.
42. Prime Minister Ekman, Andra Kammar debates, no. 14 (Feb. 17, 1932), p. 51.

agriculture in return for the Farmers' party vote on the crisis policy. The secondary place that the long-promised unemployment insurance had assumed for Social Democratic leaders was reflected in its exclusion from the agreement. The Social Democratic government taking office in 1932 was composed of men all of whom were between 40 and 50 years old and all of whom were committed to the expansion program prepared during the three previous years. Nor were the lessons of the British Labor government lost on Social Democratic leaders; in that nation "a government pledged to fight unemployment began by conceding its inability to do so" and in crisis returned to a traditional economic policy yielding only defeat and loss of office.[43] Early in 1933 Sweden's new government launched its plan for an unprecedented 200 million krona to fight unemployment, and these proposals were eventually passed with minor alteration.[44] Despite a certain amount of budgetary window-dressing, the Swedish Social Democrats had thereby established a claim to being the first practitioners of modern fiscal policy.

With help from the Liberals, the enactment of unemployment insurance was largely an incidental by-product of Labor's election to office. Möller, the new social minister, quickly established a five-man committee (composed of a leading Socialist politician, two civil servants, a representative of the powerful metalworkers' union, and a former Liberal social minister) to draw up an unemployment insurance proposal. Two and one-half months later, in January 1933, the committee presented a plan that largely repeated the 1928 Lindqvist commission's proposal for voluntary unemployment insurance, but with somewhat higher maximum benefits. Objections of the 1928 investigation that voluntary insurance excluded many of the most needy were partially accepted. As in Britain 22 years earlier, trying to meet this need implied state subsidy. To encourage the formation of funds among high-risk (notably agricultural and timber) workers, the 1932 committee agreed not merely to state contributions, but to state contributions of a proportionately larger amount for those groups with the lowest pay and highest unemployment.

Reactions outside the union movement were overwhelmingly nega-

43. Wigforss, *Minnen*, 2:362.

44. Andra Kammar motions 209, 211, 212, 216 (1933). In comparison, the previous Liberal government had considered itself bold in setting aside an extra 3 million krona for public works against unemployment in 1932.

tive. Some groups, such as the Board of Trade and Office of Paymaster, objected to any new expenditures during the current economic crisis; Social Board officials opposed the plan because of the tendency, demonstrated abroad for insurance to develop into extended benefits; employers and industrial organizations reemphasized the tie between unemployment and wages, arguing that such help to union funds would only intensify unemployment. Assured of LO support, however, the cabinet agreed on March 3 to adopt the committee's proposal almost intact. While the foremost attack on unemployment would be made through the reflationary program, unemployment insurance was still necessary to help those who could not be provided work. Echoing Beveridge, the Socialist cabinet emphasized that "in the area of cash support, primary reliance should be placed on state aid to unemployment insurance," for its "psychological effect" in creating a feeling of security. The number of currently covered workers (330,000) was predicted to more than double (to 700,000) at an annual cost to the state of 13 million krona and to the insured of 14 million krona. A small employers' contribution of 1.8 million krona was added to pay a portion of administrative and labor exchange costs. The Social Democratic government emphasized that the state's economic obligation was "quite clearly limited" and that after expiration of insurance-based benefits, need-tested benefits could be used. As the government saw it, by varying state contributions according to the needs of different union funds, "approximately the same equalization can be achieved as under obligatory unemployment insurance" and without the large administrative apparatus of a state program.[45] There was no one to worry about those unemployed and not in unions.

Parliamentary discussions changed little of substance but did demonstrate the necessity of Liberal support. The government's unemployment insurance proposal was introduced in the spring of 1933 and met strong opposition from Conservative and Farmers' parties. The Liberals' position was therefore crucial. But the Liberals were themselves divided, with Riksdag leader R. D. Hamrin having limited control

45. Proposition nr. 209, 1933. The amount of average daily unemployment insurance benefit paid by the union was taken as an indicator of variations in wages in the different occupations. State contributions would vary partly by the size of average benefit (literally translated as day-help) and partly by the extent of unemployment, expressed as the number of support days per member per year. The state would pay approximately 75 percent of day-help benefits at the minimum 2 krona per day level and 40 percent at the maximum 6 krona per day level.

over a more conservative group in the First Chamber centered around
S. H. Kvarnzelius. To gain Liberal support the socialist government
reluctantly agreed to drop employers' contributions, to require a
somewhat longer contributory period for qualification, and to allow
the offer of work to the unemployed to be at "reasonable" rather than
market wages. The government proposition was nevertheless lost when
ten of the eighteen Liberals in the First Chamber voted against the
proposal. The Liberal vote seems to have been a politically motivated
attempt to discredit the government and in fact none of the government's major proposals—among them abolition of the Unemployment
Commission—excluded from the *kohandel* agreement were passed in
the Riksdag.[46]

In 1934 the government again introduced its voluntary unemployment insurance proposal in largely unaltered form. By this time Hamrin had replaced the aged Kvarnzelius as Liberal leader in the First
Chamber. Again the plan was abridged to overcome Liberal objections
to employer contributions, and with Liberal and Social Democratic
votes unemployment insurance passed both chambers, despite the
opposition of Conservative and Farmers' parties. Conservative leader
Lindeman closed the debate by pointedly issuing the familiar warning
that parties of the Left would now compete in broadening benefits and
abandoning the insurance principle, as had Britain. As usual, policy
development was being ascribed to the simple fact of party competition
rather than to the different intellectual bases for action that parties
had learned. Social Minister Möller summed up the government's case
and replied to Lindeman that there was a basic difference between the
British and Swedish labor governments.

> The MacDonald government did not combat unemployment
> with a real work-creating program. I believe . . . that it was the
> mistake of that government—instead of meeting unemployment
> with a genuine work-creating program—to meet it mainly by
> loaning money to the unemployment insurance fund. . . . More-
> over, the idea that one must at any price maintain the gold
> standard to save the country's finances . . . the whole of this
> huge slogan was in fact a fiction.[47]

46. Olle Nyman, *Svensk Parliamentarism, 1932–1936*, pp. 138 ff. Första Kammar debate,
June 20, 1933. The vote was 67 in favor, 71 opposed.
47. Andra Kammar debate, May 30, 1934, p. 28. The final vote was 68–58 in the First
Chamber and 102–82 in the Second.

As we shall see, Möller's summary of the difference between Labor governments was fairly accurate.

Britain

In Britain, as in Sweden, the first shock of world war led to fears of rampant unemployment. During August 1914, joblessness in trade unions shot up from 2.8 percent to 7.1 percent. Britain's active war involvement, however, quickly and fully occupied the labor force before any policy response could occur. From the beginning of September the drain of manpower into the army and munitions production produced a sustained decline in unemployment. During the next four years, with the union unemployment rate at less than 1 percent, unemployment both as an economic phenomenon and as a political issue virtually disappeared from public view. Ministers, unions, employers, parties, and the public at large cared little for anticipating the problems of postwar employment policy.

Unemployment insurance did not, however, disappear from the view of civil servants responsible for the 1911 act. Again, as in Sweden, it was the institutionalized bureaucracy that provided the one center of sustained attention to public policy. The moving spirits pressing in Britain for extensions of unemployment insurance in order to take advantage of high wartime employment and to prepare for postwar dislocations were in fact the same officials who had been behind the 1911 act.[48] As a result of the concern of Board of Trade administrators for postwar industrial problems, a bill was introduced in 1916 to allow extension of insurance by departmental order to any trade engaged in or connected with munitions work; it was thought that under this guise extensions could be made to cover virtually all trades. The bill passed both Houses of Parliament and the National Insurance (Munitions Workers) Act became law on September 4, 1916, with almost no public comment.

Once in operation, however, the officials' proposed extensions of unemployment insurance met everywhere with the combined opposition of employers and workmen, both of whose representatives argued that there were sufficient orders in hand to sustain employment for years after the war. No attempt was made by the trade unions to make use of the act's provisions to frame their own schemes, wool and cotton

48. Beveridge, *Unemployment: A Problem of Industry*, p. 273. A general account is in Beveridge's "Unemployment Insurance in the War and After," pp. 230 ff.

trades successfully demanded exclusion from coverage, and the introduction of unemployment insurance in shoe and beet trades proposed by officials met passive resistance from workers and had to be abandoned. Official proposals to increase contributions in order to give better benefits in the current inflationary period also gained no support. In the end, the 1916 act brought in 1.1 million new insured workers, of whom three-quarters were women. Being poorly organized, these were the workers least capable of objecting to their inclusion but also the group most likely to strain insurance funds at war's end. Popular pressure during the war, rather than forcing extensions of this social policy, was probably the major brake on its timely advance.

In response the same civil servants made proposals for further compulsory extension of unemployment insurance but met with no response from their preoccupied political leaders. The new Ministry of Reconstruction in July 1917 established a Civil War Workers Committee to consider measures for "demilitarization" of workers after the war, and a subcommittee of experts headed by Beveridge reported in February 1918. The subcommittee found that the total war effort had obliterated any possible distinction between workers engaged or not engaged in war production and that the war's termination would affect the entire labor force. If unemployment insurance were to ease these dislocations it would therefore have to be universal; a comprehensive program would also avoid the unpopularity of the 1916 act, which had created resentments precisely among those covered while others remained outside. Immediate action would be necessary, the committee concluded, to forestall unsatisfactory, improvised methods. The subcommittee recommendation was accepted unanimously by the War Workers Committee and forwarded to the government March 1, 1918; the only government response was to forward the proposal to a subcommittee of the Labor Resettlement Committee within the Ministry of Labor, which also reported favorably in October 1918. Apart from these civil servants, no body of interested workers, employers, or reformers pressed for changes in unemployment insurance, and in the headlong rush of war nothing was done.

For all their policy expertise and prescience, civil servants could not make a major substantive contribution until events led ministers to search for alternatives. Impending demobilization provided this impetus. Suddenly in the autumn of 1918 it became clear that Germany was about to collapse and that Britain's massive civilian and military war machine would be idle in a matter of weeks. The result was a classic case of administrative expediency. The Ministry of Reconstruction, the organ responsible for postwar planning, had itself only belatedly recognized the need to plan for postwar unemployment; apart from the deficiencies of its minister (Christopher Addison) as an administrator, the "slightly bogus" ministry had to a large extent served as a public relations symbol rather than a policy analysis and planning agency.[49] After the years of delay on unemployment insurance, Addison now argued to the cabinet in October 1918 that it was too late to enact and administer any comprehensive unemployment insurance for workers immediately entering peacetime employment. Instead his ministry suggested that the out-of-work donation plan prepared for military demobilization also be applied to civilian workers for six months—later extended to one year.

The out-of-work donation was in fact one of the few plans already prepared to deal with postwar dislocations. It was now borrowed virtually intact for civilian demobilization. In essence the program provided noncontributory unemployment insurance policies to all discharged workers who became unemployed, with a weekly donation (benefit) of 25 shillings for men and 20 shillings for women, supplemented by a weekly donation of 6 shillings and 3 shillings respectively for one or more children under 15. Obviously this compared quite favorably with the total current 7 shillings unemployment insurance benefit. Emphasizing that out-of-work donations were purely an "emergency measure," the government quickly accepted Addison's plan and announced the civilian donations on November 12 following Armistice celebrations. With this program—worked out in less than three weeks—the government implicitly recognized the right of the unemployed to claim social support; with it also appeared the term "dole" in British social policy.

This landmark in British unemployment appears to have had little to do with partys' bidding for electoral support. To be sure, the donations were raised to 29 shillings four days before the December 1918 general election, but unquestionably the 1918 election appeals of the government were centered on making Germany pay; to the extent that any reconstruction program was discussed, it dealt with housing and

---

49. Bentley Gilbert, *British Social Policy, 1914–1939*, p. 7. Gilbert's is probably the best single-volume history of the interplay between politics and policy in this period, and I have built upon his account in this section.

health rather than unemployment policies. For its part the British, like the Swedish, Labor party shared in the movement toward socialist purity at war's end and gave scarcely any attention to unemployment policy. The first British Parliament elected by virtually universal suffrage would become known as a Parliament of "hard-faced businessmen" with little dedication to reconstruction or positive social policy.

In part, the government leaders seem to have been inclined to act by their own predispositions acquired during the war years. Having mobilized the country to fight, they saw it as a natural consequence that state policy should help demobilize the population for peace. Perhaps more important in generating government action was the push of indirect popular pressure expressed through leaders' anticipations. Cabinet sessions were frequently preoccupied with the danger of working class unrest. The previous year's French army mutinies, revolts in Russia, and socialist pacifism and widespread strikes in Britain were still fresh memories; a series begun in the *Times* during September 1918 concerned the revolutionary threat of organized labor and was discussed seriously within the cabinet, while accusations and answers concerning the "revolutionary" ideas being spread by the Workers Education Association were sent directly to the king.

Given this predisposition to act, the actual course chosen was a direct transplantation of the one administrative plan already worked out. The out-of-work donations program in turn created its own expectations in the public, or, more precisely, in policy makers' anticipations of these expectations. A looking-glass realm perhaps, but leaders' anticipations of public reactions were nonetheless a real force in this haphazard process of policy adaptation. The same concern over working class unrest which had initiated civilian donations also dictated that they could not be allowed to lapse with nothing to take their place. The year 1919 opened with soldiers' demobilization riots, followed by Clydeside strikes, the Battle of George Street, the threat of a national miners' strike, and a vast series of less dramatic stoppages. Between August 1 and 3 Liverpool police strikes were accompanied by widespread looting and civil disorder which ended only with the dispatch of 2,600 troops, four tanks, and a series of bayonet charges. On August 5, Lloyd George initiated a top secret review of "the whole position of the country" and told the cabinet "they could not take risks with labor. If we did, we should at once create an enemy within our own borders, and one which would be better provided with dangerous weapons than Germany. We had in this country millions of men who had been trained to arms and there were plenty of guns and ammunition available."[50]

Throughout 1919 and early 1920, the cabinet was also continually alarmed by the secret information coming to it from its domestic intelligence system headed by Basil Thompson, intelligence which covered not only subversive organizations but also private activities of the most respectable labor leaders. Increasingly the threat of leftist revolution and the power of demobilized workers was emphasized in Thompson's reports and accepted by the cabinet. On September 5, 1919, the Conservative minister of labor, Robert Horne, submitted a memorandum to the cabinet arguing that with the approaching end of the civilian donation scheme it was vital to have some new program under way. "In the face of the precedent of the Donation scheme, I think we must start from the assumption that to allow the Donation scheme to expire and to put nothing in its place is impossible."[51]

Throughout this period, civil servants in the Ministry of Labor seem to have been the main proponents of extending unemployment insurance on a universal basis. While warning of union opposition to contributions, the Conservative labor minister presented to the cabinet his officials' proposal for virtually universal unemployment insurance coverage, with contributory benefits of 15 shillings for men and 12/6 for women. From the amounts of time spent in discussion, it seems clear that, while spurred by the fear of popular violence, the cabinet's major source of reluctance on unemployment insurance policy was again the fear of further antagonizing labor. At the February National Labor Conference, union representatives had rejected worker contributions to unemployment insurance, and in December 1919 a delegation from the TUC urged the familiar labor demand that the government should provide work or maintenance as a noncontributory right. Again policy makers could be found weighing an extension of social policy in terms of its relative unpopularity. In the end, the cabinet approved the Ministry of Labor plans for extending unemployment insurance but raised benefits and provided the possibility for separate industrial funds, as the cabinet minutes put it, "in order not to antagonize the

50. Cab. 23/15, Augst 5, 1919. This and other cabinet papers subsequently quoted in this section are found in Gilbert, *British Social Policy*, chap. 2.
51. Cab. 24/88.

trade unions and labor interest." By far the greatest attention in drawing up the plan was given to such attempts at preempting labor
opposition.

As usual, the content of the plan was an administrative creation.
The cabinet received its first informal explanation of the draft bill on
December 18, 1919, only four days before the bill was first introduced
in Parliament. The basis of future disaster lay not only in the expediency with which the plan was formulated but also in the dearth of
information underlying it. Reliable unemployment statistics still did
not exist in many if not most trades, nor were projections available as
to future industrial prospects. The resulting unemployment insurance
proposal was based upon an assumed annual unemployment rate of
5.3 percent, compared with 8.5 percent posited in the higher risk
trades in 1911. In essence, the carefully devised 1911 plan for the
building and engineering trades was simply borrowed intact and
applied to the entire population of manual workers.

Within Parliament, discussions were scarcely inspired. The major
conflict proved to be between the National Health Insurance "approved societies" and a Labor party jealous that friendly societies
as well as unions should have the right to administer unemployment
insurance benefits. After some indecision, the government allowed a
free vote on the issue, which went against Labor. It was a petty and,
as it proved in practice, meaningless point. The overwhelming attention
paid to administrative proprietorship was representative of the
almost total disregard of basic issues in unemployment insurance and
postwar employment policy. The hastily devised Unemployment Insurance Act of 1920 passed Parliament in the spring of 1920, raising
the number of insured workers from 4 million to 11.4 million.

The 1920 act was to be the last reform measure attributable to Lloyd
George and contained the seeds for the virtual destruction of such insurance in Britain. Unemployment policy for the next decade was a
series of expedient liberalizations of unemployment insurance by
coalition, Conservative, and Socialist governments reacting both to
unexpectedly high unemployment and, equally important, to expectations created by the previous policy concession. Some policy
makers acted out of fears for public order, some with humanitarian
sentiments, and some in the name of party ideology. But all manipulated
unemployment insurance because it was easily available and they could
think of nothing better to do about unemployment itself.

Policy planning had lagged behind the pace of events. The 1920 act passed at precisely the moment the first signs of collapse in the postwar economic boom began to appear. In June 1920, wholesale prices started a slow decline and by midsummer intelligence coming to the cabinet showed a recession approaching. In August the new Liberal minister of labor, T. J. McNamara, reported that unemployment and unrest were certain to grow in the winter. In particular, the minister pointed out that there were 150,000 ex-servicemen unemployed, of whom 15,000 to 20,000 were in London; by November, if not earlier, these men would be leading processions of the unemployed and would "not stick at trifles." By the time the 1920 act came into effect on November 8, 1920, unemployment had more than tripled (to 5.3%) over the rate during its parliamentary debate in the spring. In October the threat of a general strike in support of the miners again arose, and the first of many postwar disturbances by the unemployed occurred in the "Battle of Downing Street." During September, October, and November, Thompson's reports again played upon the revolutionary threat posed by the unemployed and the fact that with ex-servicemen present, rioters "for the first time in history were better trained than the troops."

Anticipations of further public unrest again triggered insurance concessions. On November 4, McNamara reminded the cabinet that the out-of-work donation for ex-servicemen was about to end and that many dependent upon the donation would not be eligible for unemployment insurance under existing regulations. As a temporary expedient the cabinet decided to extend military donations until April 1921. In January 1921, while the Coalition cabinet became increasingly alarmed at radicalism among mining workers and the tendency for extremists to take advantage of unemployment, McNamara presented the Ministry of Labor's proposed extension of unemployment insurance. New extended ("uncovenanted") benefits would be paid for two special periods without reference to statutory contribution requirements. Benefits would be raised from the existing 15 shillings to 20 shillings for ex-servicemen so as to correspond to the lapsing out-of-work donations and to 18 shillings for all other workers. Although benefits would be raised immediately and contributions raised only from July 4, 1922, it was argued that the unemployment insurance fund had an ample surplus of £24 million. As Beveridge had predicted fifteen years earlier in the first unemployment insurance plans, since certain benefits were now to be provided without reference to contributions, there now also began to be applied "special," more discretionary eligibility tests for receipt of benefit.[52] On February 11, 1921, with no other alternatives before it, the cabinet approved the Ministry of Labor proposals. In Parliament, Labor sought to double proposed benefits to 40 shillings a week for all family heads and introduce dependency benefits for children. The government made the one concession of raising benefits to 20 shillings for all men and otherwise unchanged the act passed Parliament on February 23, 1921.

With the Act of 1921, the breach in the insurance principles of unemployment insurance was well under way, and the remainder of the 1920s is largely a chronicle of successive extensions through "uncovenanted," "extended," and "transitional" benefits by all governments to relieve the unemployed. In May 1921, McNamara again had to return to the cabinet for an amendment to unemployment insurance. With the continued high unemployment and a miners' strike in the spring, the insurance fund, which had been expected to remain solvent until July 1922, was at the current rate going to be exhausted by July 1921. Departmental conflict increased as the minister of labor proposed to reduce benefits slightly, to increase contributions, and to double the fund's borrowing rights from the Treasury to £20 million, and the Treasury replied by rejecting any increased borrowing and proposing larger benefits reductions instead. Eventually the cabinet compromised—lowering benefits to the Treasury-recommended 15 shillings for men and 12 shillings for women and increasing the borrowing rights to £20 million—and introduced two new periods of extended benefits for those exhausting their entitlement. Again Labor pressed in Parliament for even greater liberalizations but the second Unemployment Insurance Act of 1921 passed with little further discussion. The parliamentary, like the departmental, wrangling was merely an expression of the fundamental bankruptcy in policy ideas.

By the autumn of 1921, unemployment and labor unrest had returned

52. These requirements were roughly that the unemployed must now be "genuinely" seeking work, unable to secure it, and in insured employment 20 weeks after December 31, 1919. Determination was made by the Ministry of Labor through local employment committees.

to the serious proportions of 1919.[53] The communist-sponsored National
Workman's Movements provided some leadership but do not seem to
have penetrated far into the already agitated groups of unemployed.
In September 1921, McNamara wrote to the prime minister that
300,000 insured had exhausted the most recent July extensions of unemployment insurance. The "real danger" was that unemployed
workers were now congregating, while communists continued to ex-
ploit the situation. Regardless of the financial considerations, the
problem "has to be faced if grave civil disorder is to be avoided." In
October 1921 Lloyd George's coalition government responded to the
crisis by agreeing that the 15-shilling benefit was inadequate for
men with dependents and establishing a special distress fund paying
extra 5-shilling benefits to the unemployed with adult dependents and
one shilling for each child up to four children.

The extension of unemployment insurance was of course seen as only
the most immediate palliative to what was thought to be temporarily
high unemployment. Behind it lay—in Britain as in Sweden—the
prevailing conceptions of sound economic policy. For a basic solution
to unemployment, the government and informed opinion in almost all
quarters relied upon the established principles of classic economics:
government retrenchment and economy. With the economic downturn
beginning in mid-1920, there arose a chorus of voices in press, Conservative, Liberal, and banking circles calling for reduced government
expenditure to defeat the economic crisis, and by 1921, 170 MPs had
signed a manifesto urging retrenchment. The national economy drive
had begun. In August 1921 the government appointed the Geddes
Committee on National Expenditure, a select committee composed
entirely of leading City businessmen to suggest ways for reducing
national expenditure. Although Lloyd George and several other
Liberals queried if deflation had not gone too far, under these pressures
for economy the housing program was cut drastically, coal mines in
April were returned to private hands, the railways were decontrolled
in August, and in September the minimum wage in agriculture was
abolished. In sum, the national economy efforts far outweighed any

53. According to Beveridge, the union unemployment rate of 5.3 percent in October had
risen to 10 percent by March 1921 and 23 percent by June 1921, compared to a previous
high of 10.7 percent in 1879. Beveridge, "Unemployment Insurance in the War and After,"
p. 242.

practical effects of Lloyd George's earlier public campaign for a postwar reconstruction program.[54]

Although hoping that socialism was somehow the answer, the Labor party in reality had little more to offer in unemployment policy than its repeated demands for higher unemployment insurance benefits and abolition of the workers' contributions to its financing. The election of December 1923 provided one major opportunity for the parties' electoral appeals on unemployment to influence policy. The Conservatives again returned to and again were defeated on tariffs as a cure for unemployment, while the Liberals emphasized Lloyd George's public works approach. It was, however, the Labor party that went the farthest in its claims, asserting that only Labor had a "positive remedy for unemployment." A government that promised only insurance or maintenance was a failure; what was needed for the unemployed was "immediate employment, nothing more and nothing less." Forty-five pages of proposals for employment of the unemployed on works of public utility were said to exist already and on these "the unemployed can be directly set to work by the hundreds and thousands." Although still in a parliamentary minority after the election, MacDonald agreed to form a government "because in dealing with unemployment we believe we have a programme."[55]

In fact there was no such program. The first Labor government in British history soon came to doubt its unique capacity for dealing with unemployment and, like its Swedish counterpart at the time, reverted to established techniques. A great many of the promised employment schemes were found by their supporters to be sheer pretense. But apart from and greater than any administrative difficulties in setting up public works were the tenets of classic economics that dictated the limitations to any government expenditures. The major Labor spokesman for economic orthodoxy was the Socialist chancellor of the exchequer and former critic of the 1911 Insurance Act, Phillip Snowden. By May 1924, Prime Minister MacDonald noted that he was "not at

54. P. Abrams, "The Failure of Social Reform: 1918–1920," and Cmd. 1581. The most promising of George's capital-expanding ideas was the Trade Facilities Act, which was, however, crippled when the Bank of England informed the government that only one-half the proposed borrowing could be supported and that, anyway, "government backing would not make the difference anticipated." Cab. 23/27.

55. Labor's ambitious promises were aired in the House of Commons debates, February 24 and October 26, 1921, and August 1, 1923; Sidney Webb's election address, November 19, 1923; and MacDonald's speech at Elgin, December 22, 1923.

all sure but that we were a little bit innocent in these matters." In the end, the promised massive employment program of Labor failed to materialize, and the program presented by Snowden in August contained not one new employment plan for the winter. The so-called "Treasury dogma" enunciated by Conservative chancellors Baldwin and Churchill was but a reflection of the economic doctrine that dominated all party governments of the era; Snowden's and Mac-Donald's acceptance of the doctrine likewise forestalled any positive employment program during Labor's periods of rule. The Labor party learned nothing to put in its place. As one writer has said, when Snowden and MacDonald left the party in 1931, "they took its only economic policy with them."[56]

Thus immobilized, the first Labor government turned in 1924 to revising some of the more distasteful conditions of unemployment insurance. Benefits were raised from 15 to 18 shillings and the discretionary power of the Minister of Labor in granting uncovenanted benefits was repealed, making benefits available as a right to those who had fulfilled additional rather vague qualifications. Through a series of complicated arrangements, the possibility was created of uncovenanted benefits for a virtually indefinite period; as a condition of gaining Liberal support the new provisions were to end and be reassessed in June 1926. The Labor government, like the Coalition and Conservative governments before it, had fallen back on unemployment insurance to relieve the most obvious hardships of unemployment. As Beveridge sharply observed the following year, the danger in unemployment insurance was less that it might demoralize men and more "that it may demoralize the government of the day and cause them to give up the search for remedies. It may make easy even for a Labor government containing Mr. Sidney Webb . . . to take the easy road of perpetually extending relief."[57]

Upon again regaining office, the Conservative government in 1925 made at least one departure: the return to the gold standard, an act that was essentially an employment policy. As for unemployment insurance, the Conservative government reestablished the discretionary nature of extended benefits and created a departmental committee

56. W. Medlicott, *Contemporary England, 1914–1964*, p. 98. The growing sense of resignation can be traced in the House of Commons debates, May 20, 22, 24, 29, 1924, and Chancellor Snowden's speech, July 30, 1924.

57. Beveridge, "Unemployment Insurance in the War and After," pp. 250–51.

under the well-known Conservative Lord Blanesburgh to report on unemployment insurance prior to the 1926 expiration of the 1924 provisions. In representations before the Blanesburgh committee both the Labor party and TUC again urged full maintenance for the unemployed with the entire cost borne by the state, a course which Labor deliberately shunned when in office. For immediate implementation, Labor representatives urged raising benefits to 20 shillings a week, reducing worker contributions at the expense of the Exchequer, and replacing extended benefits with one continuous benefit paid as a right.

It was not these familiar demands of the political Left but the final recommendation of the Conservative Blanesburgh committee that actually precipitated the final transformation of unemployment insurance into a scarcely veiled form of cash relief. With only one Labor member on the committee, this change cannot be said to have been the handiwork of workers' representatives, but seems instead to have come from Conservatives' and civil servants' somewhat misguided efforts at economy, humanity, and administrative simplification. While proposing marginal cuts in benefits, the committee argued that the truly unemployed man should be relieved when in need and as long as this need lasted without the complications of covenanted and uncovenanted benefits. Against the chief government actuary's objections, the distinction between covenanted and uncovenanted benefits was to be abolished, along with the contribution rule that required six weeks' contribution for one week's benefit. Duration of benefits was therefore to become unlimited, with the payment of 30 previous contributions in two years a means of certifying previous employment and not of building up actuarial credit. For those who could not meet this qualification there would be "transitional" benefits with somewhat easier conditions. For all other unemployed with only a tenuous attachment to the labor market there remained the poor law, "which should retain the deterrent effect which now attaches to it."[58] With the ending of the contribution rule, the chief limitation on government financial obligations now resided in the worker's "genuine" search for work and the implicit assumption of work being available. The report optimistically assumed a reduction in unemployment to 6 percent and reflected the continuing faith in economic self-adjustment. In 1927 a Conservative government bill embodied the major committee pro-

58. Ministry of Labor, *Report of the Departmental Committee on Unemployment Insurance*, 1927.

posals and passed in Parliament amid the usual attempts of the Labor party to liberalize benefits.

At least potentially, the next chance for a shift in policy through electoral democracy came with the general election of 1929. The Conservative party offered a continuation of its existing policy while Labor returned to its theme of national public works and a further easing of unemployment insurance restrictions. It was within certain intellectual circles of the Liberal party that a searching attempt was made to develop and offer to the electorate a new, substantially Keynesian approach. To be sure, all parties had previously paid lip service to public works but now, largely under the personal tutelage of Keynes, the Liberals in their "Yellow Book" of 1928 (*Britain's Industrial Future*) proposed a massive program of public works, an economic general staff to coordinate economic policy and—the most decisive break with orthodox economics—deliberate deficit financing for this new government expenditure. As we have seen, Swedish Social Democratic leaders were deeply impressed. In Britain Lloyd George, after five years' in opposition and hoping to revive his and the party's fortunes, conducted an extensive propaganda campaign that succeeded in making the Liberal proposal the most discussed issue of the campaign.[59] But politics teaches about men as well as policies and both Conservative and Labor parties concentrated their responses on reviving memories of the untrustworthiness of Lloyd George's promises rather than on the substance of the Liberal program. The election on May 30, 1929, gave the Liberals an increase of 2 million votes (to 5,304,000) but only 58 seats compared to Labor's 8,365,000 votes and 289 seats. In view of their hopes, aims, and efforts, the Liberals rightly regarded the results as a lost battle. Now leader of the largest but still a minority party, MacDonald formed the second Labor government, and Snowden again became chancellor.

Although the new socialist government was no more successful than its predecessor in keeping its pledges to reduce unemployment, it did work to liberalize, as promised, the conditions of unemployment insurance benefits. Since 1924, when the requirement was first applied to standard benefits, an increasingly large number had been disqualified

59. Trevor Wilson, *The Downfall of the Liberal Party, 1914–1935*, pp. 344 ff. In response to the Keynesian campaign the Treasury brought out a closely reasoned White Paper to show that no amount of expenditure on public works could increase the level of employment. Cmd. 333.1

under the "genuinely seeking work" provision, until by 1929 it constituted the largest single reason for disqualification and was opposed by the Labor party, which had condoned it when first in office.[60] At the beginning of 1930 the government abolished the provision that the applicant prove he was "genuinely seeking work" and now put the onus of responsibility on the state. Henceforth, the unemployed person was disqualified from benefit only if he failed to apply for or accept a vacancy of which he was notified by an employment exchange or other recognized agency. All transitional benefits would now be paid directly by the Treasury through parliamentary grants rather than indirectly through the insurance fund. For the first time, aid to the unemployed was defrayed entirely through direct national taxation. The limit of state obligation was thus further reduced by being made dependent on the ability of employment exchanges to tell workers of available employment. As a condition of Liberal support, the 1930 act was to be reassessed in June 1933.

The new Unemployment Act led to an immediate spurt in the number of persons receiving benefits, with 140,000 recipients of transitional benefits in January 1930 and 300,000 in May 1930. At the same time, the spring of 1930 witnessed the first ominous increases in depression unemployment; by the end of the year, unemployment began to surpass its unprecedented 1921 peak and was still climbing.

As the depression advanced, the major roadblock to policy adaptation was a continuing adherence to old truths rather than any lack of political power. New ideas were available, but the Labor cabinet, with the help of the Treasury and Bank of England, remained transfixed by orthodox economic convictions. Oswald Mosley, for example, was a prime force in the Labor cabinet pressing for a new departure. Relying heavily on the 1928 Liberal program, Mosley argued vigorously for an expansion of purchasing power—through deficit financing if necessary—rather than deflation, but such a proposition was rejected in toto by Chancellor Snowden. On May 22, Mosley resigned from the government and carried his fight to the parliamentary Labor party, where his position was rejected by 210 to 23 votes. The subsequent revolt in the parliamentary party was easily crushed by MacDonald's appeal to party loyalty. Ernest Bevin, the leading trade union spokes-

---

60. In addition to those deterred from applying, 250, 926 of 654,491 disallowances of claim were attributable to this provision in 1929. Cmd. 3881, p. 58. The first "genuinely seeking work" test had been applied in 1921 to those seeking uncovenanted benefits.

man, was also increasingly convinced of the errors of the deflationary policy. As the only union member of the government's expert Committee on Finance and Industry, Bevin closely followed Keynes's presentations to the committee and signed Keynes's addendum calling for a program of domestic capital development. Although party loyalty prevented him from raising his doubts publicly, MacDonald and Snowden both knew privately where Bevin stood.[61]

The crisis of 1931 marked a decisive turning point in unemployment insurance, a paroxysm in the forces of economic crisis, economic orthodoxy, administrative expediency, and partisan maneuvering which had characterized policy during the previous decade. The centrality of unemployment insurance to the economic and political crisis of that year is comprehensible only by recognizing the *symbolic* importance that unemployment insurance expenditure had acquired. During 1930 unemployment had almost doubled to include one-fifth of all insured persons. In one year the annual cost to the Exchequer of transitional benefits rose from £4 million to £22 million, and between December 1929 and December 1931 the debt of the unemployment insurance fund had more than tripled to £110 million.

There is no need here to describe the full political drama of 1931. The financial and economic crash, interpreted in traditional economic terms, dictated cuts in government spending to restore confidence in the British pound. In the turmoil leading up to these expenditure cuts and the fall of the MacDonald government, unemployment insurance was of paramount importance. For the socialist government, the price for foreign bankers' pound-sustaining loans, for the Bank of England's cooperation, and for Conservative and Liberal party support was expressed largely in the hard coin of unemployment insurance cuts. It is important to recognize that this essentially *political* interpretation of the collapse of the international monetary system—rooted in the assurances of conventional economic theory—was accepted by the entire Labor cabinet, and economies were seriously sought during the

---

61. Allen Bullock, *The Life and Times of Ernest Bevin*, 1: 425, 426, 470. In January 1930, MacDonald had also established an Economic Advisory Committee of business, labor, and economic experts to advise on economic policy. Again the same divisions of economic philosophy occurred, with Keynes, Bevin, R. H. Tawney, and G. D. H. Cole arguing for measures to increase purchasing power and overcome underconsumption as well as to initiate state capital development, while businessmen and economic experts of the traditional school argued for even more deflation. As the crisis intensified in the early months of 1931, the divided committee met only three times and quickly became defunct.

week of August 12–19. The Labor cabinet was able to agree on total cuts of £56 million in the projected £170 million budget deficit, with the economy committee of the cabinet proposing a saving of £48.5 million in unemployment insurance (largely by transferring some costs to local authorities, increasing contributions, and reducing benefit duration) and the Labor cabinet as a whole agreeing to a £22 million saving in unemployment insurance. Acting Conservative and Liberal party leaders Neville Chamberlain and Herbert Samuel demanded further cuts in unemployment insurance. Bank of England representatives reported that the Labor cabinet's proposed cuts of only one-third of the deficit would not restore confidence, that a cut of one-half would, and that, "particularly from the point of view of foreign interests concerned, substantial economies should be effected in unemployment insurance. In no other way could foreign confidence be restored."[62]

On the previous day, government consultations with a TUC General Council headed by Ernest Bevin had found the union leaders firmly opposed to any cuts whatsoever in unemployment insurance. In part, this stand was a question of union leaders protecting worker interests, but in part too the union firmness sprang from the Keynes-influenced conviction of Bevin that the entire deflationary policy was misconceived and that any attempt to avoid devaluation was a useless delay of the inevitable. This union view, while certainly not dictation, was undoubtedly important in convincing some cabinet members—notably Arthur Henderson—to resist any further cuts than those already approved.[63] When MacDonald and Snowden returned to the cabinet seeking approval for cuts not of £56 million but £78 million (with a 10 percent reduction in unemployment insurance benefits) as the minimum acceptable to the Opposition and foreign bankers, the Labor cabinet was split. Although carrying a majority with him, MacDonald could not ignore the threatened resignation of eight or nine members led by Arthur Henderson. After inconclusive discussions on August 23, the Labor cabinet gave its resignation to the king, and MacDonald agreed to form a national government with Conservative and Liberal leaders.

The symbolic nature of these policy choices now became obvious. With the creation of the new National government, foreign loans were quickly arranged on August 27, before any cabinet decisions had been

---

62. Cab. 43, August 21, 1931.
63. Bullock, *Ernest Bevin*, p. 484.

taken on what economies to make. Economies eventually proposed by the National government on September 2 were in fact about £4 million *less* than had been proposed by the Labor cabinet's economy committee (which had included Henderson) and only approximately £13 million more than had been agreed to by the Labor cabinet as a whole. A memorandum prepared in the Cabinet Office the day after the National government's agreement on cuts showed that its scheme of economies was substantially identical with what a majority of the late Labor cabinet had been willing to accept. With two exceptions, the package was also identical to that which the Labor cabinet dissidents had been prepared to accept. These two exceptions were a 10 percent cut in unemployment insurance benefits (saving £12.8 million out of total economies of £70 million) approved by the National government and use of the local public assistance administration to operate a means test for transitional benefits. On the latter point the Labor cabinet had merely contemplated instead that this means test should "in some way be administered by central government machinery."[64] The point is not to question (though questions can be raised about) motives of the opposition parties in their earlier demands for cuts greater than the Labor government was likely to give and greater than the National government itself eventually made. The point lies in showing that however much a few Labor ministers might balk at certain types of marginal trimming, such as reductions in unemployment benefits, the underlying theoretical perspective was shared by virtually all ministers of all parties.

Parliament reassembled September 8 and quickly passed the National Economy Act giving the government one month's power to make economies through special orders in council. It was all for nothing. Before any of the hard-won changes in unemployment insurance could be made, the run on currency reserves had again mounted, and on September 21 Britain was finally forced off that gold standard for which so much had been sacrificed. The British pound floated and, needless to say, the feared 50 percent cut in living standards which the Treasury, Bank of England, and Labor Chancellor Snowden had so long prophesied did not materialize.

Unemployment insurance policy, however, remained fixed by the economy measures. There now occurred the one and only instance in

---

64. Cab. 21/349, September 3, 1931.

the present study where a social benefit was actually reduced in absolute terms. Even then an unprecedented economic and political crisis had been required to reverse the upward ratchet of successive governments' inheritance of and recourse to expedient policy concessions. A roughly 10 percent reduction in unemployment insurance benefits for men, women, and dependents, along with new contributions from employer, worker, and state, were introduced by orders in council the first week of October 1931. On October 7, transitional benefits were replaced by means-tested "transitional payments" administered by local public assistance committees with funds from the Exchequer. This plan was the grossest administrative expedient, using the one piece of bureaucratic apparatus available, the local poor law committees, to institute some limitation on government financial obligations. Just as the first unemployment insurance planners had eliminated poor law means-testing by contributory insurance rules, so now the 1931 reversion to such means testing was but an extension of discretionary requirements introduced in the 1920s to accompany the relaxation of rules concerning entitlement by contribution. The long 20-year series of policy moves had yielded a decision which no one chose as such but which tended to confirm the point made by Beveridge in 1907: without an entitlement based on contributory principles, aid to the able-bodied poor was likely to revert to poor law methods.

The 1931 policy had been adopted outside normal procedures of electoral democracy and parliamentary government. In the election of October 27, 1931, the electorate was given a chance to express its views on these changes. The result was a loss of 2 million votes for Labor and reduction of its parliamentary representation from 289 to 46. Bevin was defeated by a majority of 12,938 in a constituency which had a Labor majority of 16,700 in 1929; Henderson lost in the Labor stronghold at Burnley; and the only Labor ex-minister to be reelected to Parliament was the perennial George Lansbury. When the voice of democracy was heard, it overturned not the restrictive social policy but that policy's Labor opponents.

Administrative problems soon arose with the hastily commandeered local public assistance authorities. Standards and rates varied considerably and depended heavily on local authorities' attitudes toward the unemployed. In a small minority of authorities, "overgenerous" grants became the norm and attracted much press attention. This only helped confirm the lesson that politicians and top civil servants now drew from policy experiences of the 1920s: unemployment insurance must be further separated from relief and both isolated from political pressures. By 1932 even many Labor spokesmen were opposed to the haphazard local administration and blurring of insurance with relief.[65]

Again, the actual content of policy remained very much an administrative creation. From the outset the Treasury had opposed giving a blank check to local assistance committees, and by the autumn of 1932 civil servants in both the Treasury and Ministry of Labor were collaborating on a plan to establish a nationally organized system of relief committees to replace the local assistance authorities. The idea of a special Unemployment Assistance Board to isolate the treatment of unemployed workers from politics was especially favored by Chancellor Neville Chamberlain, a man some have described as "essentially a civil servant in politics."[66]

The National government's bill, prepared in the Ministry of Labor and submitted in September 1933, marked an important policy shift in its efforts to separate insurance from relief and both from politics. In the first place, there was to be created an Unemployment Insurance Statutory Committee, composed of experts appointed by the Ministry of Labor, to operate without constant recourse to Parliament. Nonpolitical and with responsibility to keep the unemployment insurance scheme solvent, the committee could set rates of contribution and benefit and, what was equally vital to a sustainable policy, finally had a defined financial target: to balance fund income and outgo over a given average of years. By 1939 the statutory committee, headed by William Beveridge, had reduced the pending debt from £106 million to £77 million and had a working balance in the fund of £57 million.

In the second place, there was to be established for relief purposes a nonpolitical Unemployment Assistance Board composed of six members with tenure at the pleasure of the crown and power to issue regulations having the force of law (unless rejected when laid before Parliament). As Ministry of Labor officials had long sought, control of all able-bodied unemployed on temporary benefits or poor law relief

65. See the TUC statement, in the appendices to Minutes of Evidence, Cmd. 4185. Part 7 (1932), pp. 477 ff. Beatrice Webb proposed a supplementary relief system clearly removed from insurance to remove the temptation to dilute the latter (p. 1319).

66. Gilbert, *British Social Policy*, p. 195. The Royal Commission on Unemployment Insurance, created in December 1930 and reporting October 1932, advocated similar ideas, as had the Ministry of Labor officials for a long period. Cmd. 4185. The commission chairman became permanent secretary of the Ministry of Labor.

now came under the jurisdiction of the new Unemployment Assistance Board, which could give cash aid indefinitely according to need. The first chairman of the board was former Minister of Labor Henry Betterton. Against this attempt to remove the unemployed from politics, the rump of the Labor party remaining in Parliament protested long and loudly but the 1934 Unemployment Act was passed by a large majority.

There now occurred one of the rare occasions when popular pressure directly altered the substantive content of a policy. It concerned only one limited part of that substance, the benefit scale, but was articulated through Conservative and Liberal as well as Labor parties. The new regulations to be used by the Unemployment Assistance Board had occasioned relatively mild criticism when laid before Parliament in December 1934. But rigid, bureaucratic implementation of the benefit scale for 800,000 workers on transitional payments at the beginning of 1935 caused a storm of public protest and widespread, almost daily, demonstrations against the new scales. With backbenchers of all parties echoing the complaints of hardship, the Ministry of Labor was forced to announce without consulting the cabinet that the scales of the "nonpolitical" Unemployment Assistance Board would be suspended in cases where the former public assistance authority grants would have been higher; later the Unemployment Assistance (Temporary Provision) Act of 1935 was rushed through by the government and authorized the relieving officer to use whichever scale was most favorable to the applicant. It was exactly 100 years since the old national poor law authority had been similarly forced to amend in practice its neat, administratively logical, but politically impractical plans.

In the end, what did it all amount to? The structure and allocation of power had changed little compared with the change in views of those in or near the centers of policy making. Unemployment insurance, to remain viable, had had to be relatively isolated from immediate questions of relief policy. The government also quickly learned, however, that questions of unemployment relief could not be realistically isolated from political life; the myth of instituting a nonpolitical social policy through the Unemployment Assistance Board was exploded in 1935. Largely by indirection, British political administrators also came to accept a national system of cash relief based on need (for the moment only for the unemployed) outside the poor law and its guiding principle of less eligibility.

Those who saw themselves losers in this process, the labor movement, also altered several of their notions. To memories of the old poor law was now added the scourge of the household means test for transitional payments. Instead of extended unemployment insurance, opposition to the means test now became the movement's espoused symbol of commitment to the unemployed. Such opposition remained the most persistent theme of labor inside and outside the legislature in the 1930s; it has colored all subsequent social policy discussions in Britain down to the present day.

Gradually declining unemployment and more discretionary practices by local relieving officers helped remove unemployment insurance from the center of the political stage during the remainder of the 1930s. Despite these improvements, however, high unemployment remained endemic throughout the decade. Only with war in 1939 did British unemployment insurance policy enter the era of full employment that Britain's economic policy had been unable to create.

UNEMPLOYMENT INSURANCE AMID FULL EMPLOYMENT

During the 1920s there had been four British and four Swedish general elections and as many turnovers in party control of government; the first socialist cabinets in each nation's history had come to, and gone from, power. But none of these political changes resolved what was probably the major concern in social policy—unemployment insurance and the treatment of the able-bodied unemployed. Even the expedients adopted or discussed in this area bore little direct relation to shifts in political power and party color. More fundamental, more realistic alterations flowed not merely from the pressure of economic events but from the ability of men in and at the fringes of policy making to learn from these events and to gain political access for their insights.

None of the interwar policies succeeded in establishing full employment in either Britain or Sweden; this remained an accomplishment of the Second World War. By the end of the 1930s, however, employment policies had gone far enough, particularly in Sweden, so that the treatment of unemployment insurance had already begun to shift from an improvised, social program of cash relief to something more of an economic tool for labor market policy. As Figure 10 shows, the coincident fluctuations in British and Swedish unemployment have not been eliminated since 1945, but they have been reduced to unprecedentedly low levels.

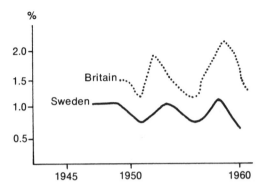

Figure 10. Unemployment as a Percentage of Nonagricultural Labor Force, Britain
and Sweden, 1947-1960

Source: Based on Phelps Brown and Brown, *A Century of Pay,* Figure 49.

In this postwar environment of full employment, unemployment
insurance had lost much but not all of its strictly partisan interest. The
essentially liberal framework of social insurance has remained intact,
while unemployment insurance itself has been increasingly seen as a
technique most directly related to economic management rather than
social relief. In Sweden the power of union organizations in maintaining
the 1935 voluntary program of union subsidy has been decisive, but
recent events have also shown that such partial coverage has the
potential ability to revive unemployment insurance debate, even in a
time of full employment. Through the efforts of several forceful and
economically progressive individuals during the 1960s, Britain belatedly
began to approach unemployment insurance as a complement to economic policy. In both nations, the civil service has remained crucial to
the actual development of new departures. Britain, however, still
lacks any integrated labor-market approach using unemployment
insurance as part of a coherent employment policy, which is also to
say that Britain has lacked any creative input comparable to that of
the Swedish Trades Union Congress (LO, or Landsorganisationen)
and its experts. Recent Swedish policy developments are subtly re-
questioning the place of leisure and labor in modern society, questions
which may, in turn, foreshadow adaptations required through future
social policies.

Sweden

From approximately the time Social Democrats arrived in office in 1933, Swedish employment began a gradual process of recovery. It was clear then and is now that the driving force behind this upswing was a revival of exports, but the expansionary fiscal policy of the Socialists did give vital support to this upward impulse in 1933–34 and contributed to continuing improvement.[67] But by no means did political controversy cease with improved economic conditions. During the mid-1930s it became clear that the interventionist economic policy of the Social Democrats was not merely a temporary crisis measure but was a normal feature of economic life. Vigorous campaigns against this trend were launched by Liberal and Conservative parties as well as industrial and financial leaders, arguing that the new Keynesian economic policy was merely a first step toward socialism.

Gradually, however, the political fears of state intervention gave way to a convergence of policy views as substantive merits of the new economic doctrine were appreciated. For Liberals, the primary agent in this conversion was the brilliant young economist and head of the Liberal youth organization, Bertil Ohlin. In 1938, Ohlin expressed the party's new orientation in a series of parliamentary motions calling for even more standby public works to combat unemployment. During the Second World War, the Conservative party also moved toward the "new economics" under the prodding of younger party members led by Gunnar Heckscher and Jarl Hjalmarson. After an electoral setback in 1944 these younger voices were able to carry through the first change in the party's program since 1919.

Amid this slowly growing policy consensus and improving employment situation, the political controversy surrounding unemployment insurance gradually diminished throughout the 1930s. What interest remained in the subject was largely centered in two political participants: civil servants responsible for the program's administration and those in charge of union funds receiving state contributions. Most postwar changes in unemployment insurance policy can be accounted for by the interaction of these two groups.

Despite hopes entertained in 1934, unemployment insurance extended its coverage quite slowly and had relatively little impact in the

67. See especially Karin Lock, *Kreditmarknad och räntepolitik, 1924–1958*.

years before World War II. Those changes that did occur were largely attributable to administrators and interest groups. During the years 1935–39, only about 20 percent of LO members belonged to unions with state-subsidized unemployment insurance funds and by 1940 the total number of persons covered was still only 196,000—compared to the 700,000 assumed during the plan's formulation. In part, increasing employment opportunities reduced the interest of workers and their unions in unemployment insurance. But a more important constraint was the limited financial incentive for unions to join the program, except in those low-benefit-paying unions which (by the 1934 formula) received the proportionately highest state contribution.

It would be tempting to ascribe the first major change in unemployment insurance, which occurred in 1941, to wartime emergencies. But this was not the case. The very operation of the plan created "affected" groups and activated their interest in detailed policy changes. By late in the 1930s better-off unions had already begun pressing for changes. On October 25, 1938, the commercial employees' union led a number of union funds in requesting alterations, and in December the LO added its voice to appeals for increased state contributions for high-benefit-paying unions and other liberalizations. In response the Social Democratic government in May 1939 authorized the Social Board to investigate what alterations in state unemployment insurance were desirable. Most of the major alterations seem to have been developed at a series of conferences between Social Board officials and union fund representatives held in the autumn of 1939.

The coming of a new European war did bring renewed fears of unemployment and led labor groups to press more strongly than they might otherwise have done for liberalizations in unemployment insurance. In many respects these proposed changes resembled those seen in Britain after World War I. Unions called for an extension of the existing limitation on state contributions (then set at a maximum of 26 support days per fund member) and increase in benefits to a level at least equal to cash relief being given by the new Labor Market Commission.[68] Disregarding the earlier equity arguments behind public

68. During the first year of war and in connection with the institution of compulsory service, the government created in May 1940 a new Labor Market Commission, superseding the old Unemployment Commission and with much greater powers over all aspects of labor market policy. Composed of labor and business representatives and a strong contingent of administrative experts, the commission could decide the mix of cash relief, relief work,

subsidy differentials, the large unions now called for equal state aid to all unions, including those paying higher benefits.

The Social Board accepted a large part of the unions' case for higher benefits, proposing an increased, though still differential, state contribution to benefits, as well as introduction of 75 percent state-financed children's supplements of 60 öre per day. The latter was a provision borrowed directly from the existing cash relief program. In addition a plan was worked out administratively inside the Social Department for a system of means-tested "supplementary benefits," which could be given in addition to unemployment insurance benefits in order to close the gap between the latter and cash relief rates.

The government's proposals in January 1941 were lost amid union opposition. On March 13, the powerful metalworkers' union urged removal of the limit on duration of state contributions and pressed for benefit increases without means-tested supplementation; a conference of unions and unemployment fund representatives reaffirmed these demands a week later. The final compromise was arranged in the Riksdag standing committee, which conferred closely with union funds' representatives and went further toward the union view than either the Social Board or the government.[69] Means-tested supplementary benefits were rejected in favor of a "spouse supplement" of one krona per day with 75 percent state financing, a proposal made to the committee by the textile workers' union representative. The maximum duration of state contributions was not abolished but increased from 26 to 36 days. In addition, the larger unions' demand for an equal percentage state contribution was accepted; now unions with the same number of support days per member per year received the same state contribution. Thus it was the unions' own insistence that ended the attempt to equalize burdens, a feature which had played such an important part in the justification of a *voluntary* plan in 1933. These changes made by the committee increased the cost to the state over

---

standby public works, and travel and training allowances appropriate in various conditions of the labor market, as well as exercise control over all labor exchanges. Generally, in higher unemployment periods the commission relied on public works and in lower periods on labor mobility devices. It was zealous in adjusting benefits to changes in the cost of living, a fact that led to the gap now complained of by unions between relief rates and insurance benefits. See *Arbetsmarknadskommissionens Verksamhetsberättelser*, 1941 and subsequent years.

69. Första Kammar, June 21, 1941, no. 42, p. 25. The committee was composed of 9 Social Democrats, 3 Conservatives, and 2 each of Liberals and Farmers. Inclusion of LO leader Axel Strand among the Social Democrats insured a full airing of the union view.

the government's original proposal by about one-quarter to 5.5 million krona. Illustrative of the extent to which unemployment insurance had ceased to be of general political interest, not a single dissent was filed to the committee report. After a very brief debate in the Riksdag, in which Social Minister Möller expressed surprise at the unanimity prevailing, the proposals were passed without a division on June 21, 1941. The only dissension expressed was filed by a Communist speaker. These new arrangements were to be the first of many instances of quiet but successful union lobbying; the departure from strict insurance principles was well under way.

Under the financial incentive of the new equal state contribution, union affiliation to the state plan increased rapidly, particularly with the addition of the metalworkers' union in 1942. The number of workers covered rose from 210,000 in 1940 to 562,000 in 1942 and 703,000 in 1943. The approaching end of the war, however, again aroused widespread fears of an economic crisis during peacetime adjustments. By 1944 the bulk of responsible opinion, particularly in the government and the labor movement, was extremely pessimistic about prospects for avoiding a postwar depression.

The lessons of the First World War had apparently been learned: everyone expected a similar surge of unemployment in 1945–46. For once, policy making anticipated events, only to find that World War I provided a false analogy. While officials in 1944 continued to use cash relief increases as the standard for improving unemployment insurance benefits, representatives of the union funds now proposed an additional special "crisis allowance" of 75 öre a day at state expense to all unemployment insurance beneficiaries. In making this and other suggestions for insurance liberalization, the unions were both giving expression to their strong fears of postwar depression and seeking to develop a framework for expandable state support. In years immediately previous there had been little strain on unemployment insurance, but "by the nature of things a reaction will arise during the unemployment crisis upon which, in some earlier or later postwar period, we must count."[70] The Social Board and Labor Market Commission approved the unions' proposals, although employers' representatives on the latter filed a strong minority protest. The major alteration

---

70. LO, *Verksamhetsberättelse*, 1944, p. 145. The LO *remiss* appears in the same volume, p. 46.

recommended by officials of the Social Board was again a graduation of crisis supplements to help equalize burdens for unions with greater unemployment risks.

Consultations showed that the unemployment insurance proposals were opposed by both state financial agencies and employers' organizations as an unhealthy reliance on state financing and departure from insurance principles. Union representatives, on the other hand, naturally supported the increase but criticized any grading of crisis supplements. As the LO put it, "from the psychological standpoint, it can be maintained for certain that members of funds with low supplements, or none at all [the better-off unions], will be unable to see the grading as just." In the end the socialist-led government accepted the proposals for higher child and spouse allowances and an ungraded, state-financed crisis supplement, arguing that, given the freeze in real wages during the war, it was unacceptable to pay for benefits with higher contributions. In rejecting the equalizing gradation of supplements, Social Minister Tage Erlander repeated intact the LO arguments against the "unjust psychological effect." Within the Riksdag, the Conservative party raised strong objections to the departure from insurance principles entailed in such special noncontributory benefits, but with government spokesmen emphasizing that the supplements were "provisional and to be ended as quickly as possible," the government's proposition easily passed into law.[71]

Since at least 1940, the union unemployment insurance funds participating in the state program had operated on an ad hoc basis, appointing special representatives to urge specific changes on the government as well as to confer on technical questions of administration and regulation. With the growing number of funds and union desires to protect themselves against postwar unemployment, the recognized unemployment funds established their own formal interest organization (Samorganisation) in 1945. This new organization would be in continual and direct contact with government departments and not wait for the state to take the initiative as had often occurred in the past.[72] It is important to recognize that such an interest organization

---

71. Proposition nr. 301, 1944, and Andra lagutskotte, *Utlatånde*, no. 7, p. 14.

72. The association's activities are detailed in yearly *Verksamhetsberättelse* of the organization (*Erkända arbetslöshetskassornas Samorganisation*). The ties between Samorganisation and LO were of course very close. The committee drawing up the 1945 proposals included LO secretary Strand, who was soon to become LO chairman.

was created subsequent to the initial policy and was responding to the opportunities offered by its ongoing existence.

Now more than ever the labor interest groups were the key actors in unemployment insurance policy. Citing declines in the real value of benefits and fears of a postwar unemployment crisis, the new association drew up a list of suggested alterations that would liberalize benefits further and underline the state's commitment to continued support. Presented to the government on December 18, 1945, the proposals called for more comprehensive family supplements, easing of a number of qualifying conditions, and removal of the 36-day limit on the duration of state contributions. Consultations revealed approximately the same division of opinion as in 1944, with employers and state financial institutions opposed, the Labor Market Commission split, and the LO and other union groups in favor. The government accepted most of the unions' proposed changes but again balked at removing limits on duration of state support, repeating Social Minister Möller's arguments of 1941 that unemployment insurance was not intended to combat a major economic crisis. Government spokesmen added that, in any event, the expected depression was not materializing. In the Riksdag, Conservative and Farmer's parties again expressed their reservations about the changes, while within the Social Democratic party backbench pressure continued to urge removal of the 36-day limit in state aid. The Social Democratic social minister responded that, given the present favorable economic conditions, the 36-day rule was not relevant, but he also promised his party members that "should an unemployment crisis occur, the government will see to it that no unemployment funds find it necessary to cut benefits to the unemployed."[73] With little more debate the new benefit changes passed the Riksdag.

Swedish unemployment insurance, like its British counterpart a generation earlier, now stood poised for transformation into cash relief. Fortunately for the integrity of the Swedish program, the government's promise never needed to be redeemed and the British post-World War I experience was not repeated. Although fluctuations and foreign exchange difficulties did occur, the new full employment economic policy avoided any serious rises in postwar unemployment. Unemployment insurance could be left to help deal with the adjust-

---

73. Andra Kammar debate, November 20, 1946, no. 37, p. 72; Proposition nr. 236, 1946.

ments of a fully occupied labor market. In 1947 the government replaced the old Labor Market Commission with the Labor Market
Board as a permanent body responsible for coordinating all efforts in
employment policy. Unemployment insurance was transferred from
the Social Board to a division within the Labor Market Board, a
substantive as well as symbolic act showing the extent to which unemployment insurance in full employment was becoming a technique
of economic rather than relief policy. Within the board, effective
guidance of unemployment insurance lay in the hands of a joint
delegation: three representatives from the recognized union funds
and two from the labor market parties (that is, employers' and workers'
organizations). It is, however, scarcely an exaggeration to say that
all of the subsequent changes in unemployment insurance until the
present time have resulted from the initiative of the union funds and
their association.

The inertial force of state-subsidized union insurance funds was
highlighted in 1948 by the one attempt at major structural change.
In 1937 the Social Democratic government had established an investigatory commission on welfare policy (*socialvard*). During a 1941 review
of unemployment insurance, it became clear to officials at the Social
Board and Labor Market Commission that a thorough study of the
existing program was required, since "[for comprehensive coverage]
the only fully effective solution in the long view . . . is the introduction
of obligatory unemployment insurance." The subject was accordingly
assigned to the investigating commission in March 1941, but only in
1948 was the commission's report finally completed.[74]

The commission found 47 percent of the work force covered by unemployment insurance; another 25 percent were thought not to need
coverage (public employees, higher-salaried workers, and so forth),
leaving about 28 percent or 700,000 persons needing but lacking
unemployment insurance. Some form of obligatory insurance was
therefore deemed necessary, although the employers' representative
dissented from this conclusion. Two basic alternatives presented themselves. The option of a British-type program organized and administered entirely by the state was supported by two (of three) civil
servants sitting on the commission. The second and majority alternative

---

74. *Remiss* statement of the Social Board, 1941, pp. 8, 9; and SOU 39, (1948), pp. 10 ff.
The major reason for the delay was the attempt to link unemployment with health insurance;
when it became clear the latter would not easily be accepted, the former had to be recast.

came from representatives of the existing union funds and met their desire to retain control of the administration of their programs. Unemployment insurance would be made compulsory for all gainfully employed persons, but the insured could join private insurance funds for higher benefits above the basic state minimum (set at the level of cash relief in sickness insurance). Each private union fund would continue to receive a state subsidy and to administer both its own and the basic state benefit to its members.

In the ensuing discussions civil servants at both the National Insurance Board and Social Board supported the first alternative of an entirely state program, while employers' groups were unanimous in rejecting both committee alternatives. The core of resistance and the decisive force preventing a restructuring of unemployment insurance in 1948 lay in the opposition of the union movement, particularly the state-subsidized union funds. The appearance of the British Beveridge Report in late 1942 (see below) had had considerable impact and in 1945 the Swedish Labor program had hinted at obligatory unemployment insurance as part of its postwar plans for more comprehensive social insurance coverage.[75] In 1948 more radical union opinion supported the state program as a means of freeing unions to become more aggressive economic advocates rather then insurance organizations. But a majority of unions and especially local union and commune labor leaders agreed that improving the existing voluntary system should take precedence over a plan which could interfere with their accumulated experience and influence in administering the current scheme. The LO and Samorganisation refused to endorse the committee proposals and urged instead an investigation of ways in which the existing program of state subsidy to union funds could be improved, particularly with a view to raising benefits to keep pace with price and wage increases. After long deliberation, the Social Democratic government decided to take no action on the commission report. With no other party willing to push the proposal and the major interested parties opposed, plans for obligatory unemployment insurance faded into the policy background.

After 1949 attention reverted to union desires for improving the existing voluntary system. Subsequent changes in unemployment

75. The LO publication *Fackföreningrörelsen* called it a "logical third step . . . of revolutionary reformism in the democratic society" (vol. 45, 1945), 15.

insurance during the 1950s and first half of the 1960s amounted largely to a series of adjustments in the union subsidy program to the somewhat unexpected persistence of full employment; without exception the changes were made on the initiative of the Samorganisation. In 1950 the "provisional" crisis supplement, which had been renewed every year since 1944, was made a permanent basic state contribution (*Grundstatsbidrag*) of the same 75 öre amount, but the current monetary crisis prevented any improvement in benefits despite an effort by some Labor back-benchers to triple the state contribution.

The major postwar adjustment of unemployment insurance occurred in 1952. A bipartisan investigating committee of experts found that unemployment insurance benefits had again lagged behind cash relief and, in fact, often lay below public assistance levels. To accommodate price and wage rises since 1935, the daily benefit should be increased from 8 to 19.8 krona per day. These increases would be paid for in part by increased contributions, but the largest portion would be financed by raising the state basic contribution, thus doubling total government expenditure from 14 million to 28 million krona. With the variable scale of state contributions, full employment had meant that what was originally intended to be the basic form of state aid— contributions to daily benefits—was actually becoming a smaller proportion of costs and was restricted largely to seasonal trades.[76] These proposed increases, which were accepted by the government, followed the arguments and figures of the Samorganisation and LO in their earlier petition to the government in September 1949. Once again the major opposition to changes came from the Conservative party in the Riksdag and the employers' organization outside; both groups argued that the proposals were another step away from contributory insurance. With only Conservative opposition, the new amendments were easily passed into law. Similarly zealous union attention led to changes throughout the 1950s that kept unemployment benefits roughly in line with rising prices and wages.

76. Proposition nr. 166, 1953, p. 65. Thus the state proportion of day benefit costs was 30–40 percent from 1935 to 1940, 52 percent in the unemployment of 1943, 22 percent in the years 1945–50, and 17 percent in 1951. All funds in the 1930s received day benefit contributions, while only 11 of the 38 did in 1951. By the new arrangements the state contribution would vary from 30 percent for funds paying highest day benefits to 40 percent for those paying lowest. *Remiss* reports are reprinted in Proposition nr. 166, 1953. See also Första Kammar debate, April 29, 1953.

Thus one important, if indirect, effect of Sweden's union-subsidized unemployment insurance was on the policy-making process itself; interest groups were activated in a new way, for intimate administrative involvement offered them a position from which to demand satisfaction before any fundamental structural change occurred in unemployment insurance. But union power, focused rather narrowly on conditions and benefits, has not remained immune from the force of outside ideas concerning the uses to which this persisting structure should be put.

These new departures in the use of unemployment benefits have sprung from Sweden's highly developed postwar labor market policy, and some appreciation of this larger policy context is essential. The basic outline of this new labor market policy originated not simply in the union movement but in that section led by the highly creative and intelligent research center of Sweden's national labor federation, the LO. The ideas were worked out in the late 1940s by LO economist Gösta Rehn and his assistant Rudolf Meidner. At a time when overmobility was generally considered a problem of industrial life, these LO economists argued that the state should intervene not with price, wage, and other controls but with a positive and coordinated policy for enhancing labor and industrial mobility: training, moving allowances, incentives for modernization and rationalization, and so forth. Initial endorsement of the Rehn theory came from the LO in its 1951 congress, but public implementation had to await the conjuncture of disciple and circumstance.[77] In 1957, Bertil Olsson was named general director of the Labor Market Board and, as a zealous supporter of the LO economists' theories, was determined to put them into effect at the first opportunity.

That opportunity was provided by a recession in the late 1950s; by January 1959 unemployment was at its highest point since the war. In reacting to this economic downturn, Olsson and the Labor Market Board were not content with trying to create employment for the unemployed but aimed instead at a "productive full employment," with new training facilities and other mobility-promoting devices. By the beginning of the 1960s, the Social Democratic party was committed to

77. Gösta Rehn, "Ekonomisk politik vid full sysselsättning." See also *Fackföreningsrörelsen och den fulla sysselsättningen,* 1951. The labor market policy was "the foremost expression of the practical political significance which LO economists' policy has had." Lewin, *Planhushållningsdebatten,* p. 435.

the labor market approach worked out and adopted by the LO. The essence of this policy was increased state activity and, more specifically, activity aimed at removing hindrances and promoting effective operation of the market—"planning in which plans act to realize that which the free market ostensibly seeks but cannot realize . . . where security is . . . created by guarantees for painless adaptation to all reasonable demands for change."[78] By 1965 the cost of Labor Market Board activities had risen to one billion krona, or ten times that in 1955, and the Swedish approach to labor market organization was perhaps the most advanced in the world. In 1965 a special expert investigation pointed out that a more extensive system of cash benefits to the unemployed was a logical complement to the other mobility promoting measures.[79]

At the same moment, voluntary unemployment insurance was becoming a partisan issue for the first time since the 1930s. By the early 1960s an economic downturn had again swollen unemployment and struck a number of groups, such as salaried workers, which had previously been relatively untouched by joblessness. A few opposition politicians began seizing upon the unemployment insurance issue, assuming that this policy's partial coverage was one point of Social Democratic vulnerability in the social policy field. In particular the one Farmers' party (now called Center party) representative in another government investigation filed a separate declaration arguing for a study of a universal unemployment insurance covering all those capable of work, since everyone seeking but unable to find work should have a "guaranteed right to compensation from insurance."[80] In 1964 the Center party began to urge introduction of a basic unemployment insurance for all citizens, above which would be maintained the existing voluntary union programs. In 1965 the Center was joined by the Liberals with a proposal covering all those aged 16 to 65 (1.4 million employees currently uninsured, 1.6 million married women, and 450,000 employers). During the 1966 municipal election campaign some mileage may have been gained by the two parties from their

78. Gösta Rehn, "Arbetsmarknad politik som samhällside," pp. 26 ff.; for a summary of LO policy see its volume, *Samordnad Näringspolitik*.
79. SOU 9 (1965), pp. 19ff.
80. SOU 40 (1963), p. 236; and government propositions 115 and 116, 1964. In 1960, of 2,809,000 employees in Sweden, about half were covered; of the 1,447,000 uncovered, over half (815,000) were not in unions.

joint program calling for, among other things, a comprehensive national unemployment insurance. The Social Democratic government was already committed to a study of the 1965 labor market investigation proposals for extended cash benefits and decided "in accordance with the wishes expressed in the Riksdag, that unemployment insurance too had better be considered anew."[81] As a result the KSA investigation (cash support in unemployment) was established in September 1966, chaired by a leading Social Democrat and with representatives from the civil service, unions, employers, and the three opposition parties.

By the early 1970s new employment benefit proposals were beginning to be acted upon, but as usual the results emerged only slowly from the long and painstaking Swedish investigation process. Some of these results continue the postwar trend of improving union-run programs. The directive from the Social Democratic government to the investigation made it clear that any proposal was expected to work in co-operation with rather than to replace state-supported union insurance. The compromise plan worked out in the committee does just that. Unions have won further improvements and a higher degree of state subsidy. Unemployment benefits are raised, the waiting period (formerly five days) for start of benefits is abolished, the duration of benefits is increased to 300 days (450 days for those over 55), and conditions for entitlement to benefits are considerably eased.[82] The greater part of additional costs involved will be met by the state, increasing the state proportion of unemployment insurance costs by approximately 10 percent or to almost four-fifths of the total.

The investigating committee has certainly accommodated the, by now, entrenched strength of union insurance programs, which cover virtually all organized Swedish workers. But the far more important fact is that the investigation began from the premise of a positive labor market policy. Widening the sphere of existing unemployment insurance funds including those for employers, is only one important part of that

81. Proposition nr. 52, 1966, p. 225. Further details on these developments can be found in Bernt Erici, "A-försäkring"; Ingemar Mundeto, *Trygghet för Alla;* Första Kammar motions 77, 596 (1964); 141, 227 (1966); Andra Kammar motions 956, 724 (1964); 296, (1966). The Conservatives joined in advocating general unemployment insurance in 1967. Första Kammar motions 635, 767.

82. Rather than needing 12 months' work and insurance contributions, a member will now be entitled to benefit with 5 months' employment in the last 12 months. Up to 2 of these 5 months can consist of time spent in military service, labor market training, or childbirth.

policy. Other cash support is also seen to be required for those outside such insurance, particularly those outside traditional definitions of the labor force. Working papers of the investigation quote with approval the Labor Market Board's view that the aim of labor market policy is no longer simply to provide some type of work for the employee who has lost his job, but "within the framework of the need for labor power in society, to give each who can and wants to work the effective support to realize his free choice of employment."[83]

Although not going as far as some, particularly civil service, advocates of labor market policy would wish, the investigating committee has proposed a new cash benefit (literally "cash labor market support"). The new benefit will go to those who have no unemployment insurance or are not qualified for benefit. Unlike the conditions for every previous unemployment benefit, the beneficiary's prior attachment to the labor force can be virtually nonexistent. This applies in particular to those who have been at home caring for an elderly or handicapped person, studying in school, or participating in Sweden's extensive system of labor market training.

To be sure, this new grant has been framed so as not to compete with the attractiveness of union benefits, being shorter in duration (150 days and 300 for those over 55) and lower in amount (about 27 krona per day compared to the union average of about 60 krona per day). Nevertheless it is a pathbreaking first step in policy with unfathomed implications. Unlike traditional relief the new benefit is given regardless of the individual's economic resources. Being entirely state-financed through general taxation, the proposed cash benefit drops even the pretense of being insurance; with the paramount role of state contributions, union unemployment benefits also can scarcely be said to constitute insurance (at least not in the sense of demonstrating any relation between individual contributions and benefits). The new cash benefit is set as a proportion of the price-related index figure and thus is automatically inflation-proofed. One of the most crucial issues is the conditions under which the beneficiary must accept a position offered or lose his benefit. Under the poor law this was easily settled by less eligibility (keeping benefits below the lowest wage);

---

83. Arbetsmarknadsstyrelsen, "Förandring och Trygghet," *Arbetsmarknadspolitik i tillämpning,* cited in SOU 42 (1971).

in conventional labor market policy prior to and including the present full employment era it was settled by requiring acceptance of the first opening offered in a man's normal occupation. The new Swedish cash benefits and unemployment insurance regulations would redefine the meaning of "suitable employment" and begin to include the individual's own preferences for a job. As the committee puts this ramification of labor market policy, "The aim is to create and preserve full, productive, and freely chosen employment. This aim is not achieved once and for all. . . . Freely chosen employment means, not only rejecting coerced work, but also that the possibilities are widened for the individual to obtain work which corresponds to his desires and abilities."[84]

It remains to be seen how well these high aspirations will be achieved in practice, even within a recently revitalized system of modern labor exchanges. All political parties and most interest groups agree to the fundamental principles of these new proposals. Having made their point in the 1966 local elections, the opposition parties have not been willing to block committee action, proposing only further extension of cash support to housewives seeking work; unemployment insurance has played little if any part in subsequent elections or political campaigning. In general, a new policy departure has been achieved through the evolving ideas of administrative and union experts acting against the background of an inherited, voluntary union-subsidy program.

While building on previous policy, the latest proposals on unemployment benefit also constitute an innovative step forward that may foreshadow major changes in future social policy concerns for many advanced nations. The relevant population of concern to Swedish, like British, policy makers has gradually broadened from groups of manual workers to the entire labor force; in the full employment era attention has been extended further to those who are not economically active (in the formal economic definition of labor force) but may at one time or another want to find gainful employment. Perhaps even more important, Swedish income maintenance for both the nonemployed and unemployed is coming to apply not merely to income lost through a lost job but to a citizen's entitlement to public support when

---

84. SOU 42 (1971), p. 78. The committee report is contained in this volume, with supplements in SOU 43, 44 (1971).

he personally chooses to seek a job that he deems more appropriate to his own interests. Potentially at least, these ideas imply new emphasis on the value of personal choice and of public support to realize these choices. It is a perspective fundamentally different from the poor law tradition of enforced, formal independence of the able-bodied from the rest of the community.

Britain

In Britain as in Sweden, unemployment insurance policy during most of the full employment era has been largely a systemization of the form given to it by political administrators in the 1930s. The fact that the British insurance was a strictly state scheme, rather than state support to union funds as in Sweden, meant far less scope for union interest group participation in the policy process. At the same time, the British attempt to integrate unemployment insurance with the rest of social security was important in delaying the appreciation and use of unemployment insurance as a tool of labor market policy. More important, the TUC cannot be said to have played anything like the constructive role of the Swedish LO in favor of an active labor market policy. While the first attention to a new departure— earnings-related unemployment insurance—came from the Labor party, the concrete proposals had already been drawn up by the civil servants serving both Conservative and Labor governments. The final push for policy change and priority for unemployment insurance came from a few key individuals in a Labor government that was anxious to improve British economic performance and willing to override the party's election pledges. Once again, the primary molding force of new policies was the perceived mistakes of past policies.

The shape of unemployment insurance in postwar Britain was elaborated during the wartime emergencies and remained virtually unchanged for 20 years thereafter. This policy sprang from the famous Beveridge Report and can hardly be said to have been the deliberate aim of any government, party, or interest group. That postwar plans for social insurance were not neglected in the Second World War as in the First was partly because of the more determined advocacy of such planning by labor, but largely because William Beveridge took it upon himself to go beyond the authority given to him by the National government. In retrospect, the fact that there ever was a Beveridge

Report now seems remarkably fortuitous, for it was created by a committee from which the government expected no policy proposals and a chairman who did not particularly want his task.

During 1940 the General Council of the TUC had concluded that the existing national health insurance benefits were inadequate, particularly since there were higher grants to an unemployed than to an ill worker. In February 1941 a TUC deputation to the minister of health argued "the necessity for the linking up of all the social services into an adequate and properly coordinated scheme."[85] With no publicity the government in May 1941 announced that it would appoint an investigating committee on "Social Insurance and Allied Services." As noted in the next chapter, proposals for "all-in" insurance were by no means new in Britain. It was Beveridge who used his quasi-official status to make these plans concrete; it so happened that he did so as a generation at war was looking for a symbol of a better postwar world around which to rally.

In the spring of 1941 William Beveridge was himself out of work, if not exactly unemployed. Originally denied the active role he wanted in Churchill's government, Beveridge in December 1940 became temporary undersecretary at the Ministry of Labor heading the Military Services Department. By the spring of 1941, Minister of Labor Ernest Bevin had decided that he did not want Beveridge as Director-General of the emerging Manpower Section and began looking for other outlets for Beveridge. He found the newly formed Committee on Social Insurance and Allied Services, announced that May. Beveridge reluctantly accepted the chairmanship.[86]

The terms of reference to the new committee called merely for a "survey of the existing national schemes of social insurance and allied services, including workman's compensation, and to make recommendations." At the beginning of the committee's work, Bevin made clear to Beveridge that the committee would be composed entirely of civil servants and that the government expected it to deal with administrative details rather than policy issues. Nevertheless by December 11, 1941, six months after his appointment and before any testimony had

---

85. Paper 3 of Memoranda from Organizations in the companion volume to the Beveridge Report, Cmd. 6405 (1942), p. 14. The Beveridge Report is Cmd. 6404 (1942).

86. "I didn't feel that welfare was up my street, and I made counter suggestions: the organization of manpower was my goal. . . . I was frankly a little sad at what I was asked to do in June 1941." Beveridge, *Power and Influence*, pp. 272, 282.

been received, Beveridge had issued four personal memoranda to the committee, one of which contained all of the essentials of the report as finally published. Upon seeing that Beveridge's memoranda did indeed involve important policy matters, the Treasury advised that the civil servants on the committee could only be considered advisory members. The result was that Beveridge's was the only name to appear on the final report, although the civil servants played an active part in its preparation.[87]

The many issues raised by the Beveridge Report cannot concern us here, but the major principles upon which it was built were the following:

1. *universality*: for the first time all citizens would contribute and be eligible for benefits

2. *classification*: the major divisions in the population would be between the employed, self-employed, and non-employed of working age

3. *flat rates*: the amount of contributions and benefits would be flat rates equal for all

4. *minimum benefits*: benefits should be adequate for subsistence but not more

5. *unified administration*: a single ministry should be responsible for all cash benefits

Despite all of the attendant fanfare, hopes, and expectations, the changes proposed by the Beveridge Report were largely ones of operational structure and not policy content. In essence, Beveridge sought to implement his ideas on comprehensive contributory social insurance, first formulated in the 1900s and amplified in the 1920s, at the same time as trying to realize the Webbs' old idea of a national minimum. As in Beveridge's first proposals in 1907, unemployment insurance was still assumed to be simply a part of this unified structure of social insurance against poverty. The basic concepts of tripartite contributory insurance, of flat rates in both benefits and contributions, and of a subsistence security remained unchanged; the aim remained that of Beveridge's youth, "the abolition of want." The Beveridge Report was

---

87. Cmd. 6404. Beveridge wrote later that the civil servants were as interested as he was in more than administrative changes. *Power and Influence*, p. 304.

the most systematic expression of liberal social policy to date and unhesitatingly subsumed unemployment insurance under its anti-poverty aims.

By the time Beveridge was preparing his report, the essentially administrative adaptations to wartime dislocations had already gone far toward creating the policy of a national subsistence minimum. In connection with the vast air-raid evacuation program, the Unemploy-ment Assistance Board in 1940 was renamed the Assistance Board and given responsibility for granting cash help adequate for subsistence not only to the unemployed and their dependents but to all evacuees what-ever their cause of need. From its new position inside the National government of Churchill, the Labor party in 1941 had also successfully insisted upon the replacement of the hated household means test with a personal test of need.[88] What Beveridge added in the area of cash relief was the proposal that this program, like all social insurance, be unified in one ministry.

As for the specifics of unemployment insurance, the impact of the Beveridge Report was comparatively marginal in relation to the policy content evolved in the interwar period. Among the major changes proposed was an increase in coverage to include all persons working for an employer under contract of service; thus there would be contribu-tions from many who faced little risk of unemployment and some redistribution of costs. Second, unemployment insurance benefits would finally be equated with sickness benefits so that it was no longer more lucrative to be unemployed than to be ill. Third, Beveridge proposed that unemployment benefits be made indefinite in duration without a needs test, but that after a certain period (normally six months) continued benefits would be conditional upon attendance at a work or training center "both as a means to prevent habituation to idleness and as a means of improving the capacity for earning." The casual manner in which Edwardian character improvement and modern job training were mixed was an accurate indication of Be-veridge's vague distinction between antipoverty and labor market policies. Finally, by including unemployment insurance along with other social security programs under the control of one social ministry, responsibility of the Ministry of Labor and any potential for even in-cidental labor market considerations was eliminated.

88. Determination of Needs Act, 1941. A description of this and other wartime policy developments is in Richard Titmuss, *Problems of Social Policy*.

The position of unemployment benefit as part of a comprehensive system of social insurance was, as in Sweden, dependent upon the development of a full employment policy, and no one realized this better than Beveridge. Of the three assumptions necessary for the successful operation of his plan, Beveridge gave greatest emphasis to "the maintenance of employment, that is to say, avoidance of mass unemployment."[89] Unlike the Swedish experience, the process by which the "new economics" came to prevail in Britain was more the result of administrative infiltration than party revelation. Despite the antagonisms surrounding the means test, a certain social and political agreement, as in Sweden, could be seen quietly growing between the parties in the 1930s, in large part because of the intellectual bankruptcy that the 1931 crisis had revealed in traditional economic approaches. In the autumn of 1939, Keynes had been quick off the mark with a series of articles in *The Times* on "How to Pay for the War," but it was not until the assumption of the chancellorship by Kingsley Wood in May 1940 that Keynes's advice began officially to gain ground. Not deeply interested in financial matters but ready to seek advice from all quarters, Wood brought Keynes back into government for the first time since 1919, first as a member of a consulting committee and by the late summer of 1940 as an adviser in the Treasury. After extended discussions and disagreements inside both the Treasury and cabinet, a Keynesian approach to financing was finally settled upon, partly it seems because of the persuasiveness of Keynes's arguments and partly because political administrators despaired of finding any other way to create stability amid the grinding of massive economic forces during the first year of war. Wood's 1941 budget was the first in British history to adopt Keynes's national income approach. During the remainder of the war, Keynes and his generation of economists rose to official influence—not only in the government but also in the Labor party.[90] Beveridge himself contributed to this new full employment policy

---

89. This and the preceding quotation are taken from Cmd. 6404, pp. 58 and 120. The Beveridge Report assumed an average unemployment level of 8.5 percent among all insured, or 10 percent of those already covered by unemployment insurance. If this seems a high rate, it must be compared to the 15 percent that the Unemployment Insurance Statutory Committee had used in its financial calculations since 1935.

90. An account is contained in R. S. Sayers, *Financial Policy, 1939–1945*, pp. 45 ff. Chapter 3 chronicles Keynes's growing influence inside the government. The development of Keynesian premises into postwar policy is discussed in J. C. R. Dow, *The Management of the British Economy, 1945–1960*.

with his privately produced 1944 book, *Full Employment in a Free Society*. Like most in the interwar period, Beveridge had fully accepted the classic idea of high wages as the cause of any "unemployment which cannot be accounted for by specific maladjustments of place, quality, and time," but by 1944 he had adopted the Keynesian approach wholeheartedly. In an unseemly competition with Beveridge, the government in the same year rushed out a White Paper on employment, making a commitment through similar Keynesian means to the preservation of "a high and stable level of employment."[91] By 1945 both political parties had accepted full employment as a primary and practical policy goal. With Keynesian economic lessons established among policy makers, the prerequisite existed for insuring that unemployment benefits would not again be use to relieve uncontrollable mass unemployment.

The reaction in late 1942 to the Beveridge Report was phenomenal, in large part due to the propaganda efforts of Brenden Bracken as minister of information. The popular hopes and exaggerated rhetoric attached to the report's appearance made it a symbol of the commitment to a better postwar world. This symbolism sprang more from the tone and assumptions of the report than its contents. It is now sometimes forgotten that before this symbolism became firmly established, the report did meet initial opposition from interest groups and a certain coolness from the wartime government. Workers' friendly societies strongly attacked the proposal, which was to end their administrative privileges in social insurance; in 1942 the insurance companies could also be found making a concerted attack on the proposals in fear, it seems, that this was to be the first step in the nationalization of private insurance. A number of employers' groups were silent or offered detailed criticisms, and the Conservative newssheet *Onlooker* proffered a mixture of praise and hostility. Churchill himself disliked the tendency of the report to divert attention from the war effort. While the national government asserted its dedication to the principles involved, Beveridge was henceforth completely shut off from official position and contacts.[92]

---

91. The quotations are taken from Beveridge's *Unemployment: A Problem of Industry*, p. 371, and *Full Employment in a Free Society*, pp. 97 ff. The government White Paper is Cmd. 6527, 1944.

92. "No member of the Government of any party, other than the Minister of Information, spoke to me about my Report after it had been made or discussed any of its proposals with me." Beveridge, *Power and Influence*, p. 333.

The symbolic importance of the report quickly precluded such
ledging. The first parliamentary debate on the Beveridge Report,
February 16, 1943, found the government spokesmen (Conservatives
Kingsley Wood and Sir Oliver Lyttelton) so ambiguous that Labor
back-benchers, with Conservative and Liberal support, tabled a motion
alling for the early introduction of legislation based upon Beveridge's·
recommendations. Although the resolution itself was defeated, both
Labor and Conservative parties eventually followed the Liberals in
ndorsing the specific approach outlined by Beveridge. But as usual
here was no clear electoral payoff connected with social policy reform.
During the 1945 election all parties affirmed their allegiance to the
new plan for social security; however, the Liberal party—which had
been the first party wholeheartedly to accept the report—gained only
marginally over its 1935 popular vote and, as a Liberal, Beveridge him-
elf lost his recently won parliamentary seat. Party views had already
onverged to the point where party competition and the 1945 election
an hardly be said to have affected the development of the Beveridge
policy.
   The 1946 National Insurance Bill proposed by the new Labor
overnment followed most of Beveridge's major recommendations.
Although scarcely recognized at the time, acceptance by Labor of this
essentially liberal consolidation of previous social insurance programs
was a crucial shift in the party's stance on income maintenance.
Formerly, the Labor party and union movement had opposed the prin-
iple of contributory social insurance, arguing against employee con-
ributions and for more redistributive financing through progressive
ate taxation. Labor's firm support for the Beveridge plan can be
ttributed in part to the events of the 1930s and in part to a revised
outlook derived from the close collaboration between Beveridge and
hose few union officials who were concerned with the substance of
ocial insurance. The 1930s policy of means-tested unemployment
enefits had sufficiently annoyed the labor movement to make it re-
eptive to Beveridge's old appeal for insurance contributions as a sure
ndicator of benefit entitlement. Unified social insurance contributions
ppeared to be the surest defense against any possible expansion of the
ated means test. None of this of course came to union leaders as a
pontaneous revelation. Many crucial discussions occurred during
Beveridge's preparation of his report and the close consultations with

his TUC friend and (since 1928) secretary of that organization's social insurance committee, Jon Smythe. Since 1911 socialists had been committed to the nationalization of the private insurance industry, but in accepting the Beveridge Report labor also accepted the principle of a state-organized minimum with reliance on voluntary insurance above that as an essential part of the total security system. It seems likely that in this unwillingness to antagonize commercial insurance interests lay the secret of the unanimous political support gained for the National Insurance Bill.[93]

The Labor government's first alteration in Beveridge's unemployment proposals was to drop the idea of an unlimited benefit period in return for attendance at work and training centers; instead, unemployed workers who had exhausted their benefit rights could apply to local tribunals in order to have their benefits extended six months at a time. These changes had little to do with Labor ideology or courting popular favor but seem instead to have been adopted by the Labor government largely on the advice of officials who, recalling their interwar experiences, feared the demise of financial limitations in unemployment benefits. Nor were benefits at a strictly subsistence level as Beveridge had suggested. Administrators assured the government that it was "administratively impossible" to tie benefits to the cost of living.[94] In addition, the Assistance Board (now renamed National Assistance Board) was continued as an autonomous agency granting general, need-tested relief rather than made part of the unified administration proposed by Beveridge.

In the House of Commons, a group of Labor back-benchers strongly but unsuccessfully opposed all restrictions upon the right to claim benefits, arguing that conditions imposed largely in order to limit the liability of the National Insurance fund should be abolished. The Labor Left, led by Sidney Silverman, assembled 44 Labor and some Liberal votes for deletion of the relevant clause but was defeated by the Labor government's votes (Conservatives abstained). Silverman's group was successful, however, in inserting a provision specifically outlawing any form of means test in the local tribunal's six-month extensions of un-

93. Robert Brady, *Crisis in Britain*, p. 350. On the importance of voluntary insurance to the Beveridge Report, see Cmd. 6404, p. 121. Anything above subsistence is considered a matter for free choice and private insurance.

94. *Parliamentary Debates* (Commons), February 6, 1946. See especially James Griffith's speech and the debate on unemployment insurance, May 22, 1946.

employment benefit. The Labor government demonstrated that National Insurance funds were not to be used against longer term unemployment by paying for the extensions from general tax revenue. Conservative leaders expressed mild dissatisfaction with any extended unemployment provision outside national assistance but made little effort to press the point.

The unemployment benefit program passed in 1946 remained virtually unchanged for the next 18 years: an antipoverty policy of secured minimum standards achieved through flat-rate contributions and benefits. The success of the full employment policy ensured that the number exhausting their entitlement to benefit remained a tiny fraction of the labor force. With no group strongly pressing the matter, unemployment benefits usually lagged in the backwaters of National Insurance and social policy. On rare occasions the old party rancor could be revived, as in the summer of 1953. The provision for six-month, non-means-tested benefit extensions expired automatically in that year, and, confident of the continuing success of the full employment policy, the Conservative government proposed to allow the provision to expire. Labor returned to its old themes, accusing the Tories of again wanting to subject the unemployed to the means test of the 1930s. With only 48,000 drawing extended benefits and many of these already on welfare supplements, the flurry of interest was temporary and superficial, and the government's bill was quickly passed.[95] Income maintenance policy toward Britain's unemployed remained a corrective to interwar experiences and largely irrelevant to most of its postwar, full employment environment.

The first important postwar change in unemployment benefits occurred in 1966 with the introduction of earnings-related unemployment insurance benefits and contributions. The process by which both major parties in the late 1950s came to accept the case for an earnings linkage in social insurance centered largely on the pension issue and is dealt with at greater length in Chapter 5. Unemployment insurance and pension policy were both reacting to the perceived failings of established Beveridge policy, which had imposed a straitjacket on any attempt to improve benefits in line with the improving standards of postwar economic life. To raise unemployment benefits to a level that

95. *Parliamentary Debates* (Commons) July 6, 1953; and *The Economist*, July 11, 1953. However, the plan also altered regulations so that ordinary benefits could be drawn for 19 months rather than for the previous maximum of one year.

higher paid workers would regard as satisfactory was impossible without putting an excessive burden of flat–rate contributions on lower paid workers.

A new economic perspective on British unemployment insurance gained ground with the economic crises in the late 1950s and early 1960s. A National Economic and Development Council was created in 1962 to bring labor and business representatives together on finding ways to improve Britain's economic performance. One of the ideas being worked on by officials inside Whitehall and economists outside was an earnings-related unemployment benefit designed to promote labor mobility. The first official mention of this proposal followed in 1963 from both the National Economic Development Council and the Ministry of Labor's Joint Advisory Council.[96] These reports cited the economic rather than social arguments: unemployment benefits were too low in relation to many workers' earnings to give adequate incentive for the labor mobility and industrial rationalization necessary for improved economic performance. Workers and industries would be encouraged to cling to the old ways as long as the consequence of joblessness brought about by any rationalization was inadequate unemployment benefits. This was particularly true for the higher paid workers who for years had enjoyed the growing returns of full employment.

By 1964 an essentially bipartisan approach was growing around the idea of graduating unemployment benefits by previous earnings. Both parties, as we shall see, had already swallowed the larger matter of graduated pensions and were unlikely, if ever they thought about it, to strain at a similar idea in unemployment grants. Conservative ministers were coming to accept the economic rationale and, while not publicly committing the government, officials in 1963 were sketching plans for earnings-related unemployment benefits. The 1964 general election and turnover in party control of the government made no important difference to this major postwar change in unemployment policy. During the 1964 election campaign each party briefly mentioned earnings-related unemployment benefits but gave little or no emphasis to the point or its possible relation to an active labor market policy.

By the time the Labor party took office in 1964, the economic situation was again considered perilous. A balance of payments deficit had

96. National Economic Development Council, *Conditions Favourable to Faster Economic Growth*. Partial accounts of developments can be found in the *News Chronicle*, October 1, 1957; the *Manchester Guardian*, September 4, 1957; *The Times*, December 1, 1963, and July 9, 1964.

mounted to unprecedented levels and recurring currency crises became familiar events. It was largely from this concern for British economic health that earnings-related unemployment aid was pushed through by the Labor government as a priority policy. The new Labor government established a Department of Economic Affairs (DEA) to encourage the rationalization necessary for economic advance. The minister of the new department was the vigorous and outspoken George Brown, and it seems that Brown personally can be given major credit for moving the Labor government quickly and decisively into an earnings-related unemployment program. Brown became convinced that such benefits would be crucial in making workers and unions more willing to accept the redundancies required for economic growth.[97]

Within the cabinet there was general agreement that the delicate economic situation precluded any immediate, massive restructuring of the social services. But there was strong disagreement on the priorities of programs that might be immediately instituted. Apparently one group of ministers argued that, in keeping with the 1964 election manifesto, priority should go to increasing family allowances and public assistance. Brown on the other hand pressed the economic arguments for earnings-related unemployment benefits and received backing from the chancellor of the exchequer, who was also probably attracted by the relatively lower cost of this course. It seems likely that in the prevailing atmosphere of economic crisis during 1965 and Prime Minister Harold Wilson's own strong interest in economic affairs, election pledges were overruled and first priority was given to earnings-related unemployment benefits by virtue of its economic justification. As the 1965 National Plan produced by the DEA put it: "To complete the structure of benefits needed to promote mobility of labor, the government has concluded that the earliest possible introduction of earnings-related unemployment benefit is essential. . . . This follows from their decision to give priority to schemes that can help to promote faster economic growth.[98]

97. In 1965 the DEA also had quickly passed a redundancy payment scheme requiring employers to make lump sum payments to dismissed redundant workers, the amount varying with earnings, age, and length of service. Largely because of its administrative simplicity, the redundancy plan was introduced before unemployment insurance amendments.

98. Department of Economic Productivity, *The National Plan*, September 1965. The earnings-related unemployment insurance plan is set out in Cmnd. 2887. A new economic attention to unemployment insurance is suggested in Mark Houser and Paul Burrows, *The Economics of Unemployment Insurance*.

The Labor government's bill was worked out in the Ministry of Pensions and National Insurance on the grounds, already settled under the previous government, that only a supplementary system could be introduced without extremely long delays and administrative upheaval. The bill was published in 1966. Throughout its consideration, this particular proposal was represented by the government as only an "interim measure" pending a thorough overhaul of the social insurance system as the Labor party had promised when in opposition. The blan gave earnings-related supplements on top of the existing flat-rate benefits, with a ceiling on both benefits combined equal to 85 percent of average weekly earnings. Extra earnings-related contributions of .5 percent (in addition to those for pensions) would be collected on earnings between £9 and £30 each week; benefits would be paid to the unemployed (and the sick) for a maximum of six months, with flat rates continuing thereafter.

Both employer and union organizations were consulted on practical points of administration, but neither seems to have had very much to contribute. Interest groups played little part in developing what was essentially an internal government plan. Apart from some employers' concern that high rates of sickness benefit would encourage absenteeism, the administrative proposals were readily accepted by both union and business groups. Nor did the Conservative party make any significant contribution. The government's bill was passed without amendment in both Houses of Parliament and received the royal assent one month after introduction on March 10, 1966. With this, unemployment benefits in Britain were at last beginning to be recognized as having an economic, labor market function as well as constituting social aid for deprived persons.

In subsequent general elections little if any mention has been made of the new earnings-related supplements. Neither side of industry has urged development of these benefits, much less played a constructive role in advancing a coherent labor market policy. The union movement in particular has contributed nothing approaching the positive force supplied by the Swedish LO. The British Department of Employment's new plans for improving government training and employment services —the essential foundation for an active labor market policy—met passive acquiescence from both employers and unions; even these plans would leave the number of British training places (14,000) in

1975 at about one-quarter the current number provided in a Swedish labor force one-sixth the size of Britain's.[99] Meanwhile, income maintenance for the unemployed has become increasingly ambivalent. As part of the effort to develop an attractive, placement-oriented service, payment of British unemployment benefits is likely to be shifted out of labor exchanges and into social security offices. Yet it is difficult to treat more adequate benefits to combat poverty in isolation from other positive efforts being proposed, largely from inside Whitehall, to encourage labor market mobility and structural economic change. As the realization of this and other difficulties related to the absence of an effective labor market policy grows, the next round of political learning—or nonlearning—in Britain will be under way.

Neither Britain nor Sweden has solved the problem of providing income support to the able-bodied. Insurance and related benefits are of course only one of a large family of state activities affecting the income security of the unemployed and nonemployed, but even within the limited area surveyed it is clear that contradictory aims are characteristic. Particularly in the interwar period, higher benefits and easier accessibility have conflicted with the goal of government economy; extended coverage has had to compete with the desires of already established administering bodies; concerns with rationalizing the labor market have had to work against inherited and equally legitimate claims that first priority must go to eliminating want. What has been achieved in Britain and Sweden are series of mixed and tentative understandings on unemployment benefit—mixed because no one has known how to make all these and other goals reconcilable, tentative because any given mixture has been open to subsequent challenge. The result is probably less than any individual policy maker desired and more than all participants intended; it was, after all, William Beveridge who in 1924 contrasted strictly contributory social insurance with the "Communism" inherent in free grants unrelated to work or services (*Insurance for All and Everything*, p. 7).

To say that action on income insecurity in unemployment has been a mixture of understandings and compromises is as easy as it is un-

99. *People and Jobs*, Department of Employment, November 1971. A most useful comparison of contemporary British and Swedish labor market policy, if somewhat exaggerated in the latter's favor, is the recent pamphlet by Santosh Mukherjee, *Making Labour Markets Work—A Comparison of the U.K. and Swedish Systems.*

satisfying. The mixtures and compromises have not been the same in Britain and Sweden. Policy contents have differed. By now we have seen enough in the record of unemployment benefits to question any view that sees these varying contents as fairly mechanical "policy outputs" at the end of an assembly line worked by the rote of political power. But before going further in trying to characterize the social policy process we should look for other evidence than that provided by the able-bodied poor. Other groups, such as the elderly, were far less threatening to social stability. Indeed, it was the quiet desperation of economic insecurity in old age that gave rise to one of the first and largest forms of public income support: old age pensions.

4   The Struggle for Old Age Pensions

For anyone who manages to stay alive, old age is as certain in human affairs as death. Debilitating injury, illness, and unemployment may or may not occur, but to survive has always been to grow old and to lose working power. Precisely for this reason, the deterrent principles of the poor law could come to seem least applicable among the aged. At most the disgrace of "falling on the rates" could be used to frighten young people into saving for their old age; once the person was old, however, deterrence could not make him less old. Deterrence could usually not hope to "improve" his behavior and return him to the universally acclaimed ideal of self-support. In 1870 the fundamental public distinction in Britain and Sweden was still whether or not one was self-supporting. By definition, if the old person could not support himself and turned to public aid, he or she became a pauper. In the 1970s it is dubious if the idea of the independent, self-supporting citizen has very much empirical meaning, although it does periodically rear its head in public debate. Apart from all of the other medical, housing, home-help, meal, day-care, and other welfare services, the elderly in Britain and Sweden receive a state pension virtually independent of the amount that they have contributed toward it. If not exactly generous, the pension provides the old person with a basic income standard that would have been unbelievable to his grandparents.

Rather than constituting a comprehensive historical account, the following narrative examines the portion of the historical record that seems relevant to the major questions outlined in Chapter 1, looking at the part played by elections, parties, interest groups, administrators, and private experts in developing the pension component of modern social policy. We shall see that the initiating agents in making pensions an issue for the political system were neither elections, parties, parliaments, nor civil service, but a small band of self-styled social reformers who were usually influenced by new intelligence inputs about both their own society and developments abroad. Elections and party competition do seem to have led to a higher degree of partisanship at earlier stages in Britain than Sweden but did not hasten the advent of pensions. In both nations, popularly organized pressure was an important initial impetus behind the first pensions but proved an ephemeral force for long-term policy development. At no time did organizations of the aged or pensioners themselves play any prominent part. With several important exceptions, the major determinants of subsequent pension development lay in outside interest group agitation, particularly in Britain; expert investigations, particularly in Sweden; and powerful government administrators in both countries. In both nations the inheritance from past policy itself was a vital force shaping the alternatives perceived and the policies adopted.

The development of modern social policy has been a continuous if poorly sign-posted road but, to the extent that landmarks can be named, the 1908 British and 1913 Swedish Pension Acts rank among the most important new departures.[1] In both nations, old age pensions were the first major breach in the traditional approach to poor relief. Prior to these reforms the citizen's claim to state support rested upon either the performance of specific services, as in the military or civil service, or the submission to disqualifying restrictions in return for general public aid. Old age pensioners were the first significant portion of the population able to gain entitlement to state support by virtue of being citizens requiring such aid and without any effect upon their status as members of the community.

Despite the British lead over Sweden in economic development and in democratic political institutions, the fact is that the initiation, growth, and legislative success of the state pension idea were approximately simultaneous in both countries. To understand this simultaneity we must look at the details of each nation's processes of political adaptation rather than solely at the different sequencing of macroeconomic or macro-political forces. But before turning to these details, it is important to recognize that different developmental sequences did create different contextual forces shaping the substance of state pension policy.

On the one hand, earlier political development of the Swedish bureaucracy meant relatively greater administrative resources for a German-type contributory scheme, as well as more advanced precedents

---

1. Much of the basic information for this chapter has been drawn from Pat Williams, "The Development of Old Age Pension Policy in Great Britain, 1878–1925"; Bentley Gilbert, *The Evolution of National Insurance in Great Britain* and his subsequent volume, *British Social Policy, 1914–1939;* Åke Elmer, *Folkpensioneringen i Sverige;* and Karl Höjer, *Den Svenska Social politiken.*

in pensions for state employees. By the end of the 1600s standard regulations for Swedish civil service pensions had been centrally established, followed by setting a uniform retirement age in the eighteenth century, and fully wage-related pensions in the nineteenth century. By comparison, British civil service pensions remained the province of each government department (usually in the form of some charge by an individual officeholder upon his successor) until the early nineteenth century. Unlike his Swedish counterpart, the British civil servant could legitimately claim at the end of that century that there was neither the accumulated experience nor administrative machinery for instituting any complex contributory scheme for the public.

On the other hand, the earlier economic development of Britain was reflected in a far greater penetration of voluntary savings organizations among workers themselves. During the eighteenth and especially the nineteenth centuries, the British friendly society movement gained a prominence without parallel in any other nation. Finding their footholds in the growing industrial centers, these societies generally drew their membership from the skilled and relatively well-off portions of the working class. Workers, in return for weekly or monthly contributions, were provided with rudimentary insurance against sickness and funeral expenses, as well as a source of conviviality and "social insurance" against the impersonality of the new urban environment. By the end of the 1880s, there were 4 to 4.5 million friendly society members in Britain, or nearly half of the adult male population.[2] There was no counterpart among Swedish workers. Inasmuch as these vast numbers of British members were also most likely to be those of the working class able to meet suffrage qualifications, it follows that the movement's political position in Britain was of considerable importance. But by the end of the nineteenth century British friendly society strength was also being threatened. Economic growth was bringing with it a dissolution of the old social ties that were central to the early friendly societies; collecting agencies could offer more businesslike insurance and the new unions could more effectively fulfill other economic and social functions. The failure to attract contributions from young recruits was also being compounded by changes in population longevity, which left the friendly societies loyally but vainly trying to pay more money to more old members who had long ago drawn in excess of their contributions. Too many brothers were surviving for the health of the

2. P. H. J. Gosden, *The Friendly Societies in England, 1815–1875.*

friendly society movement, as what was ostensibly sick pay gradually became a de facto pension to protect the member from pauperism.

That Britain and Sweden participated in a common European heritage was reflected in the fact that in each country the context of prior social provisions for old age contained all of the same elements: public pensions for state employees, voluntary savings societies for the better-off workers, and disqualifying poor relief for any citizen who might fail in his duty of self-support. That each nation was at different stages of development was reflected in the differing arrangement of these common elements. Within these similar and contrasting contexts the British and Swedish movements for old age pensions began during the last quarter of the nineteenth century.

THE FIRST EFFORTS

Britain

Industry, temperance, financial prudence—these were the key values shared by the small group of politicians, publicists, and voluntary organization leaders who thought about a policy of income maintenance in old age. They were, of course, at the core of that strange amalgam of seventeenth-century Puritan, eighteenth-century Rationalist, and nineteenth-century Entrepreneur that we recognize as the British Victorian. If capital formation by means of such virtues could build an industrial society, surely it could provide funds for the aged workers left vulnerable by that society. By the mid-nineteenth century, middle-class politicians could frequently be found calling for various schemes of state-aided savings. In 1833 the British government under Gladstone's lead had attempted directly to encourage individual prudence by providing for modest annuities purchasable in savings banks at a minimum of £4 and maximum of £20. There was little popular participation. Gladstone's plan was emasculated to placate the friendly societies and private insurance companies, and sixteen years after the act fewer than 1,000 annuities existed in the entire country. Without the insurance companies' army of collectors, with a limited number of post offices participating, and with the inability or unwillingness of those most needing such benefits to put money aside, the scheme was stillborn.

It was not to be politicians, civil servants, or leaders of established interest groups who launched the British pension movement. State pensions first gained political prominence at the hands of Canon William L. Blackley, an obscure but reform-minded curate who had learned about the pension technique both abroad and in his own profession. Educated in Brussels, Blackley familiarized himself with developments taking shape on the continent and was active in the promotion of pensions for the clergy. The 1874 report of a government commission on friendly societies demonstrated the insolvency of many funds but offered little hope for better provision through annuities.[3] This seems to have stirred Blackley into formulating his own pension plan; the friendly societies, he argued, were administratively extravagant and chronically bankrupt. According to Blackley's plan, the state would compel each working man between the ages of 18 and 21 to contribute £10 to an annuity fund; this sum would be sufficient, Blackley thought, to provide 8 shillings per week sickness benefits and a 4 shillings per week pension from age 70. It was a program designed to combat the massive improvidence which the canon identified as the major cause of aged pauperism in his Southwark parish. Blackley argued that it was morally wrong for the provident to subsidize the thriftless through the poor rates and that such pensions would greatly reduce poor rates. There was also an element of redistribution, for Blackley's plan recognized that unless the middle class participated there would be an over-concentration of bad risks, necessitating contribution rates above what the poorest could afford. Nevertheless there was no mistaking the fundamental rationale for state compulsion: only in this way would the working class be brought to save rather than waste its money. State pensions were aimed at compelling individuals who otherwise would not do their provident duty.

The pension movement began as Blackley plugged his particular ideas into the established lecture circuit of respectable, middle-class social concern. Following a vigorous lecture campaign, Blackley in 1882 organized his own independent pressure group, the National Providence League, and persuaded the Tory political leader Lord Shaftesbury to become its president. The league's efforts were crowned with success when the new Salisbury government in May 1885 appointed a select committee of the Commons "to inquire into the best system of National Provident Insurance against pauperism." This first public investigation of the pension question in Britain dealt almost exclusively with the Blackley proposal.

The committee of sixteen members of Parliament sat only 23 days in

3. C. 961 (1874).

three years, heard little testimony and undertook no statistical inquiries. Government officials offered criticisms chiefly on administrative grounds, saying that it would be difficult to prevent sick-pay malingering and that post offices would have problems in collecting and distributing the money. In 1883 the German government adopted the world's first state social insurance program against sickness and accidents. The German plan was described to the 1885 select committee and aroused much discussion among its members. In the end, however, the committee concluded that the "actuarial and administrative difficulties" were overwhelming. Statistics necessary for the actuarial calculations simply did not exist. More important, civil servants argued that any such contributory insurance would be impossible to implement given the limited British administrative resources. Of course friendly societies could not be expected to be any more favorable to German-type contributions than they were to Gladstone's or Blackley's. As the draft report of the chairman shows, there was little objection to Blackley's scheme on grounds of its compulsion or interference with the independence of workers.

While the parties remained noncommittal, administrators skeptical, and investigation perfunctory, the decisive role was played by ostensibly nonpolitical interests. The friendly societies and insurance companies in the 1874 Royal Commission on Friendly Societies had vetoed any idea of a national friendly society managed by the state. What now killed the Blackley scheme was the determined opposition of the same powerful interest groups. Both friendly societies and insurance companies saw state intervention as potentially very dangerous, not least because it was likely to compete for the contributions of workers. Friendly societies were, in fact, the only groups represented in the 1885 committee hearings and were uncompromising in their opposition. The committee of MPs pointed out that pensions were the one portion of National Provident Insurance least competitive with the societies' own sickness benefits, but finally reported that it deferred "much for the present to the opposition of the Affiliated Orders" and was "disposed to wait for the further development of public opinion."[4]

4. House of Commons, *Report of the Select Committee on National Provident Insurance*, p. v, August 2, 1887. The nature of society opposition was illustrated by an exchange with the representative of the largest society, the Manchester Unity of Oddfellows: (Q) "If you could devise some scheme which would be for the welfare of all classes in this country but which would be to the detriment of friendly societies, you would not object to it on that ground?

Despite this setback to Blackley's specific pension proposal, social reform was becoming increasingly topical in the 1880s. Through a variety of intellectual and physical disturbances Britain's middle class was coming to learn of the "Other Nation." Extension of the franchise in 1885 both reflected and promoted this discovery, but it was only one of many social stimuli pressing on politics. Violent and well-publicized disturbances, such as the Trafalgar Square Riot of 1886 and the Dockers' Strike of 1889, impinged on the socially comfortable. Probably as important as any threat of physical danger was the intellectual ferment aroused. In 1883, under the sponsorship of the London Congregational Union, there appeared what has been called the most influential single piece of writing about the poor ever produced in England, William C. Preston's *The Bitter Cry of Outcast London*. Preston's work was essentially a primitive survey based on house-to-house inquiry and provided a vivid if mawkish picture of the destitution which prevailed throughout much of London. The founding of the settlement house movement by Canon Samuel Barnet brought educated young men into direct, everyday contact with the poor and provided a knowledge that was later carried into responsible positions throughout the civil service and government. Nearly all of the major architects of British social legislation during the first two decades of the twentieth century had had settlement-house experience.

Social reform was in the air, but this offered little specific guidance for policy responses. More constructive guidance was provided through new intelligence and analysis. The most important source of these inputs to pension policy was an individual researcher named Charles Booth. A Conservative Liverpool shipper, Booth was determined to establish the facts and dispel the sentimentalism that had surrounded publicity on poverty by Preston and others. To do so Booth organized what was essentially the first serious social survey in Britain, systematically gathering evidence with trained interviewers and establishing the first operational definition of poverty. Beginning in 1887 in Tower Hamlets, Booth's surveys showed that earlier writers had, if anything, underestimated the problem. Wherever Booth looked, roughly one-third of the population was found living in want of the necessities for physical subsistence. Booth's new and unprecedentedly reliable data had a profound effect upon the development of policy discussions. The

(A) Well, I think I should object to it." (Question 909.) See also R. H. Moffrey, *A Century of Odd Fellowship*, p. 110.

figures that politicians later quoted on aged pauperism were invariably derived from Booth's data. The statistics were clear and could hardly be ignored and they provided a firm empirical foundation for those who wanted to do something about the conditions. In November 1891 Booth revealed the first systematic evidence supporting pensions: 38.4 percent of persons over 65 surveyed were paupers. By no reckoning could this proportion of the population be considered undeserving wastrels fit only for the poor law. Booth proposed his own pension plan whereby universal, noncontributory pensions would be provided by the state to all citizens at 65.[5] The announcement was made with scant publicity and aroused little initial notice. Eventually, however, Booth's idea was to grow into Britain's Old Age Pension Act of 1908.

According to some traditional democratic theories, the 1885 extension of the suffrage to virtually all adult males should have markedly increased the role of political parties and Parliament in such an ostensibly popular policy question as old age pensions. The fact is that while certain isolated politicians—men usually influenced by the ideas from Booth, Blackley, and German social insurance—became interested in pensions, their interest and promises produced no substantive policy results. At best, the partisan give and take was indirectly and largely undeliberately preparing the way for state pensions by making them an accepted topic of political bargaining; at worst it was merely delaying effective action on the basic issues.

The Liberal-Unionist Joseph Chamberlain became the first leading British politician to inject old age pensions into party political bargaining. Chamberlain had long been interested in the political organization of working men in Birmingham and produced his first unauthorized program of social reform as a Liberal in 1885. He had been kept informed of German insurance developments by Sir Charles Dilke and became interested in pensions through Blackley's earlier campaign. Chamberlain was, as he later wrote, "convinced that my fellow politicians immensely exaggerate the influence of labor," which "can easily be overcome by a political leader with genuine sympathy for the working class and a practical program."[6] In the spring of 1891, Chamber-

5. "Enumeration and Classification of Paupers, and State Pensions for the Aged." This was the first of Booth's various pension proposals, all of which remained universal and noncontributory. A review of Booth's work is found in T. S. and M. B. Simey, *Charles Booth, Social Scientist.*

6. Letter to Dilke April 21, 1893, quoted in Williams. "The Development of Old Age Pension Policy," p. 47.

lain reawakened public discussion of old age pensions in a series of speeches during a particularly important group of by-elections, elections that would test his popularity after switching from the Liberal to the Unionist party. Chamberlain repeated the statistics on aged pauperism and told his working class audiences that such large numbers of respectable workers did not deserve this fate. Although the outlines of his proposals remained vague, the ideas seem have to been based largely on Blackley's contributory scheme to overcome workers' improvidence. The Chamberlain candidates won the by-elections, and Chamberlain began work on a second unauthorized program for the 1892 general election.

By all accounts the election of 1892 was the first in which pensions were featured. Three months before the election, Chamberlain, a few members of Blackley's defunct National Providence League, and a number of Conservative politicians published a proposal for voluntary post office annuities by which the insured's modest contribution would be doubled by grants from local rates and Exchequer to provide a pension of 5 shillings per week after 40 years. To encourage membership, Chamberlain had indeed gone farther than Gladstone or Blackley by including some state grants. But he had also sought to learn from Blackley's failure by making the scheme voluntary and thus less likely to offend the friendly societies who could, Chamberlain argued, be fatal to any parliamentary proposals. During the 1892 election suggestions for pensions seem to have been made on a great many other platforms by individual candidates of both parties; but among all party leaders, save Chamberlain, the issue was ignored. Despite Chamberlain's new proposals, the election results gave Gladstone the chance to form his fourth Liberal government.

The new Liberal government yielded to pressure from Chamberlain's committee and appointed a Royal Commission on the Aged Poor to investigate the pension question. Although containing among its membership both Booth and Chamberlain, the royal commission was undoubtedly committed from the outset to opposing state old age pensions. Booth quickly became disillusioned, and the hopes Chamberlain entertained of revitalizing his pension proposals were laid to rest when the National Conference of Friendly Societies in 1893 emphatically rejected any state pensions, voluntary or not. By 1894 Chamberlain seems largely to have given up immediate hope of finding a practical solution to the pension question and advised his party leader, Lord

Salisbury, not to push the issue in any upcoming discussions of social reform. In March 1895 the royal commission reported that none of the many pension schemes it had examined was acceptable and that pensions should be left to the friendly societies. Chamberlain in a minority report called for another and less prejudiced investigation.[7] For its part, the Liberal government intended to do nothing on pensions; W. S. Shaw-Levre, president of the Local Government Board, argued that there was nothing more to be done for the aged poor once poor law guardians had been asked to inform potential applicants of more accessible outdoor relief for the deserving aged. Serious analysis of pension policy and social insurance can scarcely be said to have existed inside the British government.

The political equivocations surrounding the pension issue in the parties and Parliament had been well demonstrated a year earlier. In March 1894 due to random luck in the ballot of private members' bills, a proposal by W. Bartley introduced the first parliamentary discussion of old age pensions. The proponents clearly reflected the growing viewpoint that something less stigmatizing than poor relief should be provided for the "deserving" aged, and went on to propose a system closely modeled on the 1891 Danish plan of nondisqualifying outdoor relief for those who had kept off the poor rates, joined a friendly society, or had "exceptional misfortune." The bill gained the support of Chamberlain, Liberal Unionists, and a number of Conservatives. The Liberal government refused to agree or disagree with the bill, arguing only that it would be too expensive and that any decision should await the report of the royal commission.[8] A divided vote found the bill defeated by 205 Liberal and Irish votes to 136 Liberal Unionist and back-bench Conservative votes. Pensions had clearly become a partisan weapon but were no closer to enactment.

Electoral maneuvering continued in the campaign of 1895, as Chamberlain and other leading Conservatives castigated the Liberals for their inaction on old age pensions and gave it to be understood that a Conservative government would act on the matter. The return of a Conservative government in 1895 did not, however, bring any realistic advance toward pensions. The prime minister, Lord Salisbury, was uninterested in social reform and, as colonial secretary, Chamberlain quickly moved on to other fields of conquest. A year after taking office

7. *Report of the Royal Commission on the Aged Poor*, C. 7684.
8. *Parliamentary Debates*, April 4, 1894.

the government appointed a Treasury committee under the Liberal Baron Rothschild and composed of seven civil servants, the chief actuary of Manchester Unity, and the parliamentary agent of the Forester's Society to examine old age pensions. The government's move appears to have been designed to quiet complaints of inaction rather than seriously to consider and propose a system of old age pensions. After examining four contributory schemes, the committee concluded two years later that none was acceptable. This time it was the turn of the Liberals and a group of young Conservatives to decry the government's inaction. Most of the parliamentary discussion on pensions for the rest of 1898 and 1899 was given to unproductive partisan maneuvering, with Liberals attacking the government for breaking its promise of pensions and Chamberlain arguing that he had only "proposed" not "promised" pensions.[9] Party competition had allowed each side to score political points in parliamentary debates and elections. It led to little action on old age pensions.

During this time Booth's original 1891 pension proposal had disappeared from the view of all but a few interested reformers. To the extent that it was considered in the relevant government investigations, the noncontributory plan was quickly dismissed as being far too costly. The flat negativism of the Rothschild committee plus a stimulus from abroad brought a new policy impetus from an unexpected direction. Philanthropists, socially conscious clerics, and the young labor movement combined to make pensions the subject of an ad hoc Edwardian campaign for "social betterment." The force of labor behind pensions was scarcely organized as such; indeed pensions helped advance the organization of the British labor movement as much as the reverse.

The Reverend Francis Stead was the warden of the Browning Hall settlement house in Woolwich, a section of London with the highest proportion of aged paupers. In the autumn of 1898, New Zealand adopted a program of noncontributory pensions, and Stead asked the agent general of that nation to address the settlement on the new pensions. After the address on November 20, 1898, followed by a closing hymn and prayer, it was clear that the men attending the meeting were enthusiastic about the pension scheme, and Stead began thinking of a national campaign to promote such a plan for Britain. Stead enlisted the cooperation of his friend George Barnes, the Socialist general

9. *Parliamentary Debates*, July 18, 1898, col. 138, and April 24, 1899.

secretary of the Amalgamated Society of Engineers, with whom he had worked in previous years on the eight-hour day campaign. Booth, by now the recognized expert on aged pauperism, agreed to address a meeting in December at Browning Hall, and Stead and Barnes laid the basis of their pension movement by circularizing local labor leaders throughout Britain. In response, 40 union representatives attended the meeting, coming from most of the major industrial centers and displaying all shades of opinion in the deeply divided union movement of 1898. However, all the feuding representatives—from socialist to conservative unions—were able to agree unanimously with the concrete case put forward by Booth for universal, noncontributory pensions and asked him to address a series of northern conferences designed to interest labor in the pension issue. From the first conference in Newcastle on January 17, 1899, with 97 labor organization representatives present, the meetings gathered momentum, ending five conferences and two months later in Birmingham with over 700 present and unanimous agreement to Booth's proposals.

The Browning Hall group quickly began to organize on a more permanent basis as a mass pressure group. In May 1899 a "National Committee of Organized Labor (Trade Unions, Trade Councils, Friendly Societies, and Cooperative Societies) on Old Age Pensions" was established with the avowed aim of gaining a free state pension of 5 shillings a week for every citizen at age 65. The National Pension Committee (NPC) and its seven regional committees were, in fact, largely groups of trade unionists from London and the Midlands. Although most of the manpower of the group was supplied by unionists, the accounts show that 80 percent of the operating funds in any year came from Booth and two other businessmen-philanthropists, George and Edward Cadbury. The mixed origins of men, ideas, and money were perhaps representative of the coalition between working and nonworking class social consciences that underlay the pressure for pensions and social betterment.

In July 1899 the young pressure group hired a full-time secretary, Frederick Rogers, to undertake its pension campaign. Rogers was secretary of the small but powerful Vellum Binders Union, a respected religious activist, and seven months later became the first chairman of the Labor Representation Committee. Under Rogers's direction an extensive publicity campaign was launched to carry the case for old age pensions to the public; the committee's main publication eventually ran to 100,000 copies. The pension case, as it was expounded over and over again in the next nine years, concentrated on the facts Booth had discovered about aged pauperism.[10] Any contributory approach was rejected on the grounds that it would interfere with the friendly societies and would offer no help to women, the poorest, and those in need of immediate aid.

By 1899 the pension movement could no longer be ignored by Chamberlain and the government, particularly in view of its showing in Chamberlain's Midland stronghold. In response to a bill by a Conservative back-bencher from Tower Hamlets (site of one of Booth's most prominent investigations), Chamberlain announced the appointment of a select committee to investigate the pension question. The committee was appointed with Chamberlain's friend Henry Chaplin, a long-time pension advocate and now president of the Local Government Board, as chairman and a majority of Conservative members. Three months after its appointment the Chaplin committee submitted its recommendations for a 5-shilling, noncontributory pension to be paid partly from poor rates and partly from Exchequer grants to persons found deserving and necessitous by local boards of guardians. No one earning over 10 shillings a week or in receipt of poor relief in the last 20 years would be eligible. As the Chaplin committee pointed out, in all essential respects its proposal resembled the recently-adopted Danish system of extended, nondisqualifying outdoor relief for the aged.

The National Pension Committee welcomed the change from the negativism of the Rothschild committee but repudiated the Chaplin proposal, saying that no state functionary was competent to determine who was deserving or what income limit to apply for need. The NPC pressed on with its agitation and in September 1899 the Trade Union Congress unanimously carried a motion calling for pensions as a right to all citizens, declaring its opposition to any scheme "which makes pensions a condition of thrift or disregards the inability of a large portion of the industrious and deserving poor to make provision for the future." The latent opposition of the friendly societies and a humanitarian concern for the neediest (assumed to be those unable to save)

10. An example of a typical address can be found in Francis H. Stead, *How Old Age Pensions Began to Be*. Membership activities and financial statistics of the pension movement are discussed in the *Annual Reports of the National Committee of Organised Labour* beginning in 1900 (London: National Committee of Organised Labour).

were a powerful combination, which from the beginning turned labor against any contributory approach. The TUC in 1899 urged its parliamentary committee to make universal, noncontributory pensions a major issue at the next general election.

Almost from the beginning of the National Pension Committee's work, advocates of the traditional poor law approach also began to organize themselves in opposition to state pension proposals. Preeminent in this opposition was the Charity Organization Society (COS), founded in 1869 to coordinate private charity in such a way as to provide personal help to those who could be rehabilitated. The society unswervingly upheld the poor law's strict distinction between the deserving and undeserving poor and, in order to help the minority of those who could be morally improved, was willing to relegate the majority to a strict and austere poor relief. In 1900 the COS director, C. S. Loch, organized the Committee on Old Age Pensions to combat the propaganda of the NPC. The former could not, however, match the mass organization for pensions supplied by the labor movement and limited its agitation to several major publications.[11]

The Salisbury government would probably not have proceeded with the recommendations of its own Chaplin committee even if the Boer War had not intervened in the autumn of 1899. In November, Balfour and Chamberlain outlined to the cabinet the idea of noncontributory pensions for the deserving poor, but any chance of enacting pensions was decisively vetoed by the chancellor of the exchequer, Hicks-Beach, and the Treasury. At the heart of these objections lay anticipations of what even the limited Chaplin proposals could lead to. Chaplin's pensions were but "pensions from the public purse which can at any time be opened afresh by a Parliament depending on a working class electorate"; it was known that the Danish state's pensions had already been increased. The cabinet accepted the Treasury's suggested alternative of increasing outdoor relief to those found to be deserving and needy; "then we could not be accused of having done nothing to redeem our pledge."[12] Popular pressures were clearly important to policy making in the relatively democratic British system, but their presence could as readily serve as brake rather than accelerator in the expansion of social policy.

11. A useful history of the society has been provided by Charles Loch Mowat, *The Charity Organization Society, 1867–1913*.

12. Cab. 37/51 and *Parliamentary Debates*, April 13, 1899.

The direct force of electoral competition was scarcely any more decisive in the development of a pension program, a fact again demonstrated in 1900. Whatever slight chances the pension proposals might have had were destroyed for the next four years by the Boer War. Rapid increases in expenditures had given the Conservative chancellor a decisive argument against any state expenditure for pensions, and the interests of those within the government most concerned with the issue had shifted to South Africa. The interest of the British workingman in the 1900 election was not, as the TUC planned, directed to pensions but was captured almost exclusively by the Boer War. The National Pension Committee endorsed no candidates but conducted a vigorous publicity campaign, distributing 533,000 leaflets and tracts. Conservative campaigners on the other hand concentrated entirely upon the war and patriotic appeals. In Bristol, the chancellor told his electors that pensions would impose an intolerable burden on the taxpayers and recommended to the poor the "ancient virtue of economy."[13] The results for the pension movement were wholly discouraging. In the one election contested entirely on pensions (East Birmingham), the pension candidate lost overwhelmingly; other staunch supporters such as Steadman in Stepney (who proposed the 1899 TUC motion), Maddison in Sheffield, and Wilkie in Sunderland also lost. The Conservative Salisbury government was returned with a greatly increased majority.

Despite its electoral setback, the National Pension Committee continued to evangelize, and slowly the growing force of organized worker opinion began to make itself felt. During 1900 Barnes and Rogers, as leaders of *both* the National Pension Committee and Labor Representation Committee, were gradually gaining the incipient Labor party's commitment to universal, noncontributory pensions. In January 1901 the NPC brought 63 trades councils to petition their Members of Parliament for the committee's pension plan, and in January 1902 the pension movement gained the support of the first joint conference of trade unions and cooperatives. Undoubtedly one strategic change in the policy environment was the gradual alteration in friendly society attitudes. Faced with the growing financial strain and tendency to extend sick pay into de facto retirement pensions, the societies in the late 1890s came to look with increasing favor on non-

13. Cited in *Old Age Pensions and the Unionist Party*, Conservative party leaflet (London: Conservative Central Office, 1900).

contributory state old age pensions. Recognizing that many friendly society leaders in the past had expressed their own individual views on pensions rather than the views of their members, the National Pension Committee conducted an active campaign for the members' support, showing in a leaflet that ran to 100,000 copies how the societies could profit from state pensions. Although the friendly society leaders refused to attend the January 1902 joint union-cooperative conference, the society membership (which of course overlapped greatly with the union and cooperative membership) approved in March 1902, by three to one, a resolution introduced at the National Conference of Friendly Societies calling for state noncontributory pensions from age 65.

Thus by early 1902 the leadership of the pension movement had decisively shifted from Chamberlain, the two major parties, and the upholders of the traditional view of individual thrift, to a coalition within the labor movement. Pensions were in fact helping to make the movement as well as the reverse. On the concrete demand for noncontributory, universal pensions, the old craft and new industrial unionism were able to close ranks. For the first time the TUC, cooperatives, friendly societies, and Labor Representation Committee also agreed on a common demand. Booth's pension proposal was one concrete social reform (beyond trade union legislation) on which Labor could unite. As Frederick Rogers, the first workingman to call in print for the formation of a Labor party in the House of Commons (in 1885), said: "if the Trade Unions, Cooperative societies, and Friendly societies can follow the lines which [the National Pension Committee] has laid down and can come to a working agreement among themselves on behalf of social reform, they can govern the nation."[14] The story of pensions in the next several years is the story of Labor, with some young Liberals and Conservatives, pressing against an intransigent government and Treasury. The one sustained parliamentary impetus for universal, noncontributory pensions continued to come from that small band of Labor members connected with the National Pension Committee. More important, the committee was able to create an ambiance of policy discussion in which their basic tenet—the need for noncontributory state pensions—was accepted almost by default.

14. Frederick Rogers, *Society and Its Worn-Out Workers* (London: National Pension Committee, 1903). In May 1901, despite the opposition of its venerable leader, the Cooperative Congress had approved a resolution calling for universal, noncontributory pensions.

Between 1899 and 1908 some 30 old age pension bills were introduced by back-bench MPs of all three parties and every bill was for noncontributory state pensions.

Totally unsuccessful in its attempt to keep war taxes high and thereby produce a financial surplus for peacetime pensions, the National Pension Committee was by 1904 disillusioned with its chances of obtaining effective bipartisan support. The committee increasingly turned away from its former stance of nonpartisanship and toward full reliance on the emerging Labor party. At its historic meeting at Bradford in February 1904, the Labor Representation Committee made noncontributory, universal old age pensions the first plank in the new Labor party's social reform program. During the buildup to the 1906 general election the NPC redoubled its efforts, distributing 150,000 leaflets and urging its supporters to press all candidates for commitments to old age persions. But the leadership of both Liberal and Conservative parties carefully refused to be drawn into making any promises on the issue. In view of the subsequent developments, it is important to note that the Liberals in particular gave no prominence to pensions or any social reform and were content to attack the Conservative record, largely in terms of tariffs and the Boer War. On pensions, Asquith would agree only "to survey the problem in all its aspects and to lay a solid financial foundation for any future structure." The party leader, Campbell-Bannerman, pointedly refused to make any promise to his constituents.[15]

Undoubtedly the more important development for the future of old age pensions was not the electoral promises given but an unrelated electoral truce arranged between the Liberal party and the Labor Representation Committee. The result of avoiding three-cornered fights was the unexpected return of 29 candidates sponsored by the Labor Representation Committee, in addition to another 24 workers sitting as Liberals. An incidental consequence was thereby to gather in Parliament a group of men all of whom were committed to the universal, noncontributory pensions of the Labor Representation Committee platform.

By no means, however, did the new Liberal government simply adopt the old age pension scheme being pressed by the new parliamentary Labor cadre. The perceived political pressures called for

15. A summary of pledges is contained in the *5th Annual Report of the National Pension Committee* (London: National Pension Committee, 1907).

action, but short-term economies and the inheritance from past policy discussions determined what that action would be. As usual, there were major limitations on the government and these were strongly argued by the Treasury. Chancellor Asquith's two chief permanent officials at the Treasury had served as Gladstone's secretaries and were firmly opposed to any state pensions. On February 15, 1906, Asquith repeated the formula of financial orthodoxy to a pension deputation of the parliamentary committee of the TUC, saying that pensions depended upon obtaining the money for them "by cutting down extravagances, reducing the debt, and bringing the finances of the country into a healthier and sounder condition."[16] In accord with that position, the government's program as presented in the king's speech contained one sop to labor (a trades dispute bill), as well as an education bill, but said nothing about old age pensions.

The pension supporters continued their agitation, instigating in March 1906 formation of a committee of six Liberal, eight Labor, and four Lib-Lab MPs to demand universal noncontributory pensions in the next parliamentary session. This was in fact the first time that the Labor and Liberal members had united in Parliament to demand a specific, unified course of action. During the winter of 1906–7, the NPC organized a series of rallies throughout England, and in November sent an impressive delegation of 150 MPs from all parties to urge inclusion of old age pensions in the next year's budget. The decisive opportunity occurred in August 1906 when the government realized that its education bill would be mutilated in the Conservative-controlled House of Lords. Only then did Asquith put his private secretary at the Treasury, Roderick Meiklejohn, to work investigating the old age pension question, an issue which apart from its value as a balancing measure of working class appeal was a money measure and thus, Asquith believed, unassailable in the Lords.

What policy analysis did occur inside the government appears to have been shallow and dominated by the Treasury's financial perspective. The government's preliminary but decisive analysis of the pension question was carried out almost entirely by Meiklejohn and a group of Treasury officials. By December 1906 the first memorandum examining the issue was presented to the cabinet. The alternative of contributory pensions had been briefly examined in November, including a detailed report on the German pension scheme. Outside

16. Quoted in Stead, *How Old Age Pensions Began*, p. 78.

consultation of sorts had occurred when Meiklejohn took preliminary soundings from the friendly societies, unions, and insurance companies on a contributory approach, soundings that brought a thoroughly hostile response. The general conclusion was quickly reached by those studying the issue inside the government that workers' organizations would oppose any contributory insurance. Asquith later summed up the view in his concluding minute to the cabinet: "there is no practicable machinery by which, in a country such as this (whatever may be the case in Germany), it could be worked in the face of the hostility of such competing collecting bodies as the trade unions, friendly societies, insurance companies, etc."[17] As with Blackley's, Chamberlain's, and Booth's proposals, the power of private interests was a vital latent force shaping the alternatives deemed to be open.

The officials' report in 1906 repeated the well-known facts about the high levels of aged pauperism and dismissed completely universal pensions. A proposal along Booth's lines would be not only prohibitively expensive but also likely to lead to even greater demand for pension improvements in the future. In discussing the report that month, the cabinet agreed to what was essentially the Treasury view: a small, fixed sum might be put at the disposal of separate administrative bodies which, with information on the deserving poor, could grant pensions with no poor relief stigma attached. The cabinet agreed to a bill being drafted along these lines, and no significant alterations to this basic framework occurred during the next year of preparation. It is revealing that, immediately thereafter, Asquith delegated the task of drafting a bill to the new president of the Board of Education; the more logical sponsoring agency, the Local Government Board, remained a hostile citadel of poor law orthodoxy.

At least for the moment, the question of sound finances had been settled for pensions. In the April budget Asquith overruled his Treasury advisors and introduced graduated income taxation by reducing the one shilling on the pound income tax to ninepence for those with incomes under £2,000. War duties on sugar, cocoa, and tea were also retained, and Asquith announced that the following year would see £2.5 million on hand in the Treasury for pensions. Beyond this, Asquith and the Treasury seem to have hoped to provide for the future financing of pensions by savings that would result from the expected reform of the poor law (following the report of the sitting Royal Com-

17. "Old Age Pensions," Cabinet Memorandum, April 1, 1908.

mission on the Poor Law). In fact the question of long-term financing for pensions had been given little consideration any place within or outside the government. For all its economy-mindedness the Treasury was dominated by the annual perspective in budgeting; as long as the funds for the next full year's costing could be found, there was little further effort to assess costs.

Questions of short-term finance played probably the most important role in determining the final shape of the government's pension bill. In November 1907 Treasury estimates had shown revenues available for the first year of pensions to be about £6 million, with £4 million of this coming from the next year's estimated surplus and natural growth of revenue. The anticipated cost of pensions was based not on estimates of the likely increase in the aged or of future sources of revenue, but on the existing numbers of aged at certain income limits and the Exchequer's surplus available in the next year. Statistics dividing the aged by income groups were, as the cabinet paper said, "purely conjectural." On the basis of an expenditure ceiling agreed upon with the Treasury, the president of the Board of Education proposed a pensionable age of 70 and an income limit of 10 shillings a week.[18] Restrictions to exclude existing and past paupers were also pressed upon the Treasury drafters by an alliance of Charity Organization Society and Local Government Board representatives.

The momentum created over the years by the National Pension Committee seems to have been critical in shaping the perceived policy options. Only in September 1907, when the drafting of the government bill was well under way, did the first serious public discussions of contributory pensions since Chamberlain's appear. At the initiative of Edward Brabrook, the government's former Registrar of Friendly Societies, a number of distinguished citizens representing largely the COS viewpoint brought forward a proposal for a voluntary contributory pension plan administered through the friendly societies, with compulsory membership for those below a certain income limit. Although Asquith showed a passing interest in the idea, the TUC, NPC,

18. The final choice* was made among the following four alternatives:

Age	Income limit	Cost
65	10/ a week	£ 12.2 million
65	7/6 a week	£ 9.3 million
*70	10/ a week	£ 7.5 million
70	7/6 a week	£ 5.8 million

and Labor MPs strongly condemned the contributory approach. More important, Meiklejohn reaffirmed to Asquith that the friendly societies would vigorously oppose any contributory pensions. In January 1908, the Cabinet Committee on Pensions surveyed the results of a questionnaire to 151 friendly societies, almost all of whom by now had been won over to the NPC viewpoint. The cabinet concluded that, while any contributory plan would be opposed, the government could be satisfied there would be no concerted friendly society opposition to the drafted noncontributory pension plan. The Treasury had also strongly objected to any contributory scheme on the grounds that no adequate administrative machinery existed for the collection of contributions. Oblivious to the possible financial returns, the Treasury also concluded that any administrative structure for contributory pensions would be too expensive to create.

The draft pension bill was approved by the cabinet in April 1908. Under its provisions the state would pay a grant of 5 shillings a week to 70-year-old citizens who had resided in the United Kingdom for 20 years and had an income of less than £26 a year (10 shillings a week). Eligibility for pensions would be determined by a committee appointed by local government councils.[19] Pensions would be paid through the post office system and unlike poor relief would entail no loss of civil rights or privileges. The first full year's cost was estimated at £7.4 million. The provisions were determined more by administrative convenience than investigation of the social problem at hand. The income limit of £26 had been set with no analysis of its appropriateness but was adopted from the Chaplin committee recommendation, which apparently had chosen the limit as roughly comparable with the means limit in Denmark and New Zealand in the mid-1890s. Both age and income conditions had been fitted to the next year's financial surplus, as defined by the Treasury. One of the many things worrying Treasury officials was the fact that the government had only the roughest estimation of the number likely to fall within the income limit. Pension benefit was set at 5 shillings by rather arbitrarily taking the amount generally discussed since Booth's first proposal in

19. No person who had been in prison within the last ten years, was insane, or was receiving poor relief or had done so since January 1, 1908, could receive a pension. In addition, there was a vague "industry test" to establish that the applicant had been "habitually" employed during his working life.

1891; in any event, the Treasury opposed consideration of anything larger.

Although the pensions program had not originated through the electoral process, its acceptance by the Liberal government was accompanied by hopes of an electoral payoff. The government's proposed bill was first presented publicly in Asquith's last budget, May 7, 1908. The day before, the new chancellor-designate, Lloyd George, had written to his brother, "It is time we did something that appealed straight to the people—it will, I think, help stop this electoral rot." Despite these expectations the pension proposal seemed to arouse more derision than gratitude among electors. At two by-elections in May 1908, Liberal candidates found that references to the forthcoming pensions were greeted with laughter and sarcasm at meetings of workers, who saw little chance of living until 70.[20] It was a familiar response when policy makers sought to win votes by advocating extensions in social policy.

Parliamentary consideration of the old age pension bill brought forth no new arguments or alignment of forces on the question. The chief advocates remained a coalition of Labor and Liberals; Conservative party spokesmen could offer no informed alternative, and the major opposition resided with a minority of right-wing conservatives and defenders of poor law orthodoxy. The National Pension Committee, while objecting to limitations on eligibility, found the government's bill an acceptable beginning step toward the goal of universal, noncontributory pensions. A few days before the second reading debate, Rogers had supplied every MP with figures and arguments on the pension question and rallied supporters in the Commons' lobbies. With some justification, Rogers and Stead watched the proceedings from the Commons gallery "feeling like playwrights watching the play."

The only parliamentary opposition to the pension bill came from a small right-wing caucus of Conservatives led by Robert Cecil. None of the group's maneuvering to extend the proposed provision, a poorly disguised effort to embarrass the government and wreck the bill, met with any success and was repudiated by the Conservative leadership. At this late date Opposition leaders found themselves unprepared to do anything but accept the accomplished fact of the government's policy. Austen Chamberlain in May declared himself to be "puzzled

---

20. See, for example, Churchill's encounter with the voters of Dundee (Randolph Churchill, *Winston Spencer Churchill*, 2 : 263) and accounts in *The Times*, May 12, 1908. The Lloyd George quotation is taken from William George, *My Brother and I*, p. 220.

to see how at this stage of the proceedings we can effectively propose any alternative measure." The Conservative leaders hastily decided on June 4 not to oppose the bill but to accept it "as a temporary bridge to a complete scheme on a contributory basis." In May, the contributory approach had been belatedly and futilely reactivated by Brabrook and his supporters in *The Times* correspondence columns, and a number of Conservatives joined in the view that further extensions of "free" pensions were financially impossible; in future such grants should be made self-financing. The government bill's lack of financial provision for future years remained the major point of Conservative criticism throughout the parliamentary debates, and to this the government could give no effective reply.

The most serious critique of the government pension bill and the most informed advocacy of a contributory approach arose outside Parliament from a new and eventually crucial quarter. The young William Beveridge had recently moved from his work at the Toynbee Hall settlement house to become chief leader writer on social affairs for the Conservative *Morning Post*. Beveridge had begun as a supporter of noncontributory pensions, but reflection during 1907 convinced him that the high cost of such pensions and necessary association with a means test—which Beveridge personally despised—made a contributory scheme more desirable. A trip to Germany in August 1907, and visits to the national insurance and statistical offices there, left Beveridge more opposed than ever to noncontributory pensions and means tests. Upon his return Beveridge began a series of articles in the *Morning Post* criticizing the government's pension plans and advocating instead a contributory insurance approach.[21] Thirty years later, what Beveridge had learned was finally to be applied in creating the world's most comprehensive system of social insurance.

For the moment Lloyd George, now chancellor and responsible for defending the pension bill in the House of Commons, was learning his own negative lessons about the high cost of free grants. It was an experience that eventually shifted his support too from noncontributory pensions to contributory social insurance. During parliamentary consideration of the pension bill in the summer of 1908, amendments were offered from all parties that would have raised the initial cost from £7.4 million to £62 million. Less than a month after the passage of the

---

21. Beveridge's major articles appeared in the *Morning Post* of April 23, May 8, 11, 29, and June 16, 1908, He spoke and read German fluently.

pension bill the chancellor set out, in August 1908, on his own trip to examine the German national insurance system, a trip that helped lead to the National Insurance Act of 1911.

On July 9, 1908, the pension bill appeared for its final reading in the House of Commons. Laughter broke out in the lobbies and chamber when it became clear that despite all the Opposition arguments and doubts, only ten members dared to vote against the bill; of these, five sat for university seats. The final voting showed 217 Liberals, 47 Irish Nationalists, 30 Labor members, 11 Lib-Lab members, and 12 Conservatives voting for the bill; the bulk of the Conservative party abstained. A flutter of eleventh-hour opposition developed to no avail. In a letter to *The Times* on July 6 A.V. Dicey led a group of outstanding citizens in condemning the bill as a "social revolution" of potentially unlimited cost. The Charity Organization Society circularized both houses urging delay, as did a petition of "two thousand bankers and merchants, and chairmen of railway companies, and insurance companies and a large number of members of Lloyd's."[22] It was a belated and futile gesture. For years, inside and outside the labor movement, the National Pension Committee's efforts had permeated the intellectual foundations of policy largely by default. There was no time now to prepare an alternate approach.

In the House of Lords, former Liberal prime minister Rosebery declared the bill to be the most important bill in his 40 years in the chamber and went on to resuscitate the expressions of nineteenth-century liberalism to oppose the measure. Restrictive amendments from the Lords were rejected by the House of Commons; and on August 1, 1908, the Old Age Pension Act received the royal assent and became law. From the twisting, somewhat haphazard policy process there had occurred what later British reformers would term "the first of the measures which can be regarded as the beginning of our Social Service System."[23]

Sweden

The conception of provision for old age from which the Swedish pension movement started was not noticeably different from that in

22. *The Times*, July 6, 1908; see also *Parliamentary Debates*, 4th series, House of Lords, vol. 192, col. 1340, and vol. 193, col. 1404.

23. James Griffith, introducing the National Insurance Act, *Parliamentary Debates* (Commons), February 6, 1946.

Britain during the 1870s and 1880s. Independence and self-help were the supreme social virtues in what was still a largely agrarian society. But the gradual spread of industry was also making itself felt; by the last third of the century Sweden was increasingly caught up in the recurrent fluctuations of an international economic system. Within the Swedish legislature the growing impact of industrialization was expressed in a new identification and discussion of the *arbetarefrågan,* or worker question. From 1850 onward almost every successive Riksdag found the number of items discussed under this topic growing. The worker question encompassed one basic issue: what a preindustrial government should do about the potential danger and unrest associated with growing numbers of industrial workers. In more general terms, a search was under way for new techniques of social organization, and at this juncture German experience with social insurance provided a key guide to Swedish social policy.

Efforts to bring the *arbetarefrågan* under more active discussion began as in Britain with the efforts of individual, middle class reformers. Erik Westin, for example, was a 37-year old farmer and liberal free-trader from Gefleborg who, as a local government councilor, had become sensitized to the new income maintenance problems being created by industrialization. A Riksdag motion by Westin in 1882 argued that existing poor relief was not suitable support for the growing numbers of industrial workers and allowed employers to transfer their responsibility to the poor law system. Westin also darkly referred to the socialist threat being posed by workers in other countries. No practical proposals were offered, however, and the motion called simply for a government investigation of "ways for the betterment of the workers' condition." This and similar motions aroused little attention in or outside parliament, for as the report of the legislative standing committee report argued, "it would not be possible to have a petition to the King based on nothing more than philanthropic phrases."[24] The motion was rejected in committee and Second Chamber with little comment. Realistic changes in social policy required more specific policy ideas.

In 1883 the German imperial government passed the first of its social insurance laws and made it plain that more such legislation was to

24. Andra Kammar motion 76, 1882; *Svenskt Porträttgalleri, 1867–1904* (Stockholm: Aftonsbladet, 1905). Motions took the form of letters from the parliament to the king requesting a certain action; the quotation and parliamentary consideration are in Tillfälliga utskott, no. 2, Utlåtande, p. 5, 1882; and Andra Kammar debate, March 22, 1882.

follow. The impact was almost immediately felt in Sweden, particularly through the Liberal Adolf Hedin. In the 1884 session of the Second Chamber, Hedin introduced a motion which is now recognized as the "source document of modern social policy" and beginning of modern social legislation in Sweden.[25] By this time, Hedin was a well-known man of letters and humanitarian and, like Chamberlain in Britain, stood somewhat to the left of his Liberal colleagues. It would be misleading, however, to push the analogy, as no Swedish organizational counterpart of the British Liberal party existed at this time. Rather than a party leader, Hedin was at the head of a general intellectual current of liberal opinion, vigorously arguing for free trade, religious freedom, law reform to aid the underprivileged, and universal suffrage. Although his chosen intellectual home was with Mill and the English Utilitarians, Hedin drew upon contacts and sources of information from all over the continent. While Westin had talked only about unspecified ways of improving workers' conditions, Hedin was well-informed about specific techniques in Germany (and state guarantees to French private insurance companies) and called for a state investigation of what measures might be taken to provide "accident and old age insurance to workers." The major rationale expressed was an interest in social stability, but Hedin personally disapproved of Bismarckian paternalism to help preserve order. Rapidly accelerating industrialization, Hedin argued, was creating new problems with which neither the poor law nor the workers themselves were able to cope. Socialism was a danger, but it ought not be allowed to create unreasonable fears that paralyzed action or stimulated an overreaction prejudicing individual liberty. Hedin concluded by citing with approval a German writer who claimed that pensions were the way to achieve "reforming not revolutionary progress" so as to "make the great majority of the working population jointly interested in upholding the existing social organism."

The government reacted to Hedin's proposal with cautious tolerance. The king and his advisors raised no objection to an investigation of the subject, and the First Chamber, which was the most conservative and firmest supporter of the government, passed Hedin's motion as it stood. The only concerted criticism in fact occurred in the more popular Second Chamber and came from A. P. Danielson, leader of the parliamentary farmers group. The farmer interest, well represented in the

25. Kurt Samuelsson, *Från Stormakt till välfardsstat*, p. 230; Andra Kammar motion 11, February 27, 1884, An account of Hedin's contribution is in G. Hellström, *Adolf Hedin*.

political institutions of an agrarian era, was concerned about any possibility of being taxed to support a scheme of benefit solely to industry. Danielson moved an amendment to include farm and handicraft laborers as well as Hedin's industrial workers in the pension proposal. In the end, a compromise was arranged by which the investigation would consider pensions for workers and "all comparable persons." On the whole, members of both chambers were willing to accept an investigation of a topic that Germany had so recently made respectable, and the Second Chamber agreed without division to establish an investigation of workers' insurance.

Both Hedin's and Westin's motions illustrated the pattern which we have observed in unemployment insurance and which was typical until early in the twentieth century: individual initiatives by humanitarian, usually Liberal, legislators concerned about particular social problems. Westin had long been interested in child welfare and labor questions; among the major supporters of the motions were Count Erik Sparre, a provincial governor and former chairman of the 1877 committee on sailor welfare, and Jons Rundsäck, a farmer concerned with protection of the underaged. These agents of policy initiation were little different from those in Britain. What was different was the absence of electoral and partisan maneuvering among the poorly developed Swedish parties and, more important, the sophisticated Swedish investigation process uniting administrators and private interests.

Unlike its British counterpart of a year later, the *Arbetareförsäkringskommittee* (workers' insurance commission) established in October 1884 undertook the task of looking at all types of social insurance: old age, sickness, accident, and workers' protection. The committee, again unlike its British counterpart, was a typical example of the way in which various interests have long been organizationally integrated into Swedish policy development. Of the eleven members only three were members of the Riksdag: the chairman, a provincial governor; the farmers' leader; and Hedin himself. An additional three members could be said to represent the employers' interest, although no central organization of employers existed at this time, while in addition to Hedin the intellectual community provided a newspaper editor and a professor of mathematics, later replaced by astronomy professor H. Gylden. Finally, for the first time there appeared on a committee dealing with labor questions, a laborer: metal worker Johannes Svensson. Reflecting the orientation of the ministry in power, the committee was generally Liberal in its membership.

The investigating committee worked for the next five years, producing its report on old age pensions in 1889. A detailed comparison of the contents of British and Swedish investigations would reveal the qualitative superiority in research and analysis that underlay the Swedish group's work. The Swedish investigation, for example, included a thorough analysis of the number, costs, and sources of funds for all existing state pensions, while the British committee totally overlooked the subject. Foreign experience was covered by the British select committee with little more than a cursory review of evidence in the English language, while, with the help of the chief actuary of the Swedish Central Statistical Office, a thorough study (with over 400 sources in the published bibliography) was prepared by the Swedish commission.[26]

In their analysis the commission reached general agreement that the rapid development of industrial life was "creating greater uncertainties in the position of the working classes" and that there was a clear need for some "better provision for old age than poor relief." Research and analysis could not of course produce automatic agreement, and views diverged on the best means to meet the problem. In the commission's divided 1889 report, the chairman and two of the three employer representatives opposed compulsory state insurance, while others preferred state pensions for only the needy, paid by commune and state taxes on higher incomes. The majority proposal, however, worked out by Hedin and Professor Gylden with the concurrence of the farmers' leader, was a compulsory and virtually universal state scheme. The German old age insurance plan had not yet been publicized and in the commission's investigation a particularly thorough study of the then current Blackley scheme in Britain had been made. It was on the Blackley framework that the majority constructed their proposal. Pensions would be financed by compulsory contributions of 13 krona a year during the ten years of the workers' life between the ages of 19 and 28. This would yield pensions of 72 krona a year from age 60. There is no evidence in Sweden of any accommodation to or opposition from the fragile friendly society movement. Another divergence from British experience was to decide the issue of universal or limited coverage of the population by largely empirical analysis. As a practical matter the

26. *Arbetareförsäkringskommitteens betänkande*, 2: 254 ff.

commission found it "most difficult, if not impossible" to draw a line between who was and who was not to be considered a worker "or comparable person." The commission majority concluded, with justification, that experience abroad with voluntary associations of workmen had shown that most of those in greatest need of such protection remained outside and that the associations were composed largely of the better-off workers. It therefore recommended obligatory insurance coverage. In compulsory coverage, as in other policy details, the commission found a precedent in the long-established civil service pensions.

In 1889, as had been the custom for centuries in Sweden, the commission's proposal was sent for review to provincial governors. The provincial administrators, like the commission chairman, were overwhelmingly opposed to the compulsory insurance idea. Eight governors thought the question premature, eleven favored voluntary insurance, and only four were willing to support compulsory insurance by the state. Most reports emphasized the difficult technical questions involved, such as collecting and handling the insurance funds. Many governors also felt that a universal compulsory scheme of contributions was unprecedented "even" in Germany and would lead to bitterness among the workers.

With the divisions within the commission and the negative reaction of government administrators, Hedin's old age pension proposal was doomed, and the sponsors allowed their plan to die without being debated in the Riksdag or acted upon by the government. Loss of this particular pension proposal did not, however, signify a lack of concern on the part of Swedish political administrators. In the 1880s socialist agitation was beginning to be felt in Sweden and to many—perhaps most—leaders of the existing order, a German-style social insurance seemed a promising defensive weapon. In 1879 the first strike by organized labor had occurred at Sundsvall in the expanding timber industry. In 1882, August Palm returned from Germany to publish the first socialist propaganda in Sweden and in 1885 founded the *Social Democrat* newspaper, which soon came under the editorship of the 26-year old Hjalmar Branting. By 1889 the future prime minister Branting had been fined twice for subversive articles and in that year was sent to prison for three months. Even while disapproving of the commission's 1889 proposals for state pensions, most conservative administrators and members of Parliament expressed hopes that some form of social insurance might have a socially pacifying effect. Many would seem to have agreed with the *remiss* statement of the governor in Örebo, who said that if strife and revolution were to be avoided, "it is time to proceed with legislation which can produce reconciliation and stifle the possible outbreak of a fiery class hatred."[27]

Adoption of old age insurance in Germany in 1889 provided a new impetus to investigations of the topic in Sweden. The workers' insurance commission's proposals on accident compensation had been defeated in the Riksdag by the farmers' group in 1890 and 1891. But the results were not entirely negative. The government studies and extended public discussions were gradually building up a policy consensus, so that by 1891 the view was generally accepted that a new investigation might be able to find a way of replacing the accident insurance proposal with a general disability and old age insurance on the German model. Accordingly, a new workers' insurance commission to investigate the question was established by the conservative Farmers' government of E. G. Boström in 1891.

The six-member commission was appointed in an attempt to represent the various shades of respectable social opinion. The chairman, Viktor Ekenman, was a moderate Conservative reformer who had criticized the proposals on accident insurance as "too new and costly" but who also believed that "it would be fortunate if the Conservative elements in the Riksdag could unite to solve this worker question . . . for society's peace and welfare."[28] Other members included a Liberal professor of physiology, a noted industrialist, the farmers' leader Danielson, and Hugo Hamilton, the reformist aristocrat whom we have seen was also active in unemployment insurance policy.

The driving force behind the commission's work, however, was not a politician but a professor of mathematics and college director, Anders Lindstedt. From this time onward Lindstedt was to play a vital role in the pension question and generally became recognized as "the leading force in shaping Swedish social insurance."[29] Lindstedt epitomized the particularly Swedish (and German) mixture of academic and bureaucratic expert, a mixture which had no real counterpart in British policy

27. Öfverståthållareembetets och Länsstyrelsernas, *Underdåniga utlåtanden över arbetare-försäkringskommittens Forslag till låg, Ålderdomsförsäkring*, Remissyttrandena (Stockholm, 1890), p. 35. No exact English equivalent exists for the Swedish word *remiss*; the closest is "the circulation of a paper to interested parties for comment." Here I will use the Swedish term.

28. Första Kammar debate, April 18, 1891, p. 11.

29. Gunnar Malmquist's biography in *Kungliga Svenska Vetenskapsakademiens Årsbok* (Stockholm: Almqvist och Wicksell, 1945), p. 319.

development. Lindstedt had taught in Germany, in 1888 had been recruited by Professor Gylden to use his mathematical expertise in the earlier commission's analysis of civil service pensions, and in 1890 was appointed a state inspector of insurance companies and advisor on insurance to the Civil Department. As an acknowledged expert in the field, Lindstedt was named to the new workers' insurance committee. During the next 30 years Lindstedt was to play a central role in virtually every development concerning social insurance. By the time the new commission had met for a second time in December 1891, Lindstedt had submitted a draft proposal which was to become the basis of its final recommendations. During the following summer Lindstedt and the chairman toured Germany, and the investigation's final report in 1893 also reflected the influence of what they had seen there. Rejecting the isolated compulsory savings plan of Blackley, the new commission recommended a German-style general insurance plan. Despite the objections raised previously, the new committee retained the compulsory idea on the same practical grounds as the earlier investigation. Insurance would be compulsory for all employed persons except supervisory personnel and those above a fairly high income limit (1,800 krona a year). All contributions would be paid by employers, who would be allowed to deduct one-half of these contributions from employees' wages; pensions would be payable from age 70 or the onset of invalidism and would range from 50 to 320 krona, depending upon the amount contributed.[30] A small state contribution would also be made for administrative and pension costs. Administration would be supervised by a central state insurance board. In all essentials the commission had followed the outline of the 1889 German act.

For all its analytic sophistication, the Lindstedt plan was not politic. While there was no powerful friendly society movement to accommodate as in Britain, the investigation had failed to accommodate the one well-organized interest that did exist in semi-agrarian Sweden: the farmers. The major disagreement within the committee was expressed by the farmers' leader, Danielson, who opposed the employers' contribution and argued that, instead, the state's contribution should be raised so that the whole community bore the costs. Not only might the

30. The employers' contribution was specifically justified on the ground that, because of the pensions, poor relief could be estimated to fall by 3.6 million krona or 40 percent a year, which would benefit employers through lower taxes. *Nya arbetareförsäkringskommittens betäkande*, pp. 40 ff.

smaller farmers be liable to pay contributions, but as employers they would themselves be uncovered. When the government transmitted the commission proposal in largely unaltered form to the Riksdag, the reaction was decidedly hostile. While approving the idea of insurance for protection of workers, conservative and farmer forces united in the legislature to reject the proposal as it stood. Little coherent party activity existed in 1893–94 which could push pensions and, lacking this, the determined opposition of any section of opinion was sufficient to stymie action. The largest group of employers in Sweden at the time were farmers and, as their representatives were quick to point out, they would be responsible for paying contributions and receive little benefit in return. When it is recalled that the farmers were the only group with any degree of organization sufficient to be called a party and were dominant in the lower chamber, the result was a foregone conclusion.[31] Once again it was the one "popular" institution of the Swedish state that held back the government's effort to begin abandoning the poor law in favor of a more modern social policy.

The government responded by anticipating public reactions and sought a further investigation rather than a total rejection of pensions. As the civil minister said, "Should the whole question be left to its fate by a decisive no, it would awaken quite unpleasant notice in the country." The Riksdag agreed in 1895 to continue the investigation of old age pensions, and by 1898 the third proposal in ten years was brought forward.

Again alterations made in the proposed policy were largely the work of the civil administration in the person of Professor Lindstedt, who in the interval since 1891 had also worked out practical reforms in civil service benefits and accident insurance. Concerning pensions, Lindstedt essentially assembled the major objections to his earlier scheme and framed a revision to meet each objection. The result was a more restricted and somewhat emasculated proposal. Employers' contributions were taken over by the state, and to the compulsory insurance for lower income workers was added a voluntary system with the same state contribution. Benefits were limited to those aged 50 or over, and no one over 30 at the time of the institution of the program would be eligible. By this means state costs would be reduced but no old age pensions would be payable for 35 years from the date of the program's introduction. The amended plan worked out by Lindstedt and experts in the

31. Andra Kammar debate, April 27, 1895, p. 37.

Civil Department was accepted by the government with only minor modification.

As usual, the proposition was considered first in joint parliamentary committee where the one change of major significance occurred. Under liberal pressure, the age of exclusion was raised from 30 to 40 years, thus reducing the delay before disbursing pensions to 25 years. After a long debate, the Second Chamber for the first time passed a pension plan by the narrow margin of 109–95 votes. Analysis of the voting reveals that the adjustments made in the original plan, particularly ending employers' contributions, were sufficient to win over a vital part of the farmers' group. Liberals expressed their emerging party cohesion by forming the first solid voting blocs behind a Swedish pension proposal. The vital margin of victory, however, was provided by the support of free trade and often city-based independents, smaller farmers, and reformers in the Rural party.[32] Larger farmers who were major employers still opposed the proposition.

Whatever accommodations might be reached in the lower chamber, the conservative nobles of the First Chamber were opposed to the pension proposal in its entirety. The usual arguments were raised against compulsion in state insurance, citing the harm to workers' independence and thrift that would result. The government spokesman accepted the proposal but gave little leadership, and with the support of only a few progressive nobles the pension plan was easily defeated by 101 to 29 votes.

Hence, by the turn of the century, the issue of state pensions had reached roughly the same position in Britain and Sweden. Despite three official investigations and numerous initiatives from individual reformers inside and outside the legislatures, pensions seemed no closer than when first discussed over fifteen years earlier in each nation. British party maneuvering in a parliamentary government had produced as little policy result as the negativism in the undemocratized Swedish Riksdag chambers. As in Britain, this stagnation within established political channels sparked the emergence of a popular movement to press the case for old age pensions. However, the contrasts with the British National Pension Committee are as revealing as the similarities.

The leadership of the Swedish pension movement came not from the ranks of labor but from an ex-Army captain named Gustav Raab who

32. Andra Kammar debate, May 2, 1898. Party identifications and biographies are taken from *Portratt och Biografialbum* (Stockholm: Aftonbladets och Dagens, 1897).

had retired (at the age of 50) in 1895. Raab was the son of an estate owner and himself had acquired substantial property through marriage. Despite these unorthodox credentials as a social reformer, Raab had a long-standing acquaintance with the problems of the aged poor. As an experienced member of his local Board of Guardians, Raab had, in his words, "observed first hand the suffering which thrives under the auspices of current poor relief."[33] Raab's proposal was a fairly straight-forward system whereby all citizens between the ages of 18 and 60 would contribute a small amount (9 krona for men, 6 krona for women) each year. However only those who were needy would receive pensions after age 60. Need would be determined by an *automatic* income test so that all below a certain low income (350 krona for men, 250 for women, and 500 for couples) would receive a pension of 175 krona a year for men and 125 for women. After the defeat of Lindstedt's plan in the 1895 Riksdag, Raab began his first lecture tour in four major cities, arguing for public pensions as the substitute for poor relief to the aged.

Organizationally, Raab's movement attempted to combine the support of influential social and political leaders with what workingmen's unions existed, but the emphasis was on the former. In 1897, the organization's first committee met, a committee formally created by the Stockholm and Göteborg workers' unions but actually chosen by Raab himself. The membership was indicative of Raab's sources of support: a distinguished head of the Order of Good Templars and insurance director; a burgemeister and legal expert; and at the insistence of the unions, the head of the nonsocialist workers' union council in Stockholm, a shoemaker named Olsson. Raab's pension campaign was given an early boost through the support of the influential Göteborg newspaper editor, Henrik Hedlund. As in Britain, large contributions to finance the movement were received from several philanthropic businessmen, particularly a merchant from Göteborg and ironmaster in Bergslagen. Largely under such influential citizens as these, the movement (called the Committee for Public Pensions) gained strength. Between 1900 and 1902, working through local churches, Raab was able to gather hitherto unknown facts on income of the aged from 12 towns and 104 communes. From this he calculated the specific size and extent of benefits that his plan would entail. By September 1905 the arrangements were sufficiently specific that a

33. Quoted in Åke Elmer, "Den raabska pensionsaktionen: en utomparlamentarisk opinionsrörelse," p. 749.

detailed proposal for legislation could be solemnly presented to the king.

After a gap of seven years since 1898, Raab's agitation had again brought old age pensions into lively political discussion. In the 1905 general election, the Liberals were the first Swedish party to make specific mention of the pension issue, saying that the question of "invalidism and old age pensions is poised for a quick solution." The Social Democratic party, on the other hand, concentrated its campaign on suffrage reform and criticism of the First Chamber. By this time the Swedish Socialists had a coherent electoral party without counterpart in Britain; in this sense, pensions had little attraction as a means of helping to draw together the Swedish labor movement. More important, Swedish labor did not instigate popular agitation for noncontributory pensions as in Britain largely because its leadership was already intellectually committed to contributory social insurance. Branting, the party leader and for years the sole Social Democrat in the Riksdag, had been an insurance mathematician and, unlike the socialist leaders in Britain, accepted the contributory insurance framework. In the 1898 debate on pensions, the leader had expressed his party's position of restrained support for social insurance (with an amendment that would have increased the size of pensions and have made benefits payable before age 50) and argued for regulations which would include the present generation to the "greatest extent possible in insurance." Branting regarded the Raab proposal as amateurish and particularly objected to the flat-rate 9-krona contribution as a burden to the lower-paid, citing with approval the five income classes of contribution in Germany. Still, the Socialist leadership regarded social insurance as an extremely limited measure unable to deal directly with all of those in the working class who bore the social and economic burdens. Branting voted for the various pension propositions out of concern for their symbolic importance: pensions would establish society's duty to assist the citizen and to do so outside the realm of the poor law.[34]

Elections to the lower house in September 1905 gave the Left a majority in that chamber, increasing the Liberals' seats to 106 and the Social Democrats' to 13. In November, the first distinctively party government in Sweden was formed under the Liberal Karl Staaf, a devotee of Gladstone and British Liberalism. During the legislative session prior to the election a large number of motions from all sides

34. Andra Kammar debate, April 27, 1905.

had been introduced calling for a new investigation of state pensions. Led by Henrik Hedlund, now official head of the Committee for Public Pensions, the joint parliamentary committee had strongly urged the Raabian view that the "existence of need should constitute the condition for the receipt of a pension" and recommended establishment of a new investigation on the pension question.[35] With little debate the suggestion for yet another investigation was overwhelmingly approved in the Second Chamber, only to be defeated a month later in the First Chamber by 36 to 34 votes. Apparently influenced by the current British debate, the newly formed Liberal party demonstrated the growing discipline of party politics by introducing a motion with 31 signatories calling for noncontributory pensions; but having made what seems to have been a political gesture for the election the Liberals allowed the plan to disappear from discussion. Despite the motions and promises of the previous year, the 1905 Liberal government took no action on pensions and within six months had resigned on the question of parliamentary reform. With no party or group willing to push firmly for pensions, the momentum of Raab's movement and the 1905 motions was tending to dissipate.

The Liberal government was replaced by a Conservative government under the First Chamber industrialist, Lindman. It was this Conservative government rather than the Left which established the fourth and decisive investigation of old age pensions. The prime force behind this decision seems to have been the government's civil minister, the Conservative Hugo Hamilton. Hamilton, it will be recalled, had been an advocate of state pensions and other social policy reforms; he had participated in the first investigation of 1885 and vigorously supported the pension proposals of the 1890s. The Civil Department's chief pension consultant, Anders Lindstedt, was again called upon and became chairman of the investigating commission. Again it was Lindstedt who was the most active member, framing the alternative issues and guiding the group's researches. As usual Swedish investigation was distinguished from British procedures by involving a varied group of interests in policy development. The remaining six members were: estate owner and farmers' representative, Per Nilsson; the Social Democratic leader Branting; insurance company director and head of the insurance companies' association, Sven Palme; Conservative industrialist and member of the employers' federation, Victor Folin; and, as secretary

---

35. Andra kammaren tillfälliga utskott, no. 5, *Utlåtande* 24, 1905.

to the commission, the district judge and Radical Liberal, Assar Åkarman. The most active subgroup in the commission was composed of Lindstedt, Branting, and Åkarman.

The commission worked for five years, not producing its report and proposals until November 1912.[36] Like its predecessors, the old age insurance commission was at pains to study developments in other nations and at the same time carried much further the previous statistical studies. The difference from the relative improvisation at the top of the British civil service was striking. At least a dozen top administrators contributed to the Swedish analysis, and in the end the commission produced 250 pages analyzing foreign pension programs, 770 pages of statistical tables, and 340 pages of cost calculations worked out largely by Lindstedt himself.

As the commission analyzed the contemporary state of pensions, there were generally two alternatives: a compulsory insurance for wage-earners (Germany), and a noncontributory, income-tested system financed by general taxation (Denmark, Britain, New Zealand). In the first case, many persons needing pensions were excluded, and in the second case, aid was spread too thin to be very significant. The proposal that all of the members of the commission eventually agreed to was—typically—a compromise between the two approaches. In essence, the commission's proposal united a *universal* German scheme with a Raabian plan restricted to invalids.

In the first place there would be universal contributory insurance for old age and invalidism, extending the German system from solely wage-earners to the entire population. All men and women between 16 and 66 would contribute a minimum of 3 krona a year, with three grades of higher contributions for higher income. At age 67 (an age limit taken from civil service pensions) or the onset of disability, the contributor would be entitled to yearly benefits of 30 percent of the amount he had contributed (24 percent for women). Because of this actuarial relationship, full pensions would not be payable until 1956 after 42 years of contributions. Because of existing Swedish administrative resources and statistics there was little question raised in the commission concerning the administrative practicality of such a plan, as there was in Britain. Again, the justification for covering virtually the entire population was quite practical: any limit the commission considered would exclude a significant proportion of those who should

36. *Ålderdomsförsäkringskommitten betänkande.*

be covered by insurance. What the commission proposed would become, for all practical purposes, the world's first universal old age pension program.

In the second place, the commission proposed a tax-supported system of pension supplements for all those needy and incapacitated for work regardless of age. These supplements (*pensionstillägg*) would give a flat benefit of 150 krona a year for men and 140 krona for women, with progressive reductions in benefit for income over 50 krona, in such a way that the pension supplements ceased at about 350 krona a year. Sums would be somewhat lower during a transition period up to 1919. There was little intention in the commission's proposal of using state pensions to alter the distribution of wealth or social expenditure. Its extensive research had shown the amount currently being spent on support of the old, both by poor relief and private charity (approximately 30 million krona a year), and the commission's proposed state pensions were framed in such a way that the total expenditure on pension supplements would roughly correspond to and substitute for such existing expenditure. In this way would be realized the commission's aim "to provide an economically secure and socially valuable alternative to poor relief and private charity."[37]

The commission's report was produced in November 1912, and accepted in all its essentials by the new Liberal government of Staaf. Only the strong personal efforts of the Liberal civil minister Schotte, who pressed for a prompt *remiss* from the administrators, made it possible to have the government's pension bill ready in time for the January 1913 Riksdag. Publication of the report finally produced a lively pension debate outside the Riksdag. Most of the strongest criticism of the plan's limited scope came from within the Social Democratic ranks, particularly the party's left-wing and youth groups. The typical criticisms were that the benefits were too low, the income test was too stringent, and a greater proportion should be paid through progressive state taxation. Strong objections were also raised against the exclusion of most of the existing generation of the aged from pension insurance. The Social Democratic youth organization con-

---

37. *Ålderdomsförsäkringskommitten* betänkande, p. 70, Since the same research showed that about one-third of existing old age support came from local government communes and two-thirds from private charity, the financing of pension supplements was arranged so that the local governments would continue paying one-third and the national government would pay the two-thirds currently provided by private charity.

demned the scheme as "bourgeois social policy," adding that the plan was being criticized by most party publications whose editors were not in the Riksdag. Party leader Branting had cooperated closely in the preparation of the plan and, although filing a separate reservation arguing for a more rapid transition period, had willingly signed the final report. Branting's own experience and study of German contributory approaches had convinced him of the merits of such a plan. Before the dissident Social Democrats, Branting argued that it was important to have a unanimous report and to get something enacted, particularly since higher defense costs the following year would make even such a modest reform difficult. In any event, the plan would establish the principle of state activity in provision for old age. It would be an ameliorative first step upon which, Branting said in noting the forthcoming franchise extension, the people themselves could build. Branting's authority prevailed, and the Social Democratic parliamentary group after prolonged discussion agreed by 37 to 6 to support the proposal. The new departure in Swedish social policy was supported by but scarcely attributable to the advocacy of the political Left.

The alignment of forces showed the civil service, which had played such an important part in the plan's formulation, to be favorable; a favorable consensus among the political parties had been facilitated through the commitment of their representatives in the preceding investigatory process. As in Britain, the group which brought the most concerted opposition to pension proposals was what was called the *fattigvårdfolk* (loosely, the poor law crowd), a group of people experienced in administering and interested in perfecting the existing system of poor relief. Spokesmen for the Central Association for Social Work (*Centralförbundet för socialt arbete*) vigorously attacked the pension proposals from lecture platforms and the press. Their basic objection was that pension supplements were creating a separate and parallel form of poor relief, which was better left entirely to the poor law system. Such new benefits would necessarily lessen self-help and reduce the worker's thrift, as well as make important reforms in the existing poor law more difficult.

Within the Riksdag, the *fattigvårdfolk* were represented by Jacob Petterson heading a small group of other Liberals and several Conservatives. Petterson proposed rejection of the commission's plan and substitution of a strictly insurance-based, German-type scheme for wage earners only, so as to "lay a greater sense of responsibility upon the worker himself and his contributions."[38] State responsibility would be restricted to the present poor relief. Petterson's unsuccessful tactic was to unite his group with the opposition expressed by a number of distinguished national economists of all parties, including the Social Democrats. Economists such as the Social Democrat Gustav Steffan and Conservative Gustav Cassel argued on classic economic grounds for the German system as less likely to interfere with the market's wage-setting mechanism. Cassel went further, gaining the support of several Conservative newspapers, and attacked the pension scheme as demoralizing and creating a dangerous right to state support.

As in Britain, such last minute efforts to extend or restrict the proposed pensions were too late to affect the policy outcome. The understandings reached among the parties in the consultation process insured that none of these criticisms would wreck the bill, a fact reflected in the exclusion of Petterson from the special joint committee that considered the government proposal. The Conservative reformer Hugo Hamilton became chairman of the joint committee and worked vigorously for the plan. Within the Riksdag, the most significant answer to the poor law viewpoint came not from Branting but from the Liberals and well summed up the gradually changing social policy perspective. The most important issue, the civil minister argued, was the psychological fact that the pension recipient—even though not paying the entire cost through his contributions—would feel entitled to the benefit, as he did not under the poor law. Unlike poor law relief, pension supplements would involve no loss of franchise, freedom, or dignity.

The support of Liberals and Social Democrats assured the proposition's passage in the Second Chamber, but failure to carry Conservative support could still, as in the past, have defeated the pension plans in the First Chamber. The vital party negotiations to avoid this were carried out in the joint committee when Hamilton worked out a compromise with the Conservative leader Ernst Trygger. Trygger preferred to see insurance principles applied more strictly and was accommodated to the extent of amending the bill to provide for higher contributions from those earning between 500 and 800 krona. With this increase in the insurance base of the scheme, Trygger agreed to lead the First Chamber Conservatives in supporting the bill.

Despite the vigorous opposition of a few convinced Conservatives

---

38. Proposition nr. 126 and Andra Kammar debate, April 2, 1913.

and Independents, the pension bill easily passed each chamber with the support of all parties. Prime Minister Staaf closed the debate by calling the measure "unprecedented in the history of Swedish social policy" and quite rightly praised the civil servant Anders Lindstedt as "the man who more than any other was responsible for its occurrence."[39] Time would tell whether the foundations of a viable pension policy had been laid more firmly in Sweden or Britain.

THE MOMENTUM OF POLICY

Britain

In his valedictory to the national pension lobby, Frederick Rogers prophesied that extensions "will grow naturally out of the (1908) Act if those who have been a potent force in causing it to be passed, I mean the Labor Party, continue alert and awake to future developments."[40] In fact, the 1908 act in Britain was not the beginning of a new technique in pension policy but an ending; the dream of Rogers and many others of universal noncontributory old age pensions never came closer to realization than it did in 1908. Fears of other more conservative observers that state-financed pensions would lead to ever greater pension giveaways also came to nothing. Although marking a significant break with the poor law, the 1908 act was also, as young Beveridge observed at the time, a survival of Whig orthodoxy, a special government beneficence to the needy. The story of British pensions during the next several decades is a story of largely sterile party conflicts and eventual resolution of the contributory versus noncontributory issue within the constraints imposed by the 1908 act.

The sterile partisanship was demonstrated when pensions, ironically enough, enjoyed probably their widest electoral discussion only in the year after the act's passage. At a number of by-elections in the spring and during the general election campaign in the autumn of 1909, many Liberal candidates charged that a vote for the Conservatives would endanger old age pensions. The continuing charges agitated so many elderly persons that all post offices were forced to display an official notice affirming that "the payment of pensions . . . will continue in force for all time unless it be amended or repealed by any future Parliament."

39. The proposition was passed by 175 to 25 in the Second Chamber and 111 to 28 in the First. Andra Kammar debate, May 21, 1913; Första Kammar debate, May 21, 1913.
40. *10th Annual Report of the National Pension Committee, 1908–1909*, p. 11.

In the meantime, the leading reformers in the Liberal government were coming around to the idea of contributory social insurance. Churchill, as we have seen, had become committed by 1908 to contributory unemployment insurance; at the same time, experiences in handling the 1908 pension bill had persuaded Chancellor Lloyd George that the high costs made any further progress along noncontributory lines extremely difficult. In 1908, Lloyd George returned from his studies in Germany convinced that a practical program of social reform to revitalize the Liberal party could be built around social insurance. Contributory pensions were, however, by no means central to Lloyd George's insurance intentions and gradually faded into the background under the struggle to frame and pass the National Insurance Act of 1911. In March 1911, Lloyd George was told by consulting actuaries that the first benefits from contributory old age pensions would begin to be paid only after 25 years; Lloyd George was interested in more immediate returns and dropped the matter with little hesitation. It is unnecessary to describe how the chancellor was able to disarm union doubts and co-opt insurance companies and friendly societies into national health insurance as "approved" administering organs. The importance of the 1911 (health and unemployment) insurance act for old age pensions lay in establishing a working system of contributory insurance that could serve later as a precedent for pensions. For years the British debate on pension policy had been dominated by the assumption, fostered in part by unions and friendly societies, that workers would balk at paying contributions. The 1911 enactment of contributory health and unemployment insurance demonstrated that had there been more skillful political leadership, and realistic analysis, a contributory pension scheme might have been possible earlier.

The National Pension Committee and its popular agitation proved to be a transitory influence in the policy process. Upon achieving the substance of its objective in the 1908 Pension Act, the committee followed the route of other ad hoc groups and dissolved. Advocacy of universal, noncontributory pensions was left to the established labor organizations, which naturally had a variety of other interests to promote. During the succeeding sixteen years, in annual conferences and parliamentary debates, the TUC and Labor party pressed for higher pensions for all at age 60. But these appeals were secondary to immediate questions of wages, union rights, unemployment, and a host of other issues. Neither unions nor Labor party continued to concentrate public attention on the aged poor as zealously as had the National Pension Committee.

With somewhat desultory labor pressure for marginal changes, the diversion of Liberal reformers' attention to other areas, and the coming of the First World War, the policy of old age provision established in 1908 remained little changed until 1925. The first years of the 1908 act were marked by administrative snags and the efforts of the two departments which had originally opposed old age pensions—the Local Government Board and Treasury—to tighten administration and reduce costs. Any outside pressure reflected the fact that one major effect of the 1908 departure was precisely that it channeled most policy attention to incremental changes in benefit rate. But clearly, none of the increases ever approached the unrestrained electoral auctioneering feared by Britain's early opponents of state pensions.

With the coming of world war, British pensioners became caught up in the general struggle simply to maintain their income standards in an era of rapidly rising prices. Between 1913 and the end of the war prices rose by approximately two and one-half times, but pensions remained statutorily fixed at their 1908 level. Protests on the pensioners' behalf were given an immense but again transitory boost when they became linked with the wider worker protest against rising living costs. Demands for pension increases flowed from a variety of interested parties but not from any organization of pensioners themselves. Increases in pensions were finally achieved in 1916 and 1919 and by largely the same process as had helped create the 1908 act in the first place.

By 1916, the Miners' Federation and later the Workers' National Committee were vigorously petitioning the government for a 50 percent increase in pensions to aid the families of their often impoverished members. In each case the Liberal government's response was negative and stressed the Treasury's view that increases in pensions would be too costly to the already strained national finances. Throughout the summer of 1916 an extensive series of worker demonstrations were held to protest price increases and low wages; demands for higher pensions also played a prominent part in the agitation. Frustrated by the government's negativism, another ad hoc group was formed at the end of June. The new National Conference on Old Age Pensions contained representatives from the national Free Church Council, friendly societies, and trade unions, as well as 47 MPs from all parties. The secretary was J. L. Dennison, head of the United Order of Oddfellows; such friendly societies were by now well aware of the advantages that state pensions offered to their own seriously deteriorating finances. The national conference's primary short-term objective was an increase of pensions by 50 percent to keep pace with the rising cost of living since the war.

After a number of demonstrations and deputations from labor groups, the Asquith government finally compromised the financial objections sufficiently to announce on August 28, 1916, a special "hardship allowance" for pensioners. At the discretion of the local pension committee and only if the pensioner applied for the concession, an additional grant of up to 50 percent could be made to 5-shilling pensioners who were "suffering special hardship from the high price of food and other conditions arising from the war."[41] No such higher benefit could be received by new pensioners entering after August 1916. Only after continued pressure from organized labor and the national conference did the new coalition government of Lloyd George announce in July 1917 that the additional 50 percent allowance would be made available to all existing pensioners. But in accord with the Treasury view the amendment also stated that the measure was only temporary, pending the return of normal peacetime conditions. By this time, the 50 percent increase only partially compensated for the increase of prices since the outbreak of war.

While labor and an ad hoc parliamentary group of back-benchers continued to press for an increase in pension rates, the government finally agreed in April 1919 to appoint an eighteen-member investigating committee under Sir Ryland Adkins "to consider and report what alterations if any as regards the rate of pension . . . should be made." This committee was the first investigator of pensions since the royal commission of 1893 to contain representatives of the major interested parties: the administrative departments concerned, unions, friendly societies, and all three political parties, along with the philanthropist Arnold Rowntree. For once the needs of as well as constraints on existing pension policy were made publicly explicit. The mass of testimony from the 45 witnesses examined left little doubt that the existing 5-shilling pension, even with the extra 50 percent wartime allowance, was inadequate. Both pension committees and the Boards

41. By March 1917, some 54 percent of the 947,000 pensioners were receiving the new maximum rate and another 32 percent were receiving the old 5-shilling pension without the extra allowance. Cd. 8373.

of Guardians Association recommended 10 shillings as roughly equivalent to the prewar 5-shilling pension. Surveys showed that even a 10-shilling pension would be below the individual subsistence level and went on to demonstrate that substantial numbers of pensioners were living in severe poverty.

On the other hand, the Treasury's official representatives argued that financial difficulties prevented any further increase in state expenditure. As the war had entered its last stages, the Treasury strongly increased its pressure for economy to ensure postwar stability. The most vigorous and powerful argument in this direction was presented to the committee by John Bradbury, secretary to the Treasury, and the highest civil servant examined:

> Unless economy is effected, and unless the expenditure of the country is met out of revenue, money will continue to depreciate in value until people lose confidence in it, as happened in France after the revolution. . . . I think it is quite impossible to restore people, like the old age pensioners who are not part of the industrial machine, to as favorable a position as they occupied before the war. . . . I cannot admit any inherent natural right in an aged person to receive maintenance at the expense of the community.[42]

Coming from one of the most responsible officers in the Treasury, it was a significant piece of testimony.

Of the witnesses examined, only the Charity Organization Society pressed for a change to contributory old age insurance. Other witnesses from all sides agreed that "public opinion" would not stand the change in principle, a view to which labor leaders gave hearty concurrence. The Treasury, however, in response to the numerous demands for lowering the pension age to under 70 gave some support to the contributory approach by arguing prophetically that for financial reasons any such reduction in pension age would have to be on a contributory basis. To reduce the age limit of the existing scheme to 65 would cost an estimated £17.6 million a year, an economically ruinous sum. The Treasury also pointed out, however, that no contributory scheme should be universal for fear of establishing what would be perceived as a "prescriptive right" to pensions.

The Adkins committee reported November 7, 1919, amid deep disagreement. Not only were majority and minority reports presented,

42. Cmd. 411, p. 411.

but on the key issues of pension rates and age there were virtually four reports. The majority, composed of the Liberal chairman, friendly society, trade union, and Liberal members, supported a national 10-shilling pension (an effective rise of 50 percent), to be supplemented as needed from the poor law. On the question of means-testing pension applicants, the majority departed from Treasury advice, arguing, as the unions and friendly societies had long done, that the means test was discouraging private thrift and widely resented. Any lowering of the age limit was viewed as financially impractical, but the majority report suggested further inquiry into the question of extending contributory insurance to ages 65–70. In a separate reservation Rowntree and a Liberal MP on the committee called for universal pensions of 12 shillings and sixpence beginning at age 65. The two Labor party representatives and an Irish Nationalist MP filed a dissent to lower the age to 65 and increase pensions to 15 shillings universally, the most costly plan and one unlikely (as it proved) to be acted upon even by a Labor government.

It was the minority report that had the major practical policy impact.[43] This minority of seven, including all five of the civil service members of the committee as well as the two Unionist MPs, argued that the economy could not bear the cost of the majority recommendations. The minority suggested that a simple doubling of the means limit on existing pensions would meet past price rises and satisfy most of the friendly societies' demands. Any abrogation of the criterion of need in favor of universality was firmly rejected; once again, the major constraint was the anticipation that to do so would encourage pressure for higher pension benefits and make the potential cost of any universal scheme astronomical.

Public preoccupation with peace and reconstruction at the end of 1919 meant that the reports of the Adkins committee aroused little serious discussion even within the labor movement, the one organized champion of higher pensions. In the meantime, the first general election in British history with virtually universal suffrage had resulted in a Parliament dominated not by fervid social policy expansionists but by businessmen to whom economy was the first need of the day. Within the government this theme was, of course, warmly supported by the Treasury. At the hands of the secretary of the investigating committee, the Treasury submitted to the cabinet its reaction on the day following

43. Cmd. 410, Minority Report.

the Adkins committee report. It was accepted that in view of the 120 percent rise in prewar prices for the average working-class family, a doubling of prewar pensions to 10 shillings could be justified, but the majority's idea of a universal increase was dismissed as too expensive. Explicit support was given to the minority's argument that reliance on poor law supplementation would help limit further pressures to increase the basic pension rate. Treasury officials agreed that to try to introduce contributions for those over 70 was "not practical politics." In summary, the minority view was supported inasmuch as it would be "almost impossible to suggest a cheaper alternative." Anything less would "put pensions in a worse position than they occupied before the war and would to some extent fail to meet the objections of friendly societies and trade unions."[44]

The cabinet in December accepted the case for some general increase in pensions but a cabinet committee under the chancellor also tried again to trim the estimated £14.5 million cost of the minority report's proposal. In the end, a £4 million saving was found to be possible by raising the means limit somewhat less than the proposed doubling. With the hope that poor law supplements to a basic 10-shilling pension would obviate any further pension increases at the expense of the Exchequer, the coalition cabinet on December 17 accepted with almost no discussion the amended minority proposal. To prevent delay and the chance for "Labor and its allies" to mount even greater pressure in the next parliamentary session, the cabinet decided to push the bill through Parliament at the end of December with a suspension of the standing orders and debate in most stages. In a poorly attended House, Bonar Law introduced the bill, saying he was informed "that if we succeed in passing this bill it will have a quieting effect on the general unrest which exists in the country."[45] Ryland Adkins objected that the pension increase gave even less purchasing power than existed nineteen years earlier with the first act. The Labor spokesman merely pointed out that he accepted that the government had to bow to financial pressure but that the bill did not meet the necessities of the case. In a little over 30 minutes from its introduction, and with no MP having seen the proposition prior to this time, the bill passed through all stages in the House of Commons.

The efforts at economizing which had played such an important

44. Cab. 24/5, November 13, 1919.
45. *Parliamentary Debates* (Commons), December 19, 1919.

part in shaping the 1919 pension increases were but a foreshadowing of the forces that were largely to underlie pension policy in Britain during the 1920s. The nature of Britain's economic malaise during the 1920s has been dealt with in the earlier discussion of unemployment. Its effect on pension policy was that, under the prevailing economic conceptions, economic recession necessarily had to be met by strict government economy and tax reduction. It was an expenditure climate amply suited to the introduction of contributory pensions.

The new movement toward a contributory pension policy began with the discussion of unified social insurance. Once again the concrete policy proposals came from the rather haphazard interventions of individual reformers in and at the fringes of government, rather than being coherently developed by any of the party, interest group, or government bureaucracies. An appendix to the Geddes committee report on economy in government was added by the chief actuary of the government, who had signed the Adkins committee minority report, and suggested that significant economies could be achieved by combining the separate national insurance schemes into one unified administrative system, with one set of records and one contribution. The concept of "all-in" insurance quickly became a fashionable policy topic in the economy drive then under way, arousing much discussion in the press and political circles. A number of people, including some who had formerly supported noncontributory pensions, were convinced that any further advance would be difficult if not impossible on a noncontributory basis. Both Dennison, the friendly society leader and former chairman of the National Pension Conference, and the *National Insurance Gazette* had supported noncontributory pensions but switched in 1922 to contributory pensions on the grounds that present taxation was "ruining" the country and could not possibly be increased.[46]

One of the first well-developed schemes was worked out by a group of back-bench MPs advised by the Liberal Thomas Board, producing in September 1923 "An All-In Insurance Scheme." A single administrative system would pay sickness, unemployment, and old age benefits in return for contributions from all gainfully employed, their employers, and the state. The scheme gained great currency, being supported by *The Times*, *Spectator*, and the National Conference of

---

46. *National Insurance Gazette*, September 1922; the tendency was well represented in a study by Joseph Cohen, a Cambridge economist and former Labor parliamentary candidate, *Social Insurance Unified*.

Friendly Societies (who as approved societies would administer most benefits under the plan). In the 1923 general election the popular currency of comprehensive social insurance was briefly recognized in both Conservative and Liberal party programs, largely as part of an overall emphasis on economy in government.

In the meantime an official investigation on the unification of health and unemployment insurance had bogged down under the disagreements of unemployment insurance officials and approved societies, both of whom opposed any surrender of independence through amalgamation. The Ministry of Labor was influenced by its extremely active permanent secretary, Horace Wilson, and eager to gain control over all aid going to the unemployed. In conversations with Warren Fisher, permanent secretary at the Treasury and head of the civil service, agreement was reached on the desirability of an orderly examination of recent comprehensive insurance proposals. In December 1923 the Baldwin government had been defeated at the general election, and on December 13 Conservative ministers hastily approved Fisher's suggestion for a somewhat informal investigatory committee under John Anderson, permanent secretary at the Home Office. The remaining six members of Anderson's committee were also civil servants. Terms of reference for the committee, which were drafted by Horace Wilson at the Ministry of Labor, called for "a general survey of possible rearrangements of the existing system of National health insurance, unemployment relief, and old age pensions . . . in the light of suggestions which have been made for the better coordination and extension of such social services." Wilson's private secretary became secretary to the new committee. The major interwar change in pension policy was eventually to evolve from the work of this committee of officials.

Within three weeks, on January 9, 1924, the Anderson committee gave its first interim report to the departing Baldwin government. On the advice of Anderson, Baldwin deleted a section from the royal speech calling for "dealing in a comprehensive manner with the various insurance systems of the country." The civil service committee had examined and criticized Board's unified insurance approach on the grounds that the insured class would be too small to cover all benefits for the needy; as a result the plan would undoubtedly lead to further expansions and end by being too costly to the state. While recognizing difficulties with the means test in pensions, the committee argued as had the civil service minority of the Adkins committee that the effect of any thrift disqualification could best be dealt with by raising the means limit on allowable income (to 25 shillings a week). Universal pensions at 70 were quickly dismissed as too costly, as was any extension of noncontributory pensions to the 65–70 group. The committee stated that it would proceed to examine a contributory scheme for this younger age group.

At this point, on January 22, 1924, the first Labor government in British history took office. Labor's public pronouncements on old age pensions could reasonably have led one to expect a decisive redirection of policy discussions away from the contributory direction developing out of the economy drive, Conservative government, and civil service. Throughout the creation of the 1908 act as well as during World War I, the Labor movement had pressed for extensions of universal old age pensions at Exchequer expense. In 1921 Arthur Henderson, the Labor party domestic policy spokesman, had moved a resolution in the House of Commons to abolish any means limit in noncontributory old age pensions and to establish 20-shilling pensions at age 60; the same resolution had been repeated in 1922 and 1923.[47] In the autumn election of 1923 Henderson had vowed that a Labor government would lower the age limit for noncontributory pensions at the first opportunity and see to it that money from any other sources did not affect pension size. All TUC annual conferences had followed a similar line.

The Labor government was, however, by no means its own master. In the Commons it relied on the votes of the 159 Liberals to remain in office; the budget estimates that it inherited had been prepared by the Baldwin government. But the most restrictive force on the Labor government's policy, as noted in Chapter 3, seems to have been its own acceptance of prevailing economic theory and the resulting policy implications. Responsibility for sanctioning changes in pensions rested with Chancellor of the Exchequer Phillip Snowden and his Treasury advisors. Snowden expressed to the cabinet the orthodox view that "it is necessary in the present financial conditions to proceed cautiously." Abolishing the means test, even for present pensioners, was rejected by the chancellor as too expensive. Quoting the statistics of the

---

47. *Parliamentary Debates* (Commons), May 11, 1921; April 4, 1922; February 21, 1923. At Burnley, February 23, 1924, in the by-election for the new Labor government's Home Secretary, the government's plan for increasing pensions from 10 shillings to 15 shillings, lowering the age to 65, and removing the means limit was outlined. *Campaign Addresses* (London: Transport House, 1924).

first Anderson report, Snowden argued that the soundest financial approach was a modest rise of the existing means limit. Despite objections from some ministers, MacDonald and Snowden carried the cabinet for this limited pension adjustment.[48] The old age pension bill that the Labor government introduced in July 1924 disappointed almost all Labor supporters and was severely criticized in the House from all sides, particularly Labor back-benchers. Roughly in line with the Anderson committee recommendations, the government bill raised the income limit for pensions. The Labor party's previous decades of advocacy on behalf of noncontributory universal pensions were substantially discredited when Snowden, for the 1924 Labor government, announced in the second reading debate that "the case for universal pensions is not really logical. I can imagine circumstances where [they] might be justified if the country had means to squander and it knew of no other purpose to which they could be devoted."[49]

With defection of the major defenders of the 1908 Pensions Act, it was now only a matter of time until British policy finally turned to contributory old age pensions. The major question concerned how comprehensive contributory insurance should be. While out of office in 1924, Neville Chamberlain, minister of health in the first Baldwin government, maintained a continuing interest in social policy reform. As chairman of a Conservative party study group Chamberlain submitted his first memorandum on all-in insurance to the party leader in March 1924. Any program, Chamberlain argued, should be contributory, compulsory, and cover the four main needs of unemployment, sickness, old age, and widowhood. Specific rates of contribution and benefits were worked out between Chamberlain and Duncan Fraser of the Liverpool Royal Insurance Company, but any graduation in contributions was rejected by the Conservatives as administratively too complex. The Conservative study group accepted the comprehensive social insurance proposals as policy and Chamberlain planned to

48. The economic preconceptions and influence of the Treasury and Anderson's committee behind the 1924 Pension Act were revealed even more strongly by the provision that income earned as a result of work was to be excluded from the exemption. Thus the first distinction in British social legislation between earned and unearned income was introduced to the advantage of *unearned* income by a Labor government because, as Snowden argued, "it would be wrong to do anything which might act as an encouragement to wage-earning over 70 in the present condition of unemployment."Cab. 24/165, cited in Williams, "The Development of Old Age Pension Policy," p. 317.

49. *Parliamentary Debates* (Commons), June 25, 1924.

implement the plan upon his return to office and the Ministry of Health. Throughout this period, Chamberlain seems to have been largely ignorant of the work of the Anderson committee.

In July 1924 the Anderson committee of civil servants submitted its second report. It concluded that comprehensive social insurance would be far more costly to the state than anyone had calculated and on this basis was unacceptable. Yet any further development of noncontributory pensions "would be so costly that the necessary funds . . . could only be found at the risk of stopping social development in other directions." The committee then faced the dilemma of what it could recommend in terms of contributory pensions. A parallel contributory pension for the insured over 70 would be regarded as offering excessive total benefits, while any contributory supplement to existing pensions would be an admission that present pensions were inadequate; it would moreover reinforce pressures for a pension increase. Faced with this dilemma, the committee chose what it considered the least objectionable compromise. A contributory pension scheme could be instituted for those between 65 and 70. At age 70 the contributory pensioners and their widows could be regarded as qualifying automatically—without means tests or other investigations—for the noncontributory pension. Thus, implicitly, the committee acknowledged that contributors were to be regarded as somehow more deserving than others by the differential treatment if not the sums they would receive at age 70. As in the National Health Service, entry into contributory pensions would be based upon employment in an insurable occupation with income below £160 a year, and thus would be limited largely to the working classes.

Without considering the Anderson committee findings, the Labor government fell on October 8, 1924, amidst a flurry of publicity on the Zinoviev letter. The general election, with virtually nothing new presented by any party on pensions or social insurance, brought an overwhelming Conservative victory, and Chamberlain returned to the Ministry of Health with a four-year, 25-point program, including reform of the poor law, local government, national health insurance, and introduction of contributory pensions. Two weeks after the election Chamberlain submitted the pension plan of the Conservative policy committee to the cabinet, which tentatively agreed and referred the matter to the Anderson committee. In its report in February 1925, the Anderson committee gave a devastating critique of the Chamberlain-Fraser proposal. For technical reasons the proposal had assumed static economic, social, and demographic conditions until 1975, when the first contributor became eligible for the full 25-shilling pension. It was also "administratively impractical" in its complex requirements. Above all, the committee of officials leveled the standard financial objections at the proposal: because of its arrangements for widows, orphans, and late-age entrants, the plan would require a £25 million state contribution at a time when expenditures were supposed to be held back; employers' contributions would increase production costs 5 percent a year when the urgent need was to reduce costs. Finally, a contributory pension of 25 shillings per week would set a subsistence standard and this in turn would generate pressures for increases in noncontributory pensions, which the reform was intended to prevent.

In the face of these arguments Chamberlain declared himself to be convinced that his plan was unworkable and set his department to work drafting legislation based on the Anderson committee recommendations of the previous July. Chamberlain reluctantly retained the 10-shilling pension as "the highest figure admissible on financial grounds."[50] A powerful force smoothing the way for pensions was the new chancellor of the exchequer, Winston Churchill. As always, the chancellor's position on the question was central, and in effect Churchill made a deal with Chamberlain. Eager to reduce income taxes in order to promote economic recovery, Churchill was also eager to be able to announce something of offsetting benefit for the working classes and looked to pensions for this purpose. If the plan could be ready to announce in his first budget, Churchill would agree to support the pension plan as proposed by the Anderson committee. On April 28, 1925, Churchill announced in his first budget a £42 million tax reduction and the outline of the government's forthcoming contributory old age pension scheme.

In all essentials, the Conservative government's proposal corresponded to the second report of the Anderson committee. During the second reading debate the Labor party strongly protested, but having taken no action when in power and with no agreed proposal of their own, Labor spokesmen could only bewail the low benefit rates and departure from noncontributory principles. No constructive policy alternative had been developed in the Labor party. Apart from labor, the main

50. Cab. 24/173, quoted in Williams, "The Development of Old Age Pension Policy," p. 354.

parliamentary objections were raised by industrialists advocating a suspension of employers' contributions. Although there was considerable debate about the details of the plan, its basic contours aroused remarkably little disagreement. Chamberlain argued, for example, that the only way to bring in the poorer uninsured would be to vary the rate of contribution, an impossibly complex task for which one "would have to have a completely new administration."[51] Thus flat-rate contributions became established as a policy of administrative convenience with virtually no public discussion; it was to survive and restrain higher benefits for another two generations.

Judging from past experience, the most potentially dangerous reaction was to be expected from the friendly societies. Several weeks earlier, however, they had given their support to the government's draft proposals in anticipation that, as in health insurance, considerable administrative responsibility and rewards from the new scheme would devolve upon them. The government, in fact, was deliberately vague on the administrative arrangements and only on the second and final day of major debate did it become clear that approved societies would have a far smaller administrative role than anticipated. By then it was too late to organize opposition, and in any event the societies were now far more concerned with sickness than old age insurance.

Against Labor opposition, the bill passed its second reading in the Commons on May 19. In July 1925, the Widows', Orphans', and Old Age Contributory Pensions Act became law. In one sense, the new program was an important break with the 1908 policy, for it finally established the contributory principle in state old age pensions. In another sense, however, virtually everything about the 1925 act had been predetermined by its predecessor. The 1908 act had been based on the noncontributory principle, and the prevailing economic interpretations condemned further expansion on this basis as financially irresponsible. Contributory pensions were the one feasible alternative, being both relatively inexpensive and, by linking up with the benefit rate for noncontributory pensions, also likely to constrain further pressure for increases in the latter. Past policy molded the 1925 act in other ways. All of the leading participants regarded it as politically impossible to *substitute* a contributory plan for the existing noncontributory scheme. The major problem then became how to mesh the two; contributory pensions could be fitted in for the insured 65–70

51. *Parliamentary Debates* (Commons), May 18, 1925.

age group; their benefits at 70 would have to correspond to the non-contributory pensions, although without the means-tested conditions of the uninsured. As nature took its course, the ranks of the 1908 noncontributory pensioners gradually would be replaced by the 1925 contributory pensioners. It was a policy change upon which the effect of elections and party competition seems to have been marginal. A superficially clear division between party appeals on the financing question had been denied in practice. Potential interest group opposition had also been effectively muffled. Apart from a pervasive consensus on expenditure restraint, the decisive changes since the formulation of the 1908 act were, first, the far more active part being played by national administrators, and second, the experience derived from the previous policy itself.

Apart from several technical consolidating measures, the pension approach established by the 1925 act continued with no substantial alteration until the Second World War. Pensions were no more immune from the dictates of prevailing economic theory and fiscal stringency than any other policy involving public money. Indeed, two central features of pensions went far to ensure that, in the existing economic context, the substance of the 1925 policy remained particularly static. The first feature was the immense and automatically growing cost of the pension program itself. Virtually every Treasury presentation on the subject of national expenditure could be expected to highlight the heavy burden of old age pensions. The new Labor government of 1929, for example, had begun with a warning from Chancellor Snowden that inherited and economically unproductive obligations were outrunning revenue (widows' pensions for instance would "relieve hardships and anomalies but they will not increase the production of wealth"), that new obligations were being incurred too quickly, and that in these circumstances a cautious eye would have to be turned toward "proposals for further increases in expenditure upon Social Services."

The 1930, pre-crisis budget judgment amply confirmed these forebodings. Budget prospects for 1931 were described as "grim"; as unemployment climbed relentlessly the chancellor told his colleagues that "this country cannot afford a Budget with any sort of deficit." The Labor cabinet was warned that social service expenditures had more than doubled since 1924 (an increase of £55 million) and that over half of this increase was attributable to pensions, with most of the remainder going to unemployment benefits. Apart from an improvement in the unemployment situation, "the only means of securing any large and immediate reduction of this [social service] group of expenditures would be the reduction of Pension rates." It was not a prospect likely to warm the heart of a Labor minister or to lead to further pension expansion. A similar 1939 Treasury review responded to outside labor pressures seeking to use "more of the taxpayers money on the amendment or expansion of the system of old age pensions." The study showed an "astonishing increase in social service expenditure since 1925" (£116.7 million compared to a £79.4 million increase in other civil expenditures and £110 million for defense). This—in view of the meager increases in economic resources, the "bespoken" character of any prospective revenue, and higher defense spending—meant that "sooner or later the question is bound to arise of a general cut such as that experienced in 1931. In the meanwhile the gravity of the issues now before the country is itself a sufficient answer to claimants for new expenditure for social ends."[52] Within a year the Second World War was making a shambles of this economic interpretation, but the scramble for a yearly balanced budget in the interwar years had had sufficient impact to render pension improvements a subject to be dismissed out of hand.

If high pension expenditures and economic stringency precluded expansion, political sensitivities made any pension cutbacks extremely unlikely. Pension rates had been one of the few social service expenditures to remain untouched by the economies of 1931. Subsequent scourings for economies found that, while pensions were one of the only areas where large savings might be found, the political costs of cuts were likely to be unbearable. As a 1932 Treasury memorandum concluded:

> It is very doubtful whether either Parliament or the public would tolerate a cut in say the Old Age Pension, unless at the same time there were a compulsory reduction in the interest charged on the National Debt, which would mean repudiation, temporary and limited perhaps, but still repudiation. . . . The loss of confidence would itself be a further blow to our trade and to our national revenue.

52. T.175/114 (1939), p. 10. Preceding statistics and quotations are taken from T.171/287 (1931), and T.172/1684 (1929).

It was not a prospect likely to attract any Conservative chancellor. Given the additional difficulties involved in distinguishing foreign from domestic holders of government debt, the Treasury concluded that the idea of pension cuts and debt repudiation was "hopeless" and that even a change in the price of the pound was preferable.[53] Squeezed between economic stringency and political sensitivities, it is not surprising that the next important changes in pension policy had to await the upheaval of world war. These major changes in British policy can be more appropriately dealt with in the next chapter.

Sweden

Passage of the 1913 Pension Act in Sweden established the direction pensions were to take for the next 25 years: a small insurance-based contributory system overlaid with means-tested supplements. The intention of the act's framers was that the former insurance portion would constitute the major state aid in provision for old age. In fact, pension policy undeliberately evolved into a system placing major reliance on the latter supplements, with contributory benefits playing a fairly insignificant part in old-age support. The 1913 act itself remained substantially unaltered until 1935, with all of the significant amendments occurring within the first eight years of the act and largely under the impact of wartime conditions. In large part, it was precisely because this basic framework remained unaltered in the midst of changing circumstances that the framers' intentions were unconsciously subverted. As noted throughout this volume, one of the easiest ways to change a policy is to fail to change a program to accord with the movement of events.

We should begin by recognizing how the administrative apparatus bequeathed by the original Swedish pension program differed from the British. The noncontributory British pensions of 1908 required no separate, central agency to administer the collection and dispersal of funds. A network of locally appointed pension committees to examine and decide on pension applications could suffice. Central control was a rather ramshackle arrangement of functions divided among the existing departments. Actual payment of pensions occurred through the post office; to each pension committee was attached an Inland Revenue officer who, in safeguarding the Treasury's interests, made the necessary inquiries and recommendations on the applicant's

53. T.172/1790 (1932), p. 3.

means. Those few central statistics gathered on the operation of the program were the responsibility of the Board of Customs and Excise; appeals by pension officers or individual applicants against a committee decision were made to the Local Government Board. When contributory pensions became established in Britain they were administered entirely separately by the Ministry of Health. The Swedish pension administration, on the other hand, provided for central collection of contributions and funds under the auspices of one National Pension Board. Administration and suggestions for revision of the law rested with the board, which worked through a series of local commune pension committees whose meetings included an official of the National Pension Board. In 1914, the omnipresent Lindstedt became the first head of the new board, and this central administrative body remained crucial for whatever further development of pension policy occurred.

As early as 1914, Lindstedt and the board proposed extending benefits to complete the coverage intended for invalids. Some 165,000 persons were already invalids when the 1913 act came into operation, and the board recommended including all of these in the pension supplements. Because of the uncertainty of state finances in wartime, the Conservative government would agree only to propose an extension that covered 35,000 of the total. Within the Riksdag, however, the Pension Board view was upheld by motions from both Liberal and Social Democratic parties and accepted by the joint committee under former Liberal civil minister Schotte. The government acquiesced to Riksdag pressure, and the extended version passed both chambers without public debate. This expansion also seems to have entailed almost no discussion in the press. According to its provisions, invalids who before 1914 were 67 or wholly supported in private care would receive one-half the standard pension supplement.

Although spared the physical ravages of the First World War, Sweden could not escape its economic effects.[54] By the end of 1918 the cost of living had risen 167 percent over 1914; it paused in 1919, and rose another 10 percent by the end of 1920. Compared to Britain, however, the agitation and pressure for pension increases was small. Only the National Pension Board brought any persistent effort to policy development. In 1918 a small pension change was made at the sug-

54. A general description of social policy responses is in Olof Exblom, "Sociala Förhållanden och social politik 1914–25," in *Bidrag till Svenska ekonomiska och sociala historia*, ed. Eli Heckscher.

gestion of the board in order to take some account of rising prices. For those newly entering into supplements—but not those already receiving them—60 percent rather than 100 percent of outside income over 50 krona was to be deducted from the pension supplement. In the 1919 and 1920 general elections the Social Democrats were the sole party to propose improvements in pension benefits, but even this was well overshadowed in the party's appeal by other, more radical, issues. Like most of the Left parties in Europe, the Social Democrats in 1918–20 turned to the more far-reaching issues of socialization and industrial democracy.

Only in 1921 was a hesitant and long overdue attempt made to increase pension benefits in some rough correspondence with the increased cost of living. Studies at the National Pension Board showed that the real value of pensions had declined so far that a doubling of benefit rates was necessary to restore their original value. At what seems to have been its own initiative, the board drafted a measure to provide for a doubling of supplementary pensions and adjustment in the reckoning of contributory pensions to take account of when the contributions were paid. A new contribution class for incomes over 3,000 krona was also introduced, raising the maximum contribution from 13 to 33 krona and thus increasing the intake from the better-off. The caretaker von Sydow government duly transmitted these proposals to the Riksdag. By this time a reaction not unlike the British economy drive was occurring in many Swedish political circles and prescribing reduced government expenditures as the means to restore economic health. Opposition to the board's proposed pension increases developed within the Riksdag among both Conservative and Farmers' parties. A compromise worked out in the joint committee increased pension supplements by only 50 percent rather than the 100 percent proposed; even then a hard core of Conservative and Farmers' party members voted against the increases.[55]

This modest improvement, which did not fully compensate for the rise in prices since 1914, was even less generous than it seemed, for the new supplement rates applied only to those persons becoming incapacitated for work after January 1, 1922. Pensioners already on supplementation continued to receive their old rates until the 1935 change in

---

55. The proposition passed 60–38 in the upper chamber and 145–42 in the lower (Proposition nr. 284, 1921). By an earlier amendment in 1920, full supplementary pensions were paid to those who by the 1918 law had become entitled to half supplements (Proposition nr. 59, 1920).

the law. An unexpected fall in the cost of living during the 1920s made this less of a hardship than it might have been; but it is still, at first glance, difficult to understand excluding from a cost-of-living adjustment the holders of pensions whose value had deteriorated. The explanation lies in the administrative perspective through which such changes were shaped. Unlike the case in Britain, where the pressure for change came largely from outside agitation aimed at compensating a group of state beneficiaries, the initiative for pension increases in Sweden rested with a central administrative body that concentrated on bringing the administration, not past benefits, up to date. In this sense, higher pensions for the new entrants after January 1922 maintained administrative standards first applied in 1914.

In a similar way, the generally accepted administrative standards of the 1913 policy facilitated changes in supplements rather than any adjustments in insurance pensions. Lindstedt in 1913 had expressed the premises behind the 1913 act and the way in which it was operated by the Pension Board. The aim, he said, was not to raise the material standards of those incapacitated for work but to shift the sources of their support from poor relief and charity to contributions and, to a smaller extent, the state. A fairly strict insurance approach was thus called for and nowhere was it suggested that anything other than a funded system of accumulated premiums should be used. The fears of Lindstedt and many others that a large state fund might interfere with the private capital market were necessarily translated into low contributions and low pensions.[56]

After these few relatively minor changes, the substance of Swedish pension policy from 1921 to 1936 remained virtually unchanged, despite the intervention of four general elections and ten changes in party government. However, a number of proposals for change were generated, and an examination of these proposals will elucidate how the existing policy was able to resist demands for both its extension and contraction.

The fall in prices dating from the summer of 1920 was welcome to pensioners' budgets but disastrous for the economy. As in Britain, unemployment began climbing steeply from mid-1920. As in Britain too, the growing economic crisis stirred a chorus of appeals for government retrenchment. Rather than "economy drive" the Swedes spoke of *"positiv naringspolitik"* (literally, a positive industrial policy), by which

56. *Nationalekonomiska föreningens förhandlingar* (Stockholm: Norstedt, 1913).

was meant less state expenditure, lower state taxes, and less state regulation. Despite the advent of parliamentary government and virtual universal suffrage, the issue had now become not expansions in social policy but whether or not the existing pensions should be cut back. Pensions, like unemployment policy, became subject in the 1920s to the interpretive analysis of liberal economic doctrine; unlike unemployment insurance, state pensions already existed in Sweden and had all the force of administrative and intellectual inertia behind them.

At the beginning of 1923 the pension system came in for its strongest criticisms. Gösta Bagge, its enemy in 1913 and now a respected professor of political economy and director of the Social Institute in Stockholm, argued that state pensions were destroying private initiative, discouraging thrift, and hence were economically dangerous. The policy debate was taken up in the National Economic Association with Bagge and a number of conservative economists on one side and the new head of the National Pension Board, Adolf Jocknick, on the other. Again, the most informed defender of pension policy was the administrative body charged with its operation. Bagge contended that supplemented pensions were becoming simply a parallel form of poor relief. Administrators in the pension committees were extending the supplements in such a way as to make the originally small grants to invalids a de facto form of noncontributory benefit without the conditions of poor law relief. Even more dangerous, the costs were becoming so great as to endanger not only state finances but the entire economy. Ideally, Bagge would have preferred a completely voluntary old age insurance, but as second-best was willing to see those low-income persons unable to contribute to existing pension insurance transferred to local poor relief. Jocknick's answer to these charges was revealing. The basic difference between pensions and poor relief, he argued, was a "psychological reality." Local pension committees reported that pensioners considered themselves entitled rather than "relieved," with all of the loss of dignity and independence that the latter entailed. If this first argument was not likely to convince his economist opponents, his second was little solace to pension sympathizers. Jocknick argued that the rise in the cost of pensions had been quite moderate, and that the sums spent on pensions had not risen as much as the fall in the value of money.

In April 1923 the Social Democratic government of Branting fell and without a general election was replaced by the Conservative government of Ernst Trygger. Although an economic upswing was by now under way, the government was sufficiently concerned by the arguments of Bagge and the other economists to appoint the State Economy Committee (*Statens Besparingskommitte*) and requested it to investigate the costs of social insurance. In making this appointment the Conservative government had in mind the model of the British Geddes committee, but in practice the new Swedish investigative body more closely resembled the Anderson committee. Rather than prominent financiers, the Swedish committee was composed of six civil servants, all but one of whom seem to have been conservatively oriented.[57] As a group they were deeply pessimistic about the economic situation and shared the prevailing interpretation concerning the dangers created by what was considered an overextension of state finances. The investigatory commission's report appeared early in 1925 and not surprisingly was fairly favorable to the Bagge viewpoint. The relief aspect of pensions, it found, was being emphasized at the expense of the contributory insurance principle. The commission proposed that contributions should be raised (thus allowing contributory pensions to become somewhat higher in the long run) but that pension supplements should at the same time be reduced for all who had any form of outside income—including contributory pensions. The commission concluded that the nation was in a precarious economic position, a position that could be easily upset by excessive expenditure on social policy.[58]

As in Britain, the economic difficulties of the 1920s generally left Swedish labor unions more concerned about jobs and bargaining rights than old age pensions. The LO gave the commission proposals a surprisingly favorable reception, agreeing that pensions in principle should be financed with contributions but doubting that premiums could be raised as much as the commission proposed. The most vigorous interest group opposition to the commission report came, in fact, from another direction: the insurance companies, Taxpayers' Union, and savings associations, all of whom felt threatened by the large state fund-building entailed in the commission's proposals. Such forced savings would, these interests thought, lessen the scope for private voluntary saving and interfere with the operation of a free capital market. In essence, the direction and rationale of opposition from these business enterprises were quite similar to the bases of the earlier op-

---

57. Karl Höjer, *Svensk socialpolitisk historia*, p. 153.

58. SOU 8, 1925, p. 8. The *remiss* statements appear as supplements to Proposition nr. 109, 1926.

position of friendly societies in Britain, although one represented capital and the other workingmen. The opposition of these rapidly growing Swedish business groups in the 1920s suggests some of the difficulties that probably would have faced the 1913 contributory plan had these interests developed more vigorously in earlier years.

Even without these largely negative *remiss* statements, the commission's proposal was doomed from the beginning. Following their election victory in 1924, the Social Democrats had again assumed office and were not inclined to cut pension supplements. At the general election of 1924 the only party program to deal with old age pensions was that of the Conservatives, who called for an investigation of social insurance "which is threatening to submerge us." The Social Democrats had paid little attention to the issue but concentrated upon the high level of unemployment. The social policy brochure prepared by Möller for the campaign made no mention of old age pensions.

There is some uncertainty about what happened in the next two years to give the pension issue a prominence in the Social Democratic party that it had never had before. As in Britain, the party organization as such seems to have played little part, nor was the LO particularly concerned with pensions. The evidence that exists suggests that the new priority given to pensions was the result largely of Möller's own activity and learning during his first term as social minister. The Danish model of social insurance seems to have impressed him; what was more important, Möller's everyday work in the ministry awakened him for the first time to the far-reaching social impact social insurance could have. Before any action could be taken by Möller, the Social Democrats in 1926 again lost office on the unemployment issue, and now in opposition the party took up improved pensions as an important political demand. With the shift in party leadership from the generation of Branting and Sandler to Hansson and his close friend Möller, the question of social insurance became increasingly central. Möller declared the new theme in his election brochure of 1926: existing "pension insurance gives nothing except a meager livelihood in certain exceptional cases." The existing contributory pension of 10 krona a year was declared to be meaningless; only pension supplements were of any real significance and these were far too small. Pensions should be raised "to give a tolerable existence." The Social Democrats declared that they could not, without further investigation, say how the pensions should be paid for but stated that they would not shrink from a complete change from the current contributory pensions system.[59]

In preparation for the upcoming 1928 general election, Möller personally drafted a motion which was presented by the Social Democratic group in each chamber of the Riksdag. Here at last was a thorough Social Democratic critique of the existing pension system and demand for changes. The party argued that existing pensions forced too many to depend on poor relief and would take entirely too long to come into full effect. What was required was a complete reform "by which every citizen without delay is assured old age and disability pensions sufficient to live on." Although the motion called for an investigation to examine all alternatives for achieving this aim, Möller and other Social Democratic leaders in the 1928 general election expressed a clear preference for tax financing without contributions, on the Danish model. Regardless of this new electoral appeal, the Social Democrats suffered a resounding defeat at the general election in 1928.

In response to Socialist initiatives, Conservatives in the Riksdag had also sponsored their own motion under the authorship of Otto Järte, who, as mentioned in Chapter 3, was active in the same direction on unemployment insurance. The viewpoint of the State Economy Committee was taken up in the strongest possible terms. Like the Social Democrats, Conservatives called for an investigation but one which would treat the unforeseen and unfavorable effect of social insurance on the people's "psychological health." State pensions in particular had stimulated "parasitic elements within the population."[60] Pensions were clearly beginning to break out as a fully partisan issue, but it was not party competition that was to create the specific policy departure.

In view of the interest generated on social insurance, the Riksdag readily voted to establish another instance of that typical Swedish policy-making device, the representative investigatory commission. Jacob Pettersson, the 1913 Liberal opponent of pensions and by this time social minister in the Ekman government, wrote the directive to the investigatory commission, offering the familiar guideline that state support as far as possible should be in the nature of "help to self-help."

59. *Arbetslöshetsförsäkringen jämte andra sociala försäkringar*, 1926; and Första Kammar motion 169; Andra Kammar motion 294, 1928. These proposals should be compared with the Social Democrats' earlier policy document, *Vad vi Vilja, en Socialdemokratisk appell till väljarna*, 1924.

60. Andra Kammar motion 229, 1928, pp. 1 ff.

The new Conservative government that came into power in the autumn of 1928 appointed as chairman of the investigatory commission the Conservative Linnér, who had also been chairman of the State Economy Committee. The Conservative government was clearly hoping for recommendations along the lines of the previous civil service investigation. But as was the custom with major investigations of controversial matters, the commission also contained representatives of all parties, including Möller (until he again became social minister in 1932) and Järte. Among the experts involved were both Bagge and von Koch. Pensions as a political issue subsided into the accepted quietude of the Swedish investigatory process.

The commission took six years from its appointment in 1928 to produce a report but from the mass of factual information gathered was able to achieve substantial agreement among its diverse membership. Extensive statistical studies of pensions, their effect on thrift and relation to poor relief, provided facts where before there had been only conjecture and assertion. From this evidence there could be little doubt that higher pension supplements had reduced reliance on poor relief *and* had done so without discouraging private thrift. It was also established that the number on poor relief would have been some 30 percent, or 100,000 people, greater without pensions and their supplements. At the same time, evidence on the program's operation showed that the intentions of the 1913 act were not being achieved. Because of the small scale of contributory pensions, pension supplements had frequently, perhaps typically, been used by local pension committees for what were at best dubious cases of invalidism. To this extent the Social Democratic criticisms of contributory pensions and the unsatisfactoriness of the existing system were given empirical support.

After literally years of discussion, the commission was able to reach unanimity on most major issues. On the problem of supplements for invalids, it was agreed that the most effective and administratively efficient approach would be to allow *all* persons over 67 with sufficiently low income and regardless of the degree of disability to have a right to pension supplementation; rather than a pension supplement, the new benefit was to be called a supplementary pension (*tilläggpension*). A supplementary pension of 200 krona (compared to the current 225 for most men and 210 for most women on disability pensions) would be paid to most persons, but the country was to be divided into three cost-of-living areas and pensions of 250 and 350 krona paid in the more expensive areas. The idea of cost-of-living areas was pushed by Möller, who had been impressed with a similar arrangement in Denmark.

Probably the most far-reaching question concerned whether the commission would endorse the continuing emphasis on strict insurance principles of the 1913 funded pension system, as the State Economy Committee had, or would turn toward more state-supported pensions, as urged by both Social Democrats and insurance interests. The result of commission analysis and discussions was a compromise leaning toward the latter view. The premium reserve funding of the 1913 act was abandoned, a change symbolized by the use now of the term *folkpensions* (literally, peoples' pensions) rather than the earlier pension insurance. Any close correspondence between the pensions to be paid and previous contributions was eliminated. Instead, a basic yearly pension (*grundpension*) of 100 krona plus 10 percent of the sum contributed was to be paid to all persons qualified at age 67. The minimum contribution would be doubled to 6 krona and the maximum contribution raised from 33 to 50 krona for those with a yearly income over 5,000 krona. Only a portion of contributions would be put in a pension fund, with the rest going to pay for current pensions. The net result was an increase in contributory pensions for those who paid the smallest contributions and a lowering for those who paid the highest contributions.[61]

Two reasons were advanced for this change from what in former times had been regarded as self-evident insurance principles. On the one hand, the funding system was burdening the present generation by making them pay for both the present aged and their own future pensions. The unspoken premise was that the present aged could not be abandoned to their own fate, and the unspoken expectation was that the children of present contributors would feel the same way about their elders in later years. In the second place, it was argued that the aims of the 1913 act could be achieved only with stable money values, which, in the light of postwar experience, did not seem likely. Pension policy was accommodated to the accumulated experience of inflation. On the whole question of funding, the commission was particularly influenced by the analysis of one of its consulting experts, the young economist and future Liberal leader, Bertil Ohlin. Ohlin's was one of the earliest and most clearsighted views of social insurance's indepen-

61. SOU 36, 1932.

dence from private insurance principles.[62] But the commission did not choose a purely pay-as-you-go system on the grounds that some small funding would lessen the cost imposed on future generations by an aging population. The overall result of the commission's analysis was a compromise, with less funding in the insurance system but also a smaller part played by means-tested pensions than had been the case under the 1913 act.

While the commission was engaged in its deliberations, the chief outside agitation for improved pensions continued to come from the Social Democratic party. In the 1930 commune elections the party called for "folkpensions on which the old can live," and in the crucial 1932 election the party repeated the demand, emphasizing that action "must be taken in the next Riksdag session." In both 1928 and 1932 Liberals had campaigned on a program "to improve old age insurance." The Conservatives, on the other hand, recommended a review of all social provision in order to improve controls and reduce costs. The election of 1932 gave the Social Democrats an impressive victory and, in alliance with the Farmers' party, control of the government. Möller again returned to the Social Ministry with his party committed to achieving some sort of improvement in state pensions. With the unanimity it had been possible to achieve in the recent pension investigation, the future of the commission's 1934 proposals looked bright.

On the whole, the commission's approach was welcomed by the major interest groups and press. The LO agreed with almost every recommendation, expressing support however for the Social Democratic commission members' individual proposal for higher supplementary pensions. The farmers' organization objected to raising the minimum contribution to 6 krona and suggested delay until better economic conditions returned. The employers' federation accepted all major points of the proposals. As might be expected, the National Pension Board and Conservative press strongly criticized abandoning the insurance principle and the fact that those who paid the highest contributions would not get insurance value for what they had paid. The

---

62. *Nationalekonomiska föreningens förhandlingar* (Stockholm: Norstedt, 1930); and SOU 36 (1932). Ohlin argued that, unlike private insurance, state compulsory insurance did not need to give individual value for paid-in contributions in order to attract customers, nor did it need to build a large fund for its future obligations on the chance that the number of new entrants into insurance might suddenly fall. The obligatory and comprehensive nature of state insurance obviated both requirements.

nonparliamentary Social Democratic press, on the other hand, generally complained that the proposed benefit sums were too small.

The Social Democratic party leadership was, in fact, surprised at the small amount of contention the new pension proposals generated. In part, public attention was diverted to the massive problem of depression unemployment, but in addition, the acceptance of the basic change from 1913 insurance by the party representatives was a function of the extended consultations that had occurred in the investigatory process. This was especially true of the Conservative party, which might have been expected to object most strongly to the proposed abridgement of insurance-based old age insurance and extension of supplementary pensions. The Conservatives were, however, also extremely sensitive to the views of the insurance companies and financial interests, which saw the large fund entailed in an extensive contributory scheme as a direct threat to their own interests in a privately controlled capital market; this view was also accepted by the employers' association. Pressed to a choice between the general dangers of higher state social expenditures and the direct threat of a large state insurance fund, the conservative groups chose the former.

The debate became somewhat more lively in 1935 when the government submitted its propositions on pensions. As has been the case since the first British and Swedish pensions, the new proposition was introduced by stressing the need to free pensioners from reliance on poor relief.[63] In the main, the Social Democratic government followed the recommendations of the investigating commission. However, in accordance with the reservations of the commission's Social Democratic members, Möller proposed raising the supplementary pensions from the recommended 200, 250, and 300 krona in the three cost-of-living areas to 250, 350, and 450 krona respectively, thus particularly aiding the elderly in urban areas (where lay the bulk of Social Democratic support). Apparently in hopes of appeasing the better-off, Möller responded to criticisms of the proposed increase in the maximum contribution (from 33 to 50 krona) and recommended instead a reduction of the maximum contribution to 20 krona for those with incomes over 5,000 krona. On the grounds of cost, the basic pension was set at 70 krona plus 10 percent of contributions rather than the recommended 100 krona plus 10 percent. The total effective pension increase to the pensioner without private means was therefore 20 krona for most of

63. Proposition nr. 217, 1935.

the nation and 70 and 120 krona for the two higher cost-of-living areas.

The Social Democrats' proposed changes in the commission proposals aroused general conservative criticism inside and outside the Riksdag as being entirely too costly given the existing economic depression. In particular, the higher supplementary pensions would add 25 million krona to the state's total pension costs. In the debate on the government's bill, however, the basic principles of pension reform were generally lost from view amid an uproar created by Finance Minister Wigforss's stated intention to finance part of the higher state pension expenditure by establishing a state monopoly on the sale of coffee and petroleum. In making this suggestion the Social Democrats were merely taking a page from the Conservative Hammarskjöld government, which in administering the new 1913 Pension Act had established a monopoly on tobacco sales in 1917 to cover the cost of pensions. In fact, the proceeds from the tobacco monopoly came to far exceed the state costs of pensions. Despite this precedent, Social Democratic plans were seen as confirming the worst fears of conservatives about the party's socializing tendencies and aroused an extensive public debate on state ownership rather than pensions.[64] A petition with 100,000 names was organized against the monopoly suggestion, while under a union initiative a counter-petition with one million names was submitted demanding higher pensions, no mean achievement in a nation of five to six million people. The way in which the demands of two petitions tended to bypass each other was typical of a largely incoherent public discussion.

Within the Riksdag, the working compromises on pension policy were established among the parties within the joint parliamentary committee. The Farmers' party vigorously objected that different pensions for different cost-of-living areas were totally unfair to the party's largely rural constituents. The Conservatives generally opposed higher pensions and cost-of-living areas, although the party's representative on the commission had accepted the latter idea. The Liberals had no objections in principle to the government's proposals, but saw in the cost-of-living issue a clear chance to break the Social Democratic–Farmer coalition government and perhaps return to office at the head of a bourgeois-center government.[65] An agreement was reached among

64. Financially, the proposed monopolies were less important than assumed, yielding an expected 30 million krona in relation to the total estimated increase in state pension costs of 100 million krona.

65. Gustaf Andersson, *Från Bondetåget till Samlingsregeringen*, pp. 160 ff.; Ernst Wigforss, *Minnen*, 3: 68.

the three parties to abolish the cost-of-living areas and keep a higher uniform pension supplement of 250 krona. The Conservative leader on the committee filed a separate opinion, emphasizing the importance of lowering pension benefits in the future if the consequent built-in expansion of state expenditures was not to lead to higher taxation. In all other essential respects the government's proposal was approved by the committee. On the floor of the Riksdag, isolated individual criticisms were heard from Bagge, von Koch, and several other Conservatives and Liberals who objected to the higher state expenditure and feared that the proposal might "lead to a general raising of poor relief standards and thereby forfeit the economic gain to the communes while state expenditure expands greatly." There was almost no discussion of the bill's basic principles and, regardless of these individual objections, the proposition passed both chambers almost unanimously at the beginning of June 1935. The social minister let it be known, however, that the government intended to reintroduce the matter of cost-of-living areas at the earliest opportunity. It was the one major policy issue on which party maneuvering in the legislature can be considered to have had a direct, if temporary, effect.

Predictably, the government immediately established an investigatory commission on cost-of-living areas. The membership was made up entirely of government experts and Social Democrats and duly recommended a scheme substantially the same as the one lost by the government in the joint committee.[66] In March 1936 Möller again submitted his proposal for pensions graded according to three cost-of-living areas. The investigation had found that by increasing the contribution from high cost-of-living communes to correspond with their savings on poor relief, the proposal's cost to the state would be reduced from 20 million krona to 10 million. Moreover, Moller said, the improved economic conditions in the nation should make the financial question of less concern.

Having been excluded from the investigatory preparation of the government's renewed proposal, the Liberals, Conservatives, and Farmers were for once completely united in their opposition to the Social Democrats. In cementing their antigovernment alliance, the Farmers again decried the injustice to the aged rural population, the Conservatives criticized the large spending increase, and the Liberals looked hopefully to the chance of defeating the government. Social

66. SOU 62 (1935).

Democrats made the Riksdag vote on their pension proposal a matter of confidence and, with the opposition of the Farmers' party, lost the vote and office in June 1936. The issue of cost-of-living area adjustments now became one of the few items in Swedish or British pension policy ever to be posed and decided electorally.

This pension issue was, in fact, intimately bound up with the question of defense spending, inasmuch as the Social Democratic government under the leadership of Hansson and Möller insisted that bourgeois demands for higher defense spending would not be met at the expense of expenditures on social reforms. When a compromise to this effect could not be reached, the pension issue became largely a symbol of the Socialists' view of spending priorities rather than intrinsically of confidence-vote stature. The Social Democratic cabinet decided largely as a matter of electoral tactics to resign and go to the nation on the cost-of-living area question.[67] The election was fought in the autumn of 1936 with Social Democrats campaigning under the theme, "Remember the Poor and Old," and keeping the defense issue well in the background. None of the three opposition parties mentioned pensions in their programs, preferring to emphasize to various degrees the need for a stronger defense sector and the dangers of socialism.

Election results gave a clear if modest victory to the Social Democrats, increasing their representation in the Second Chamber from 104 to 112 and giving the party its first majority in that chamber over the three bourgeois parties together. The Social Democrats were still, however, in a minority in the First Chamber and after some hesitation Hansson again invited the Farmers' party into a coalition government, on the understanding that part of the government's program would be pension scales based on cost-of-living areas. The election was accepted by all parties as a mandate for such a provision, and early in 1937 the proposal was again laid before the Riksdag and approved by a large majority in each chamber. Liberal and Farmers' party representatives supported the government; even the Conservatives raised no strong objections but generally abstained from the vote.[68] The major controversy on pensions during the interwar period had ended; in the process had begun the period of Social Democratic government that continued to the 1970s.

The interwar period had seen major policy changes: Britain had large-

67. Sten Carlsson, "Folkhemspolitiken," p. 105 ff.
68. Proposition nr. 15, 1937.

ly abandoned its original tax-financed, noncontributory pension approach in favor of social insurance contributions; Sweden, after drifting away from its original insurance-based scheme, had decisively seized on a largely noncontributory policy financed by general taxation. Certain policy forces—a pervasive economic doctrine prescribing lower state spending for economic recovery, a constructive policy role by government administrators—were substantially the same in both countries. Other factors were quite dissimilar; here we may recall, for example, the presence in Sweden of an ongoing state pension bureaucracy, of a heavily empirical and analytic investigatory process able to involve a broad range of interests in more consensual policy development, and of a Labor party leadership more constructively involved in the reform of social insurance.

Whatever these similarities and differences, perhaps the major fact is that the momentum from past policy had itself decisively shaped the perceived outlines of a "new" policy departure. What British and Swedish governments came to do scarcely seems to have depended on the ideology (if any) of the party in power, or on the electoral turnover of party control, or on interest group pressures. The substance of the "new" interwar policies consisted essentially of a sequence of correctives for the perceived difficulties of past policies—the burdensome cost of noncontributory pensions in Britain, the inadequacy of insurance-based benefits in Sweden. After a 20-year period of improvement in pension rates, for which no party or group can claim exclusive credit, the next major change in policy has come in the contemporary era—that is, the overlaying of basic subsistence pensions with earnings-related state superannuation. The story of pensions can be brought up to date by turning to this important and highly controversial policy development in Britain and Sweden.

5 From Pensions to Superannuation

State old age pensions clearly did not originate as a substitute for voluntary retirement provisions. Public pensions in Britain and Sweden were invented and developed as a means of providing a certain minimum level of support, a minimum which above all would be clearly distinct from the poor law. Above this minimum there might or might not be private occupational pension plans; that was a voluntary matter left to market forces. Such occupational pensions usually have been and remain a reflection of existing social inequalities, with the best pensions going to upper-grade businessmen and salaried employees, lesser benefits going to lower-salaried employees, and meager or nonexistent private pensions for manual and casual workers.

From at least two directions, contemporary changes in Britain and Sweden have brought this spontaneous division of the pension market into new prominence and called for new policy responses in each country. On the one hand, the affluence of the postwar, full-employment era has tended to blur distinctions between salaried employees and higher-paid wage earners. Large numbers of manual workers have for the first time found their economic rewards improved to such an extent that their primary concern is not so much physical subsistence as maintenance of their high income standards after retirement. In the second place, the growth of existing state pensions has itself raised the question of how far such uniform general pensions can continue to be increased to take account of rising living standards. When, for whatever reason, worries occur about the feasibility of further indefinite increases in basic state pensions, the likely reaction is to consider the possibility of earnings-related contributions and benefits on the model of private occupational schemes. The result is a shift of policy attention to state superannuation.[1]

In this chapter we will look at the way such forces have been expressed through policy deliberations in Britain and Sweden. How does

1. The word *superannuation* is used to distinguish an earnings-related program comparable to private occupational pensions from the earlier minimum state pensions described in Chapter 4. In Swedish, the word roughly equivalent to superannuation is *tjänstepension*.

227

the recent policy process concerned with superannuation compare with the earlier developments in state pensions? Again elections and public votes will appear at most to be of marginal direct significance. Apart from the ever present deficiencies inherited from past policy, the primary agents behind the creation of these new policy departures seem to have been the labor movements in Britain and Sweden. However, as already foreshadowed in the discussion of unemployment insurance and pensions, a fundamental difference will become apparent between the two nations' labor movements, in particular the constructive policy role of the Swedish LO compared to the British TUC.

The continuing difference between the private insurance sectors in Britain and Sweden must also be borne in mind. Extending back to the collecting societies of the nineteenth century, the insurance industry's development in Britain has consistently exceeded that in any European nation—including Sweden. By the mid-1950s, when superannuation became a political issue in each nation, Sweden had one-ninth the number of Britons in group pension plans and one-tenth the number of private employees in private occupational pensions of all types, or substantially less than any population differences would justify.[2] But such comparisons can acquire more meaning when put in the context of actual social policy making. In the subsequent discussion, a certain amount of rather difficult detail will be unavoidable, for state superannuation represents what is probably the most technically complex social policy ever undertaken by national governments. In its long-term implications it may also be one of the most important.

Sweden

After the conflicts of the mid-1930s, the legal provisions of Swedish pensions remained largely unchanged until 1946. Only in the early 1940s did the first interest groups of pensioners begin to make themselves felt in Swedish pension policy. Both of the two major pensioners' organizations, *Sveriges folkpensionärers Riksförbund* (RF) and *Sveriges folkpensionärers Riksorganization* (RO), were created directly or indirectly by political parties rather than by pensioners themselves—the former organization by Left Socialists and the latter by the Social Democrats. At no time have the organizations covered more than 20 percent of

2. The general differences between the nations can be appreciated by comparing Svenska Försäkringsbolags Riksförbund, *Sweden, Its Private Insurance*; Cmd. 9333; and *The Economist*, July 29, 1967, pp. xxvii ff.

pensioners, and only on several minor points have these interest groups, particularly RO with its ties to the Social Democratic party, effected marginal changes in pension programs.[3]

While pensioners' organizations did support the changes of 1946, the new liberalized policy of that year can scarcely be said to have been the product of their agitation. During 1943 the British Beveridge Report received a great deal of attention in Sweden; a similar background of popular feeling already favored a commitment to a better postwar life for all citizens. Once again, however, the Swedish investigatory process and civil service were crucial in working out the concrete policy departures. The central role in specifying the pension changes contributing to a better postwar life was played by the previously mentioned investigatory commission on social provision (*socialvård*). With the commission's decision for state-subsidized, private health insurance, any amalgamated Beveridge approach was ruled out, but the extensive statistical inquiries left little doubt in the commissioners' minds that substantial improvements in pensions were needed. The factual evidence showed, for example, that, in 1943, 17 percent of pensioners with supplementary pensions were forced to rely on public assistance payments to obtain subsistence incomes. There was also unanimous agreement that—for administrative simplicity—benefits should be paid without the formality of keeping individual records of contributions. But earmarked contributions distinct from general taxation were retained, as in 1935, for their "psychological value" in creating feelings of entitlement to benefits.[4]

Opinions were divided, however, on alternative approaches to pension improvement—with Conservatives and civil servants, not Socialists, proposing the more generous approach. The option supported by three of the four Social Democratic commissioners, one Liberal, and one civil servant proposed substantially higher basic pensions but a fairly large amount of income-testing to reduce the cost of the higher benefits. As the commission was finishing its work, another alternative was brought forward by two civil servants. Commission secretary and head of the Pension Board Rolf Broberg had developed a plan with its general-director, Karl Höjer. Under this plan, pensions raised by sub-

3. For a review of RO activity and criticism of this supposedly nonpolitical organization's Social Democratic line, see Rolf and Lena Norberg, *Pensionärernas Riksorganization och Partipolitiken.*

4. SOU 46 (1945), pp. 123 ff.

stantially the same amount as the majority proposed would go equally
to all pensioners and do so without a means test; only housing supplements (to account for different areas' cost of living) and disability
pensions would be reduced for outside income.

To the administrators involved, the practical simplicity introduced
by avoiding detailed investigations of income was an important advantage of such an approach. For the Conservatives the question of party
advantage was more central and, as a deliberate strategic move, the
Conservative party's new election program and the party members
on the commission rejected income testing in favor of the Broberg alternative. With the Conservatives favoring the more generous plan
(costing 831 million krona compared to 360 million krona under the
old law) which would remove income tests from three-fourths rather
than only one-third of pensioners, the reversal of party stances was not
at all to the liking of back-bench Social Democrats. Most Social Democratic ministers, however, felt restrained by immediate fears of a
postwar economic crisis. With the backing of Prime Minister Hansson,
his designated successor Tage Erlander, and others, Finance Minister
Wigforss cited the limitation in state funds, which were already committed to preserving full employment, and observed that such higher
expenditure on pensions would make other reforms in family assistance,
health, and housing far more difficult. Social Minister Möller on the
other hand argued that only the Broberg proposal would really fulfill
previous Social Democratic promises on the pension issue.

The disagreement was carried from the cabinet to the party executive, which after a two-hour debate decided by a large majority for the
Broberg proposal. Although with somewhat higher contributions, the
Social Democratic government's 1946 proposal repeated most features
of the Broberg plan. Unlike the 1935 reform the new pension proposal
was passed with overwhelming support of all the parties. While Conservatives claimed a "triumph for the Right," it was a victory achieved
by the Social Democrats' preemption of the Conservative position.
Substantially higher, largely flat-rate *folkpensions* financed mainly
through general taxation remained the basic state pension policy for
the next decade.

Until superannuation began to dominate public debate in the mid-
1950s, Swedish discussions of pension policy concentrated upon three
types of adjustment: price index, wage index, and housing supplements.
In many cases the policy scenario of 1946 was followed: bourgeois

party initiatives, socialist government reluctance, and back-bench Social Democratic insistence. Price index supplements were essentially a formalization of the ad hoc and rather haphazard past increases in pensions granted to meet rising prices; with continuing postwar inflation, allowing for such adjustments automatically through price indexing seemed a logical development. In the 1946 pension debate, the Liberal leader Ohlin had urged that pension rates be tied to a cost-of-living index, a view that the government and Riksbank in particular rejected as an admission of future inability to master inflation. In responding to the Liberal challenge, Möller did, however, pledge that the government would adjust pensions to any future price rises. By 1948 prices had risen substantially (from 151 in 1946 to 173; 1935 = 100), but the Social Democratic government felt strongly restrained by the current monetary crisis from authorizing any added expenditure at that time. Only by threatening to resign was Möller able to win consent from his colleagues for a 5 percent income-tested supplement to the most needy pensioners. Within the Riksdag, the Social Democratic parliamentary party would have none of its government's proposed income-testing and supported the bourgeois parties' proposal for an unconditional 5 percent pension increase. Rather than provoke a crisis the government accepted the proposal, partly it seems because of the upcoming election and partly because the efforts to control inflation had not succeeded. After this difficulty, Möller changed his views on the advantages of automatic index regulation and proposed its enactment. Only then did the pensioners' own organization urge introduction of price indexing.[5]

If automatic cost-of-living adjustments were an accommodation to postwar inflation, wage index supplements (called standard-of-living supplements) were a response to the continuing real economic growth. Here too past adjustments had been ad hoc policy responses; in 1944, for example, RO seems to have used its public deputations and close ties with the Riksdag to persuade the government of the case for an increase in pension benefits that would give the pensioners a part of the higher real income standards realized during the war. The joint parliamentary committee's decision to establish an investigation was overturned on the Riksdag floor by all-party support for an immediate, special increase in the real value of pensions. During the 1950s the

5. Descriptions of these events are in Åke Elmer, *Folkpensioneringen*, pp. 90 ff.; and Wigforss, *Minnen*, 3: 389.

opposition parties were again prominent in pressing for increases. In 1951 a Farmers' party representative urged new standard supplements to take account of real standard improvements since the 1940s, and in 1952 the Liberal party and RO joined in the demand. The point was not lost on the government, and in 1953 pensions were raised proportionately to changes in industrial workers' wages between 1946–52. As we shall see, this compensatory approach to pension policy became formalized in 1956 in connection with the superannuation issue. Clearly, party counterbidding and legislative pressure were significant for marginal changes in rate, timing, and means-testing of benefits within the existing pension framework. But for the major postwar policy change we must look elsewhere than the parties and legislature.

Superannuation in Sweden had its origins in the union movement and developed amid a breakdown in relations between employers' and workers' labor market organizations. Prior to the 1940s the chief political attention to occupational pensions had come from conservative quarters mainly concerned with state aid to guarantee and/or encourage employers' voluntary pension plans. In 1935 however, an obscure Liberal Riksdagsman did propose an investigation of obligatory, low-level superannuation as a means of encouraging early retirement and easing the unemployment situation. Three years later a number of Liberal supporters joined in urging legislation that would have required companies to make pension provision for employees, but again the proposal aroused little attention. Apart from these abortive Liberal efforts, the general assumption remained—as the 1936–46 *socialvård* investigation illustrated—that superannuation was a matter of concern to salaried employees and not manual workers.

In the meantime, and outside the public view of politics, pressure for a new policy departure was developing within the union movement. It was this pressure that resulted twenty years later in a Swedish national superannuation policy.[6] During the late 1930s and early 1940s, wages in certain skilled trades had already achieved relatively high levels. Nowhere was this more true than among the strongly organized metalworkers. At a number of local branches of the metal and foundry workers' unions, particularly in Norrhammar and Jonköping, there were growing unionist demands for the same pension rights for manual workers as were enjoyed by salaried employees. The story cannot be

6. Much of the following account is based on Björn Molin's excellent study, *Tjänstepensionsfrågan.*

followed in detail here, but through pressure at local and regional conferences in the late 1930s and early 1940s, the metalworkers' union and, through its power, the LO, were gradually sensitized to this issue as one of vital concern to workers. Subsequent development of superannuation revolved around the LO's failure to achieve its desires in three policy arenas: through private negotiations with employers, within the Swedish investigatory process, and between the political parties. Eventually Swedish superannuation escalated to the point that the Social Democratic party was led into a dramatic public campaign during 1956–57.

The first involvement of parliamentary institutions began in 1944, when LO member and Social Democrat Osker Åkerström proposed an investigation on the feasibility of establishing occupational pensions through national legislation. The most important point of the motion was its emphasis that only public legislation could assure the necessary income security to *all* employees. During the first half of 1944, negotiations between the LO and SAF (the employers' organization) within the Labor Market Commission had broken down on precisely this point of the need for legislation. LO representatives insisted that the voluntary arrangement of employers' plans would inevitably fail to include many workers who needed coverage. Although the Riksdag with little discussion approved the proposal to establish an investigation of all possible alternatives on the question, it was two years before this investigation was established. In large part the delay stemmed from the desire of Social Democratic party leaders to concentrate attention first on the other pending social service reforms, and, in any event, the negotiations between LO and SAF had not yet irredeemably broken down.

Union organizations refused to countenance such drift. At the 1946 LO Congress, pressure arose from metalworkers, foundryworkers, and other unions urging the LO to spur the government into establishing the promised investigation. With an assurance that the LO executive would make a strong case to the government, the issue was not pushed to a vote. On January 24, 1947, Commerce Minister Gunnar Myrdal finally authorized establishment of an investigation into obligatory occupational pensions. Under the chairmanship of O. A. Åkesson, director of the state insurance inspectorate and secretary of the *socialvård* investigation, the new commission contained no political party representatives as such but was composed of three representatives each from the LO and the major employers' federation, one employer from small industry, and one representative of the supervisors' union. This membership and the fact that the investigative body was appointed by the Commerce Ministry clearly expressed the general assumption that, even if state activity might result, the creation of a superannuation policy would be a nonpolitical, semitechnical question to be settled between the labor market parties themselves.

The preliminary report of the investigation limited itself to basic principles, but even at this abstract level important divergences appeared among the groups represented. All could agree that occupational pensions should be related to the employee's living standard, should be inviolable, and as far as possible be part of an interrelated pension system.[7] On the question of fund-building, however, employers' representatives, as in the 1920s, generally opposed any large accumulation of contributions. Workers' representatives, on the other hand, argued in the opposite direction; *more* than the strictly actuarial contributions should be gathered in a large fund. This would provide benefits and security to workers currently approaching retirement as well as lower the coming burden of a proportionally aging population. Consultations with outside groups generally reflected these differing views. The labor movement was scarcely united behind the idea of state superannuation, the divergences largely reflecting the extent to which each interest group's members were already covered by private provision. The Cooperative Society, one of the largest private insurers, wholeheartedly opposed any state scheme. With their already extensive pension arrangements, the salaried employees' union (TCO) urged that no action be taken until satisfactory means were found of coordinating any state system with existing pension programs. As the most powerful of the union federations, the LO affirmed what was by now becoming its established view; only an obligatory and comprehensive state occupational pension plan could provide adequate coverage for all workers—including the LO's largely manual labor membership.

During the next year the Social Democratic government digested these comments and took no action on the issue. Pressure was growing within the LO, however, to give clear priority to the superannuation issue. The powerful metalworkers' union was now firmly convinced that the employers' negative attitude pointed inescapably to the conclusion that a general superannuation plan would have to be legislated.

7. SOU 33 (1950), pp. 70 ff.

At the 1951 LO Congress, nine major motions were presented urging a speedy solution to the question and removal of the unjustified difference between workers and salaried employees; the government's investigatory work should be accelerated. In all essential respects the foremost spokesmen for labor on the superannuation issue remained the former local unionists, by now rising to positions of leadership in the LO, who had ten years earlier begun pressing the issue.[8] At the suggestion of the LO executive the congress declared itself in favor of a speedy solution through legislation rather than employers' contracts.

Hopes for the development of a superannuation program now shifted to the Swedish investigatory process and its thorough examination of the possibilities of political compromise among the affected interests. The new investigatory commission established in 1951 included five of the former commission members (Åkesson again was chairman) and added four new members, including a Social Democratic representative, a Farmers' party representative, and Paul Steen of the metalworkers' union—who in 1946 had been instrumental in urging the LO into a more active role on the issue. If anything, the policy views of the two major interest groups now became more insistent. While the second investigation deliberated, the LO continued to demonstrate its strong interest in the subject, and during 1952 and 1953 a number of motions by LO Social Democrats in the Riksdag called for a hastening of the commission's work.

Within the SAF the policy position was becoming more obdurate and at the beginning of 1952 a special subcommittee was appointed to help develop the employers' position on occupational pensions. The superannuation question was seen to hinge, for private industry, on the method of financing; it was better, the subcommittee concluded, to consider occupational pension costs as a delayed wage benefit and cost of production rather than to finance the costs through public means. State fund-building would discourage thrift and threaten the private capital market. Superannuation should therefore be arranged through negotiations between employers and unions rather than by state means, with occupational pensions always considered a part of the total negotiation on wage benefits. The outlines of the government investigation's

---

8. On the metalworkers' position, see the various editorials in *Metallarbetaren,* vol. 25–26, 1950. Foremost among the 1951 activists in the Riksdag was Harold Almgren of the metalworkers, who had first become involved in the late 1930s in Jönköping; LO, *Kongress Protokoll,* 1951.

proposals were already known, and it seems clear that the SAF sub-committee proposals were intended as an alternative to the upcoming commission plan, which would be too costly and depend upon large fund-building. Although the SAF did not commit itself to any plan, it did submit its subcommittee's report to the Labor Market Board and tried to begin further negotiations with the LO in May 1954. LO chairman Axel Strand and chairman-designate Arne Geijer, former head of the metalworkers' union, gave the employers' report a cool reception and decided to delay discussion until after the government investigation's report. With this, the attempt to evolve an occupational pension policy through negotiations between the major labor market parties came to an end.

Events soon proved that the investigatory process had also failed to develop a generally acceptable superannuation policy. The second Åkesson investigation finally reported in September 1955.[9] In contrast with the unanimity on principles prevailing in the first report, the second contained no less than ten separate statements and reservations. The majority views, supported mainly by union representatives and Social Democrats, accepted the case for compulsory state superannuation. Pensions ought to be universal, without the possibility of contracting out, if the system were not to be made financially unstable by the withdrawal of large and important groups. The majority repeated the LO's long-standing arguments that only a state scheme could ensure coverage of all workers, ensure inflation-proofing, be part of a unified pension system, and come into effect within a reasonable length of time. More generally, the superannuation advocates contended that to separate state and private pensioners through contracting out would "endanger social solidarity." The commission majority refused to agree to the salaried (TCO) and professional (SACO) unions' demands for preferential treatment of income in later years, and also maintained the first commission's arguments for building a large fund during a 20-year transition period.

Alternative proposals were presented in a series of separate statements by nonlabor commission members. Brodén of the SAF argued the employers' case for voluntary pensions through private negotiations. The other major alternative was presented by the Conservative, E. Ahlberg, who rejected the state system and proposed instead a further strengthening of the existing general folkpensions, a plan he had un-

9. SOU 32 (1955).

successfully presented to the commission in 1953.[10] Folkpensions would be successively raised and income tests abolished; this would be more fair, Ahlberg argued, to groups such as those already old (who would get no improvement in pensions through superannuation), home and agricultural workers, and housewives—in short, all those not earning regular income through employment.

Outside consultations on the commission report were at least as varied as opinion within the commission itself. Of the 89 bodies responding (43 being state organs), only five were generally favorable to the majority recommendations. Not surprisingly, the major supporter was the LO. The other major unions, TCO and SACO, decided to withhold judgment until it became clear what arrangements would be made for their existing private pension schemes. Twenty-six bodies, including the private insurance companies, the SAF, and the Farmers' Association supported Ahlberg's proposal for higher folkpensions and voluntary occupational pensions. Both pensioners' organizations supported the call for improved folkpensions but were dubious about superannuation.

Clearly no policy consensus on superannuation could be said to exist in Sweden. In the face of this disagreement even among union organizations, the Social Democratic government temporized and appointed a new investigatory commission. The hesitancy of the Social Democratic party, as well as its desire to split the Liberals from the Conservative and SAF view, was illustrated by this further delay and by the government's instructions to the new investigation to consider *all* possible alternatives, both legislative and other solutions. Only at this point in the development of superannuation did the political parties begin to be seriously involved in the issue. Now that a private solution between the LO and SAF had proved impossible, both in the Labor Market Board and the investigatory process, the new commission included representatives of all political parties. With the further breakdown of this party-consultative approach in the next two years and continued LO insistence that an adequate solution required a state program, the superannuation question finally escalated into a partisan issue of first-rank importance.

Prior to this time none of the political parties had taken a public

10. Ahlberg was the representative of the supervisors' union in the first Åkesson commission, where he argued strongly for extensive contracting out. He had just been elected to the Riksdag as a Conservative.

position on superannuation. In the 1956 Riksdag and general election, however, all political parties did offer clear public alternatives on the issue. In line with Ahlberg's proposal, the Conservative party urged a large rise in folkpensions but argued that beyond this basic level pensions should be a matter of voluntary private arrangements. The Farmers' party joined in the demand for higher folkpensions and considered insignificant any further need for superannuation. During 1954 the Liberals had spoken of "clarifying the issue through further investigation," but in 1956 the party began advocating a rise in folkpensions, with some state aid in ensuring the real value of occupational pensions acquired voluntarily through private labor market contracts. Under Ohlin's leadership, the Liberal party was nearer to a positive approach than either of the two other bourgeois parties, and in the spring of 1956 the Liberal representative on the new investigation came close to allying with the Social Democrats. Such a course was eventually vetoed by the parliamentary Liberal party, partly it seems because of an unwillingness to alienate industrial and financial supporters and partly because of a miscalculation that political advantage would be gained through white-collar opposition to superannuation.

The most crucial question was the position of the Social Democratic party. By no means was the LO case for immediate introduction of state superannuation readily accepted by the party leadership. Until 1954 the party platform had ignored the issue and even in that year had simply declared the general issue to be "urgent." During the Riksdag debate of January and the party congress debate of May 1956, the government spokesmen agreed on the importance of occupational pensions and the need to ensure legal rights to such pensions, but declared that the government was withholding its judgment on an actual solution until the report of the third investigation. The exact means by which the LO position was adopted by the party remains unpublished. It does seem clear, however, that Social Democratic party leaders were extremely hesitant to push the matter, both because it would virtually guarantee a break with the Farmers' party (their coalition partner in the government) and because large numbers of white-collar workers with private pension rights could be expected to oppose state superannuation. By whatever means—and reliable sources report that this involved some extremely severe LO threats—the Social Democratic leadership at some time during 1956 adopted the LO view favoring a state superannuation policy roughly in accord with the Åkesson investigation's earlier proposals. At the September 1956 LO Congress, Prime Minister Erlander declared that the question of occupational pensions could not be solved except through legislation laying upon the employer the duty of contributing to the pensions of all his workers.

It was hardly electoral pressures that were forcing the advent of superannuation. The 1956 election results gave a setback to both government parties, the Social Democrats and Farmers, while the Conservatives and Liberals gained support. Although the actual voting changes were small, the psychological effects were not. Here at last was the first general election setback to the Social Democrats since the war; no matter how slight the margin, the bourgeois parties for the first time since 1930 had actually gained a majority of the popular vote (50.1 percent). Although each party had emphasized its particular pension approach, the data do not allow one to determine the extent to which this influenced the election results. The important point however is that, to both Liberal and Conservative parties, the results seemed to confirm the electoral advantage of pushing their opposition to occupational pensions. Similarly, the Farmers' party became much more reluctant to tie itself to the Social Democratic view on superannuation. On October 13, 1956, a new coalition government was established between the Social Democrats and Farmers, with the superannuation question left in an uneasy limbo awaiting the investigatory commission's report.

All parties had by this time agreed to a substantial rise in folkpensions. From an early point in the discussions, the bourgeois parties had been pushing for such increases as an alternative to state occupational pensions.[11] The Social Democrats again preempted the opposition parties' position and supported guaranteed folkpension increases quite apart from whatever was done on superannuation. One of the first acts of the new government was to agree to such a general increase. In all essentials the government in doing so accepted a preliminary ten-year plan worked out by the third investigatory commission. After some objections by the LO representatives, agreement had been reached for a separate plan of folkpension increases, which would in successive steps increase the real value of such pensions by two-thirds between 1958 and 1968. By this means existing pensioners somewhat accidentally became the beneficiaries of party maneuvering on superannuation.

11. A summary can be found in Andra lagutskott, no. 30, 1956; and the Andra Kammar debates, January 19 and May 26, 1956.

The growing partisanship surrounding any proposed superannuation policy finally came to a head when the third investigatory commission brought forward its final report in February 1957. This time the divergence of views was almost complete. Liaison between the commission members and their respective interest groups had been especially close during the entire deliberations and helped destroy the supposed neutrality of the investigation. The chairman, along with the LO economist Nils Kellgren and LO Social Democrat Harold Almgren, supported obligatory occupational pensions organized by the state. After certain compromises,[12] the TCO member associated himself with his fellow labor members' stand. The proposed system would apply to all wage-earners and all wage income from 300 to 30,000 krona, with occupational pensions set at 50 percent of the worker's average income during his fifteen best years of earning. This "supplementary pension," along with the higher folkpensions, would give a total state pension of approximately two-thirds of his income. All benefits would be price-indexed to assure real values. During the transition period full pensions would be provided after 20 years of contribution, but thereafter 30 years of contribution would be required. Both employers and employees would contribute (for administrative reasons, all contributions would be paid by employers). It was a revealing illustration of the Swedish confidence in its industrial relations process that even now the exact proportion that each party would contribute was left to be determined in wage negotiations. Like its predecessors, the commission proposed setting contributions at a higher level than that required by actuarial costs; thus during the transition period a considerable fund would be accumulated, which it was thought could be made available for capital borrowing by industrial enterprises as well as by state and national authorities.

Again the proposal of state superannuation was rejected by the representatives of the employers' federation, as well as the Conservative and Liberal parties. The three argued that the nature of the pension question was fundamentally altered by the coming reform of folkpensions, which they of course supported, and that compulsory occupational pensions were now unnecessary. After some disagreement these spokesmen united behind a plan presented by the Liberal rep-

12. Most notably, the average of the 15 best years was substituted for total average income as the basis for pension amounts; TCO members, of course, had a more steeply rising income curve than manual workers.

resentative Aastrup, which called for higher folkpensions with some fairly vague state cooperation in the arrangement of private occupational pensions on a voluntary basis. Given the stance of the other parties, the Farmers' party was obviously in an exposed position. It had taken a cool attitude toward superannuation but was allied in the government with the one party supporting such a policy. In the end, the Farmers' representative on the commission presented a separate proposal criticizing both majority and minority presentations, the former for being too costly and the latter for being too vague. Instead it was proposed that folkpensions should be raised, possibly higher than already proposed, and occupational pensions left to voluntary arrangements.

Nor was the Swedish consultation process able significantly to advance discussion of superannuation policy. The fundamental lack of consensus still remaining among the well-organized groups of Swedish society was amply demonstrated in the *remiss* statements on the commission's report. The proposal for compulsory superannuation was objected to by almost all reporting bodies; apart from several county administrators, the only two statements definitely in favor were those of the LO and Cooperative Union. As usual, the minority proposal was supported by business, financial, and Conservative groups. The union movement itself was far from united behind the LO approach. The professional workers' federation and the national association of government employees rejected all such alternatives to private provision. Despite the concessions achieved in the commission, the TCO found its own executive body strongly divided and was unable to arrive at any agreed view. LO remained the vital force in promoting superannuation policy, saying that the basis was now laid for a legislative proposal in the 1957 Riksdag along the lines of the majority report. The LO statement also went to the unusual length of threatening that its support for higher folkpensions was dependent upon settlement of the superannuation issue. Unless this issue was satisfactorily and quickly resolved "then according to LO's view, the entire folkpension question would have to be reexamined with regard to the altered premises."[13]

Given the stalemate among interest groups and parties, the last mediator on superannuation policy remained the electoral process. However, neither a referendum nor two general elections gave any clear guidance during the next two years. After receiving the strongly

---

13. The LO *remiss* is in *LO Verksamhetsberättelse*, 1957, p. 254. A summary of *remiss* statements is in SOU 16 (1957).

divided *remiss* statements, the Social Democratic party leadership and parliamentary party decided in March 1957 to invoke a public referendum on superannuation.[14] For at least a year before, first the Liberals and then Conservatives and Farmers had pressed for this course. With the subsequent failure to achieve a policy consensus, the Social Democratic leadership now resigned itself to a popular vote in order to achieve some sort of denouement. The LO for its part was decidedly cool to the referendum idea, but its leadership was determined to see the issue through. Prime Minister Erlander had proposed to retire in the spring of 1957 but was now persuaded, by LO leaders among others, to stay on for the fight.

Even the format of the referendum became the subject of intense partisan conflict. Disagreements on the wording of the various alternatives were strong, but the government rejected any idea of allowing the parties to draft their own wording. Also rejected was a Conservative plan that would have allowed the voter to choose first between voluntary and obligatory approaches and, if choosing the former, then be allowed to express a preference for one of the two voluntary schemes that had been advanced. With both Conservatives and Liberals criticizing the government's abuse of power, the referendum format was finally established. An introduction on the ballot would explain that folkpensions were to be raised in successive years, and the voter could then choose one of three alternatives or vote blank. Alternative One was the commission majority's plan for compulsory state superannuation for all wage-earners. The second was the Farmers' party plan for voluntary occupational insurance with the state guaranteeing the real value of benefits up to a limited sum. The third alternative was that of the SAF, Liberals, and Conservatives advocating voluntary occupational insurance (organized by group or individual plans) through collective contract or other private agreements. With typical Swedish thoroughness, each alternative was provided with a publicly financed organization to campaign in the referendum. Chairman of the national committee for Alternative One was LO chairman Arne Geijer, although the Social Democratic party would have preferred the venerable ex-social minister, Gustav Möller; of the 121 national committee members, 50 came directly from groups associated with the LO, and 31

---

14. This was only the third occasion when Sweden used a national referendum, the first being in 1922 on prohibition and the second in 1955 on switching to driving on the right-hand side of the road.

others were active Social Democratic politicians. In a similar way, Alternative Two was closely tied with the Farmers' party organization at all levels. The third national committee, led by the head of a private insurance company, included the chairman of the employers' federation and prominent Liberal and Conservative politicians and also succeeded in involving a relatively larger number of nonpoliticians than the other two groups. The salaried workers' union remained neutral in the campaign, while the private pension organizations and salaried employees with established pension rights tended to support the third alternative. The major pensioners' interest group (RO) had originally been extremely skeptical of the LO superannuation proposals and continued to insist that any future increases in folkpensions should not be jeopardized. However, in the partisan conflict of 1957, RO sided loyally with the Social Democrats—as some saw it, to the detriment of its members' interests. In the referendum campaign the pensioners' own organizations were, at most, marginal factors.

The referendum of October 13, 1957, saw approximately 3.5 million Swedes vote on the superannuation issue, or 72.4 percent of those qualified. Potentially, it was the clearest opportunity for direct "democratic" input that any social policy question has ever had in either Britain or Sweden. The results were entirely indecisive and subject to contrary interpretations. The voting, by percentages of the total vote, was as follows:

Alternative 1	45.8
Alternative 2	15.0
Alternative 3	35.3
Blank	3.9

As recipients of the largest number of votes, the LO and the Social Democrats claimed the referendum results were a mandate for superannuation. The three bourgeois parties on the other hand claimed that a majority had voted against obligatory and for voluntary occupational pensions. Conceivably, there was an element of truth in both views.

The result of the referendum led to the resignation of the government on October 26, 1957. The Farmers' party (after the preceding summer known as the Center party) would not be the partner in a government introducing state superannuation; the Social Democrats would not agree to a government of the four democratic parties; the Center party refused overtures to form a government of the three bourgeois parties.

Thus on October 31, the Social Democrats formed a minority government. Even now attempts at compromise continued. In October the SAF initiated consultations with the LO, but these were inevitably stillborn, given the continued LO demand that occupational pensions be established through national legislation. In February 1958, discussions between the four major parties were mercifully ended, with the Liberals expressing strong desires for a compromise but pointing out that the government's insistence on a public program made the discussions pointless.

By January 1958, drafts of the government's superannuation bill were prepared and the first copies sent to members of the government, top civil servants, and—revealingly enough—LO chairman Geijer and vice chairman Steen. The Liberals saw this as an act of bad faith while the four-party deliberations were still proceeding. On February 11, two days after the party talks broke down, the cabinet formally decided in favor of a plan for state superannuation. In all essentials the government's plan corresponded to the 1957 majority proposal of the third investigatory commission. The one concession added was that any group which had already established a collective pension contract could, as a group, contract out of the state scheme but only under quite strict conditions.

If ever the Swedish opposition parties were to be united, now clearly was the time. Their good faith in the four-party talks was scarcely greater than the government's and, at the Liberals' initiative, the three bourgeois parties had assembled in December a committee of experts to develop a unified alternative to the Social Democrats' forthcoming plan. The result was largely in line with the previous Liberal proposals but insufficient to unite the three parties. In the Riksdag, Conservatives took an entirely negative line, moving for the rejection of any legislation on occupational pensions. The Center also opposed the government's proposal but argued for income security to be guaranteed entirely through folkpensions and a government commitment to higher folkpensions after the ten-year program of increases ended in 1968. The Liberals argued for their own plan of permissive legislation based upon a limited premium reserve system.

The government's proposal was laid before Parliament on April 23, 1958. Former Social Minister Ericsson pointed out that folkpensions alone were unlikely to be adequate for many years and that occupational pensions were far less costly to the state than reliance solely on folkpensions. Ominous words came from LO chairman Geijer. Any solution to the problem through the private labor market organizations was impossible since the employers were never willing to deal with the social issues involved; if the Riksdag did not approve the superannuation plan, the continued loyalty of the union movement to the goal of stable economic growth would necessarily be lessened. After three days of debate, in which all of the well-known arguments were repeated by each party, the voting found the government defeated in the Second Chamber by the united force of the three bourgeois parties, 117–111. On April 28 the cabinet announced the dissolution of the Riksdag with a new election scheduled for June 1, 1958.

The 1958 election was inevitably based almost entirely on the parties' conflicting superannuation appeals. Again however, the popular voice was indecisive. Considering the total distribution of votes between the two socialist and the three bourgeois parties, the result was virtually identical to that of 1956—50 percent of the popular vote for each side. In terms of Second Chamber composition, the bourgeois parties lost four and the socialist parties gained four seats, meaning that with a Social Democratic speaker each side had exactly 115 votes in the chamber. Both antagonists in the pension dispute could take heart. The Social Democratic vote rose 1.6 percent and the party gained five seats. Among the opposition parties, both Center and Conservative parties gained, largely at the expense of the Liberals.[15] The Liberals' attempt to find a "middle way" in pensions had led for the first time to their replacement by the Conservatives as the largest opposition party. Basically the same trends were repeated at the commune elections in September.

In response to the election results Social Democrats claimed a mandate to proceed with their superannuation proposal, Conservatives and Center parties were encouraged to declare their opposition to any form of obligatory provision, and Liberals claimed there was no mandate for any action on superannuation. At the Liberal party congress in June, the party declared its intention to hold firmly to its own pension position and the following January again refused all overtures from the Social Democrats to come over to the government's plan. The political forces were clearly set for a stark confrontation, a confrontation con-

15. The Conservatives gained 2.4 percent in the popular vote and three seats; the Center gained 3.3 percent and 13 seats; and the Liberals lost 5.6 percent and 20 seats.

tradicting the theory of supposedly bland, nonideological development of postwar social policy.

Even in the well-organized, sophisticated group relations of modern Sweden, there is no escaping the personal factor in policy development. On January 22, 1959, Ture Königson, a Liberal Riksdagsman from Göteberg, announced that he would not vote against the government's proposition. Viewed variously as a burst of treachery or statesmanship, it was in all events an explosion upon the pension scene. Königson had entered the Riksdag from a working class area of Göteberg. As a former worker himself and member of the LO, he had often been subjected to Social Democratic jibes for defecting to the Liberal party. Throughout the pension debates Königson had vigorously defended the Liberal line, had participated in drafting the Liberal resolution on the subject in 1956, and had served on the national referendum committee for Alternative 3. According to his own account, the most important thing to Königson by the beginning of 1959 was to achieve some decision on superannuation; now that the electorate had rejected the Liberal approach, even cooperation with the Social Democrats was justified in order to reach a solution.

The government plan submitted to the Riksdag on March 13, 1959, differed only slightly from its 1958 proposal. Any right to contract out would be ended in July 1961, and a somewhat reduced advance pension could be received between ages 63 and 70. The Riksdag debate on May 13 repeated the unaltered positions of each party, with Conservative and Center parties firmly opposed to any legislation and Liberals arguing vehemently for their voluntary plan. Königson was the first speaker after the luncheon break. The truly decisive point, he maintained, had occurred on June 1, 1958, when the electors repudiated the Liberal approach on superannuation and left the Social Democratic proposal as the only possible positive action. He still thought the Liberal plan was superior, but it was better that the workers had the government plan than nothing at all. Königson would not vote against the government proposition. The Liberal parliamentary party had earlier unanimously condemned Königson's behavior as "contrary to fundamental democratic doctrine."[16] Voting in the First Chamber found the government's proposal approved 81–60 on a strictly party vote. In the

16. Andra Kammar debate, May 13, 1958, p. 78. Königson was later expelled from the Liberal party in Göteberg and joined the new Christian Democratic party, a fairly conservative group emphasizing Christian principles in government and society.

Second Chamber the proposal was carried 115–114, with Königson abstaining. Thus by one vote the Swedish superannuation plan became law in 1959.

In view of the intense party feeling that had been generated, the defection of one Liberal Riksdagsman was not likely to lead to a general accommodation of views on the new superannuation policy. If the electoral process had been an uncertain guide in the development of this policy, it did play an important part in bringing about an accommodation after the policy's adoption. Immediately after the Riksdag outcome, the Conservatives made it clear that they did not accept the decision and would work for abolition of superannuation legislation, a view supported by the Center in somewhat milder language. Liberals argued that the new system should perhaps be modified but not abolished. During the following Riksdag debates and 1960 general election campaign, each party made its appeals according to these respective positions. The 1960 election results gave the Social Democrats a further increase of 1.6 percent over the 1958 special election, the Center gained .9 percent, Liberal losses were cut to .7 percent, but the Conservatives lost 3 percent of their 1958 vote. Again, although margins were small, the impact of the trend was not. All bourgeois party gains from the early 1950s, which by 1956 had given them their first popular majority since 1930, were now wiped out and the Social Democrats were again in a majority position. In the Second Chamber the socialist-bourgeois division was changed to 119–113. The Liberal leader declared that the election results showed the new superannuation system to be accepted by the people, and at the parliamentary party meetings in the autumn of 1960 both Conservative and Center parties decided to end their opposition. The Riksdag debates in 1960 demonstrated that superannuation was no longer a partisan political issue.

With state superannuation an accomplished fact, the detailed negotiations with private groups went surprisingly well. During the several years after 1959 the superannuation program was rather smoothly implemented through discussions with the groups concerned. Negotiations were held to ensure, as all investigatory commissions had recommended, that no worsening of conditions occurred for those already possessing accumulated pension rights. Salaried employees' and supervisors' unions were satisfied that their additional private pensions would provide unaltered pension conditions (such as age of retirement and transition period arrangements). Wage increases also compensated these groups for the pension benefits now received by formerly un-covered groups through state superannuation.[17] It quickly became clear to the groups concerned that contracting out of the state scheme would involve great inconveniences, and no group did so by the 1961 deadline.

By 1961 the issue of folkpensions had become removed from whatever might have been the slight postwar tendency for party counterbidding. The ten-year program of automatic increases was deemed such a success that in 1968 all parties agreed to an administrative plan for another ten-year agenda of pension increases. With this plan, the government became legally committed to a series of pension increases, improvements following not only price rises but also improvements in the real standards of industrial earnings, or a total pension increase of probably 5 to 6 percent a year. Thus there was formalized within the policy process the compensatory approach to basic pensions that had been developing over the past 50 years; adjustments in basic pensions now became a largely automatic administrative operation.

The development of state superannuation has, however, brought with it new and far-reaching policy implications scarcely imagined before. One does not overdramatize the issue in saying that for retirement purposes superannuation has made all wage-earners de facto employees of the state. The new and major policy conflict involves the uses to which the mammoth state pension fund might be put. Although seen by some as an insidious socialist-inspired plot, the funding issue is largely an unintended by-product of the superannuation plan adopted in 1959. Earlier, in 1957, the Socialist government had appointed a specialist commission to examine the complex matter of fund admin-istration in national superannuation. The commission was chaired by the head of the state bank and composed of distinguished economists, and its report in January 1958 established the principles on which the government's plan for fund administration was based. There would be not one but three pension funds: one paid into by public authorities for their employees, one for the normal employers' contributions, and a third paid into by those employers and self-employed persons who voluntarily joined the scheme. The first fund would be used to buy obligations of public authorities and the other two funds loaned out to

---

17. Employers agreed that wage increases would be based on the pension benefits salaried employees were entitled to immediately before the state scheme was implemented and would equal at least the amount previously contributed to the pensions by employers, meaning usually about an 8 percent wage increase.

the contributors (business enterprises) in the manner of any normal credit institution.[18]

From an early point in the consideration of superannuation, the state fund to be created by the proposed scheme was looked upon, particularly within the LO and its sophisticated economic staff, as a valuable device for relieving the extreme shortage of capital in the Swedish economy and increasing net community saving. But this was a secondary argument little mentioned in the political passions surrounding the issue in the 1950s. The 1959 act provided for a 20-year transition period before full benefits became payable. Since contributions began in 1960, it was obvious that there would be a large interim fund, but the magnitude of this fund seems to have been something of a surprise for most policy makers. The superannuation fund of 480 million krona at the end of 1960 had unexpectedly risen 10-fold, to 4,840 million krona by the end of 1963 and was at 19 billion krona at the end of 1967. By the end of 1973, fund assets exceeded 55 billion krona (£5.5 billion) and were projected to surpass the resources af all Swedish banking, insurance, and credit institutions by 1978.

Criticisms of this fund from Conservative and business circles were soon forthcoming. During 1963 and 1964 these groups increasingly complained that the state pension fund was diverting savings from innovative, risk-bearing sections of the economy; industrial spokesmen lamented the reduced savings and inadequate financial resources for industrial expansion. More far-reaching than these fears for private saving were arguments that vital dangers were attached to giving the government such extensive power through control of a massive credit source. The state could be a formidable force in not only directing the rate of economic development but also penetrating private industry to affect its form, scope, and activity—what some of the more sensational writers called a "backdoor to socialism." In 1964, the Conservative party leader launched a strong counterattack on the state superannuation fund and proposed instead that the unexpected accumulation of money be used to pay full benefits to the million or so persons over 50 who, under existing provisions, would receive only partial benefits. The Social Democrats responded by charging the Conservatives with deceit, inasmuch as the party which had earlier opposed the very creation of superannuation was now trying to sabotage it; not only would the Conservative proposal be unfair to those who had paid their full con-

18. SOU 4 (1958). Up to 50 percent of fund resources could be so invested.

tributions for full benefits, but it would dissipate the collective saving of the pension fund, which was needed for financing housing and other projects of social value. The view of Conservative and financial interests had changed little since the 1920s debate on funded basic pensions, but the Socialists had clearly learned more about the potential issues at stake.

Factual analysis of the situation showed that Conservative groups' claims concerning diminished private saving had little foundation. In the mid-1960s the National Institute of Economic Research demonstrated that neither the fears of the Conservatives nor hopes of the Socialists had been fulfilled in the initial years of the superannuation fund's operation. Personal saving between 1960–64 rose rather than fell; there was no clear trend in corporate savings. Net savings seem to have been neither positively nor negatively affected in these years although the composition of saving had changed (net contributions to private insurance companies clearly stagnated while other forms of collective saving rose). As for its effect on the credit market, pension fund activities had scarcely changed the pattern of lending by private credit institutions. The national pension fund was found to be a very minor factor in the borrowing needs of private enterprise and far more heavily involved in the market for government obligations, particularly in housing; the result was actually to redirect private lending from these areas and toward private enterprise. The state pension fund portfolio was found to be similar to that of a large private insurance company, with the same criteria as the private sphere—profitability and security of investment.[19] As an instrument of government direction, the superannuation fund could hardly be termed revolutionary.

In light of these findings, strong pressure now arose from the opposite direction. Labor spokesmen, particularly those connected with the LO, began criticizing the passiveness with which the superannuation fund was being used. In its major statement on the new and active labor market policy in 1961, LO and its economic experts had argued that the superannuation fund was one of the most important tools available to the government for influencing the capital market and encouraging

19. *Occasional Paper no. 4* (Stockholm: National Institute of Economic Research 1965). In 1965 the insurance companies' savings revived, and the 1959 rate of growth was again resumed in such private saving. By 1967 the net effect of the state superannuation had been to raise annual inflows of public and private savings from 1,200 million krona to 6,000 million krona. *The Economist,* July 29, 1967, p. 28.

structural rationalization in the economy. Spokesmen at the 1965 metalworkers' union congress agitated vigorously for the free placing of the state fund along the lines proposed in LO's active industrial policy. After the election of 1966, in which the Social Democrats suffered one of the greatest reverses in their history, discussion of the government's passive use of the insurance fund was at the center of the party stocktaking.[20] At the January 1967 party executive meeting, the Social Democratic leader presented the new theme of increased state activity, repeating many of the arguments used by Gösta Rehn twenty years earlier in developing his ideas for a positive labor market policy. To provide for the accelerated rationalization necessary in modern economic life, the state would have to provide a guaranteed and large supply of capital for industrial adaptation, as well as a labor market policy to ease the effect of these adaptations upon workers.

In February 1967 the Social Democratic government laid out its plans for establishing a state-owned credit institution to finance industrial rationalization and development. The finance minister made it clear that the institution would provide risk capital which commercial banks were by bank law prevented from undertaking; the minister concluded that "the existing Swedish capital market operates exclusively according to the profit criterion. The new credit institution will have an opportunity to direct lending according to its benefits to Society as a whole."[21] The initial share capital of the institution would be 5 billion krona and would allow lending up to five times that amount, making the development bank the nation's single largest credit institution. Funds would be obtained both through the bank's issuance of obligations and by use of the state superannuation fund.

Predictably enough the reaction of business and financial leaders was negative. Marc Wallenberg, Jr., chairman of the Association of Swedish Banks, urged that the law restricting private bank lending be amended and that no new state institution be established. The head of the SAF argued strongly that no such institution was necessary for the financing needs of private enterprise, especially if restrictions on foreign borrowing and corporate taxes could be reduced. Within the Riksdag,

---

20. See the article of metalworker Hans Hagnell, "Medinflytande ockso genom våra pengar"; on the 1966 reaction, see articles by Hagnell and LO economists, such as Hagnell, "Varför satter regeringen våra företrag i strykklass"; Nils Kellgren, "Regera! För Guds skill regera"; Per Holmberg, "Valet och ideerna."

21. Andra Kammar debate, February 1, 1967.

spokesmen for the three opposition parties vigorously protested against the government's proposal, arguing that the government should restrict itself to maintaining full employment rather than attempting to direct the credit market and private enterprise itself. Against opposition from the Center, Liberal, and Conservative parties, the Riksdag approved the Social Democratic proposition on July 1, 1968.

Activities of the new credit institution have scarcely lived up to the unionists' expectations. Pressures again welled up inside the LO during 1971–72 to call for more active, socially oriented use of the state superannuation fund. In accord with decisions of the 1972 congress, the LO executive urged the Social Democratic government to revise the administrative regulations and membership of the superannuation fund administration. Regulations were changed to encourage placing the fund's loans as risk-bearing, rather than passive, capital in private and public enterprises. Because this activity is expected to be "substantially more controversial" than earlier loan placings, the unionists seek a clear majority for themselves on the fund's governing board. Nor are union representatives likely to shrink from claiming complete workers' control over the fund, given the fact that employees are said to have provided the capital themselves and given the immense resources at stake (Swedish private insurance funds totaled 31 billion krona in 1970 compared to a state pension fund of 38.3 billion krona in January 1971).[22] In January 1974 the state pension fund was authorized to begin its first purchases of common stock in private companies.

Developments in Swedish superannuation are only one manifestation of dissatisfactions in many parts of the labor movement by the end of the 1960s. During the middle of that decade small, informal groups of mostly younger union officials, civil servants, academicians, and, perhaps most prominent of all, a few economists within the LO itself began to notice and study the social and economic inequalities that persisted amid complacent satisfaction with economic growth. Eventually, through a mixture of public propaganda in the press, private persuasion among Social Democratic leaders, and the inevitable investigations, the efforts of the agitators paid off; both the LO and the Social Democratic party declared the theme for domestic policy in the 1970s to be "increased equality." In pensions, superannuation, and all realms of social policy the aim is said to be not the bankrupt liberal notion of assuring the right to compete from an equal start and under equal

22. LO Kongress *Protokoll*, 1972, pp. 859 ff.

conditions, but the provision "to all persons of an equal right to live a rich and developed life." Social policy should "provide to all the same freedom to form their own lives, more through cooperation than competition . . . to provide such choice over the entire adult life as well as equal opportunities at the beginning."[23] Eventually convinced that the patterns of wage settlement have done little to reduce and probably much to increase inequality, the LO began in 1969 to negotiate tough national wage agreements in an attempt to close wage differentials both between manual and salaried/professional unions and between its own groups of better- and worse-off manual workers. The result was a rash of strikes by many who felt their income advantages diminishing and the most intense ferment since the Depression over the pros and cons of egalitarian social policy. In this setting, the issue of greater deliberate control and use of state pension funds for social purposes, far from being only a technical detail, focuses renewed attention on the uncertain line between private aims and collective welfare. And all this is happening in the supposedly bland era of welfare state consensus.

Britain

Swedish struggles over superannuation suggest that any final "solution" or consensus on the important welfare issues at stake is unlikely. Indeed, given its complex social ramifications, conscious planning in superannuation is likely to increase the scope for dissension. British experience suggests that this development is far from a uniquely Swedish phenomenon and that national adaptations can be retarded as well as advanced by the play of political power and learning. Not only are agreed conceptions about equity likely to be infrequent, transient, and nontransferable between policy areas, but self-interest is not self-defining. Strong British labor groups have not necessarily perceived the same interest in superannuation as have strong labor groups in Sweden. Nor is a party, by virtue of being labeled Conservative in Britain, necessarily led into the same position as a party labeled Conservative in Sweden. Processes by which some men adapt collective arrangements in the name of all men is far more complex than that.

As usual, a policy inheritance provided the starting point. Previous

<hr>

23. These and related arguments are set out in Socialdemokratiska Arbetareparti, *Jämlikhet*, p. 2 ff. Preliminary analyses of this renewed concern with inequality are in Karl Jungefelt, *Löneandelen och den ekonomiska utvecklingen*; Per Holmberg, *Arbete och löner i Sverige*; and Donald Hancock and Gideon Sjoberg, *Politics in the Post-Welfare State*.

pension policy served not only as a premise for Britain's departure into superannuation but as an active agent in setting the policy lessons that emerged. The basic pension format of 1925 had remained unchanged down to the Second World War: a distinct contributory system for wage earners at age 65; a meager, means-tested, noncontributory pension for those aged 70 who had become entitled before the 1925 act; and largely automatic pensions from age 70 for those who had earned contributory rights at 65. Only with the economic upturn and urban evacuations at the beginning of World War II was policy attention directed away from the mass unemployment of the interwar years and toward the gross poverty of many aged Britons. The device chosen to alleviate their distress was the already existing Unemployment Assistance Board. Rechristened simply the Assistance Board, this body was authorized in 1940 to grant means-tested "supplementary pensions," and within two years almost one-half of the 500,000 noncontributory pensioners were receiving cash assistance from this new board.

The vital policy context for British superannuation was unknowingly laid by the reaction of William Beveridge and his 1941 committee of civil servants to this ramshackle pension structure. Chapter 3 has already recounted the largely unintentional way by which the committee, in close consultation with the TUC, came to refashion the entirety of British social insurance. Since 1908 a few observers had periodically suggested an integrated, contributory insurance program but none had done so more consistently and in a more comprehensive manner than William Beveridge. It was a classic instance of influence on social policy by a man with an idea. The Beveridge Report expressed the traditional liberal aim, the "abolition of want," and nowhere was want deemed to be more severe and more hopeless than among the aged. In terms of recipients to be benefited and amounts to be spent, old age pensions were the dominant element in Beveridge's proposed system of subsistence security. The noteworthy point for present purposes is that Beveridge was committed first to the "contributory principle" and second to contributions of a particular kind.

For three decades Beveridge had argued for a universal, contributory insurance providing a minimum subsistence in old age and consolidated as far as possible into one universal contribution for provision against unemployment, disability, and widowhood. The merit of a national insurance contribution separate from general taxation lay not in the moral or financial superiority of contributory insurance but in the fact that it was the one comprehensive and administratively least objectionable way to provide a minimum of security for all. Contributions were an automatic administrative device capable of settling questions of entitlement to benefit and thus of avoiding subjective devices such as the means tests. In view of organized labor's intense and accumulated detestation of the previous decade's household means test in unemployment assistance, entitlement by contribution was now warmly supported by TUC leadership—even more warmly than labor had opposed contributory insurance for the preceding three decades. For once the British labor movement and leading expert opinion in the field were agreed on the fundamentals of a major social policy change. As Beveridge summarized in his report, "it is felt rightly and strongly that contributions irrespective of means is the strongest ground for repudiating the means test." To officials, and particularly a Treasury interested in limiting Exchequer obligations, such contributions also served as an important restraint on demands for higher expenditure; the citizen "should not be taught to regard the state as the dispenser of gifts for which no one needs to pay."[24]

The actual form of contributions was settled almost by default. Given labor's aversion to testing means, graduating national insurance contributions by level of income was dismissed as undesirable and politically impossible. A proportionate contribution, i.e. a fixed percentage of income, would require a proportionate return in benefits. Not only would such proportionalism conflict with the desire to leave voluntary private insurance unhindered but it would be superfluous to Beveridge's basically liberal desire to guarantee only a subsistence minimum. Any possibility of an earnings-related contribution in return for one, uniform (flat-rate as it is called in Britain) money benefit was regarded as completely inequitable; for the next 30 years the idea that the same benefit required the same contribution would hold sway in British social policy. All of this suggests, however, a greater degree of deliberation and canvassing of alternatives than actually occurred. In general, flat-rate (that is, the same number of shillings) contributions

24. Quotations are taken from Cmd. 6404, pp. 12, 108. That there was immense continuity in Beveridge's views can be gathered from his 1924 pamphlet, *Insurance for All and Everything*, p. 8. There he argued for "welding all of the schemes into one harmonious system" attacking the five major risks to income; such a comprehensive contributory insurance would prevent political parties from competing in "easy promises of higher doles," raise more money than could otherwise be extracted through taxation, and offer "manifest administrative advantages in defining the classes to benefit."

and flat-rate benefits were imported into the postwar British welfare state because that is the way things had been done since 1911.

Neither the Beveridge plan nor its legislative manifestation in the National Insurance Act of 1946 succeeded in guaranteeing a subsistence income to the elderly or in obviating their reliance on means-tested cash relief from the Assistance Board. Not only were the data used by Beveridge for defining his subsistence level somewhat out of date, but the rates eventually introduced by the Labor government in 1946 were, if anything, below the income standard he proposed. The 31 percent increase in rates intended to compensate for price changes since 1938 (the income survey year used by Beveridge) was in fact based on an obsolete price index, which accounted for only about 60 percent of the real cost-of-living changes since that time.

Probably the most important constraint on subsistence pensions from National Insurance sprang from the budgetary ceilings bargained with the Treasury. As in Sweden, memories of post-World War I economic dislocations played an important part in setting the limits on old age pensions, but the British Treasury was far more, if not entirely, successful in holding the government to such a policy. A government spending ceiling of £100 million per year for pensions during the first five years was bargained out between Beveridge and Keynes, in return for which Keynes agreed to support the Beveridge Report from within the Treasury. By this arrangement subsistence rates of benefit in pensions would be paid, but only after 20 years of contribution. As Beveridge expressed this compromise, economic conditions after the war and the need to conserve resources made it "unreasonable" to give immediate subsistence pensions or "be in any way lavish" with those not in need or contributing.[25] Moreover Beveridge's own inclinations favored a long 20-year transition period to build up funds to pay for contributory pensions. In the interim, needy pensioners approaching retirement age would have to rely on public assistance.

The concrete policies introduced in 1946 were the result of internal government analysis, bargaining, and consultation with the TUC. The one exception to this generalization and the one substantial change in the Labor government's proposals was, as in Sweden, a result of back-bench pressure from the government's own parliamentary Labor party. Rather than imposing a 20-year delay, full pension rates were to be

25. Cmd. 6404, para. 204, 236, 240, 241. The deal with the Treasury is discussed in Beveridge, *Power and Influence*, pp. 308–09.

made immediately payable to those insured since 1925; for those still contributing, full pension rights would be earned in 1958 after ten years' contribution. British pension policy had always been equivocal on whether to pay pensions from an income-earning, funded scheme or to use current contributions for current pensions; the 1946 back-bench amendment created a shorter transition period and ensured that an unfunded upsurge of expenditure would be on the political agenda in the late 1950s.

In Britain and Sweden back-bench pressure for major policy change proved to be a fleeting postwar incident, applicable only as the overall structure of pension policy was being fixed for the next decade. Despite prevailing assumptions that pensions have been particularly subject to back-bench political maneuvering, or to "pensioneering" through party competition, or to left-wing pressure in the Labor party, actual policy development reveals little such adaptability. What has usually been left to the influence of partisan maneuvering has been the timing of pension increases by the government of the day. Of the eight separate pension increases between 1946 and 1970, six occurred during or immediately preceding a general election campaign. But the absolute base from which increases were made has been little affected by partisan competition and, despite general protestations from both parties favoring larger increases in the abstract, party counterbidding does not appear to have accelerated the rate of increase. The postwar record of British old age pensions has been one of occasional ad hoc increases to give some approximate compensation for price and wage increases.

The question of any automatic cost-of-living adjustment mechanism was rejected by the 1945 Labor government, largely (as in Sweden) because of an official reluctance to institute what seemed an abdication to forces of inflation. As in Sweden, the immediate postwar years revealed the government's inability to control rising prices. Continuing inflation actually left the National Insurance benefit with less purchasing power than the prewar unemployment assistance benefit. But unlike Sweden, with a Treasury more firmly imposing ceilings on further government expenditure and a government unwilling to increase flat-rate contributions, the British Labor government took little action. Only in 1955, under the Conservatives, was the real value of pensions restored to the 1946 level and then less because of changes in party or interest group power than because of a freer spending climate following the post-Korean decline in defense expenditures. Pension increases in 1958,

1961, 1963, 1965, and 1967 began to give to pensioners some part of the improvements in real standards. By and large, decisions on pension increases have been fairly mechanical decisions taken to adjust pensions every two or three years for the intervening price changes; less often, when the Treasury view of economic circumstances permitted, the increases gave some real improvement in benefits.

The fundamental constraints on British pension policy arose less from an inherent fund of Treasury power and more from the structure of Beveridge flat-rate policy operating in a political world. Pension increases depended on increases in flat-rate contributions. Here was a burden for lower-paid workers which no government contemplated lightly. The contrast to the Swedish policy context is revealing. The contributory principle (which as in Sweden justified distinct national insurance contributions on the "psychological" grounds of entitlement to benefit) could be and was carried through far more extensively among British policy makers who were still recalling the means test of the thirties. While the proportion of postwar pension costs paid from general tax revenues in Sweden has varied between one-half and three-fourths, it has not risen above one-fifth in Britain and usually has been much less. Even that portion paid by Swedish contributions has been based on a levy proportional (generally less than 5 percent) to income rather than the flat-rate sum of British contributions. Although Britain has made a considerable effort (given its lagging rate of economic growth), Swedish postwar pensions started from a higher relative base (26 percent versus 19 percent of average industrial wages in 1948) and have outpaced British pensions, both in terms of keeping up with increases in cost of living and average earnings, and in providing a minimum subsistence budget.[26] As a result, while the proportion of aged receiving public assistance in Sweden has rarely been over (and usually under) 5 percent since the beginning of the 1950s, the proportion in Britain has never been under 20 percent and often over 25 percent (though it must be borne in mind that rent assistance included in British public assistance is often provided under a separate housing program in Sweden).

Although the fundamental limitation in British pensions stemmed from the flat-rate structure of the national insurance system itself, this was not a situation that the Treasury was averse to using in order to

26. Comparative data can be found in Paul Fisher, "Minimum Old Age Pension," and Elmer, *Folkpensioneringen*, Tables V6 and IIIB.

limit Exchequer obligations. During the first years of operation, financial constraints were eased as British National Insurance accumulated a surplus from Beveridge's overestimation of postwar unemployment. Subsequently, attempts were made to use the existing contributory structure to finance those benefit increases that did occur. In the ten years after the 1946 act, the British Exchequer actually reduced its proportionate expenditure by deliberately transferring costs to private contributions, with the familiar rationale that relying on this contributory foundation would restrain demands for future pension increases.[27] Although both the Labor party and TUC could invariably be found protesting against each increase in employees' National Insurance contributions, Exchequer payments in the 1950s were consistently below the level projected at the time of each pension increase.

Charging contributions in excess of actuarial contributions could only postpone the onset of an annual deficit of expenditure over receipts. In 1958 the number of British pensioners was substantially increased by 400,000 late-age entrants who, under the 1946 formula, were allowed to draw full pensions after ten years of contribution; in addition, of course, each previous pension increase had created an increased financial obligation for which pensioners could not be expected to contribute retroactively. With this financial pressure on existing pension policy, administrators began thinking about, or at least became potentially receptive to, the idea of changing from the Beveridge flat-rate straitjacket to an approach varying contributions and benefits with earnings. Such financial considerations were a more important conditioning factor for state superannuation in Britain than in Sweden largely because of the inherited Beveridge policy.

The innovating force behind the introduction of British superannuation came not, however, from the government nor—as in Sweden—from pressures within the union movement, but from a group of Labor party intellectuals. Prior to this time the Conservative government and party had demonstrated little interest in superannuation, apart from a desire to limit rising expenditures. The major policy investigation of the period was the 1954 Phillips committee, which was composed large-

---

27. The Treasury rationale was expressed in the comments of the financial secretary to the Treasury, *Parliamentary Debates* (Commons), April 26, 1951. The proportion of the actuarial contribution paid by employers and employees was 73 percent under Beveridge's proposal, 78 percent in the 1946 act, 91 percent in the 1951 act, 97 percent in 1954, and 102 percent in the 1957 act. See reports of the government actuary, Cmd. 6730, Cmd. 8212, Cmd. 9332, Cmnd. 294.

ly of Conservatives. This investigation commended private pension plans since, by such means, "there need be no eventual burden on the rest of the community"; the committee even dismissed the idea of contributory subsistence pensions.[28] Organizations of the elderly were scarcely any more constructively involved in the emerging policy.

In 1940, that is, about the same time as in Sweden, the first interest group of British old age pensioners had organized into the National Federation of Old Age Pensions Associations. Unlike its Swedish counterparts, the British organization was largely a creation of pensioners themselves and constituted a nonpartisan body willing to support any politician who took up the cause of higher pensions. From its meager beginnings in Manchester, the association has grown to somewhat less than 300,000 members (of some seven million state pensioners). A fairly small and amateur body, the National Federation is composed largely of local associations of the elderly and has always limited itself to the simple demand for higher pension rates; although occasionally supplying graphic publicity on the poverty of the aged, by all accounts but its own the association has played little substantial part in postwar policy developments.

The impetus behind British superannuation policy came from a group of socialist academics and, through them, a Labor party initiative that the Conservative government could not ignore. As professor of social administration at the London School of Economics, Richard Titmuss had by the mid-1950s attracted a group of students who were socialist, intellectually acute, and dedicated to the study and improvement of British social policy. Foremost of these students were Brian Abel-Smith and Peter Townsend. Detailed evidence coming to light by this time suggested that in the postwar era of full employment the key reason for poverty had become not unemployment but old age.[29] Incensed by the negativism of the Phillips committee, the Titmuss group's foremost policy concern became old age pensions. Through a

28. Cmd. 9333, para. 212. The committee's controversial recommendations, which were never acted upon, would have raised the pension age from 65 to 68 as well as increased contributions, the insurance principle being a device that encouraged "social discipline" (para. 167).

29. Seebohm Rowntree and G. R. Lavers for example found that old age as a cause of all poverty in York had increased from 15 to 68 percent. *Poverty and the Welfare State*, p. 35. The development of the academics' thought can be traced in Brian Abel-Smith, *The Reform of Social Security*, Fabian pamphlet, 1953; Abel-Smith and Peter Townsend, *New Pensions for Old*; Townsend and Dorothy Wedderburn, *The Aged in the Welfare State*.

series of conversations, informal seminars, and some of the first systematic investigations of the actual conditions of the aged, their conviction grew that the existing Beveridge system was not only inadequate but, by limiting benefits to those flat-rate contributions which the lowest wage-earners could afford, constituted a brake on the development of adequate pensions.

In 1955 Titmuss and Abel-Smith, as leading experts in the field, had consulted with the Conservative government and Labor party on the costs of national health insurance. Amid growing dissatisfaction with what was considered to be the Conservative government's retrenchment in social security, a Labor party study committee was established in the same year; Titmuss, Abel-Smith, and Townsend served as advisors. The three academics were quickly able to convince the committee that the Beveridge flat-rate concept led to a dead end for social policy. A persuasive case was presented to the effect that "two nations" of aged were developing, one including the recipients of flat-rate pensions who were often forced onto public assistance, and another of some 6.5 million better-off persons covered by private occupational pensions—who were also receiving a vast £100 million government subsidy in the form of tax concessions. Given the opposition of Conservative government and Treasury to any increased use of general taxation, only earnings-related contributions could provide the necessary resources for substantial improvement in pensions without burdening the lowest paid; only earnings-related contributions had a serious chance of bringing benefits into line with prices and earnings. Meetings of the Labor study group were, however, somewhat chaotic affairs, held once a week in the late afternoon at the House of Commons. Neither the MPs nor the Labor party retained any staff with the resources or expertise to develop concrete policy proposals; after gaining general consent to the earnings-related principle, Titmuss volunteered to draft a specific scheme that could form a basis for action by the next Labor government.

The superannuation plan which resulted was largely the work of Titmuss, Abel-Smith, and Townsend in 1955–56, with some aid from the Labor party research department at Transport House. Innovative as the turn to earnings-relation was, socialist planners still carried forward two fundamental premises of existing policy. First, it was accepted as virtually self-evident that earnings-related contributions would have to be accompanied by earnings-related benefits if popular support was to be won. A fair return on a fair contribution was an idea deemed to be deeply imbedded within both the union movement and population at large. Second, and somewhat inconsistent with the first premise, pension policy should retain as its primary goal the elimination of poverty among the aged. Hence not only a fair return but also some redistribution to the lower-paid and existing pensioners would have to be built into the plan. There was nothing uniquely British in this tension between individual equity and increased equality, but planning on superannuation in Britain differed from that in Sweden because it had fallen to men dedicated to upholding a large measure of redistributive justice within the state plan.

Until the intervention of the Titmuss group, the Labor party's position was ambivalent on the entire pension issue. Strong as they were, forces of party competition and parliamentary opposition were insufficient to crystallize thought into agreed policy proposals. One important section of the Labor party, led by Aneurin Bevan, was seeking to move in a more purely socialist direction, and at the 1955 party congress Bevan returned to the ancient party call for "free" pensions financed by Exchequer and employers. TUC leaders remained insistent, as they had since the trauma of the 1930s, that contributory principles had to be retained to prevent any possibility of means testing; in 1955 the TUC had also reaffirmed its commitment to equal benefits and equal contributions for all. So divided was the labor movement that it fought the May 1955 election without any agreed pension policy.

The policy analysis eventually uniting the Labor party was scarcely the cerebration of abstract and isolated intellectuals. From the onset of their work the academics made deliberate efforts to involve and gain the support of important and potentially important Labor politicians and leaders, including possible future chancellors of the exchequer such as Harold Wilson. The most fervent political recruit to the superannuation cause was Richard Crossman, then a young Labor MP and leader-writer for the *Daily Mirror*. Working closely with the Titmuss group, the former university don was schooled in the ways of earnings-related pensions and, with the immense enthusiasm of a new convert, soon replaced the more restrained chairman of the Labor party study group. Twelve years later, as secretary of state for the social services, Crossman would finally try to bring this learning to fruition.

If the Titmuss plan was to have any chance of being accepted by the Labor party, the most important converts to the new approach would have to come from within the trade union movement. Unlike LO's dominant leadership position on superannuation in Sweden, the British TUC was at most a reluctant supporter of the proposed policy departure, preferring instead to emphasize the need for continuing increases in flat-rate benefits. Through Beveridge's personal contacts with the TUC leadership (contacts developed during their membership on the 1930s Unemployment Insurance Statutory Committee), the TUC had been closely involved in the development of the Beveridge plan; unionist thinking on social policy had advanced little since that time. In part, the hesitancy toward the Titmuss plan seems to have stemmed from TUC fears of endangering certain union pension plans, not least those affecting union officials. But in large part the TUC reluctance was bred by the organization's lack of expertise and a basic ignorance within the organization itself. In contrast to the LO's strong analytic capability, the TUC Social Insurance Committee since its founding in the 1930s has normally consisted only of one underpaid head and one or two amateur assistants.[30] Union bargaining with employers has concentrated on wages, not retirement plans, and in the mid-1950s the TUC approach toward earnings-related state provision reflected the same apathy. The process of amending the unions' traditional commitment to flat-rate equality was carried out in long and painstaking sessions between Titmuss and the TUC staff. An invaluable ally was gained in the person of Alfred Roberts, head of the TUC Social Insurance Committee. Having spent years in frustrated attempts to gain higher benefits without inflicting crippling contributions on lower-paid workers, Roberts quickly became convinced of the advantages of the new approach in reducing reliance on Treasury goodwill for each meager pension increase.

The importance of TUC sanction and the reeducation of its leadership was illustrated when the Labor party Home Policy Committee first considered the academics' scheme and decided that an issue so fundamental would have to be backed by the TUC before it had any chance of approval by the party's National Executive Committee. After extensive discussion and questioning, the TUC General Council in March 1957 accepted Roberts's advice and gave the go-ahead to the pension plan. On April 17, the Labor party executive also accepted the basic principles of national superannuation, saying that general sup-

30. The qualitatively different effort of the Swedish LO is described in Rudolf Meidner, "The Research Department of the Swedish Confederation of Trade Unions."

port of the TUC had been achieved but that discussion was proceeding on details.

It was approximately at this time—the beginning of 1957—and in response to what had already become known of Labor planning, that Conservative ministers and senior civil servants began to give serious consideration to possible pension alternatives. At one of the prime minister's weekend conferences at Chequers the first week of May 1957, the superannuation issue was discussed in detail, with the aid it seems of a complete draft of the Labor party plan. On the basis of an official analysis, the Labor plan was seen to be "actuarially unsound," inasmuch as it was vague on the extent of its self-financing and likely to add to inflation. Nor, apart from the information minister, did Conservative ministers feel that the Labor plan required any immediate response from the government. Labor party activity may have focused Conservative attention on superannuation but it hardly precipitated an effort to outbid the Opposition for popular support. Instead, the prime minister and ministers instructed their experts to proceed unhurriedly along different lines, completing a plan designed by administrators to relieve the emerging deficit in the National Insurance fund and provide encouragement to private occupational pensions.[31] As with the Labor party, the point of departure for the new proposals was a reaction against a policy that was proving inadequate; at this early date an earnings-related approach—although largely for financial rather than antipoverty reasons—was unanimously accepted as more adequate than flat rates.

Six days before the proposed publication date (May 19, 1957) of the Labor superannuation plan, sufficient information had leaked for most newspapers to be discussing the proposal in detail. Here we can consider only the broadest outline of what was a very complex and detailed Labor proposal.[32] In the first place, and apparently the most important issue to the TUC in the plan's formative stages, the existing flat-rate pension for current pensioners would be increased 10 shillings, to three pounds a week. In addition, there would be added an earnings-related portion designed eventually to give the average worker a total pension of one-half of his average earnings. The employee would pay 3 percent

31. For partial published accounts of the meeting, see *Financial Times*, May 8, 1957; *News Chronicle*, May 8, 1957; *The Observer*, May 12, 1957; *Daily Telegraph*, May 15, 1957; and *Yorkshire Post*, October 15, 1958.

32. Labour Party, *National Superannuation*.

of his yearly earnings, his employer would pay 5 percent of the earnings of each employee, and the Exchequer would contribute 2 percent of total earnings (or about 24 percent of total contributions) to the national superannuation fund. In addition to the immediate increase in flat-rate pensions, redistributive aims were also to be achieved by a rather complicated formula designed to ensure a pension of at least half earnings for the average worker, somewhat less for those with above average earnings, and somewhat more for those below. Although the Titmuss group was originally opposed to any contracting out from state superannuation, party leaders' counsels prevailed. Without a chance for those already possessing good pension rights to contract out, the plan would arouse immense middle class hostility as well as confirm TUC fears that union pension plans would be ruined by the state scheme's absorption of new entrants. It was therefore decided to allow approved private occupational schemes to continue if they fulfilled certain desirable criteria, including transferable pension rights and benefits comparable to the proposed national superannuation.

As in Sweden, the basic method for financing state superannuation was a modified pay-as-you-go system, which at maturity would maintain an equilibrium between current income and outgo. But the fact that during a transitional period contributions would be collected in full while few benefits were being paid meant the accumulation of a large interim fund. Estimated fund size was £800 million in 1960 (when the plan would begin), £4,000 million in 1970, and £6,000 million in 1980. This fund would have been relatively the same magnitude as in Sweden, that is, slightly more than three times the size of current expenditures in the tenth year of the plan. Unlike their Swedish counterparts, however, British planners made it clear from the outset that an active use of the state fund was contemplated. The Titmuss group spoke of "boldly investing" superannuation funds as an essential part of the plan, and the Labor party statement concluded by saying that the trustees of the pension fund "should have the same opportunities to carry out profitable investment of their funds as private insurance companies." In Britain this meant not only holding government obligations and long-term bonds, but active investment in equities to ensure a good return on fund assets. Special regulations would also keep superannuation benefits adjusted for changes in average earnings during the period of contribution and adjusted for price changes once pensions were received.

Although finally ending in vigorous controversy, the Swedish policy-making process had first exhausted all possibilities for compromise; in Britain these possibilities had scarcely been explored among parties or interest groups. British superannuation immediately burst into public discussion as a fully partisan issue. In most quarters the fundamental point—changing from flat-rate to wage-related contributions and benefits—was accepted. But this basic issue was quickly lost from view in the flood of partisan and interest group criticism. Following the Labor announcement, Conservative party chairman Oliver Poole condemned the plan as "half-pie in the sky rather than half-pay on retirement"; many would never get half pay and many others would do so only in A.D. 2000. Once again the specter of nationalization of insurance and other industries was raised: Poole accused Labor of sinisterly planning the piecemeal takeover of industry through socialistic investment of the pension fund. Nationalization was quickly picked up as the basic theme of Conservative party spokesmen. On May 18, the chancellor of the exchequer claimed the Labor party's purpose to be one of collecting public contributions in order "to buy off bits of British industry." On May 20, Minister of Labor Ian Macleod called the plan a "wild attack on private insurance companies . . . by the party which always intended to nationalize the insurance companies." The minister of pensions on May 29 claimed that the plan was "above all a socialist plan . . . of nationalization by takeover bid." Finally on June 1, Prime Minister Harold Macmillan made his first speech on the issue, attacking Labor's plan as "nationalization by stealth." Within four days of the publication of the plan, £2.4 million were wiped off the value of Prudential Insurance Company shares on the London Exchange.

Industrial and financial interest groups shared in the shouting match. The British Chambers of Commerce, representing some 56,000 firms, condemned the plan as inflationary, likely to devastate savings through its redistributive bias, and an oppressive restriction on the continued growth of private pensions. Other employers' organizations, such as the National Association of British Manufacturers and Federation of British Industries, were somewhat more restrained in their comments but nevertheless hostile. The most considered reaction came from the insurance industry. Private pension insurance for employees is generally of two types in Britain: a pension plan internally administered by the company with its own independent fund, or an individual contract with one of the private insurance companies (life offices). The National

Association of Pension Funds (NAPF) since 1917 has represented the interests of the former and the Life Offices Association (LOA), the private insurance companies. NAPF was fairly inactive in the 1950s and in reaction to the Labor plan did little more than issue a public statement on the need to protect existing pension funds.

By far the most important, well-organized, and well-staffed interest group concerned with superannuation was the Life Offices Association. To many LOA member companies, the provision of private pensions was a major part of their insurance business and an especially fertile source of accumulated funds for investment. Covering firms that handled 99 percent of all ordinary life insurance business, it was the LOA that launched the most comprehensive and informed attack upon the Labor plan. The Labor party plan, it was said, would discourage saving and stimulate inflation; because of miscalculations by the Titmuss group, running costs would be approximately twice those anticipated; the fact that higher paid workers would get less from their contributions than the lower paid was said to be an "unreasonable [attempt] to force one section of workers to subsidize others." Finally, recalling the earlier socialist proposals for the "mutualization" of the insurance industry, the LOA concluded that the greatest danger of all was that the state "will cast covetous eyes on insurance company assets." Apart from left-wing members of the Labor party, the LOA was in fact the only important advocate for maintaining the existing flat-rate system (although on grounds of preserving opportunities for private insurance rather than socialist equality); any state pension scheme should be strictly limited to ensuring that the basic needs of the elderly were met "with the same benefits for everyone."[33]

Framers of the Labor plan may have intended their original statements about using state superannuation funds for "bold" investment as merely a bargaining counter which could eventually be traded for closer regulation of insurance companies' assets. If so, the vast amount of concern and publicity concerning Labor's supposedly sinister intentions clearly showed it to be a counterproductive gambit. There was some irony in the fact that Labor party leader Hugh Gaitskell, who firmly supported the superannuation plan and its break with established

33. Life Offices Association, "The Pensions Problem." Reactions of the Conservative party and industrial groups are in *The Times*, May 16; *Daily Telegraph*, May 16; *Daily Telegraph*, May 21; *Yorkshire Post*, May 30; *Sunday Times*, May 19, June 2; and *The Guardian*, June 25 (all 1957).

socialist ideas, should now be forced to spend much of his time denying any intention of government takeovers—and to have to do so precisely as he was leading the Labor movement away from its traditional commitment to nationalization.

Even in late 1957 the British union movement could scarcely be said to be enthusiastic about national superannuation. A number of trade unions, including building trade operatives, railwaymen, engineers, and electrical workers' representatives, attacked the published plan, either for fear of its effect on their own pension plans or because of the plan's insufficient state financing. In its *Annual Report* on August 20, 1957, the TUC expressed a certain coolness in its endorsement of Labor's plan by saying simply that it was "sufficiently attractive in general to justify detailed examination." The 1957 TUC *Annual Report* went on to stress the traditional TUC view that superannuation concerned only a "future policy" and that the major aim of the TUC would remain immediate and substantial increases in national insurance benefits. The negativism that distinguished much of British from Swedish union leadership was well expressed in July, when the Transport and General Workers Union (comprising one-seventh of the TUC membership and a powerful force in the organization) criticized the proposed use of pension funds to buy equities as a "blood transfusion for private enterprise." At the September TUC national conference Sir Alfred Roberts vigorously defended the plan as "the greatest single contribution in our history towards social wellbeing for those in the evening of their lives." Roberts's arguments expressed well the rationale which, however slowly, was leading the TUC to alter its traditional view. Ever since the war, Roberts said, the unions had brought pressure to bear on the successive governments for substantial increases in flat-rate benefits, "but these efforts had failed," and increased reliance by the old on national assistance was the result. The General Council "had come to the conclusion that so long as they stick to the flat-rate system they could not hope to secure a proper minimum level of pension benefits." At the end of the TUC debate, a motion by Frank Cousins of the Transport and General Workers' Union was unanimously accepted, welcoming "in general principle" the superannuation plan but demanding too that the government should make an immediate and substantial increase in existing pension rates; the "welcoming" of superannuation was given third place in the motion.

Even the restrained TUC endorsement seems to have been received with a certain relief by superannuation's promoters in the Labor party. Yet the Labor party conference the first day of October 1957 showed that traditional party views on pensions did not change easily. An otherwise apathetic conference was stirred to life by a series of constituency resolutions calling for the rejection of the contributory superannuation plan in favor of substantially increased, tax-financed, flat-rate pensions. Investment plans for the fund were condemned as "perpetuating capitalism almost to infinity." What was more, earnings-relation would simply carry over the inequality of working life into old age; as one speaker of Bevanite sympathies concluded, "these are not socialist proposals." But the party leadership had become convinced of the practical merits of the new approach and, by all accounts, Crossman's rebuttal speech for the party executive was a personal triumph. Any proposed increase in tax-financed, flat-rate pensions would require an unwelcome rise in income tax as the first act of a Labor chancellor, but the "real reason" such a course was rejected was that, as the TUC argued, the contributory insurance principle safeguarded the pensioner from any future chancellor's efforts to cut pensions or apply a means test. Though investment in private companies was not exactly socialist, there was no reason the community should not gain returns on its money the same way as did private insurance companies. Finally, to the old socialist argument that earnings-related pensions would perpetuate inequality, Crossman replied that "it is really for the trade unions to decide whether wages should be equal or unequal and so long as trade unions are prepared to have unequal wages it is a little tough to ask for all pensions to be equal." Moreover, the plan was definitely weighted in favor of the lower paid. In the end, the Labor conference gave overwhelming support to the executive's and Crossman's desire "to get the scheme started after the first two years of a Labor government."

In this way the most prominent upholder of flat-rate national insurance and the uniform equality that it implied—the Labor party—became reoriented in a new policy direction. There was nothing inevitable about the Labor party's particular view before or after this change. Without a concentrated analytic effort and considerable ventures in persuasion, British labor would undoubtedly have remained oblivious to superannuation. Throughout, electoral influences had played no direct part in the policy-making process, and anticipation of electoral payoff seems to have been an afterthought. During the Labor party conference there were indications that some felt national superannuation to be an "election winner." A Gallup poll two weeks after the plan's publication seemed to bear out this feeling, showing three-quarters of all voters aware of Labor's scheme: 45 percent approving, 16 percent disapproving, and 16 percent unsure. Even 34 percent of Conservatives approved, compared to the 29 percent who disapproved. Nevertheless, any lingering hopes that popular pressure would fuel the superannuation issue were soon to be disappointed, as they had been in Sweden.

In accordance with the decision of Conservative ministers in May 1957, Ministry of Pension officials had continued working on a Conservative plan for earnings-related pensions. Labor and Conservative plans shared at least one common point of departure: both were reacting against inherent limitations in the previous flat-rate insurance policy. Beyond this premise, however, the two approaches differed substantially. The Labor movement and its academic mentors laid primary emphasis on the failure of flat-rateism to provide adequate subsistence benefits. As the introduction to Labor's superannuation statement said, "the next Labor Government must abolish poverty among our old people." If the motivating thrust of Labor's plan was poverty, that of the Conservatives was the health of state finances. Earnings-relation in social insurance offered the only feasible way of meeting an emerging deficit in the National Insurance fund. The Conservative dilemma was clear: to find a plan extensive enough to meet state financial needs and limited enough to leave private insurance schemes unhindered. Unlike Labor planners, the ministry held informal consultations with LOA, NAPF, and other interested business groups, doing so well before the government White Paper appeared for public discussion. Available evidence suggests, however, that these consultations concerned only technical points of implementation.

The Conservative government's proposal finally appeared publicly on October 15, 1958.[34] The Boyd-Carpenter plan (named for the energetic Conservative minister of pensions) provided for contributions of 4.5 percent on earnings between £9 and £15 a week, thus leaving those below £9 on the flat-rate pensions and severely limiting any tapping of higher incomes (average earnings in Britain at the time were approximately £13 a week). By comparison, Labor's proposal required 3 percent contributions on all earnings up to £50. Pension benefits under the Conservative plan were to be meager at best, yielding at the full £15 contribution level only £1 for every £2–7–0 contributed and

34. Cmnd. 538.

making no provision to protect pensions against future wage or price increases. Fairly generous terms for contracting out would be allowed to private pension programs containing transferable benefits equivalent to the maximum of the state plan; it was estimated that 2.5 million employees eligible would contract out. In a separate act earlier in the year, the government had already raised the existing flat-rate pensions from 40 to 50 shillings in what was the first significant increase in the real value of old age pensions since the 1946 act.

There can be little doubt that the primary consideration in the structuring of the government's plan was the desire to restore the soundness of the existing National Insurance fund without an increased Exchequer contribution. In introducing the plan, the minister of pensions announced that the purpose of the proposal "is to put National Insurance on a sound financial basis and to introduce the social concept of graduated contributions and pensions for those who do not have the advantages of being in private schemes." In a subsequent speech to the Office Management Association, the minister put the point more bluntly:

> No responsible government could leave National Insurance as it was, since it was running into irretrievable financial deficits. . . . It would be a tragedy if anything checked [private pension insurance's] development. . . . As a matter of social philosophy it was wrong to compel people to do what they had shown they could do for themselves. The real function of the state was to bring along the laggards.[35]

Figures used in the preparation of the government plan showed that despite the higher flat-rate contributions introduced in 1954 and 1958, expenditure in 1961 would exceed the income of the National Insurance fund by £144 million and in 1981 by £428. Under the Conservative plan, the vast bulk of earnings-related contributions would go toward financing this deficit in flat-rate pensions, rather than toward graduated pensions, and thus help reduce the Exchequer commitment.

Although orientations of Labor and Conservative plans clearly differed, there should be no mistaking that fundamental policy departure which had emerged from the adaptations of both parties. The comments of Beveridge, now 80, revealed how far outdistanced the assumptions behind his earlier policy contributions had been. Labor's plan was

35. Reported in the *Financial Times*, June 30, 1960.

"not a serious contribution. . . . State provision should be at a basic level above which private insurance operated. . . . The Individual should share some responsibility for himself and not be spoon-fed by the Welfare State." The Conservative plan was similarly inadequate, and Beveridge returned to advocating higher flat-rate pensions at a subsistence level.[36]

The public debate on the Conservatives' proposed policy was understandably divided. All of the formerly hostile organizations—LOA, NAPF, British Chambers of Commerce—offered their cautious approval, while Labor launched a vigorous attack on "this shoddy copy" of its own proposal. Nothing in this public debate changed the substance of the policy put forward. After a heated parliamentary debate, the Conservative plan was passed without major alteration in November 1958.

A general election in 1959 provided an opportunity for popular participation to affect the development of superannuation policy. In introducing the Labor party's election manifesto, Gaitskell declared that pensions would be the major domestic election issue. Labor pledged that one of its first acts in office would be to introduce a 60 shilling pension, which would be revised yearly for price changes, and that national superannuation plans would be quickly brought into effect. The Conservative party during the election emphasized its record of past pension increases, attacked the Labor superannuation plan as financially ruinous, but made little of its new earnings-related plan. To the existing pensioners, R.A. Butler pledged for his party, "you will take your share in the rising prosperity of the country." Labor's proposed superannuation policy can hardly be said to have proved a major election asset; election results showed the Conservative popular vote at 49 percent compared to 50 percent in 1955, while Labor's dropped from 46 to 44 percent, with the Liberals gaining the difference. Conservatives retained their parliamentary majority with 58 percent of the seats. In a post-election review Crossman admitted that perhaps "our scheme last time was too complicated to understand."[37]

Following the hyperactivity of the late 1950s, pension policy entered

36. *Parliamentary Debates* (Lords), December 4, 1958, and *Yorkshire Post*, November 30, 1957.
37. *The Times*, October 4, 1960. Accounts of the campaign treatment of pensions are contained in *The Guardian*, September 22, 1959; and *The Times*, September 24, September 25, and October 1, 1959.

a quiescent phase for most of the 1960s. Within the Labor party, a special study group led by Titmuss and Abel-Smith developed far more comprehensive plans for putting all British social insurance on an earnings-related basis, as well as introducing a form of minimum income guarantee to obviate most public assistance. Throughout the Labor party policy deliberations, the question of poverty provided the basic orienting force. Policy makers inside government remained preoccupied with implementing the Boyd-Carpenter scheme.

The Conservative government's new pension plan, which came into effect in April 1961, not only avoided hindering the development of private occupational pensions but provided a positive fillip to the entire private sector. Pension fund experts and brokers generally seem to have counseled their clients, particularly those firms with a high proportion of workers earning over £12 a week, to contract out. By April 1961 the number of contracted-out employees was 4.1 million rather than the 2.5 million originally estimated by the government; all of the state's own civil service employees, including the Ministry of Pensions workers, contracted out of the state's limited superannuation plan. Although the minister of pensions originally reported that extensive contracting out would not affect the government scheme "to any great extent," financial strains in 1963 required an increase in the ceiling on contribution-bearing income from £15 to £18, and by the end of 1967, 5.3 million employees had been contracted out. The accounts in that year showed the financial importance of the new earnings-related contributions in relieving obligations incurred under the separate, basic pension scheme. Of total graduated contributions of £42 million, only £5 million went to graduated pensions and by far the greater part of the remainder was devoted to meeting the deficit in flat-rate pension accounts. In the meantime, private occupational pension business expanded vigorously; under the spur of new business, insurance shares on the 1961 stock market rose 31 percent while the all-share index remained unchanged.

Labor party spokesmen continued their periodic attacks on "the Tory pension swindle" and made superannuation the linchpin of comprehensive reform in social insurance. Employers were warned that the Labor superannuation plan "would be very difficult to contract out of." As for the existing graduated pension scheme, one of a Labor government's "first decisions would be an amending act dealing with contributions, benefits, and the rate of Exchequer contribution."[38] In the buildup to the 1964 general election, both Conservative and Labor parties endorsed the concept of earnings-related social insurance, but only Labor offered a distinctively new pension plan. The results gave the Labor party its first victory since 1951, but the evidence available shows superannuation to have played little part. Immediately prior to the election, two-thirds of those intending to vote Labor identified that party's pension policy as "increase them," and only 2 percent knew of the party's superannuation scheme.

As usual, British civil servants had closely followed the policy statements of both parties and, well before the 1964 election, experts brought into the Ministry of Pensions and National Insurance were at work developing an outline of alternatives for earnings-related pensions upon which an incoming government could act. However, the new Labor government did not act immediately on superannuation as had been expected. In part this was due to the narrow parliamentary majority of three produced by the election, but even after the 1966 election provided a comfortable majority, the Labor government hesitated on its promised pension plan. Another two years were lost as the policy makers grappled unsuccessfully with the immense administrative problems of the Labor party's proposed minimum income guarantee and with recurring balance of payments crises. Undoubtedly the major reason for delay in superannuation stemmed from Britain's delicate economic position and the Treasury's firm refusal to see any such massive financial scheme undertaken at a time of economic crisis. Only with revived economic hopes following the 1967 devaluation and the arrival of Crossman as head of the newly unified Department of Health and Social Security (with Crossman's colleague from Labor study group days, Abel-Smith, brought in as a senior economic advisor) did political steam build up behind the superannuation issue. In January 1969, the Labor government's new pension proposal was finally announced, to come into effect at the beginning of 1972.[39]

The real world and policy makers' perceptions of it had moved on since 1957 and *National Superannuation*. With memories of the previous furor, the Labor proposal carefully avoided any mention of "bold investment" for the superannuation fund. Even assuming no contract-

38. *Daily Herald*, September 30, 1963; the preceding quotations concerning Labor's pension plans are taken from the *Daily Mail*, April 12, 1961; and *The Times*, October 2, 1962.
39. Cmnd. 3883, 1969.

ing-out, the fund would be but a fraction of the size foreseen in 1958; and the assumed rate of return (3 percent) suggested that, far from being actively invested, superannuation monies would be tied up in government obligations. But lessons learned since 1957, largely uncalculated though they were, went far beyond administration. The key theme in relations between state and private insurance had become "partnership." Understanding British superannuation policy requires a closer look at how this altered perspective was politically acquired.

One important measure of this search for partnership was the degree of consultation undertaken as the Labor government prepared its superannuation plan. Crossman went much farther than any of his Conservative counterparts in seeking early consultations with the groups concerned. Formally a White Paper is designed to serve as the basis of policy discussions with public groups. However the government had begun confidential consultations on superannuation with employer, insurance, and other interest groups almost a year before the appearance of the White Paper in January 1969. Besides the government's reluctance to revive the intense clashes of the late 1950s, the strong expansion of private pensions since that time made an accommodation with the private sector even more important. Many employers had used the savings derived from contracting out of the Boyd-Carpenter scheme to start their own pension plans, so that between 1956 and 1967 the membership in private pension plans rose by 50 percent to cover one-half of all employed persons. This mass of contractual relationships could not be ignored by the Labor government.

Yet consultation would have mattered little if an intellectual breakthrough had not occurred and been assimilated to make partnership in superannuation possible. Since the mid-fifties two problems and one dilemma had bedeviled the business groups, civil servants, and party experts interested in superannuation. The first problem was that though private occupational pensions could not do everything they had done too much to be ignored. Second, decent flat-rate pensions could not continue to be financed by flat-rate contributions without severely penalizing those earning low incomes. Thus the dilemma: state superannuation terms comparable to private plans would draw in those who were out, crippling the private occupational pensions and their crucial contribution to national savings. But state terms not comparable would leave out too many who should be in—crippling the financial intake necessary to improve flat-rate pensions and to give concessions for those already nearing retirement. Moreover any subsequent improvement in state benefit automatically reneged on the terms by which some had contracted out. What to do?

A solution was hit upon as early as 1959—namely, to deny the distinction between being totally in or totally out of a state scheme. By allowing only partial contracting out, or "abatement," the state scheme could provide and improve its benefits without cramping the ability of private occupational pension schemes to provide and improve their own benefits. Under abatement, a certain percentage of state pension would be given up for a correspondingly reduced contribution to the state scheme, with the condition that the employer must provide a pension of at least the same size. The gap between reduced contribution rate (say 1.5 percent) and reduced benefit (say 5 percent) was the economic breathing space that would make private schemes profitable or unprofitable.

The abatement idea was created by a senior representative of the insurance companies' interests, and through a series of informal talks within the close network of London actuaries, the idea gradually spread among experts. Abatement was not a panacea but it did offer some hope of settling the basic dilemma behind state/private relations on superannuation. Persuading the insurance interest groups was a good deal more difficult, but civil servants concerned were quick to seize on the new approach. After initial talks between the creator of abatement and Ministry of Pension officials, little more was heard, but two years later civil servants commended the concept to the insurance interests before they themselves had accepted the idea. This in turn assisted the efforts of those trying to turn the organization around from the inside. By 1965 the major insurance interest group had accepted abatement as its own.

In essence, debates behind the acceptance of abatement within these interest groups revolved not around self-interest per se but an altered conception of self-interest. In 1957 this interest had been expressed as flatly negative; state activity should be strictly limited to flat-rate provision. Yet before the Labor government could formulate its own plan, the Life Offices Association (LOA) had been persuaded to the view that its member companies' interests would be served by a partnership that accepted a state role in providing earnings-related pensions.[40] In the

40. The results of this new view are set out in the LOA pamphlet, *Progress by Partnership* (London: Life Offices Association, 1969); and a paper by one of LOA's experts, C. S. Lyons,

first place, it was clear that significant gaps in coverage would always exist if earnings-related pensions were restricted to private plans. In the second place, abatement could allow state and private superannuation to exist side by side without detriment to each other. Complete contracting-out, as opposed to abatement, might actually create difficulties for private occupational pension plans, particularly if they were forced to match the benefits of a state scheme incorporating the present flat-rate pensions or containing any guaranteed protection against inflation. At least as important, a *positive* abatement rate of contributions over benefits could be of financial benefit to the private pension sector, as well as reduce further the size and dangers of the state fund (by replacing part of the surplus income in the state scheme with equivalent contributions to privately funded schemes).

Abatement was taken almost as axiomatic during preparation of superannuation policy inside Whitehall, and by the time Labor's plan appeared almost all relevant interest groups of employers, unionists, and pension industry had absorbed the new approach. Controversy there was, but this concerned the terms, not the fact of abatement itself. Essentially this meant that, with virtually no public debate, a policy consensus had grown that the state had a legitimate claim to provide an immense insurance program well above any minimum requirements of Beveridge-type subsistence.

The 1969 Labor government plan related all contributions and benefits to earnings. In return for a straight percentage contribution on individual earnings up to one and one-half times the national average, a wholly earnings-based pension would be provided: redistributive aims were incorporated in the plan by weighting lower earnings (up to one-half national average earnings) with a 60 percent pension return and higher earnings with only a 25 percent pension return. All benefits would be inflation-proofed by a guaranteed adjustment every two years. Although the plan did not include increases for existing pensioners, these too were guaranteed an annual adjustment at least in line with price changes; this was of course a formalization of de facto procedures of the previous decade. Only twenty years of earnings-related contributions would be required for the full pension return, thus offering a particularly favorable bargain to those currently middle-aged. As an addi-

---

"The Case for Earnings Relation in State Pensions" (London: mimeographed, 1968). Private pensions, for example, would seldom cover casual workers or small firm employees, and the private plans could not ensure future purchasing power of pensions.

tion to rather than a substitute for these state provisions, private pension schemes would be allowed to reduce contributions and benefits in return for higher levels of provision on top of the state plan. It was complicated no doubt, but Labor's redistributive aims would be advanced, Beveridge flat-rateism well and finally overturned, and a working relationship established between private insurance and large-scale state provision.

After the long consultation process, initial reactions by employers and private pension interest groups to the January 1969 White Paper were largely favorable, with LOA spokesmen saying that the plan "looks realistic in principle." For the next ten months the government and interest groups engaged in a series of long and complex negotiations on the precise rates of abatement the state plan should offer. In November 1969 the Labor government finally offered abatement terms of one percent in pension in return for 1.3 percent in contribution reduction, a figure rejected by the LOA and employers, who continued to hold out vehemently for a one percent and 1.5 percent formula. Only now did a number of unions begin taking superannuation seriously, leading to still further delays as Crossman tried to win over his own party supporters. A number of unions including local government officers, railwaymen, white collar staff associations—in short unionists with already good private pension schemes—condemned the Crossman plan as an infringement. Despite these objections the Labor government's plan was finally introduced in January 1970 and began moving inexorably toward passage in the House of Commons. Computer facilities and programs stood ready to undertake the mammoth social bookkeeping involved in superannuation.

That Britons are not now living under Labor's superannuation policy can only be put down to political accident. As the bill moved toward its final reading before passage, Prime Minister Wilson declared a general election for June 1970. In a few more months Crossman's plan would have committed administrative resources to an extent that it would have been almost impossible for any future government to reverse. The election was called and conducted with little reference to superannuation; Labor's new plan, far from being an election winner, probably had little positive impact on either the party leader or voters.[41]

41. Harold Wilson, *The Labour Government, 1964–1970.* Following the government's superannuation announcement in January 1969, and amid comprehensive publicity and press coverage, polls found voting intentions were 32 percent Labor and 55 percent Conservative, compared to 33 percent Labor and 49 percent Conservative immediately before the an-

The election returned the Conservatives to power with no clear idea of a pension policy. In this sense, the loss of Labor's plan was accidental. But the more important point is the context of policy development which made superannuation vulnerable to such an accident. Whereas Swedish socialists had called elections specifically to enact superannuation, leaders of British socialism condoned an election that directly endangered its passage. Superannuation was not considered sufficiently important to merit high priority among the Labor party leadership, either after victory in 1964 and 1966 or before an election in 1970. And party uninterest was in turn a function—at least compared to Sweden— of apathy and misunderstanding in the British union movement, so much so that union hostility was itself an important cause of the delay that led to the plan's demise. For the second time since the 1950s it fell to the Labor party to propose on superannuation and the Conservative party to dispose.

The Conservative party in opposition cannot be said to have been particularly alert or informed about superannuation. Out of office and without the informational resources of government ministries, the party had to rely largely on its own inadequately staffed research department; not only did the Conservatives lack academic experts for policy analysis such as Labor had in the mid-fifties, but party figures took far less interest in the entire pension issue. Serious work on a superannuation alternative started only with the appearance of the Labor government's plan at the beginning of 1969. At an initial meeting of the shadow cabinet, skepticism was expressed about the cost and inflationary effect of the Crossman plan. In the end it was agreed simply that the party would work to ensure that private occupational pensions were not impaired. Meanwhile, a study group of MPs and several outside experts continued working on an alternative plan.

The proposal eventually produced by the Conservatives in office[42] affirmed several features of the policy consensus that had gradually and without deliberation developed since the 1950s. The purchasing power of existing pensions was to be adjusted for price changes every two years, as had become normal political practice. Earnings-related rather than

---

nouncement. The Opinion Research Center concluded that superannuation's impact was negligible and that the important issues were the government's mishandling of the postal strike and the Opposition leader's speech on immigration. Opinion Research Center, *Reports*, February 1969.

42. "Strategy for Pensions," Cmnd. 4755.

flat-rate contributions were necessary to finance pensions. Above all, the Conservatives recognized a state responsibility for extending provision beyond flat-rate subsistence and providing wage-related pensions to those without adequate private pensions. This crucial third point was not the result of spontaneous sociological enlightenment. During the late fifties and again in the late sixties, Conservative leaders had approached the LOA and other insurance interests to explore the possibility of relying solely on compulsory private insurance. Insurance interest groups were quick to veto the idea. Welcome though the first years' profits would have been, insurance industry leadership was sufficiently enlightened in viewing its self-interest to realize that the greed of marginal companies could easily lead to abuse. Increasing state controls would inevitably follow and destroy what was and is an exceptional degree of freedom from state regulation. Conservative policy makers concluded that some small state reserve scheme would be necessary for those outside adequate private plans.

It would be misleading however to discount the fundamental changes introduced by the Conservatives' own approach to superannuation policy. Partly because the new Conservative leadership was eager to encourage private enterprise and competition, partly because Conservative isolation from the preceding policy debates had left them less conditioned by its assumptions, the new British superannuation plan incorporated two unique features. The policy result was direct, relatively clear, and more far-reaching than probably anyone in the Conservative leadership realized. In the first place, superannuation was to be treated as completely separate from the questions of redistribution and antipoverty which had inspired Labor planning since the 1950s. The existing flat-rate pensions would continue but now be financed by earnings-related contributions (5.25 percent from employees and 7.25 percent from employers on earnings between one-quarter and one and one-half times the national average). We have seen that before the 1908 Pension Act, through Beveridge in the forties and socialist pension planners in the fifties and sixties, it had been regarded as politically impossible and inequitable to make people pay differential amounts without getting differential benefits in return. Now, to keep social considerations from getting mixed up with the hard business facts of superannuation, the Conservatives made explicit what had been concealed in the previous decade of Boyd-Carpenter pensions: people were to be taxed in accord with their earnings to pay for equal benefits.

With little fanfare and almost no public notice, the formerly impolitic course of overtly increasing intake from higher earners to finance better flat-rate pensions for all was used in September 1971 and October 1972 to improve the cash value of basic pensions by a third.

The second unique feature of the Conservative proposal was operating superannuation on a strictly commercial basis. No question here of abatement or contributions from the national exchequer. The government's earnings-related pension program would be a discreet business, sharing the market with private insurance and supporting itself financially from its own contributed fund and returns earned on that fund. The Conservatives' assumption was that most people will acquire coverage through private occupational pensions, with the state reserve program left for that residue falling outside private insurance. There can be no doubt that, as first intended, the Conservative plan is less generous than the Crossman proposal. Forty years of contribution is required for full benefit, rather than Labor's foreshortened 20 years; widows' benefits are halved; and benefits as a proportion of earnings tend to be lower than under Labor's plan. Though the immediate impact of the Conservatives' proposed superannuation is highly limited, its policy implications are immense.

Basic pensions have finally been freed from the straitjacket of having either to increase flat-rate contributions (and hurting the lowest earners) or to spring a few extra shillings from the Treasury. Largely without meaning to, the British Conservatives have introduced the intrinsically more redistributive approach (that is, graduating contributions but not benefits) vetoed by Labor in the fifties and implemented by Swedish Socialists in the forties. Moreover, the state will also enter the private pension business as a full participant. Undistorted by social objectives, it is now value for money that counts in both state and private plans.

Although publicly welcoming the opportunities for growth, private insurance interests have also had private doubts. Earlier, in endorsing the abatement approach, the Life Offices Association summed up the implications of a totally separate state scheme in its booklet, *Progress Through Partnership:* "A state scheme covering a limited range of employees would be in direct competition with occupational schemes in such matters as the scale and range of benefits, the rate of contribution and the method of dealing with rises in earnings levels or cost of living. It would become the yardstick by which all occupational schemes would have to be measured." Conservatives have now introduced just such a yardstick.

Even assuming that the government has not underestimated gaps in existing occupational coverage and the inclination of some employers to shift their pension headaches completely to the state, there are to be an estimated seven million policyholders in the state insurance company, or over a quarter of the labor force. Welfare issues in the future are likely to center around not only the performance of private schemes but also how equitably and adequately state beneficiaries are being treated vis à vis any number of reference standards among the privately insured. Moreover, the state's commercially run scheme requires a permanent, immense, and performance-managed fund if beneficiaries are to receive a reasonable return. On the assumption of seven million state policyholders, the fund will have £200–250 million to invest every year and in 25 years will be worth £5,000 million (compared to the total of £1,500 million of new funds currently invested each year by the private occupational pensions). Since Labor's 1957 plan for "boldly investing" its fund created howls about back-door nationalization, there had been general agreement that any state fund would be small, temporary, and conservatively managed. According to the Conservative White Paper, the pension fund will not be able to buy over 5 to 10 percent of voting capital in any company. Otherwise, the pension board investment managers will be free to invest as they wish "to secure the best pensions for the scheme members." Welfare policy making can therefore be expected to involve not only the rate of return to state beneficiaries but, as in Sweden, the use of state power and workers' contributions throughout the credit market. Conservative business sense may thus turn out to be as radical in its policy potential as any socialist concern with equality.

Experience with superannuation policy leaves no doubt that the important welfare issues surrounding state provision for old age are far from settled in either Britain or Sweden. British superannuation proposals in 1970 claimed to be addressing the greatest social problem of the second half of the twentieth century: "How to abolish poverty in old age."[43] It was almost exactly a century since Canon Blackley had begun drafting a "National Provident Insurance Scheme" to deal with the same question. Many of the basic problems encountered in modern social policy were equally familiar and intractable to nineteenth-

43. *Parliamentary Debates* (Commons), January 19, 1970.

century policy makers. What level of collective provision should the citizen expect? How can the state provide a dignified form of support that meets human needs? Who will share the cost? Where will the line be drawn between state and private provision? The fundamental continuity behind social policy choices remains strong. Yet there has also been change. Consciously or unconsciously, choices have been made and amended through time. New standards have been set, though often imperfectly. State pension aims have been transformed from incidental income supplements, to basic subsistence, to wage-related guarantees for living standards. Simple notions of relieving distress among a class of the aged have carried ever wider ramifications for social policy making. Between the reaction against the poor law and the state use of collective savings for social management an important distance in public policy has been traversed. We are now in a better position to assess the political process through which change and continuity have been accommodated.

6 Social Policy and Political Learning

Democracy? Don't understand the word—something to do with decisions.

Working class respondent

Social politics is enveloped in paradox. Universal adult suffrage, competitive democratic parties, and socialist movements have all arrived and persisted without producing the massive government giveaways and social expropriations anticipated in the nineteenth century. Yet social policy has also undergone immense sea changes. Deterrent relief for a pauper caste has given way to devices to encourage working class saving, which have shaded in turn into collective provisions as a right of citizenship. Standards have grown from temporary subsistence dispensations into more comprehensive minimum levels of support, and from there into guarantees of individual living standards. These lines of development have not been straight, simple, or fully accomplished, but the changes are nonetheless real for that. Certainly it would seem that the results achieved in British and Swedish provision for unemployment and old age compare favorably to the practice of other nations; the two countries' achievements seem great even in relation to the idealistic and consciously planned income-maintenance aims used to help justify the violence of the 1917 Russian Revolution.[1] It is time to return to our original questions and take stock of British and Swedish experiences with income maintenance policies. How have these immense and largely indeliberate changes been brought about?

The Agents of Policy Development

In the first chapter I suggested that the development of modern social policy might be seen as the natural by-product of economic development, the outcome of popular electoral control of leaders and party competition, the result of interest group pressures, or the emer-

---

1. For two of the few detailed international comparisons, see Gaston V. Rimlinger, *Welfare Policy and Industrialization in Europe, America and Russia*; and Arnold Heidenheimer, "The Politics of Public Education, Health and Welfare in the USA and Western Europe," *British Journal of Political Science*, 3 (1973).

gence and growth of administrative expertise. The term "or" is used advisedly inasmuch as we also suggested that no one of these emphases necessarily excludes any other. Before considering possible interrelations, it will be useful to summarize the accumulated evidence for each interpretation, recalling that any generalizations are drawn from only a limited sample of social policies. In such an exercise there is sometimes an unfortunate tendency for each discipline, or specialty within a discipline, to develop a proprietary interest in a variable, taking it as a matter of honor to prove that its variable is most important or at the very least is not cast into the outer darkness of statistical insignificance.

As it turns out, the development of social policy is sufficiently complex and varied that almost any of these loyalties to particular variables can be accommodated to some degree; the more interesting problem is to see how they might fit together.

Socioeconomic Development

In a fundamental sense it is true that the social policies discussed here reflect the course of socioeconomic development in Britain and Sweden during the last 200 years. In both nations, policy grew out of a historically unprecedented acceleration in agricultural output, industrial product, and population growth. In both, a primary demographic security had gradually infiltrated social life without conscious planning; profligate creation was no longer necessary to counter the profligate destruction of disease, famine, and plague. In both nations modern social policies were initiated amid broad-based and substantial improvement in real incomes. Despite all of the qualifications that must be made, the welfare policies discussed are basically the accompaniments of affluence rather than poverty. If sheer destitution were the stimulus, then surely the fourteenth or seventeenth centuries would have been more likely candidates than the twentieth for major policy innovation.

Periods of economic growth had, of course, occurred before without generating anything comparable to modern social policies. What shaped contemporary policy responses was not some abstract phenomenon of economic growth but the substantive nature of this change. Of paramount importance was the altered human condition itself. The consequence of increased reliance on the isolated wage-earner was an increased vulnerability to interruption in those wages, particularly through unemployment or old age. In modern industrial society, wage insecurity implied a comprehensive economic insecurity which, with the poor law looming in the background, implicated the family's entire social position. Human insecurity had, more than ever before, become cumulative and wage-based. Men were moving not from a pastoral security to urban insecurity but from one mix of security and insecurity to another mix. The problem of income maintenance gave concrete expression to the paradox that in modern society men could simultaneously become more autonomous and more interdependent, more wealthy and more vulnerable. Like the need to defer wants in favor of industrial investment, income maintenance issues sprang from the nature of economic growth itself rather than capitalism or any particular form of economic organization.[2] Techniques of income maintenance policy were and are compatible with the range of market, mixed, and centralized economies.

In addition to a cumulative income vulnerability, modern economic growth involved a sustained course of essentially cyclical fluctuations. Sustained growth naturally made better provision for the future seem a more realistic proposition. But equally important, periodic swings of the business cycle encouraged the tendency for both workers and the state to set aside funds in good times to prepare for the bad—an elementary form of insurance. Such pulses in the rate of economic improvement also provided particularly noticeable stimuli to policy makers' searches for ways of relieving the results of these recurring and apparently inevitable phenomena. In both Britain and Sweden, economic downturns (as in the 1890s, 1905–07, 1919–21, the 1930s depression, and the 1959 recession) or anticipations of such downturns (as after the Second World War) occasioned far more concentrated attention to social policy alternatives than occurred in more normal times. Above all, exposure to recurring economic crises made it much more difficult to contend that those who became unemployed and destitute during these times did so as a result of personal failings. New social policies at the turn of the century were typically justified precisely on the grounds of separating the cyclically unemployed and distressed from "ordinary paupers."

In these fundamentals, therefore, one can reasonably argue that the crucial forces shaping policy have been social movements largely beyond the control of politicians.[3] This is not to suggest, however, that

2. Similar phenomena are analyzed in Emile Durkheim, *The Division of Labor in Society*, and Karl de Schweinitz, Jr., *Industrialization and Democracy*.

3. See for example George Kitson Clark, *The Making of Victorian England*.

the substantive policies discussed here have been simply automatic by-products of socioeconomic development. Aggregate relationships between economic level and social security programs are, as suggested in Chapter 1, far from simple, and the international diffusion of new programs has not followed the straight path signposted by economic development. In examining Sweden's experience in the nineteenth century as a "poor" nation, the most obvious feature in the policy record is that regardless of a substantial lag behind Britain's industrial and economic development, effective agitation for old age pensions and unemployment insurance began at approximately the same time in both nations. Apart from a largely fortuitous delay in Swedish unemployment insurance, the first enactments of these social policies also occurred almost simultaneously. If anything, by the time of World War I Sweden led Britain in terms of its approach to social insurance as a right of citizenship.

A second reason for rejecting any one-to-one correlation between socioeconomic development and social policy is that the former has been largely indeterminate for substantive policy contents. Growing rural proletarianization in Sweden and an increased number of urban wage-earners in Britain suggested that the old poor law policy in each nation would come under growing strain; it did not determine that the policy response would be social insurance. Economic recession at the end of the First World War and continuing high unemployment suggested that some policy response would be forthcoming, but it did not dictate a government policy either of retrenchment and unemployment insurance expedients as in Britain or of Keynesian expansionism as in Sweden. The modern era of full employment cast doubts on the adequacy of policies of guaranteed minimums; it did not determine that unemployment insurance should become a tool of an integrated labor market policy in Sweden but not in Britain or that superannuation should evolve in the form it has taken in each country.

Anyone willing to follow the detailed twists and turns of contemporary social policy cannot fail to be impressed by the ever changing kaleidoscope of new problems overlooked and/or created by each preceding "solution." If the experience of the last century is any guide, continued economic growth, far from generating a self-corrective spread of well-being, will raise more issues of state social policy than it settles. Spurs to workers' thrift have only led to new concerns for a satisfactory minimum income in old age; a universal pension floor has prepared the way for arguments not only on the level and standards for upgrading the floor but on guarantees of individual living standards, which in turn foreshadow renewed interest in balances between individual equity and increased social equality. Socioeconomic development is not the end but the beginning of social policy choices.

The fact of economic development is little help in accounting for policy leads and lags, for substantive policy contents, and for ever emerging policy problems with indeterminate outcomes. In short, there is no valid either/or choice—political versus socioeconomic variables—in understanding the growth of modern social policy. The match is a non-contest. Through politics, society has been supplied with the effective perceptions and substantive responses for adapting collective arrangements to meet the problems raised by economic growth. Apart from the policy process there were no "problems," only conditions. The grand choice between economic and political explanations turns out to be little more than a difference in analytic levels, a difference between the socioeconomic preconditions and the political creation and adjustment of concrete policies. The distinction, in terms of Aristotle's classification of causes, is between a material cause—socioeconomic factors as the underlying conditions calling forth a policy response—and an efficient cause—political factors as the energizing agents by which specific responses have been made.[4] To appreciate the process underlying this efficient causation we must return to the detailed evidence on elections, parties, interest groups, and administrators.

Elections

To say that elections have had a direct impact on policy would seem to imply the following corollaries: (1) that a policy choice has been presented to the electorate; (2) that the electorate has responded in an identifiable way; and (3) that those elected have then acted in line with this response. The presumption in the interpretation of social policy is, of course, that the electorate has responded positively rather than negatively to proposed extensions of state welfare policies. The evidence suggests, however, that elections were of little direct significance to the programs studied. Consider, for example, the treatment of old age

---

4. To complete the classification, the "formal cause" could be said to be the functionalist's view of systemic adaptation to an outside stimulus, and the "final cause" to be the parliamentary enactment and administrative implementation of new legislation, along the lines of the older institutionalists' approach.

pensions, now the largest social expenditure in each national government's budget. In most elections, the question of old age provision has given rise to no clear alternative presentations to the electorate. More often the important policy departures have been made subsequent to an election in which the victor was noncommittal on the subject. In the second place, where a distinctive electoral appeal has been made on this issue, the advocate as often as not has lost in the election. Finally, there have also been a number of significant instances where the policy advocate, although elected, has taken no action, or action contrary to the promised policy.

As one would expect, pensions did become an election issue earlier in Britain than in Sweden (as in the 1892 and 1895 general elections). Although the various and largely unofficial election promises seem to have aroused a good deal of public attention, they led to few practical results from those elected. As often as not, the major pension advocates lost the election (1892, 1900) and at the crucial election of 1906 the subject of state pensions was carefully avoided by responsible spokesmen of the party which eventually instituted the first law; electoral success of the Labor pension advocates seems to have been due less to their advocacy and more to a tactical electoral arrangment with the Liberals. In Sweden, the course of events leading to the first universal pensions was well under way before the major extension of suffrage in 1909, and there was no direct action by the Liberal government that was elected after making the first pension promises in 1905. Nor was there very much indication in the Liberal appeal of 1911 that the world's first universal pension system would be introduced two years later.

In later periods the same lack of a direct relationship between elections and social policy expansion held true in each nation. In Britain the major electoral choice between the generous, noncontributory pensions proposed by Labor and the insurance-based approach of the Conservatives was rendered meaningless when the Labor government of 1924 repudiated its own prior claims. The new Conservative government which took over and instituted the change to a contributory policy made no different pension appeal in its 1924 victory than it had in its 1923 defeat; it had in fact appointed what proved to be the crucial administrative investigation only after its defeat in 1923. In Sweden the numerous succession of elections and governments during the 1920s effected no change in pension policy at all. The Social Democrats under

Möller's influence were by 1926 awakening to the inadequacy of existing provisions, but in the 1924 election that had given them office the party leaders had scarcely mentioned pensions. In 1932 the Social Democrats made no different social insurance appeal in winning than they had in losing overwhelmingly in 1928. The 1936 Swedish general election stands out precisely because it is the only clear case in which the pension issue (cost-of-living areas) was directly affected by an electoral outcome. In the more recent development of superannuation in Britain and Sweden, initial electoral reactions to the Labor and Social Democratic parties' plans have been either negative (1959, 1970 in Britain, 1956 in Sweden) or indecisive (1957, 1958 in Sweden).

Much the same can be said of the electoral impact on income maintenance for the unemployed. In the first stages, the innovative Liberal unemployment insurance plans played no discernible part in the relevant British elections but were developed administratively only after the party gained office. Despite persistent appeals by the Swedish Social Democrats in the 1920s for the introduction of unemployment insurance, the electoral results were either negative or failed to lead to action when the party did obtain office. The election of 1932, which led the Socialists back into power and preceded Sweden's introduction of unemployment insurance, was actually characterized by a reversal of the party's emphasis on unemployment insurance in favor of a new Keynesian "crisis policy." During the same period in Britain, the crucial changes in unemployment insurance began only after an election in which neither unemployment insurance nor any other social reform was emphasized in the Coalition appeal (1918); Labor promises on unemployment in 1924 were not kept; and the Liberals' new Keynesian approach in 1929 aroused no decisive support. Undoubtedly the most clear-cut election involving unemployment insurance policy occurred in 1931 between a National government bent on economizing and a Labor party which by popular account had vastly increased unemployment insurance expenditures. The result was a massive defeat for the advocates of the expanded social policy—including the former Labor ministers considered responsible. In 1945 Beveridge himself lost his parliamentary seat following his proposed restructuring of the social services, and in 1964, despite election promises for more general welfare improvements, it was the almost unmentioned graduated unemployment insurance that was given priority by the Labor government. To put it mildly, the social policies studied have clearly been much more than an accumulating sum of commands issued by democratic electorates and subsequently put into effect.

The indirect impact of elections seems more important, but hardly the predominant motive power in the course of policy development. We have noted at various points how individual politicians—from Joseph Chamberlain pushing Conservatives toward pensions in 1886 to Richard Crossman trying to sell superannuation to Labor in 1956— have operated with rather vague assumptions that such proposals would have popular, electoral appeal. Rarely, however, does the evidence allow us to say that a policy has been consciously designed to evoke anticipated electoral payoffs. Policy making has been emmeshed in the anticipated reactions of others but at least four major points illustrate the limited scope of anticipated electoral accountability as a spur to social policy expansions.

In the first place, elections per se have not been required for the operation of a psychological responsiveness to popular needs. In predemocratic Sweden there was clearly a form of "defensive modernization" that occurred in the period before mass suffrage and well-organized parties. Social insurance was seen as a palliative technique to prevent social unrest and diminish the appeal of socialism. Nowhere was this defensiveness better expressed than in what is now recognized as the source document of Swedish social policy, Hedin's Riksdag motion of 1884. Even where there were elections, policy could develop with little relation to electoral aims but with similar aims of social stabilization. The dramatic expansion and corruption of unemployment insurance during the 1920s in Britain was only marginally concerned with elections; the popular force energizing policy makers had much more to do with immediate and vivid fears of popular violence if nothing were done.

It would be as easy as it would be wrongheaded to slip over from the recognition that policy has been used for indirect purposes of social control to the conclusion that all social policy development has been a series of sops to the lower classes, to keep them in line or at least off the streets. While Sweden was facing the rise of an industrial working class, Britain had already met this situation without instituting the social policies discussed. Equally significant, any indirect popular impact through policy makers' anticipations was by no means entirely in the one "democratic" direction favorable to extensions of social policy. One of the more persistent themes in the deliberations on pensions in

Britain, for example, was the fear that popular pressures would in the future lead to disastrous extensions of whatever modest first step was taken. Because of such anticipations, inaction or scaled-down proposals were the rule in the 1890s, during the drafting of the 1908 act, and during deliberations on the possibility of expanding pensions during the First World War. If "defensive modernization" was more common in predemocratic Sweden, such "anticipatory stagnation" was more common in democratic Britain.

In more recent times, policy adjustments resulting from indirect popular influence have frequently been aimed at minimizing the unpopularity of what was to be done, not currying public favor. Often the anticipation of potential democratic reactions has served to restrict rather than extend state social policy. Early British fears of workers' reactions to contributory insurance, for example, only presaged a later assumption that constricted pension improvement for at least a generation—the idea that it was politically impossible to charge higher contributions to some people without providing them with higher benefits at the same time. Many Swedish Social Democrats in the mid-fifties demonstrated similar misgivings about possible public hostility to comprehensive superannuation proposals. Debates on unemployment in both countries during the 1920s were typically concerned with finding the least objectionable way of expressing policy presumptions that were going to be carried out in any event. In the end, much of what has been specifically accomplished in state provision for old age and unemployment has depended on calculations of what the public would stomach rather than what it demanded.[5]

Finally, any interpretation of policy expansion in terms of anticipated electoral or popular reward is seriously limited by the fact that policy makers in neither country have been able to judge with assurance what policy alternatives would in fact be popular. It may be that Liberals in the first decade of this century did believe their new policies for pensions and unemployment insurance would reap a rich return of popular favor. It was a cruel miscalculation in each case. In both Britain and Sweden, the one party most obviously responsible for instituting the change from poor law provision to pensions and unemployment

5. My interpretation of the evidence is similar to Paul Smith's findings that earlier social reforms, 1866–80, were little related to party programs or attempts to win working-class favor and more clearly "shaped by results of formal inquiry, public opinion pressure and the promptings of civil servants." Paul Smith, *Disraelian Conservatism and Social Reform*, p. 322.

insurance was thoroughly beaten within a decade of introducing such measures. The governments which enacted the first old age pensions and made a beginning in unemployment insurance were the last clearly Liberal governments to hold office in either nation. Reforms in social policy may have occasionally been the high road to public favor but at least as often they have been a shortcut to the political graveyard.

In summary, elections appear to have had little direct impact on social policy and even the power indirectly asserted through policy makers' anticipations of popular reactions seems difficult to define and identify. Forms of self-styled responsiveness operated without electoral accountability; fears of popular enthusiasm could stagnate as well as advance policy development; public feelings were often considered to be substantially negative toward the policy in preparation; at other times public reactions could not be anticipated with any assurance at all. Elections, past and forthcoming, were one of many forces that sensitized policy makers to the need for action. Exactly what to do was another matter.

Parties

By suggesting the restricted part that electoral decisions seem to have played in most policy changes, the preceding section has also indicated the limited usefulness of seeing parties as strictly electoral devices— passive petitioners to and executors of a defined electoral will. Parties have not served as the unfettered transmission lines between public demand and government social policy, partly because those responsible for the latter were not interested in or could not understand the messages but mostly because the public was sending no clear signals on concrete social policies. Another approach more strictly oriented to relations among parties themselves argues that it is their competition, rather than their articulated public directives, that serves as the proximate source of important policies. In some sense of the term, parties "produce" policy alternatives.

Our evidence yields little support for this view if it is taken to mean that particular policies have been outgrowths of party contests. Certainly little in the record of policies studied here shows that alternatives evolved by the competing and relatively well-organized European parties have been the basis for concrete policies eventually adopted by the state, as some reformers of U.S. parties would lead us to believe.[6] In terms of political parties, the significant contrast between Britain and Sweden was during the last two decades of the nineteenth century and involved the question of old age pensions. In neither nation was a positive pension policy adopted. There was an early tendency in Britain for individual Conservatives and Liberals to offer competing claims, but a decade of such claims led to little practical result in British pensions (with fruitless recriminations in 1895 from the Conservative opposition against a Liberal government's inaction and in 1898 from a Liberal opposition against a Conservative government's inaction; the process no doubt reached its nadir in 1899 with the dispute on whether Chamberlain had "promised" or only "proposed" old age pensions). The result of party competition was a higher level of public partisanship in Britain but little clear effect on the creation or adjustment of policies.

Particularly in the current postwar period, it has been popular to explain expansions of social policy in terms of parties counterbidding for the votes of client groups. "Pensioneering," as the term goes in Britain, can scarcely be said to be any more prominent now than it was at the beginning of the century. And in any event, when they have occurred, counterbids have been more in the nature of marginal adjustments in the timing of increases and rates of benefit than major policy changes. Much of the scope for even this competition has been restricted by the institution of automatic benefit adjustments to price indices in each nation. Where major issues have been involved, for example in the recent reintroduction of unemployment insurance as a partisan issue in Sweden or Conservative reactions to Labor superannuation in Britain, the actual content of the new policy departure has come from nonparty sources and has scarcely been more generous than the original opposition offers. Modern social policies are much more than the accumulated residue of party "bids" in the political marketplace.

Traditionally there has also been a tendency to assert that differences in the preparation of policy alternatives result from the number of parties competing. A multiparty system is said to be less aggregative

---

6. See, for example, Stephen Bailey, *Political Parties in the United States*, and J. M. Burns, *The Deadlock of Democracy*. The effect of parties on policy making is probably the most poorly investigated topic in the entire vast literature of political parties. For critiques, see Frederick Engelmann, "A Critique of Recent Writings on Political Parties," in Harry Eckstein and David Apter, *Comparative Politics*, pp. 378–89; Fred Greenstein, *The American Party System and the American People*, pp. 99–101.

of the relevant interests, while the two-party system has often been seen as the ideal means for providing a smooth alteration of responsible governments as well as a reconciliation between the extremes of opinion. Our review suggests little evidence of such differences between two-party Britain and the multiparty Sweden. Perhaps the clearest example of an "unaggregated" interest in Sweden has been the Farmers party, which, as noted, has always been careful to preserve the particular interests of its unemployed or elderly clients. But this care has not prevented the achievement of compromises among the parties at most major junctures in policy (with the Farmer interest often finding its accommodations in coalition government with the Social Democrats). In light of the considerable policy changes since the Social Democrats began their rule in 1933 and what seems the persistently higher level of unproductive partisanship in Britain, it is difficult to conclude that Swedish social policy development has been marked by less responsible government or fewer attempts at conciliation.

The major impact of political parties on pensions, unemployment benefits, and superannuation has been in organizing general predispositions to policy choices. Occasionally parties have helped clarify alternatives, organized opinion behind alternatives, and provided long-term commitments to these positions. Typically, however, the alternatives in question have been expressions of a general sense of urgency or ease, sensitivity to some problems and not others. Parties have competed in expressing moods toward social policy change; concrete proposals for implementation have come in a distant second. Neither party functionaries nor organizational structures have been prominent in the creation of specific new policy departures. In Sweden, for example, contributory social insurance was not the product of party competition, but its early acceptance was significantly advanced by Branting's consolidation of Social Democratic attitudes in favor of employee contributions. In Britain, on the other hand, the Labor Party's early pension approach was first crystallized at the time of the party's formation and initiated over forty years of continuing, ingrained opposition to contributory insurance. Subsequent restrictions in unemployment relief during the 1930s raised Labor opposition to means-testing into an article of faith capable of prejudging any attempt to improve on flat-rate equality.

On rare but important occasions political parties have gone beyond the facilitation to the actual creation of policy choices. The most important examples were the new Swedish "crisis" policy of the early 1930s and the Socialists' superannuation plan in Britain during the late 1950s. It is important, however, to emphasize again that parties could be equally effective in entrenching predispositions that prevented the development of new policy choices. While the Swedish Social Democrats and British Liberals at the end of the 1920s succeeded in arriving at a more adequate departure in unemployment policy, the British Labor party used its powers against potential reformers to remain committed to an outworn policy.

So far I have discussed the interacting parties as interchangeable commodities, a method that V.O. Key would have identified as "taking politics out of political behavior."[7] What has been the effect on policy of parties as distinctive programmatic actors? It clearly cannot be contended that any individual party had a monopoly on the development of modern social policy; in particular, such policy has not been the consequence of the rise to power of a working class Labor party which then legislated its own interests. This does not mean however that the differences between the parties have been insignificant. The initial stages of policy development in both unemployment insurance and old age pensions show that the successful first efforts have come from Liberals rather than the Socialist Left. While one can rarely trace these policies to specific party programs, there does seem to be a common strain of origin from liberal opinion in its various forms—party members, philanthropists, and individual reformers—in the period between 1880 and 1914. From Hedin's original efforts in 1884 to Churchill's unemployment bill of 1911, the Labor and Social Democratic parties were either faintly interested or actually hostile. The major exception to this generalization is the 1908 British Pension Act, which was strongly pressed for by the Labor party; but this first act was in fact the terminal achievement of the Socialists' noncontributory approach in British social policy rather than its beginning.

While all parties have contributed to the subsequent development of social policy, by no means has the substance of these contributions been identical or randomly varied. Conservative parties in both nations can be found generally promoting a more strictly contributory system and expressing a particular concern with the state of national finances (we may recall, for example, Swedish Conservative opinion on pensions

7. V. O. Key and K. Munger, "Social Determinism and Electoral Decisions," in *American Political Behavior*, ed. E. Burdick.

and unemployment benefits in 1913, 1914, 1922, 1928, and 1933; and British Conservatives in 1898, 1906, 1925, and 1934). The Labor parties on the other hand have historically placed major emphasis on immediate relief of need and benefit adequacy (as in Sweden and Britain on the scope of pension proposals during the first decade of the century and unemployment insurance during the 1920s). Often these opinions were not reflected by practice in office or workable proposals out of office, but the difference in party orientations does seem a persistent theme in the policy record. Far from disappearing in a postwar "decline of ideology," the distinctions have only shifted their reference from already established policies to newer, ever emerging issues. On recent and significant policy questions, the differences between the parties by no means seem smaller than at earlier periods. One would, for example, have to be particularly obtuse not to recognize the important differences—in content and orientation—between British Labor and Conservative superannuation proposals in the 1950s and again in the 1960s, or between the superannuation plan adopted and pension funds actively used by the Swedish Social Democrats against bourgeois parties' preferences. These party orientations have frequently had unintentional policy consequences, crippling where they would strengthen policy (for example, Labor on noncontributory pensions) and expanding where they would limit state activity (one may guess current British superannuation falls into this category). Social policy has been shaped as much by the party moods and promises unfulfilled as by those realized, by the consequences unintended as much as those intended.

Interest Groups

There is a tendency to consider interest-group influence in policy as a peculiarly modern phenomenon, and in particular a phenomenon of the consensual, postwar era of full employment. A historical study of old age pensions and unemployment insurance makes clear that, although there may currently be a more formal institutionalization of interest organizations (as there is also in parties and government departments), the existence of consultation, bargaining, and accommodation with the "nonpolitical" interests has been of persisting importance throughout the development of social policy. British friendly societies, for example, were at least as central to social policy issues in the late nineteenth century as are any interest groups of the modern period. Over the course of the last century—with a few important exceptions— these interests appear to have operated as veto groups rather than initiators of particular approaches and alternatives.

One exception is the ad hoc group occasionally impinging on the policy process. We have identified two major types of interest organizations concerned with social policy: cause groups, entailing public agitation to achieve some specific reform, and spectrum groups, uniting individuals to pursue some common but more generalized economic interest on a permanent organizational basis. Cause groups seem to have been a limited and transitory influence in the policies considered. Two major instances of their impact occurred at the turn of the century when, in both Britain and Sweden, such groups pressed for the introduction of a particular form of old age pension. With the support of organized labor—in fact by helping to create an organized labor— the British National Pension Committee was of considerably greater consequence than the Swedish Committee for Public Pensions. Unlike Gustav Raab's group the British committee created a popular, issue-specific agitation uniting philanthropists, religious bodies, cooperatives, friendly society members, and unionists. By virtue of the close ties between unions and the NPC leadership, the British Labor party from the moment of its birth became committed, somewhat indeliberately, to a particular noncontributory policy approach. Cause groups also arose to defend the traditional poor law approach in each nation but seem to have been far less significant in their opposition. In both Britain and Sweden all cause groups have faded away rather quickly once the initial issue was settled (although under union sponsorship the pension movements briefly revived again during World War I).

Being fairly permanent but also issue-specific, organizations of beneficiaries themselves exhibit characteristics of both cause and spectrum groups. They seem to be a phenomenon of only the last 30 years, summoned forth by, rather than creating, the state's activist policy role. Pensioners' organizations have helped maintain the visibility of pensioners' needs and created a climate for marginal improvement in some benefits. But these bodies cannot be said to have been in the vanguard of or crucial to any major changes in postwar policy. Beneficiaries' groups have been of more lasting significance when crystallized into existence by being given a cooperative role in policy administration, as in the case of Swedish unemployment insurance funds; at the same time, such organizations have seemed likely to be interested in continuing more of the same rather than promoting policy change.

While cause groups have usually been temporary advocates of a particular positive course, spectrum groups have been more permanent and pervasive actors, often exerting a negative or delay-inducing influence. In Britain, for example, the first pensions were shaped not only by the push of the National Pension Committee but also by the pull of the friendly societies. From Blackley to Joseph Chamberlain to Meiklejohn, the perceived opposition of the long-established and powerful friendly society movement effectively stifled any attempt to institute contributory pension insurance. Such opposition usually did not need to be overtly mobilized in order to have its effect. Policy makers needed merely to anticipate friendly society hostility in order for the alternatives to be shaped and for what was essentially a non-decision on contributory British pensions to be taken. By the same token, the first introduction of flat-rateism was partially justified in Britain by the scope it would give to existing private union funds above the flat-rate level; a similar argument was used in the Beveridge Report 35 years later for uniform minimum benefits that would not interfere with the benefits of voluntary private insurance. As a result of its later industrialization, Sweden lacked any such vigorous friendly society establishment or private insurance sector during the early phases of social insurance and seems to have encountered little outside pressure against contributory insurance. Yet even in these very early stages Swedish techniques of ad hoc group consultation and involvement foreshadowed the deliberative process in evidence later.

It is an obvious but far from trivial point that the effect of any interest group upon social policy has varied with the perception of its own rather than anyone else's interests. This means that neither capital nor labor, employers nor employees have consistently been on one side or the other of the question of an expansionary social policy. Groups take their advantages where they find them; social policies change by indirection. Conservative business and financial interests, for example, have usually resolved their general opposition to higher social expenditure and their immediate interest in a free capital market in favor of the latter, supporting general pension increases over any large, funded scheme that might upset the capital market. Nor on the other hand have workers' interest groups been particularly zealous in the expansion of social policy where union members' immediate interests were not recognized to be directly at stake. While both the LO and the TUC have often expressed desires for general pension improvements, these desires have almost never been firmly pressed with a significant commitment of organizational resources, and in the interwar period of high unemployment were scarcely pressed at all. Undoubtedly the most significant and successful interest group initiative in either country was the LO's analysis and sponsorship of state superannuation but even here it was acknowledged by the organization that the agreed large increases in general pensions could be made a bargaining counter for the superannuation plan, which was of greater interest to the LO's manual workers. Much the same thing can be said about unemployment insurance. From the first experimental Swiss schemes, organized worker interest has been less in the introduction of a policy of comprehensive unemployment insurance and more in the protection and expansion of existing privileges, a fact illustrated again in 1948 by union hostility to the introduction of a general Swedish unemployment insurance. The first British state contributions to unemployment insurance were specifically justified as a means of allowing the better-off worker to avoid supporting his higher-risk brethren. More comprehensive income maintenance programs have usually flowed from concerns of those in or at the fringes of government civil service rather than from the sum of sectional interests. In Sweden, for example, it was union pressure that altered provisions on scaled state contributions—provisions that had originated to give greater protection to the worst-risk groups and had served as the justification for a voluntary rather than compulsory and comprehensive state insurance plan. Usually welfare of the unorganized and inarticulate has been a vulnerable ward if left solely to the concern of recognized interest groups.

Interests are self-serving but they have not been self-defining in the policy process. Substantive pressures from any group have depended on the capacity of the organization to recognize its interests to be at stake and to define what that stake is. Perhaps the clearest and most important illustration of this point is the different policy contributions of the Swedish LO and British TUC. With the unusual exception of the Beveridge Report, the TUC has rarely played anything approaching a creative role in the development of policies. The Swedish union movement has, particularly in the postwar period, taken a key part in the creation of new policy departures. It is difficult to separate the exact interrelations between the closely tied LO and Social Democratic party, but the policy analysis behind the new labor market approach, which in turn has given rise to new unemployment benefits, seems to have been adopted almost intact from the LO. On the question of superannuation, the British TUC has even more clearly remained an inert body, eventually persuaded by others, while the LO was the prime instigator and advocate of the Swedish policy and its subsequent elaborations.

Similar groups not only recognize their interests differently, but the same group can perceive its interest differently over time. Interests have not necessarily been immutable in their policy implications. For example, British private insurance groups, whose reservations had precluded superannuation in the 1950s, had embraced the advantages of state partnership by the end of the 1960s. Even the TUC eventually came around to supporting wage-related social insurance. Interests change, depending on the willingness and ability of men to see things differently.

Administrators

If policy is understood not simply as intended action but as what actually occurs consequent to intentions, then the place of civil servants in the development of modern social policy has been crucial. Forced to choose one group among all the separate political factors as most consistently important (though there is no good reason to force choices in this way), the bureaucracies of Britain and Sweden loom predominant in the policies studied.

One dimension of this administrative importance is implied in the term "consistently." While parties and interest groups did occasionally play extremely important parts, it was the civil services that provided the most constant analysis and review underlying most courses of government action. Parties and interest groups typically required a dramatic stimulus, such as a spurt in unemployment, to arouse their interest, but administrative attention remained relatively strong throughout these fluctuations. We may recall, for example, the important administrative efforts behind the extension and improvement of British unemployment insurance both during and after World War I, or the adjustments in Swedish pension policy at times when other political actors had lost interest (as in 1914, 1918, and 1921).

Apart from the persistence of influence, the substantive administrative effect on policy content has been immense. Insofar as policy has evolved as a corrective to social conditions, civil servants have played a leading part in identifying these conditions and framing concrete alternatives to deal with them. The contrast between British and Swedish administrations at the beginning of our period of analysis is enlightening. Influence of the more well-developed Swedish administration on the positive construction of a pension policy was without counterpart in Britain. Between 1890 and 1913, Swedish administrators played a key and probably primary role in developing the basic analysis and exhaustive information which underlaid the construction of a Swedish pension policy. From the beginning, contributory insurance was seen to involve no serious burden on Sweden's relatively well-developed bureaucratic resources. The investigatory and *remiss* procedures, which were eventually applied to outside interest groups, were administratively developed routines of long standing.

Given the weaker central administration, most important British research at this time remained extragovernmental (as in the work of Charles Booth) and the early investigatory process was at best perfunctory. By their own estimation, British administrators also lacked the necessary administrative resources to make a scheme of contributory pensions realistic. The policy effect of this difference between the two nations was well illustrated by the manner in which the extent of pension coverage was decided upon. From the beginning of deliberations, acceptance of a universal scheme in Sweden grew out of a relatively objective analysis of needs, existing provisions, and administrative practicality. Eventually the extent of coverage of British pensions was shaped by the haphazard play of forces between reformers' demands for noncontributory pensions and the resistance of the Treasury; on the basis of the amount of money surplus in the next year, the second least expensive coverage was finally chosen. The result was a noncontributory pension payable immediately in Britain and a Swedish contributory pension fully payable only after years of contributions. While British policy offered more immediate gratification to some outside demands, the Swedes had planned a more viable system of social insurance that could be extended, rather than circumvented as the British were led to do by 1925. The work of the 1925 Anderson committee on contributory pensions suggested that the British lag in administrative inputs to policy had been quickly eliminated during and after World War I.

As the first social policy initiatives have become established, the full scope of administrative influence has come into play in both Britain and Sweden. Social policy has most frequently evolved as a corrective less to social conditions as such and more to the perceived failings of previous policy. To officials has fallen the task of gathering, coding, storing, and interpreting policy experience. A policy "problem" may involve public demands, and/or conflicting alternatives presented by competing political parties, and/or a group's definition of its own injured interest; it always involves the government bureaucracy's own conception of what it has been doing. Substantive pension, unemployment benefit, and superannuation policies have evolved out of precisely this web of understandings on the current state of collective action.

The policy record suggests that administrative influence has not necessarily been directionless, in favor of the status quo, or concerned with reconciliation at the "lowest common denominator of opinions among affected interests."[8] Administrative policy making has preserved the status quo only if that term is given a peculiar definition—trying to correct what was done last time around. Attention to corrections in ongoing policy is scarcely directionless, though it may not yield predetermined policy courses (what party program or group interest does that?). Nor is it a peculiarly American phenomenon (said by some to be due to America's separation of powers and disorganized parties) to find administrators promoting and organizing the political basis of a policy. Our evidence suggests the activist civil service role is a pervasive policy phenomenon rather than the exception. It is a phenomenon unmistakable even in the home of the ideal of administrative neutrality. British administrative consultations with outsiders have seemed more often aimed at persuading interest groups than reconciling their positive pressures. The world's first state program of unemployment insurance was largely the creature of British civil servants; in both Britain and Sweden the new concern with unemployment at the turn of the century was reflected in policies administratively developed at the Boards of Trade; the "work approach" of the new administrative Unemployment Commission dominated Swedish policy in much of the interwar period; it was the British Ministry of Labor's plans to universalize unemployment insurance and eventually to take over relief of all unemployed that

8. Such an interpretation is discussed in Richard Rose, "The Variability of Party Government." pp. 442 ff. For an early emphasis on the importance of administrative power resources, particularly in the United States, see Norton Long, "Power and Administration," and *The Polity.*

was adopted in Britain. More recently, postwar plans for earnings-related unemployment insurance reflect the same administrative contributions to policy in each nation. This theme can also be traced in old age pensions, from the 1925 introduction of contributory pensions in Britain and 1941 development of the Beveridge Report, to the investigation that laid the foundation for Swedish pension policy in 1935 and its alteration in 1946. Apart from the general recognition of the need to act, the determination of what has been and should be the substantive content of these actions has often, and perhaps usually, been the primary administrative contribution to the development of modern social policy.

Administrative influence has, of course, periodically restricted as well as promoted the growth of social policy, particularly with regard to the financial scope of the policies in question. We may recall, for example, the early Treasury vetoing of even the limited Conservative pension plans, the financial limitations imposed on the 1908 pension and 1911 unemployment proposals, the restrictions in pension increases at the end of World War I, or the more recent restrictions in pension financing, delays in superannuation, and limitations imposed on the Beveridge proposals. The British refusal—as contrasted with the Swedish attitude —to acknowledge the "political" contribution of administrators to policy has not meant the elimination of their influence, only its public obscuration.

In both expansionary and restrictive directions, administrative actors have been crucial in giving concrete substance to new policy initiatives and in elaborating already established approaches. What officials have rarely been able to do is to fire up, by themselves, sufficient political steam to create new policies *ex nihilo*. This corrective—or if one prefers, reactive—role does not minimize the administrative contribution, for much of social policy development has been and remains an elaboration rather than redirection of the original liberal framework. But it does alert us to the cramped view that results from considering political factors seriatim and in isolation from each other. Social and political events *move*. To understand public policy we must try to appreciate the mobile connections between factors—the real-life process of policy development and social politics.

POLITICS AS LEARNING

Tradition teaches that politics is about conflict and power. Where there are conflicting opinions, there will be politics; where men agree about who gets what, when, and how, there is no politics. Governments reconcile conflict and through public policy give authoritative expression to the resulting courses of action; these policies change when there is a change in the possession and relationships of power among conflicting groups.

This is a blinkered view of politics and particularly blinding when applied to social policy. Politics finds its sources not only in power but also in uncertainty—men collectively wondering what to do. Finding feasible courses of action includes, but is more than, locating which way the vectors of political pressure are pushing. Governments not only "power" (or whatever the verb form of that approach might be); they also puzzle. Policy-making is a form of collective puzzlement on society's behalf; it entails both deciding and knowing. The process of making pension, unemployment, and superannuation policies has extended beyond deciding what "wants" to accommodate, to include problems of knowing who might want something, what is wanted, what should be wanted, and how to turn even the most sweet-tempered general agreement into concrete collective action. This process is political, not because all policy is a by-product of power and conflict but because some men have undertaken to act in the name of others.

Axiomatically, a nonrevolutionary change in social policy required that the external tensions in society find corresponding tensions within existing political institutions. But a pure power approach, like a circular "systems analysis" (input, blackbox, output, feedback), fails to flesh in how this actually occurred. The creation of modern social policies, at least those discussed here, cannot be said to have resulted from the electoral rise to power of a working class intent on legislating its own interests; alternations of party power in government have far more frequently maintained the momentum of existing policy than given expression to parties' deliberately announced and campaigned-for alternatives. Interest group concern in policy has been sporadic and limited largely to specific issues of immediate self-interest; when active, these interests have been differently perceived both by similar groups and by the same group at different times. Much the same variability holds true for the alternative moods expressed by political parties. The arrival in power of a British Socialist party in 1929 and Swedish Socialists in 1932 was not itself a denouement in unemployment policy, and in each case carried different implications for government action. Even increases in administrative power have had as their basis less the ability to issue authoritative commands than the capacity to draw upon administrative resources of information, analysis, and expertise for new policy lessons and appropriate conclusions on increasingly complex issues. In short, the possession and relationships of power have not necessarily decided the substance of policy.

To observe that particular policy contents have not flowed from innate qualities, interests, or demands of powerholders is not to say that power considerations have been negligible. It is to suggest that a great deal of policy development—its creation, alteration, or redirection—has been settled prior to or outside of substantial exercises of power. In the end, when analysis, deliberation, and persuasion have failed to achieve agreement—as in the case of Swedish superannuation in 1956–57 or British unemployment insurance in 1931—political power has been resorted to and sometimes proven decisive. Yet these events, which onlookers in each country invariably termed "crises," stand out precisely because they are so rare. More frequently, changes in the relationships of power—wider political participation, election results, party government turnovers, new mobilizations of interest groups—have served as one variety of stimulus, or trigger, helping to spread a general conviction that "something" must be done. But there have been other triggers besides power contributing to these convictions and, in any event, the possible range of specific policy responses regarding what to do seems almost limitless. The question is how can we adequately conceptualize the broad political process supplying this "what to do"?

Our review of social policy development suggests the fruitfulness of viewing politics through the concept of learning. Much political interaction has constituted a process of social learning expressed through policy. In its most general sense, learning can be taken to mean a relatively enduring alteration in behavior that results from experience; usually this alteration is conceptualized as a change in response made in reaction to some perceived stimulus. Unfortunately, learning theory has concentrated almost exclusively on learning by individuals; our understanding of how groups learn is, to say the least, fragmentary. To speak of learning by society or groups should not imply reifying society into a discrete organic mind responding to holistic stimuli. Social learning is created only by individuals, but alone and in interaction these individuals acquire and produce changed patterns of collective action. Even where individual views may not be changed, sometimes in fact precisely because men's views do not change and circumstances do, the collective actions expressed through public policy may be altered. Social politics constitutes one increasingly important vehicle for such learning, and social policy is its result.[9]

Political learning may encompass a variety of analytic levels. Internationally, the spread of social policy innovations can be mapped, as in Chapter 1, to show a familiar diffusion pattern. Another range of group learning occurs within particular organizations themselves, growing from their accumulated experiences and capacities for response. Our attention has centered largely between these levels, on British and Swedish societies at large and the way in which their political interactions have led to the creation and adaptation of policy responses. Clearly, however, each level impinges on the other, with national policy contingent on influences from both national subunits and international examples. There is nothing simple about this cobweb of interaction and one preliminary generalization from the evidence must be that there is no one pattern of learning in either nation or in any of the policy areas studied.

If not necessarily comforting to those looking for simple explanations, this multiplicity is at least a useful corrective to the idea that there is something called "the" policy process (though we have used this as a useful shorthand term) and that it is adequately conceived as a matter of problem solving. Most taxonomies salami-slice the policy process into a series of stages in which policy is treated as a problem grappled with by a collective "decider" analogous to an ideal individual decider. A situation arises (perhaps because conditions have changed and policy has not, or vice versa, or because both have changed); the problem is identified; alternatives are sought; through being weighed in controversy, one is chosen; the choice is implemented; it in turn reacts on social conditions, and so on. A few portions of the social policy record (for example, the prelude to the first Swedish pension act) do bear a family resemblance to this model. Sometimes, however, a choice has been made prior to canvassing alternatives and has then been sent out, not only to do battle with other alternatives but to find a problem

9. This approach builds upon the earlier work of Karl Deutsch, *The Nerves of Government*, which emphasized the importance of political feedback networks for the acceleration of social learning. My use of the term is of course completely distinct from its use in social learning theory to designate the study of how individuals learn to behave in social relationships, as in the work of J. B. Rotter, *Social Learning and Clinical Psychology*. One of the few psychological studies of collective learning is reported by Herbert Gurnec, "Group Learning."

(as in the case of British noncontributory pensions). A pattern much more prominent than that of abstract problem-solving finds administrators actively mobilized by the first efforts to deal with a social condition and then using their new positions to generate more continuing interest in identifying issues and possible settlements (for example, early twentieth-century Boards of Trade, or the British turn to contributory pensions).[10] At still other times, policy seems to proceed more in the manner of a random walk (Conservative superannuation plans?). A better image for social learning than the individual is a maze where the outlet is shifting and the walls are being constantly repatterned; where the subject is not one individual but a group bound together; where this group disagrees not only on how to get out but on whether getting out constitutes a satisfactory solution; where, finally, there is not one but a large number of such groups which keep getting in each other's way. Such is the setting for social learning. Yet the fact that there is learning and nonlearning rather than random bumping can be highlighted by returning to three familiar features in the history of modern social policy: individual agents of change, organizational inter-relationships, and the impact of previous policy itself.

The process we have discerned from a study of pensions, unemployment benefits, and superannuation within the two democracies involves parties, interest groups, and bureaucracies, but it is misleading to think of these as discrete, bounded political corpuscles. In the ongoing policy processes it is more accurate to think of these structures as crannied hosts supporting individual agents of policy change. Typically, social policies have been most directly influenced by middlemen at the interfaces of various groups. These have been men with transcendable group commitments, in but not always of their host body.[11] While not the most powerful participants, these agents of change have usually had access to information, ideas, and positions outside the normal run of organizational actors. Their formal party allegiances have differed greatly but all have used their varied positions to bring pensions or unemployment insurance or superannuation questions onto political

10. This pattern has been identified in the detailed administrative studies of Oliver Mc-Donagh, *A Pattern of Government Growth, 1800–1860: The Passenger Acts and Their Enforcement.*

11. In the terms of diffusion theory, these individuals have ranked high in "cosmopoliteness," i.e., the degree to which orientation is external to a particular social system. Everett Rogers, *Communication of Innovations: A Cross Cultural Approach.*

agendas. The nonpartisan clergyman–insurance advocate Blackley; the Conservative businessman, social scientist Booth; the Liberal-Unionist, businessman Chamberlain; the Socialist-leaning Reverend Stead; the Liberal journalist-administrator Beveridge; and the Socialist academic and insurance expert Titmuss. In Sweden there were the Liberal man of letters Hedin; Conservative philanthropist-aristocrat Hamilton; Liberal army officer Raab; nonpartisan administrator Lindstedt; Liberal von Koch; Socialist Wigforss; and LO economist Rehn—all began policy analysis and advocacy far more in their individual capacities than as group representatives. In common with the innovators in new industrial and engineering techniques of a century earlier, most of these innovators and reformers of new social techniques were talented amateurs in the subjects rather than established professionals and experts. As advocates of new policy approaches to unemployment for example, Beveridge and Wigforss had little or no formal economic training; Lindstedt moved to pensions from the academic study of mathematics, and Titmuss had never received an advanced academic degree. Together, these men were leading figures in mediating a market for social policy ideas.

We have seen how the actual processes for injecting these ideas were not unique to any country, period, or policy. They ranged (in terms S. E. Finer has used for the earlier context of Benthamite influence)[12] from irradiation (attracting and convincing a wider school of disciples) to suscitation (exciting public interest through public inquiries, press agitation) to permeation (acquisition of public office), with possibilities for further irradiation and suscitation from the inside. The difficulty of finding any one-for-one relationship between these activities and a particular policy is obvious; often their effects have piled up over time and, like a succession of seemingly light winter snows, accumulated a weight eventually sufficient to move the vast glacier-like inertia of existing policy. Often the content of their contribution has taken the form of new factual and well-publicized intelligence on internal social conditions in the nation. The beginnings of modern social policy were imbedded in a new era of empirical studies and political investigations of social conditions. Nowhere was this perspective better illustrated than in the contributions of Charles Booth, who in 1886 wrote to his young research assistant Beatrice Potter (later Webb):

12. S. E. Finer, "The Transmission of Benthamite Ideas, 1820–50," in *Studies in the Growth of Nineteenth-Century Government*, ed, Gillian Sutherland.

> what I want to see instead [of *a priori* theory] is a large statistical
> framework . . . to receive accumulations of facts out of which
> at last is evolved . . . the basis of more intelligent action. . . .
> The *a priori* reasoning of political economy, orthodox and unortho-
> dox alike, fails from want of reality.[13]

Sometimes too, the contribution of reformers was simply an appreciation for the possibilities of a new technique of social organization, for
example, Lindstedt's dedication to social insurance and Möller's
realization of its wider possibilities in the 1920s, Beveridge's campaign
for labor exchanges and unemployment insurance, or Titmuss's and
Abel-Smith's appreciation of the positive financial possibilities of
earnings-related insurance.

Very frequently, the contribution of reformers to adapting new policy
responses consisted in perceiving and transmitting foreign experience;
misconceptions could be as effective a stimulus as accurate reports.
We have seen how the consideration of old age pensions and unemployment insurance began at approximately the same time in both
economically developed, democratic Britain and underdeveloped,
predemocratic Sweden. This simultaneity is surprising only in terms of
a narrowly national and power-oriented perspective. Much of the
development of earlier poor law policy had depended on the communication of policy techniques throughout an international community;
similarly, the growth of pension and unemployment proposals in
Britain and Sweden at the end of the nineteenth century was part of a
general European phenomenon expressed in a great many countries by
the handful of persons thinking about such policies. In old age pensions,
for example, Blackley and Hedin, Stead and Lindstedt, Chaplin and
Branting—in short, almost all the major characters active in originating
British and Swedish pensions—followed international developments
on the subject and drew inspiration from one or another foreign example. Experiences in Denmark and New Zealand were important in
Britain, while Blackley's proposal strongly influenced the first Swedish
investigation. At the turn of the century municipal innovations and
experimentation in unemployment insurance were reported and im-
itated throughout Europe. Above all, however, it was experience in

13. Quoted in T. S. Simey, "Social Investigations: Past Achievements and Present Difficulties," p. 125. See also O. K. McGregor's article, "Social Research and Social Policy in the
19th Century," in the same volume.

Germany that stirred greatest international interest. Invention there of the new compulsory state insurance technique was studied and repeated, earlier in Sweden by Lindstedt, later and more expediently in Britain by Lloyd George and Churchill.

Any learning interpretation would only replace one form of myopia with another if it suggested that enactment of social policy has been solely a matter of information and analysis and has nothing to do with power. Each without the other has been inconsequential for policy. But while knowing "what to do" has been mutable into a capacity to do it (particularly when those formally in power did not know), power has not usually been transformable into knowledge. Political institutions provide one vital means of facilitate the former transmutation. If socioeconomic conditions have been the primary signals for adjusting policy, these have had to be expressed in practice, first, by being discerned, discussed, and interpreted into secondary signals, and second, by formulation of an appropriate response. As disorganized purveyors of internal intelligence, appreciators of technique, and interpreters of foreign experience, policy middlemen have been particularly prominent in both tasks. The resulting variations in any interest group's definition of its interest, and party inconsistencies in the priorities of their election appeals or expressions of alternative moods, have been important, practical ways in which this adaptiveness in collective behavior has been expressed through time. The importance of policy middlemen has sprung not from any unique powers of abstract thought, but from sensitivity to the changes going on around them and access to powerful institutions.

In learning theory, responses depend not only on the nature of the stimulus but also on the internal set (sometimes called a state of response readiness) in those affected. The networks of policy middlemen in a society constitute one factor in this state of readiness; so too do their organizational hosts. These organizations may be permeable, but they are not passive vehicles for anyone with a bright idea. Members of the same family of political institutions do differ; in terms of learning capacities not all socialist parties, for example, are the same. This difference has been one of the basic distinctions between the LO and the British TUC across a range of social policy issues; much the same can be said for the Labor parties of the two nations. While British Labor remained tied to the original flat-rate, non-means-tested approach, Swedish Social Democrats under the prodding of Branting and

Möller found ways to make positive use of the contributory approach in social insurance. A study of this breadth has not been able to pursue questions of internal organization or to determine whether a lack of learning is due to lack of stimulus, to structure, to the nature of problems, or—a factor unduly neglected by academics—to sheer stupidity. Here I can only observe that social policy has been a product of not only positive and negative learning (finding out what to do and what not to do) but also "nonlearning," that is, the unadaptability of policy makers and institutional perspectives.

Nowhere is the importance of such learning and alteration of perspectives more clearly demonstrated than in the economic doctrines prevalent in any given period. There is some, but perhaps not too much, exaggeration in saying that social policy has developed in the interstices allowed to it by "sound economic thinking." As we have seen, the established economic approach was instrumental in the delay of British pensions, in their improvement, and in creating the turn to a contributory basis. In both Britain and Sweden, economic doctrines of retrenchment to recover economic health were the dominant social policy theme in the 1920s. Paradoxically it was the same economic doctrine, inhibiting any positive government expenditure to cure unemployment, which left little alternative to the continuous expansion of unemployment benefits at the same time that pensions were being economized. It was not a simple question of sinister conservative interests in command of the policy process. The same economic doctrines were accepted and acted upon by the Socialist parties in office in both countries, including even the former supporters of noncontributory social insurance. Significantly, one of the closest observers of the expansion of British unemployment insurance to disastrous proportions in the 1920s laid the blame not on party counterbidding or Socialist party liberalities, but on failures in political learning; it was "but a part of the general problem of persuading governments to see economic problems steadily and to see them whole, and not either in the fits and starts of inexpert cabinet committees or sectionally through the eyes of administrative experts concerned with some one object."[14] Eventually these economic perspectives were changed, again earlier and more successfully in Sweden through Wigforss's and the Social

14. William Beveridge, *Unemployment: A Problem of Industry*, p. 409. One of the rare accounts of the effects of economic doctrine on politics, and the learning process involved in its changing impact, is H. V. Emy, "The Impact of Financial Policy on English Party Politics before 1914."

Democratic party's "crisis" policy and the LO's postwar labor market policy, later and more hesitantly through administrative infiltration in Britain. Whether the newer post-Keynesian economic doctrines are any less decisive for social policy today is doubtful, but for some reason the role of individuals and ideas in policy making arouses little interest among political scientists.

Usually, the interactions of political institutions have produced collective learning by indirection. Parties, by taking as given most policies of a previous government, unwittingly have moved forward the center of consensus concerning what is accepted as routine. On rarer occasions a competitive urge in parties, or more commonly among government departments, has led to unplanned searches for policy alternatives. Social inequities have become policy issues through comparison, and interest groups seeking benefits for their own members have sometimes indeliberately given scope to powerful new comparisons for others in the policy process. Cause and beneficiary groups, by the infrequency or predictability of their interventions, have offered little stimulus to policy makers to improve their responses or their analysis of needs; policy responses become patterned into routine. Administrative organs, by being more continuously involved in substantive policy, have constituted some of the most important learning outposts occasionally available for capture by agents of change. More subtly, political institutions have served as social assemblers, bunching activists into cohorts whose common exposure to outside stimuli evolves into rough bodies of shared interpretation. In time, these generations of policy makers may rise to positions allowing them to express in policy their own generational views of the issues and presumptions for action (as Edwardian poor law opponents, Keynesian reformers, anti-means-testers from the 1930s and so on). Social policy in any period acquires a molar quality through these bodies of common interpretation.

A few institutions have been more consciously designed to aid in political learning. This is best demonstrated in the prominent part played by expert investigations throughout the period of this study. While such formally constituted inquiries have been used in both nations, little in the British policy process can compare with the substantial contributions of Swedish investigatory committees (*utredning*). In general, Swedish discussions of particular social policies have begun from an assumption that the primary requisite for policy decision is more information, clarification, and analysis among the interested parties; British discussion has generally begun from the assumption of divergent interests resolvable only through partisan conflict and certainly not through joint committee work. One can trace this difference throughout the Swedish investigation of pensions in the 1880s and 1890s and the largely perfunctory partisan investigations in Britain at the same time; it is seen also in the exhaustive attempts to arrange a compromise on Swedish superannuation through interminable investigations in the 1950s, contrasted with the immediate birth of British superannuation proposals in an atmosphere of direct, irreconcilable partisan clashes.

The evidence examined seems to leave little doubt as to which assumption has been most productive in policy making (what the effects are for the clients of social policy no one knows). Certainly, at various important junctures in Swedish policy, diverging interests have been found to be irreconcilable; in a number of other cases, however, a mutually acceptable policy has been found. The 1907 Swedish pension investigation, for example, entailed an analysis qualitatively superior to anything in Britain and produced a plan acceptable to most groups concerned, a plan capable not only of pre-empting a good deal of partisan conflict but of being developed and extended to all citizens in subsequent years. The British pensions of the same period, involving what analysis and consultation could be hurriedly arranged by several civil servants, created from the moment of their passage a persisting and largely sterile party division between contributory and noncontributory antagonists. The point is not that partisan clashes are necessarily unproductive, but that through the British method they remained largely mock battles; they were irresponsible in the sense that the supposed opposition (usually Labor) was unwilling or unable to act on most of its own pension or unemployment proposals when finally in office. In the same way, the 1928 Swedish investigation, which ostensibly was a manifestation of economizing forces, exerted its own independent impact, providing factual and analytic intelligence that seems to have obviated any strong party clash on the basic lines of a new and more adequate pension policy adopted in the 1930s. Much the same can also be said for the current Swedish investigation of unemployment benefits. The most successful British departure, the Beveridge Report, seems to have been the one British investigation with the greatest amount of serious (though informal) consultation and analysis among the interested parties. By no means has the Swedish approach prevented partisan clashes; investigations on a number of important issues have been unable to reach agreement. But the direct consequence of this has been that partisan conflict—for example in superannuation in the 1950s or unemployment in the late 1920s—has been concentrated on precisely those issues of significant disagreement, in contrast to the more vague, often fanciful clashes that have characterized much of British policy.

The responses mediated through policy middlemen and institutional relations shade into the third and probably most pervasive manifestation of political learning in the development of social policy: the impact of previous policy itself. For some reason there is a reluctance in policy studies to identify policy as an important political variable. The point of emphasis here is not to suggest that all development is the replay of past policy; but what is normally considered the dependent variable (policy output) is also an independent variable (in an ongoing process in which everything becomes an intervening variable). We have seen throughout that policy invariably builds on policy, either in moving forward with what has been inherited, or amending it, or repudiating it.

Two types of learning can be identified in the policy record. Much of the time, policy responses have resembled what is known as classic conditioning (or respondent behavior); the repeated coincidence of conditional with unconditional stimuli has over time led to highly predictable patterns of response. Policy makers may not exactly salivate at the sound of the usual bell, but there is something of a conditioned reflex in a great deal of their behavior. Once implemented, a technique such as social insurance has tended to be readopted, to be considered the "natural" policy response for other types of income risk; repeated representations on client distress have come to be taken as undiscriminated signals for continual increases in benefit rates rather than indications that the existing structure of policy requires reexamination; certain political parties and interest groups have learned to respond to every proposal for selectivity as a threatened reinstitution of the hated household means test. Even more adaptive forms of policy response share something of this form of learning; for if new events were seen as totally novel, with no relation to what is already known, the only possible response would be total bafflement. The incrementalism pervasive in policy making is one manifestation of the more general tendency to respond by analogizing. Typically, steps taken with regard to a new situation are small (compared to the almost infinite variety of possible responses) because the new situation is responded to like something already known, or some element of it. It is this facet of learning that more than anything else lies at the heart of the essentially liberal continuity evident in social policy since the first insurance efforts to deal with the cumulative insecurity of industrial society. The inheritance of income maintenance policies has served as a path through the immense complexity facing social policy makers and has facilitated the creation of subsequent responses.

To take only a few examples, the interwar changes in British unemployment insurance scarcely seem attributable to the lesser desire of British policy makers to economize—which they were doing in pensions—but rather to the fact that there was an unemployment insurance program at hand to be expanded; Sweden, on the other hand, responded to the 1920s high unemployment by continuing to operate a work relief policy inherited from the administrative innovations of the First World War. After the establishment of Swedish unemployment insurance, liberalizations were similar in their general thrust to those made in Britain after the First World War; it was the intervening creation of full employment policies which ensured that Sweden would not repeat Britain's virtual destruction of unemployment insurance finances. In its fundamentals the Beveridge Report was similarly a further restatement of early Liberal aims for a comprehensive subsistence insurance against want.

If classic conditioning has been most relevant to policy continuity, instrumental conditioning (or operant behavior) has been most directly applicable to policy change. The distinctive feature of this second type of learning is the addition of environmental consequences (reinforcement) to the basic stimulus-response model, so that reinforcement is not paired with a particular stimulus but is contingent on the response emitted. What one learns depends on what one does (as well as on the original stimulus and internal set), and nowhere is this more true than in the contingencies of reinforcement produced by preexisting policy. In both its self-instruction and self-delusions, the cobweb of socioeconomic conditions, policy middlemen, and political institutions reverberates to the consequences of previous policy in a vast, unpremeditated design of social learning. Operant conditioning is a process underpinning policy development at the earliest as well as the later, more interventionist, periods of social policy. Inherited policy not only creates analogies but also sets in train many of the stimuli for future policy making.

Major shifts in social policy predated anything that can be called democratic politics or parliamentary government. Rather than resting on an inherent policy view of the English magistracy, of 1832 suffrage reformers, or of a new industrial middle class, the essential outlines of the Speenhamland system or the 1834 reforms seem best accounted for by the substantive policy techniques that had been inherited and found wanting. Probably the single most important force molding the policies discussed in this volume was the reaction against the poor law. Without exception, the point of departure for reformers of all parties in both Britain and Sweden was the desire to find something better than the opprobrious poor law for the deserving poor. New evidence on the extent of aged pauperism in industrial society, the recurring cycles of unemployment, these and many other pieces of intelligence were cited in the attempt to find an alternative to poor relief for those whose poverty "was not their own fault." To those searching for this alternative, social insurance seemed to offer an answer to the administratively justified poor law techniques of deterrence, workhouses, and means-testing. Now insurance contributions could provide entitlement to benefits, argued the initiators of pensions and unemployment insurance in both nations. Nowhere was this conscious effort to break the poor law's conceptual grip better expressed than in the work of William Beveridge, both in the creation of the world's first state unemployment insurance and in his exposition of the postwar system of comprehensive social insurance. It was the more stringent poor law inheritance, institutionalized administratively in the British Local Government Board, that seems to have particularly aroused hostility against and fears about any means testing in Britain—fears that were not so seriously aroused by Swedish administrative institutions or subsequently ingrained in the Swedish Labor party.

The same process of operant conditioning underlies many policy changes of the modern era. Interwar developments in pensions saw Britain move from a relatively free-grant to insurance-based system and Sweden move from a relatively strict, insurance-based scheme toward a free-grant system. This basic change of policy in each country occurred during a period when there were over a dozen general elections and even more frequent changes in party government. More relevant than changes in possession of political power were the momentum and

experiences generated by established policy. Almost every major provision of the 1925 British Pension Act was in some way designed as a
response to the 1908 act. Contributory pensions for the 65–70 age
group were selected as a device to avoid the unacceptable costs of
further increases in the existing noncontributory pensions; benefits
were arranged to correspond to those of the existing program for fear
of stimulating further demands for increases in the latter; the actual
implementation of contributory pensions was modeled on the existing
National Health Insurance program.

Similarly, Swedish policy discussions underlying the 1935 and 1937
pension reforms revealed the influence of the twofold framework
created in 1913. Other conceivable alternatives, such as a move to flat
rates or noncontributory pensions, were scarcely discussed. In almost
every quarter the implicit premise was that the two types of pension
provisions would remain in existence but that, compared to the past,
the insurance portion should play a somewhat smaller role than supplementation. Sweden's earlier start with contributory pensions had
itself been a vital factor in bringing policy analysts to see earlier the
inadequacies of such an approach. While Swedish changes in 1935 were
reacting to the failures of the 1913 insurance policy, British policy
changes after the Second World War went on to react against the 1925
policy. Recent discussions on British superannuation have been shaped
by the perceived failures of the Beveridge system; in particular, the
Socialist party's initiation of earnings-related—which can be called
inegalitarian—social insurance proposals is incomprehensible except
as understood against the backdrop of limitations discovered in the
older policy of uniform contributions and benefits. The more radical
potential of subsequent Conservative superannuation plans springs not
from spontaneous socialist enlightenment in Tory circles but from a
reaction against Labor's specific plans.

To view the development of social policy in Britain and Sweden in
terms of a political learning process is to throw into a different light the
classic debate between pluralism and elitism. Previous comments have
suggested the limited extent to which electoral accountability of elites,
or their competition through party and interest group mechanisms,
have been involved in the development of policies. If one were forced
to hold the policy process static and choose between an essentially
pluralistic or elitist interpretation, then our tentative conclusions about
interest groups, administrators, and the significance of fairly small

groups of individual reformers would suggest the greater interpretive power of the latter. In terms of political learning, however, pluralist and elitist approaches are but different ways of looking at the same phenomenon of adaptation through politics—depending upon whether one adopts an essentially static institutional view or a dynamic societal perspective.

At some risk of oversimplification we may say that, in the policies considered, elites in each nation have functioned as the agents of institutional learning, while the plurality of interests and techniques of influence over time has functioned as the agent of societal learning. Only relatively small groups of people have provided the vital new sources of domestic and international intelligence in the social policy process. To have a political impact, such views have had to become attached to some institutional or popularly organized group; examples are Booth's tie to the National Pension Committee, Lindstedt's to the Swedish administrative apparatus, Wigforss's to the Social Democratic party, Rehn's to the LO, or that of Titmuss to the British Labor party. Policy changes have flowed from the influence of these individuals through their affiliated groups.

The significance of pluralism for political learning and policy has been at the societal rather than institutional level of analysis. The pluralism we have identified is not necessarily that usually assumed by American observers, that is, a large number of semi-independent power units at a fairly narrow cross-section in time. At various points policy has been decisively shaped by one or a very few principal actors. The plurality affecting the creation and development of modern social policy has been longitudinal. Over the course of policy development, no particular group, party, or administrative organ has finally captured a monopoly of influence on any policy; no one device of electoral determination, party competition, interest group pressure, or bureaucratic politics has provided "the" technique of policy making. All have played an important part at one time or another.

In this longitudinal plurality, the societal process of policy making in Britain and Sweden has achieved a rough accommodation to the unstable market it faces. Variations in social policy stimuli have occurred along all three possible dimensions of fluctuation: regularity (is it predictable?); amplitude (how severe are peaks and troughs?); and frequency (how long is a cycle?). Some variations have been sufficiently moderate to be manageable, regular enough to be forecastable, and frequent enough to be perceptible (for example, cyclical unemployment); they have facilitated regular investigation and routinization through insurance techniques. Other phenomena have sent unforeseeable and severe shock waves and have often been amenable to only the grossest expediency (for example, depression unemployment). Still other events have been of such long-term variation as to be only gradually recognized (for example, demographic aging or changes in family structure). Surrounded by this instability, a variable policy process may have proved superior to any one coherent system, even a system that would have been more efficient for each individual type of stimulus. In any event, the actual development that has occurred—the "how" of politics' effects on social policy—has been piecemeal, ad hoc, and largely unplanned, using a variety of techniques. It can be called a process of "opportunistic unawareness," "a fit of absence of mind," or in Karl Polanyi's more perceptive phrase, "spontaneous order," an order attained by allowing each part to interact on its own initiative.[15] Compared to the other spontaneous social orders we know about, the social policy process in Britian and Sweden seems closest not to the strictly economic or power politics order of completely competitive interaction, but to an order achieved through a mixture of consultation, some competition, and persuasion. The result has been a vast number of specific policy adjustments which, taken as a whole over time, add up to something of a learning process.

We are still the children of the liberal reformers, patching the mechanisms haphazardly bequeathed to postwar societies proud of their supposed uniqueness. Yet in the end there has also been change, for the underlying process of group learning is capable of moving through a variety of policy patterns. Social policy has moved from undifferentiated responses, such as the poor law, to more differentiated provisions for a variety of income maintenance problems. New capabilities (full employment benefit or superannuation) have grown out of already established, subordinate capabilities (such as earlier forms of basic contributory insurance). There may even be a slight tendency for policy responses to have become less matters of chance encounter with reward and punishment and more self-conscious realizations of the relation between the state's policy behavior and social consequences.

15. Michael Polanyi, *The Logic of Liberty*, pp. 154 ff. The other descriptions are from Gunnar Myrdal, *Beyond the Welfare State*, p. 12; and Bentley Gilbert, *British Social Policy, 1914–1939*, p. 308.

The social learning involved in the play of power and puzzlement is not necessarily "better" than nonlearning, nor is it necessarily the product of individuals becoming "smarter." But gradually individual attitudes have also changed and, like adaptive group interactions, affected the content of collective provision. Social policy was not created by the bumping of impenetrable billiard balls of power, but by men who could learn and whose viewpoints could change. Such learning, mediated through the perceptions of political actors and their organizational hosts, has helped shift the terms of policy debate toward a new perspective—a fact that is easier to illustrate than to prove conclusively. Consider the following four comments made at various points in the consideration of old age pensions in each country:

A secure position does not diminish thrift but favors it; on the contrary, it is insecurity and hopelessness which feeds indifference and carelessness.

If terror be an incentive to thrift, surely the penalties of the system which we have abandoned ought to have stimulated thrift as much as anything could . . . It is a great mistake to suppose that thrift is caused only by fear; it springs from hope as well.

It is not despair or fear that makes people save but hope. . . . There would be something to save towards if a man is sure that if he gets old he will have a certain income.

Experiences . . . ought to have taught us that hopelessness in the working class's struggle to protect itself against need in old age must completely wreck feelings of responsibility.

The first was made by the Swedish reformer, Count Hamilton; the second by the young Liberal, Winston Churchill; the third by the philanthropic businessman, Charles Booth; and the last by the Swedish Conservative aristocrat, Count Treffenberg.[16] The point under discussion in each case was whether or not state intervention in old age provision might hinder individual thrift; in each case the response stemmed from an emerging perspective fundamentally different from the deterrence ideas of the old poor law, a perspective that seems to have

16. Hugo Hamilton in Första Kammar debate, May 21, 1913; Churchill in a 1908 speech at Dundee; Booth in a speech at Birmingham, March 25, 1899; Treffenberg in Första Kammar debate, April 27, 1895.

had little to do with election fears, party programs, or interest group pressure. If the larger result of this changing perspective has been to add new social rights of citizenship to existing civil and political rights, then the ongoing process of sequential policy adjustment has brought not only immediate political settlements but a result greater than the sum of contending interests or parties. It is a result that none of the politicians, reformers, interest representatives, or administrators, immersed as they were in the immediate policy questions, ever decided they wanted and deliberately set about to create.

None of this is to offer an apologia or to suggest that social politics in either Britain or Sweden has served as a smoothly adaptive servomechanism. Discontinuities have been prominent—for example, in the neglect and ineptness of beneficiaries' own organizations, the meager study of policy impacts, the strong leverage of interest groups on issues of direct self-interest and vulnerability of the unorganized, the immobility resulting from failures to adapt economic doctrine, the self-evident priority of narrow financial criteria, and so forth. Much of social policy has remained at the level of chance discovery and ad hoc invention, with little attention to accumulated evidence, experimentation, or questions of how the learning process itself might be improved. Despite all this, however, the collective process of social policy making in Britain and Sweden has remained open, which is to say that it has retained the potential for future political learning. On the policies we have considered, what have been achieved are settlements rather than solutions. Democratic social politics has failed to provide or convince itself that it has any comprehensive, final answers to the profound issues of human welfare. In this failure may lie its greatest success.

Epilogue: The Rediscovery of Inequality

After the substantial alterations in social insurance following World War II, a general assumption prevailing in Britain and Sweden seemed to be that in some once-and-for-all sense, "the" Welfare State had been created. Social policy had been established on what was widely regarded as a satisfactory basis, and during the late 1940s and 1950s this complacency was reflected in a reduction of partisan clashes on the recently revised social programs. British and Swedish Labor parties—usually the prime sounding-boards of dissatisfaction—had a particular interest in extolling the achievements of policy changes they had introduced when in office in the immediate postwar era. So muted were disagreements on welfare that some foreign observers were led to proclaim an age of consensual politics and decline of ideology.

By the 1970s these easy assurances had been thoroughly unsettled. Politics in both Britain and Sweden, nations usually considered the archetypical models of the welfare state, were again being agitated by the classic questions of poverty and social inquality. Once again economic growth had brought not an abatement but a renewal of interest in social policy expansion; again there had been no cloture in the policy process.

In the buildup to the 1970 general election, for example, the British Labor party's domestic policy proposals returned to the themes of poverty, inequality, and social injustice. Socialists reasserted claims for "a society based on cooperation rather than competition . . . ; a massive reemphasis of our commitment to egalitarian principles . . . ; and positive discrimination to deal with poverty and special categories in need." The new Conservative government implemented its earlier vague appeals for greater selectivity in social benefits with an unexpectedly sweeping version of the negative income tax. Income tax deductions and family allowances would be abolished in favor of a basic tax rate and positive tax credit; those whose credit exceeded their bill would receive automatic cash payments from the government. Although costing at least an extra £1,300,000 and covering that 90 percent of the population in employment or with National Insurance benefits, the plan was presented as only a supplement to, rather than replacement for, most other income maintenance programs. It wisely made no claims to be "the" solution for poverty or social inequality.[1]

In Sweden, the Social Democratic party went further, calling for a deliberate and comprehensive attack on all forms of economic, political, and cultural inequality. As usual in Sweden, a special investigatory body—the Låginkomstutredning (low income investigation) with one of the LO's young antipoverty agitators as secretary—was appointed; but as with the unemployment investigations of the 1920s, investigation and analysis was only a part of the political process and not the final solution to issues arousing fundamentally divergent views. The investigation's work constituted one of the most thorough empirical studies of social inequality ever undertaken in any nation, and its initial finding that almost one-third of the nation's working population lived at or below a relative standard of poverty was only the tip of the controversial results produced before the commission was closed down.[2]

The new evidence emerging at the end of the 1960s suggested that, if anything, the social inequalities in both nations were more intense and persistent than first thought. Britain and Sweden are not in social upheaval but neither is there the self-satisfaction of a decade earlier. Vigorous reformers are dissatisfied with the degree of socioeconomic inequality and with the different ways in which people are treated by the state. To judge from historical experience, it is doubtful if all the hopes of the latest groups of social policy reformers will be realized in practice. By no means is there a consensus on the nature or limits of the social equality and collective provision desired. "Relative" poverty means that there is no foreseeable end to social crusades; a minimum standard defined as relative to changing conditions among the better-off is an elastic yardstick. But believers in an absolute minimum standard of need are also rarely found in agreement on what (or whose) standard to use and whether or how to adjust it through time. And even if the poverty minimum is agreed to be either relative or absolute, the far more difficult problem remains in affluent societies of deciding how to treat inequalities and differentials above that minimum. Those condemning any redistributive intervention and those insisting on nothing less than complete uniformity in personal conditions have at

1. See the Labor party's policy document, *Labour's Social Strategy*; and the Conservative government's Green Paper, "Proposals for a Tax-Credit System," Cmnd. 5116, 1972.
2. SOU 39 (1971).

least the advantage of simplicity. Other observers face the familiar problems of conflict, ambiguity, and puzzlement in modern social politics.

Social policies in British and Swedish welfare states are easy targets to advocates of both more and less radical change. Unemployment benefits, old age pensions, superannuation, and a host of other state activities quite possibly have failed to do more than compensate for problems created by modern industrial society; no one can claim they have directly forestalled the causes of income insecurity. These policies may have generated, or at least exposed, as many new problems as they have ever helped to solve. They have never offered a fundamental transformation either forward to a hoped-for society or backward to a cherished old society. It is proper that the social policies already won should be exposed to and made to answer these and other criticisms, for each criticism, well and persuasively made, may itself become a contribution to the ongoing mosaic of policy adaptation. Indeed, we have observed at length that it is precisely those bringing salient criticisms to bear on inherited policy who can be expected to make the major mark on future policy development.

Dissatisfactions with specific results should not, however, be allowed to obscure the essential service performed by the societal process of policy adaptation itself. No one has come up with ideas for social policy that can win general and permanent assent. Tensions between the logic of economics and the logic of sociology are inevitable. The former emphasizes relationships of exchange, individual wants, and pecuniary transaction; the latter concentrates on unilateral transfer, collective needs, and affective ties. Economics is the realm of marginal calculations, division of labor, and tradeoffs amid limited resources; sociology usually deals in holistic values, the integration of subunits, and intrinsic qualities. Economics is concerned with the marketplace equality of opportunity, sociology with the community equity of results. Or putting such questions within the terms of this study, if the market results in income inequalities, how far shall state pensions allow these inequalities to continue into old age? What should be the relation between economic pressures for employment on the one hand and collective support in unemployment or in the search for a more personally satisfying job on the other? Where shall we fix the balance between income from the economic market and income from social provision? Obviously there are and have been no clear answers to such questions. It is politics that mediates these claims of economic and social perspectives. Political interaction does so not only by serving as a battleground on which the assembled hosts of policy makers carry out tests of strength but also as the playing field on which men learn to adapt their collective responses to uncertain, if not intractable, puzzles.

In both Britain and Sweden, notice has been served that the social politics of the 1970s will not necessarily be a bland, consensual slumber where nothing really changes. On all sides it is increasingly fashionable to point out that the welfare state has not made us happy, to lament the state's inability to "do good," and to deprecate the possibilities of an ethical or emotional attachment to what is only a super-insurance company on a national basis. But no one familiar with the course of past policy development should be tempted to identify old programs with the full meaning of social policy. If the modern welfare state is now only a patched and refurbished liberal social insurance state, an affluent gloss on what H. G. Wells once called "copious, low-grade living," there is no reason this must inevitably remain the content of social policy for all time. Quite the opposite. All the evidence suggests that politics is likely to continue as the agent of substantive policy adjustment at the hands of those with a commitment to knowledgeable action.

Works Cited

1. Government Papers

Great Britain

CABINET AND TREASURY, Public Record Office

Cabinet Office, Minutes series 23, "Civil Disorders," volume 15, 1919.
Cabinet Office, Minutes series 23, "Trade Facilities Act," volume 27, 1919.
Cabinet Office, Minutes series 23, "Economies in Public Spending," volume 47, 1931.
Cabinet Office, Memoranda series 24, "Old Age Pensions," volume 52, 1919.
Cabinet Office, Memoranda series 24, "Out of Work Donations," volume 88, 1919.
Cabinet Office, Photographic Copies of Cabinet Papers series 37, "Old Age Pensions," volume 51, 1899 (cited as Cab. 37/51, etc.)
Cabinet Office, Photographic Copies of Cabinet Papers series 37, "Old Age Pensions," volumes 89, 90, 92, 96; 1908.
Cabinet Office, Registered Files series 21, "Conclusions of the Labour Government and the National Government," volume 349, 1931.
Treasury Papers, Chancellor of the Exchequer's Office series 171, "Budget and Finance Bill Papers," volume 287, 1931 (cited as T.171/287).
Treasury Papers, Chancellor of the Exchequer's Office series 172, "Miscellaneous Papers," volume 1684, 1930.
Treasury Papers, Chancellor of the Exchequer's Office series 172, "Miscellaneous Papers," volume 1790, 1932.
Treasury Papers, Hopkins papers series 175, "National Expenditure," volume 114, 1939.

PARLIAMENTARY DEBATES

Parliamentary Debates, 4th series, vol. 22, April 4, 1894.
Parliamentary Debates, 4th series, vol. 62, July 18, 1898.
Parliamentary Debates, 4th series, vol. 69, April 13, 1899.
Parliamentary Debates, 4th series, vol. 70, April 24, 1899.
Parliamentary Debates (Commons), fifth series, vol. 25, May 4, 1911.
Parliamentary Debates (Commons), fifth series, vol. 26, May 25, 29, 1911.
Parliamentary Debates (Commons), fifth series, vol. 30, November 2, 1911.

Parliamentary Debates (Commons), fifth series, vol. 32, December 6, 1911.
Parliamentary Debates (Commons), fifth series, vol. 123, December 19, 1919.
Parliamentary Debates (Commons), fifth series, vol. 138, February 24, 1921.
Parliamentary Debates (Commons), fifth series, vol. 141, May 11, 1921.
Parliamentary Debates (Commons), fifth series, vol. 147, October 26, 1921.
Parliamentary Debates (Commons), fifth series, vol. 152, April 4, 1922.
Parliamentary Debates (Commons), fifth series, vol. 160, February 21, 1923.
Parliamentary Debates (Commons), fifth series, vol. 167, August 1, 1923.
Parliamentary Debates (Commons), fifth series, vol. 173, May 20, 22, 1924.
Parliamentary Debates (Commons), fifth series, vol. 174, May 29, 1924.
Parliamentary Debates (Commons), fifth series, vol. 175, June 25, 1924.
Parliamentary Debates (Commons), fifth series, vol. 176, July 30, 1924.
Parliamentary Debates (Commons), fifth series, vol. 184, May 18, 1925.
Parliamentary Debates (Commons), fifth series, vol. 418, February 6, 1946.
Parliamentary Debates (Commons), fifth series, vol. 486, April 26, 1951.
Parliamentary Debates (Commons), fifth series, vol. 794, January 19, 1970.
Parliamentary Debates (Lords), fifth series, vol. 212, December 4, 1958.

PARLIAMENTARY PAPERS (The following classification of command papers is modeled on the tabulation of volume numbers and command paper numbers in Edward Di Roma and Joseph Rosenthal, *A Numerical Finding List of British Command Papers Published 1833–1961/62.* New York: New York Public Library, 1967.)

P.P. 1874, vol. 23. "Fourth Report of the Commissioners Appointed to Inquire Into Friendly and Benefit Societies." C. 961.
P.P. 1887, vol. 11. "Report of the Select Committee on National Provident Insurance."
P.P. 1893, vol. 82, "Report on Agencies and Methods for Dealing with the Unemployed." C. 7182.
P.P. 1895, vol. 14. "Reports from Commissioners, Inspectors, and Others on the Aged Poor." C. 7684.
P.P. 1909, vol. 37. "Report of the Royal Commission on the Poor Law and Relief of Distress," together with "Separate [Minority] Report," pp. 719 ff. Cd. 4499.
P.P. 1911, vol. 73. "Tables Showing the Rules and Expenditure of Trade Unions in Respect of Unemployed Benefits." Cd. 5703.
P.P. 1913, vol. 36. "First Report of the Board of Trade Under Part II of the National Insurance Act." Cd. 6965.
P.P. 1916, vol. 23. "Treasury Scheme for the Award of Additional Allowances to Old Age Pensioners." Cd. 8373.
P.P. 1919, vol. 27. "Report of the Departmental Committee on Old Age

Pensions." Cmd. 410

P.P. 1919, vol. 27. "Appendix to the Report, Including the Evidence." Cmd. 411.

P.P. 1928–29, vol. 16. "Memoranda on Certain Proposals Relating to Unemployment Insurance." Cmd. 3331.

P.P. 1930–31, vol. 32. "Twentieth Abstract of Labour Statistics." Cmd. 3831.

P.P. 1931–32, vol. 13. "Final Report of the Royal Commission on Unemployment Insurance." Cmd. 4185.

P.P. 1942–43, vol. 6. "Report of Sir William Beveridge on Social Insurance and Allied Services." Cmd. 6404.

P.P. 1942–43, vol. 6. "Appendix G, Memoranda from Organisations." Cmd. 6405.

P.P. 1943–44, vol. 8. "Statement of Government Policy for the Creation and Maintenance of Full Employment." Cmd. 6527.

P.P. 1945–46, vol. 13. "Report by the Government Actuary on the Financial Provisions of the National Insurance Bill." Cmd. 6730.

P.P. 1950–51, vol. 16. "Report by the Government Actuary on the Financial Provisions of the National Insurance Bill." Cmd. 8212.

P.P. 1954–55, vol. 6· "Report by the Government Actuary on the Financial Provisions of the National Insurance Bill." Cmd. 9332.

P.P. 1954–55, vol. 6. "Report of the Committee on the Economic and Financial Problems of the Provision for Old Age." Cmd. 9333.

P.P. 1957–58, vol. 15. "Report by the Government Actuary on the Financial Provisions of the National Insurance Bill." Cmnd. 294.

P.P. 1957–58, vol. 24. "Provision for Old Age: The Future Development of the National Insurance Scheme." Cmnd. 538.

P.P. 1962–63, vol. 11. "Report of the Committee on Higher Education." Cmnd. 2154.

P.P. 1968–69, n.v. "National Superannuation and Social Insurance." Cmnd. 3883.

P.P. 1970–71, n.v. "Strategy for Pensions." Cmnd. 4755.

P.P. 1972–73, n.v. "Proposals for a Tax-Credit System." Cmnd. 5116.

MISCELLANEOUS DEPARTMENTAL REPORTS

Conditions Favourable to Faster Economic Growth, National Economic Development Council, 1963.

The National Plan, Department of Economic Productivity, 1965.

People and Jobs, Department of Employment, 1971.

Report of the Central Advisory Council for Education, England, Ministry of Education, 1959.

Report of the Departmental Committee on Unemployment Insurance, Ministry of Labour, 1927.

Sweden

ARBETSMARKNADSKOMMISSIONENS VERKSAMHETSBERÄTTELSER,   Arbetsmark-nadskommission, 1941–present.

BIHANG TILL RIKSDAGENS PROTOKOLL

Andra kammaren tillfälliga utskott nr. 2, Utlåtande nr. 5, 1882.
Andra kammaren tillfälliga utskott, nr. 5, Utlåtande nr. 24, 1905.
Andra kammaren tillfälliga utskott, nr. 1, Utlåtande nr. 25, 1909.
Andra lagutskott, Utlåtande nr. 7, 1944.
Andra lagutskott, Utlåtande nr. 30, 1956.
Första kammaren tillfälliga utskott nr. 1, Utlåtande nr. 26, 1909.
Första kammaren tillfälliga utskott nr. 1, Utlåtande nr. 24, 1910.
Kungl. Maj:ts. proposition nr. 126, 1913.
Kungl. Maj:ts. propostion nr. 279, 1914.
Kungl. Maj:ts. proposition nr. 59, 1920.
Kungl. Maj:ts. proposition nr. 284, 1921.
Kungl. Maj:ts. proposition nr. 109, 1926.
Kungl. Maj:ts. proposition nr. 209, 1933.
Kungl. Maj:ts, proposition nr. 217, 1935.
Kungl. Maj:ts. proposition nr. 15, 1937.
Kungl. Maj:ts. proposition nr. 301, 1944.
Kungl. Maj:ts. proposition nr. 246, 1946.
Kungl. Maj:ts. proposition nr. 166, 1953.
Kungl. Maj:ts. proposition nr. 52, 1966.
Motioner i andra kammaren, nr. 76, 1882.
Motioner i andra kammaren, nr. 11, 1884.
Motioner i andra kammaren, nr. 152, 1900.
Motioner i andra kammaren, nr. 32, 1908.
Motioner i andra kammaren, nr. 193, 1909.
Motioner i andra kammaren, nr. 185, 1910.
Motioner i andra kammaren, nr. 276, 1924.
Motioner i andra kammaren, nr. 129, 229, 294; 1928.
Motioner i andra kammaren, nr. 54, 1929.
Motioner i andra kammaren, nr. 119, 1930.
Motioner i andra kammaren, nr. 209, 211, 212, 216; 1933.
Motioner i andra kammaren, nr. 956, 724; 1964.
Motioner i andra kammaren, nr. 296, 1966.
Motioner i första kammaren, nr. 123, 1924.
Motioner i första kammaren, nr. 169, 1928.

Motioner i första kammaren, nr. 108, 1929.
Motioner i första kammaren, nr. 133, 1931.
Motioner i första kammaren, nr. 188, 1932.
Motioner i första kammaren, nr. 77, 596; 1964.
Motioner i första kammaren, nr. 141, 227; 1966.
Motioner i första kammaren, nr. 635, 767; 1967.

HISTORISK STATISTIK FÖR SVERIGE, Statistiska Centralbyrån, 1955.

RIKSDAGENS PROTOKOLL

Andra kammaren, March 22, 1882.
Andra kammaren, April 27, 1895.
Andra kammaren, May 2, 1898.
Andra kammaren, April 27, 1905.
Andra kammaren, April 2, 1913.
Andra kammaren, May 21, 1913.
Andra kammaren, April 1, 1909.
Andra kammaren, June 3, 1919.
Andra kammaren, March 4, 1921.
Andra kammaren, March 15, 1921.
Andra kammaren, April 14, 1924.
Andra kammaren, March 2, 1929.
Andra kammaren, May 16, 1931.
Andra kammaren, February 17, 1932.
Andra kammaren, May 30, 1934.
Andra kammaren, November 20, 1946.
Andra kammaren, January 19, 1956.
Andra kammaren, May 26, 1956.
Andra kammaren, May 13, 1958.
Andra kammaren, February 1, 1967.
Första kammaren, April 18, 1891.
Första kammaren, April 27, 1895.
Första kammaren, May 21, 1913.
Första kammaren, March 2, 1929.
Första kammaren, May 13, 1931.
Första kammaren, February 17, 1932.
Första kammaren, June 20, 1933.
Första kammaren, June 21, 1941.
Första kammaren, April 29, 1953.

STATENS OFFENTLIGA UTREDNINGAR (unnumbered series)

"Ålderdomsförsäkringskommitten betänkande och förslag angående allmän pensionsförsäkring." Civildepartmentet, 1912.

"Arbetareförsäkringskommittens betänkande." Civildepartmentet, 1889.
"Fattigvårdskommittee betänkande angående fattigvården i riket." Fattigvårdkommittee, 1837.
"Nya arbetareförsäkringskommittens betänkande." Civildepartmentet, 1893.
"Promemoria angående arbetslöshetsförsäkring." Riksförsäkringsantalten, 1907.

STATENS OFFENTLIGA UTREDNINGAR (numbered series)

SOU 1922, vol. 59. "Betänkande och förslag angående offentlig arbetsförmedling och statsbidrag till arbetslöshetskassor." Socialförsäkringskommitten.
SOU 1925, vol. 8. "Betänkande med utredning och förslag angående socialförsäkringens organisation." Statens besparingskommittee.
SOU 1928, vol. 9. "Betänkande och förslag angående arbetsloshetsförsakring, arbetsförmedling och reservarbeten." 1926 års Arbetslöshetssakkunniga.
SOU 1932, vol. 36. "1928 års pensionsförsåkringskommittee och organisations-sakkuniga, statistiska undersökningar." Socialdepartmentet.
SOU 1935, vol. 62. "Utredning med förslag rör dyrortsgraderade folkpensioner." Socialdepartmentet.
SOU 1936, vol. 32. "Svensk Arbetslöshetspolitik åren 1914–1935." Socialdepartmentet.
SOU 1945, vol. 46. "Utredning och förslag angående lag om folkpensionering." Socialvårdskommittens betänkande 11.
SOU 1948, vol. 39. "Utredning och förslag angående lag om obligatorisk arbetslöshetsförsäkring. Socialvårdskommittens betänkande 16.
SOU 1950, vol. 33. "Allmän pensionsförsäkring." Handelsdepartmentets pensionsutredningen.
SOU 1955, vol. 32. "Allmän pensionförsäkring." Handelsdepartmentets pensionsutredningen.
SOU 1957, vol. 16. "Remissyttranden." Socialdepartmentet.
SOU 1958, vol. 4. "Promemoria med förslag om fondforvaltning." Socialdepartmentets 1957 års pensionskommittee.
SOU 1963, vol. 40. "Arbetslöshetsförsäkringen." 1960 års Arbetslöshets_försäkringsutredning.
SOU 1965, vol. 9. "Arbetsmarknadspolitik." 1960 års Arbetsmarknadsutredning.
SOU 1971, vol. 39. "Den svenska köpkraftsfördelningen 1967." Låginkomstutredningen.
SOU 1971, vols. 42, 43, 44. "KSA-utredningens betänkande." Inrikesdepartmentet.

STATSRÅD PROTOKOLL ÖVER CIVIL ÄRENDEN, Riksarkivet, October-November 1911; January-February 1914.

2. BOOKS

Abstract of British Historical Statistics. Cambridge: Cambridge University Press, 1962.

Anderson, Ivar. *Otto Järte-en man för sig.* Stockholm: Bonnier, 1965.

Andersson, Gustaf. *Från bondetåget till samlingsregeringen.* Stockholm: Tiden, 1955.

Arbetsmarknadsstyrelsen. *Arbetsmarknadspolitik i tillampning.* Stockholm: Prisma, 1967.

Aristotle. *Politics, Book III.* The Works of Aristotle, edited by W. D. Ross. Oxford: Oxford University Press, 1952.

Ashley, Sir William J. *An Introduction to English Economic History and Theory.* Part 2. 2d ed. London: Longmans, Green and Co., 1893.

Bailey, Stephen. *Political Parties in the United States.* Chicago: Rand McNally & Co., 1960.

Barker, Ernest. *The Development of Administration, Conscription, Taxation, Social Services, and Education.* European Civilization: Its Origin and Development, edited by Edward Eyre, vol. 5. Oxford: Oxford University Press, 1930.

Berggren, Hågan, and Nilsson, Gören. *Liberal socialpolitik, 1853–1884.* Uppsala: Almquist and Wicksell, 1965.

Beveridge, William H. *Full Employment in a Free Society.* New York: Norton, 1945.

————. *Power and Influence.* London: Hodder and Stoughton, 1953.

————. *Social Insurance and Allied Services.* New York: Macmillan, 1942.

————. *Unemployment: A Problem of Industry.* London: Longmans, Green and Co., 1930 (originally published 1909).

Blaug, Mark. *Economic Theory in Retrospect.* Homewood, Ill.: Irwin, 1962.

Brady, Robert *Crisis in Britain.* Berkeley and Los Angeles: University of California Press, 1950.

Bruce, Maurice. *The Coming of the Welfare State.* New York: John Day, 1961.

Bullock, Allen. *The Life and Times of Ernest Bevin.* Vol. 1. London: Heinemann, 1960.

Burdick, E., ed. *American Political Behavior.* Glencoe, Ill.: The Free Press, 1959.

Burns, J. M. *The Deadlock of Democracy.* Englewood Cliffs, N. J.: Prentice-Hall, 1963.

Butler, David, and Freeman, J. *British Political Facts, 1900–1960.* London: Macmillan, 1963.

Cairncross, A. K. *Home and Foreign Investment, 1870–1913.* Cambridge: Cambridge University Press, 1953.

Carlsson, A. B. *Den svenska centralförvaltningen, 1521–1809.* Stockholm: Beckmans, 1913.

Carr-Saunders, A. M., and Jones, D. C. *Survey of Social Structure: England and Wales.* Oxford: Clarendon Press, 1913.

Childs, Marquis. *Sweden: The Middle Way.* New ed. New Haven: Yale University Press, 1961.

Churchill, Randolph. *Winston Spencer Churchill.* Vol. 2. London: Heinemann, 1967.

Clokie, H. M., and Robinson, J. W. *Royal Commissions of Inquiry: The Significance of Investigations in British Politics.* Stanford: Stanford University Press, 1937.

Cohen, Joseph. *Social Insurance Unified.* London: P. S. King and Son, 1924.

Comte, Auguste. *A Discourse on the Positive Spirit.* Translated by E. S. Beesley. London: William Reeves, 1903.

Dahl, Robert A. *A Preface to Democratic Theory.* Chicago: University of Chicago Press, 1956.

————, And Lindblom, Charles E. *Politics, Economics, and Welfare.* New York: Harper & Row, 1953.

Deane, Phyllis, and Cole, W. A. *British Economic Growth, 1688–1959.* Cambridge: Cambridge University Press, 1964.

Deutsch, Karl. *The Nerves of Government.* New York: The Free Press, 1963.

Dicey, A. V. *Law and Public Opinion in England.* 2d ed. New York: Macmillan, 1914.

Dow, J. C. R. *The Management of the British Economy, 1945–1960.* Cambridge: Cambridge University Press, 1964.

Downs, Anthony. *An Economic Theory of Democracy.* New York: Harper and Row, 1957.

Durbin, E. F. M. *The Politics of Democratic Socialism.* London: G. Routledge and Sons, 1940.

Durkheim, Emile. *The Division of Labor in Society.* Translated by George Simpson. Glencoe, Ill.: The Free Press, 1947.

Eckstein, Harry, and Apter, David. *Comparative Politics.* New York: The Free Press, 1963.

Eckstein, Otto, ed. *Studies in the Economics of Income Maintenance.* Washington, D. C.: The Brookings Institution, 1967.

Elmér, Åke. *Folkpensioneringen i Sverige.* Lund: C. W. K. Gleerup, 1960.

————. *Från fattigsverige till välfärdstaten.* Stockholm: Aldus, 1965.

Ericsson, Lars, and Hellstrom, Mats, eds. *Valständsklyftor och standardhöjning.* Stockholm: Prisma, 1967.

Fleisher, Wilfrid. *Sweden: The Welfare State.* New York: John Day, 1956.

George, V. *Social Security: Beveridge and After*. London: Routledge and Kegan Paul, 1969.

George, William. *My Brother and I*. London: Eyre and Spottiswoode, 1958.

Gerdner, Gunnar. *Parlamentarismens kris i Sverige vid 1920-talets början*. Stockholm: Almquist and Wicksell, 1954.

Gilbert, Bentley. *British Social Policy, 1914–1939*. London: Batsford, 1970.

———. *The Evolution of National Insurance in Great Britain*. London: Michael Joseph, 1966.

Gordon, Robert A. *The Goal of Full Employment*. New York: Wiley, 1967.

Gordon, T. J. *A Study of Potential Change in Employee Benefits: National and International Patterns*. Vol. 2. Middletown, Conn.: Institute for the Future: Riverview Center, 1969.

Gosden, P. H. J. *The Friendly Societies in England, 1815–1875*. Manchester: Manchester University Press, 1961.

Greenstein, Fred. *The American Party System and the American People*. Englewood Cliffs, N. J.: Prentice-Hall, 1963.

Hancock, Donald. *Sweden: The Politics of Post-Industrial Change*. Hinsdale, Ill.: The Dryden Press, 1972.

———, and Sjoberg, Gideon. *Politics in the Post-Welfare State*. New York: Columbia University Press, 1972.

Hanser, Charles J. *Guide to Decision: The British Commissions*. New York: Bedminister Press, 1965.

———. *Investigatory Commissions: An International View*. Unpublished manuscript, mimeographed, 1970.

Harris, José Chambers. *British Unemployment Policy, 1870–1911*. Ph.D. dissertation, Oxford University, 1970.

Heckscher, Eli. *An Economic History of Sweden*. Cambridge: Harvard University Press, 1963.

———, ed. *Bidrag till Sveriges ekonomiska och sociala historia under och efter världskriget*. Economic and Social History of the World War, Scandinavian series. Stockholm: Norstedt, 1926.

Heckscher, G. *Några drag ur representationsfrågans sociala bakgrund*. Uppsala: Almquist and Wicksell, 1941.

Heilstrom, G. *Adolf Hedin*. Stockholm: Norstedt, 1948.

Hesslen, G. *Det svenska kommitteväsendet intil år 1905*.

Höjer, Karl. *Svensk socialpolitisk historia*. Stockholm: Norstedt, 1952.

———. *Den svenska socialpolitiken*. Stockholm: Norstedt, 1968.

Holmberg, Per. *Arbete och löner i Sverige*. Solna: Raben and Sjogren, 1963.

Höök, Erik. *Den offentliga sektorns expansion*. Stockholm: Almquist and Wicksell, 1962.

House, Mark, and Burrows, Paul. *The Economics of Unemployment Insurance* London: Allen and Unwin, 1969.

Hutchinson, T. W. *Review of Economic Doctrines, 1870–1929.* Oxford: Clarendon Press, 1953.

Inglis, Brian. *Poverty and the Industrial Revolution.* London: Hoddert and Stoughton, 1971.

Jungefelt, Karl. *Löneandelen och den ekonomiska utvecklingen.* Uppsala: Almquist and Wicksell, 1966.

Key, V. O. *The Responsible Electorate.* Cambridge: Harvard University Press, 1966.

Keynes, J. M. *The General Theory of Employment, Interest, and Money.* New York: Harcourt Brace, 1936.

Kihlberg, Leif. *Karl Staaf.* Vol. 2. Stockholm: Bonnier, 1963.

Korpi, Walter. *Fattigvård i välfärden.* Stockholm: Tiden, 1961.

Kuznets, Simon. *Modern Economic Growth.* Studies in Comparative Economics 7. New Haven: Yale University Press, 1966.

Landgren, K. G. *Den nya ekonomien i Sverige: Keynes, Wigforss och Ohlin, 1927–1939.* Stockholm: Nationalekonomiska Institutionen vid Göteborgs Universitet, 1960.

Landsorganisationen. *Fackföreningsrörelsen och den fulla susselsattningen.* Stockholm: Tiden, 1951.

———. *Kongress Protokoll.* Stockholm: mineographed, 1951, 1972.

———. *Samordnad naringspolitik.* Stockholm: Tiden, 1961.

———. *Verksamhetsberättelse.* Stockholm: Tiden, 1921 to present.

Lewin, Leif. *Planhushållningsdebatten.* Stockholm: Almquist and Wicksell, 1967.

Lindeberg, Sven-Ola. *Nödhjälp och samhällsneutraletet.* Lund: Uniskol, Akademisk Avhandling, 1968.

Lipset, S. M. *Political Man.* New York: Doubleday, 1960.

Lock, Karin. *Kreditmarknad och rantepolitik, 1924–1958.* Stockholm: Bonnier, 1961.

Long, Norton. *The Polity.* Chicago: Rand McNally, 1962.

Lowi, Theodore. *The End of Liberalism.* New York: Norton, 1969.

Lubove, Roy, ed. *Social Welfare in Transition.* Pittsburgh: University of Pittsburgh Press, 1966.

Marsh, David C. *The Changing Social Structure of England and Wales, 1871–1961.* London: Routledge and Kegan Paul, 1965.

Marshall, J. D. *The Old Poor Law, 1795–1834: Studies in Economic History.* London: Macmillan, 1968.

Marshall, T. H. *Class, Citizenship and Social Development.* New York: Anchor Books, 1965.

Masterman, L. C. *C. F. G. Masterman.* London: Nicholson and Watson, 1939.

McDonagh, Oliver. *A Pattern of Government Growth, 1800–1860: The Passenger Acts and Their Enforcement.* London: MacGibbon and Kee, 1961.

Medlicott, W.N. *Contemporary England, 1914–1964*. New York: McKay, 1967.

Meijer, Hans. *Kommitteväsendets utveckling, 1905–1954*. Lund: Gleerups, n.d.

Moffrey, R.H. *A Century of Odd Fellowship*. Manchester: G. M. and Board of Directors, 1910.

Molin, Björn. *Tjanstepensionsfrågan*. Göteborg: Akademiförlaget, 1965.

————, and Stromberg, Mansson. *Offentlig förvaltning*. Stockholm: Bonnier, 1971.

Montgomery, Arthur. *Industrialismens genombrott*. Stockholm: Almquist and Wicksell, 1966.

————. *Svensk socialpolitisk under 1800-talet*. Stockholm: Almquist and Wicksell, 1966.

Moore, Barrington, Jr. *The Social Origins of Dictatorship and Democracy*. Boston: Beacon Press, 1966.

Mowat, Charles Loch. *The Charity Organization Society, 1867–1913*. London: Methuen, 1961.

Mundeto, Ingemar. *Trygghet för alla*. Stockholm: Skandia, 1968.

Murie, Allen. *British Postwar Pensions*. Master's thesis, London School of Economics, 1969.

Myrdal, Gunnar. *Beyond the Welfare State*. New Haven: Yale University Press, 1960.

Neumann, Sigmund, ed. *Modern Political Parties*. Chicago: University of Chicago Press, 1956.

Nicholls, Sir George. *A History of the English Poor Law*. London: King and Son, 1898.

Norberg, Rolf and Lena. *Pensionärernas riksorganization och partipolitiken*. Stockholm: Kihlströms, 1966.

Nordström, Gustal H. *Svensk arbetslöshetspolitik, 1914–1933*. Stockholm: Kooperative Förbundets Bokförlag, 1949.

Nyman, Olle. *Svensk parliamentarism, 1932–1936*. Uppsala: Almquist and Wicksell, 1947.

Ohman, Bertil. *Arbetslöshet i svenska historia*. Fil. lic. dissertation, Uppsala University, 1967.

Pechman, Joseph; Aaron, Henry; and Taussig, Michael. *Social Security: Perspectives for Reform*. Washington, D.C.: The Brookings Institution, 1968.

Peltason, J. W., and Burns, J. M. *Functions and Policies of American Government*. 3d ed. New York: Prentice-Hall, 1967.

Phelps Brown, E. H., and Brown Margaret. *A Century of Pay*. London: Macmillan, 1968.

Piven, Frances, and Cloward, Richard. *Regulating the Poor*. New York: Pantheon Books, 1971.

Polanyi, Karl. *The Great Transformation*. Boston: Beacon Press, 1957.

Pryor, Frederick. *Public Expenditure in Capitalist and Communist Nations.* Homewood, Ill.,: Irwin, 1968.

Ranney, Austin, ed. *Political Science and Public Policy.* Chicago: Markham Publishing Co., 1968.

Redford, Emmette. *Democracy and the Administrative State.* New York: Oxford University Press, 1969.

Rimlinger, Gaston V. *Welfare Policy and Industrialization in Europe, America, and Russia.* New York: John Wiley and Sons, 1971.

Robinson, W., ed. *Social Security.* London: Allen and Unwin, 1948.

Rogers, Everett. *Communication of Innovations: A Cross Cultural Approach.* New York: The Free Press, 1971.

Rooke, Patrick. *The Growth of the Social Services.* London: Weidenfeld and Nicholson, Ltd. 1968.

Rotter, J. B. *Social Learning and Clinical Psychology.* Englewood Cliffs, N.J.: Prentice-Hall, 1954.

Rowntree, Seebohm, and Lavers, G. R. *Poverty and the Welfare State.* London: Longmans, 1951.

Samuelsson, Kurt. *Från stormakt till välfärdsstat.* Stockholm: Raben and Sjögren, 1968.

Sayers, R. S. *Financial Policy, 1939–1945.* London: Her Majesty's Stationery Office, 1956.

Schattschneider, E. E. *Politics, Pressures, and the Tariff.* Reprint. Hamden: Archon, 1963 (originally published 1935).

Schumpeter, Joseph. *Capitalism, Socialism, and Democracy.* New York: Harper and Row, 1947.

Schweinitz, Karl de, Jr. *Industrialization and Democracy.* Glencoe, Ill.: The Free Press, 1964.

Simey. T. S. and M. B. *Charles Booth, Social Scientist.* London: Oxford University Press, 1960.

Smellie, K. B. *A Hundred Years of English Government.* London: Duckworth, 1937.

Smith, Paul. *Disraelian Conservatism and Social Reform.* London: Routledge and Kegan Paul, 1967.

Stead, Francis, H. *How Old Age Pensions Began to Be.* London: Methuen, 1909.

Sutherland, Gillian, ed. *Studies in the Growth of Nineteenth Century Government.* London: Routledge and Kegan Paul, 1972.

Svennilson, Ingvar. *Growth and Stagnation in the European Economy.* Geneva: United Nations Economic Commission for Europe, 1954.

Tate, W. E. *The Parish Chest: A Study of the Records of Parochial Administration in England.* 2d ed. Cambridge: Cambridge University Press, 1951.

Thoenas, Piet. *The Elite in the Welfare State.* New York: The Free Press, 1966.

Titmuss, Richard. *Commitment to Welfare.* London: Allen and Unwin, 1968.

————. *Problems of Social Policy*. London: His Majesty's Stationery Office, 1948.

Trevelyan, G. M. *British History in the Nineteenth Century, 1782–1901*. Oxford: Oxford University Press, 1922.

Verney, Douglas. *Parliamentary Reform in Sweden, 1866–1921*. Oxford: Oxford University Press, 1959.

Vernon, R. V. and Mansergh, N. *Advisory Bodies*. London: Allen and Unwin, 1940.

Vinde, Pierre. *Hur Sverige styres*. Stockholm: Prisma, 1968.

Webb, Beatrice. *Our Partnership*. London: Longmans, 1948.

Webb, Beatrice and Sidney. *English Local Government: English Poor Law History*. London: Longmans, 1927–1929.

Wigforss, Ernst. *Minnen*. Vols. 2 and 3. Stockholm: Tiden, 1950, 1954.

Williams, Pat Thane. *The Development of Old Age Pension Policy in Great Britain, 1878–1925*. Ph.D. dissertation, London School of Economics, 1970.

Wilson, Harold. *The Labour Government, 1964–1970*. London: Weidenfeld, and Nicholson, 1971.

Wilson, Trevor. *The Downfall of the Liberal Party, 1914–1935*. London: Collins, 1966.

Woodward, Sir Llewellyn. *The Age of Reform, 1815–1870*. 2d ed. Oxford: Clarendon Press, 1962.

Wraith, R. E., and Lamb, G. B. *Public Inquiries as an Instrument of Government*.

3. ARTICLES AND PAMPHLETS

Abel-Smith, Brian. *The Poor and the Poorest*. Occasional Papers in Social Administration, London: London School of Economics, 1965.

————. *The Reform of Social Security*. London: Fabian Society, 1953.

————, and Townsend, Peter. *New Pensions for Old*. London: Fabian Society, 1955.

Abrams, P. "The Failure of Social Reform: 1918–1920." *Past and Present* 24 (1963).

Angman, Berndt. *Socialist Theory or Welfare State Reality: Ideological Conflict within the Social Democratic Workers Party of Sweden 1932–1940*. Maryville, Mo.: Northwest Missouri State College Studies, 1960.

Auteri, Oskari. *Arbetslöshetsförsäkringen i utlandet*. Helsingfors: n.p. 1909.

Beales, H. L. *The Making of Social Policy*. L. T. Hobhouse Memorial Trust Lecture. Oxford: Oxford University Press, 1946.

Beveridge, William. *Insurance for All and Everything*. London: Daily News, Ltd., 1924.

————. "Labor Exchanges and the Unemployed." *Economic Journal*, 17(1907).

————. "Unemployment Insurance in the War and After," in *War and*

Insurance, edited by Sir Norman Hill, Economic and Social History of the World War, British series. London: Milford, 1917.

Bjurling, Oscar. "The Baron's Revolution." *Economy and History* 2 (1959).

Booth, Charles. "Enumeration and Classification of Paupers, and State Pensions for the Aged." *Journal of the Royal Statistical Society* Series A, 54 (1891).

Boulding, Kenneth. "The Boundaries of Social Policy." *Social Work* 12 (1967).

Briggs, Asa. "The Welfare State in Historical Perspective." *Archives Europeennes de Sociologie* 2 (1961).

Burnham, Walter Dean. "Some Relationships between Electoral Politics and Policy Outputs in the United States." Mimeographed. Boston: Massachusetts Institute of Technology, 1971.

Carlsson, Sten. "Folkhemspolitiken." In *Den svenska historien*, vol. 10, edited by Gunvor Grenholm. Stockholm: Bonnier, 1968.

Centralförbundet för Socialt Arbete. *Berättelse ofver förhandingarna vid kongressen för fattigvård*. Stockholm: n.p., 1907.

———. *Reformslinjer för svensk fattigvårdlagstifting*. Stockholm: Ekmans, 1910.

Clark, George Kitson. *The Making of Victorian England*. Cambridge, Mass.: Harvard University Press, 1962.

Elmér, Åke. "Den raabska pensionsaktionen: en utomparlamentarisk opinionsrorelse." *Sociala Meddelanden*, Spring 1957.

Emy, H. V. "The Impact of Financial Policy on English Party Politics before 1914." *Historical Journal* 15 (1972).

Erici, Bernt. "A-försäkring." *Tidskrift för allmän försäkring* 8 (1968).

Fenton, John, and Chamberlayne, Donald. "The Literature Dealing with the Relationships between Political Processes, Socio-economic Conditions, and Public Politics in the American States." *Polity* 1 (1969).

Fisher, Paul. "Minimum Old Age Pensions." *International Labour Review* 102 (1970).

Fry, Brian, and Winters, Richard. "The Politics of Redistribution." *American Political Science Review* 64 (1970).

Gilbert, Bentley. "Winston Churchill versus the Webbs: The Origins of British Unemployment Insurance." *American Historical Review* 71 (1966).

Gurnec, Herbert. "Group Learning." *Psychological Monographs: General and Applied*, edited by Norman Munn, 76 (1962).

Hancock, K. "Unemployment and the Economists in the 1920's." *Economica* 27 (1960).

Hagnell, Hans. "Medinflytands ockso genom vara pengar." *Fackföreningsrörelsen* 65 (1965).

———. "Varför satter regeringen våra företrag i strykklass." *Metallarbetaren*, no. 46 (1966).

Hansson-Preusler, K. "Den kommunala fattigvården i arbete." *In Hundra År under Kommunal forvaltningarna, 1862–1962*, edited by Sven Ulric Palme. Stockholm: Godvil, 1962.

Heclo, Hugh. "Review Article: Policy Analysis." *British Journal of Political Science* 2 (1972).

———. "A-försäkringens utveckling i Sverige." *Tidskrift för allmän försäkring* 9 (1969).

Holmberg, Per. "Valet och ideerna." *Aftonbladet*, September 30, 1966.

Hoshino, G. "Britain's Debate on Universal or Selective Social Services: Lessons for America." *Social Service Review* 43 (1969).

Huss, Gunnar. *Arbetslöshets och arbetslöshetsförsäkring*. Uppsala: Föreningen Helmdals Småskrifter, 1908.

Kellgren, Nils. "Regera! För Guds skill regera." *Aktuellt* 16 (1966).

Labour Party. *Labour's Social Strategy*. London: Transport House, 1969.

———. *National Superannuation*. London: Transport House, 1957.

Life Offices Association. *The Pensions Problem*. Mimeographed. London, September 1957.

Long, Norton. "Power and Administration." *Public Administration Review* 9 (1949).

Macleod, Roy. *Treasury Control and Social Administration*. Occasional Papers in Social Administration. London: London School of Economics, 1968.

Marshall, T. H. "Value Problems of Welfare Capitalism." *Journal of Social Policy* 1 (1972).

———. "The Welfare State: A Sociological Interpretation." *Archives Europeennes de Sociologie* 2 (1961).

Marwick, Arthur. "The Labor Party and the Welfare State in Britain, 1900–1948." *American Historical Review* 73 (1967).

McGregor, O. K. "Social Research and Social Policy in the 19th Century." *British Journal of Sociology* 8 (1957).

Meidner, Rudolf. "The Research Department of the Swedish Confederation of the Trade Unions." *Skandinaviska Banken Quarterly Review* 39 (1958).

Mukherjee, Santosh. *Making Labour Markets Work—A Comparison of the U.K. and Swedish Systems*. PEP broadsheet 532. London: Political and Economic Planning, 1972.

Paukert, Felix. "Social Security and Income Redistribution: A Comparative Study." *International Labour Review* 98 (1968).

Perrin, Guy. "50 Years of Social Security." *International Labour Review* 99 (1969).

Phelps Brown, E. H., and Hopkins, S. V. "Seven Centuries of Builders' Wage Rates." *Economica* 23 (1956).

Rehn, Gosta. "Arbetsmarknad politik som samhällside." *Femton År med Tage Erlander*, edited by Olle Svensson. Stockholm: Tiden, 1961.

———. "Economisk politik vid full susselsättning." *Tiden* 40 (1948).

Reviglio, Franco. "The Social Security Sector and Its Financing in Developing Countries." *International Monetary Fund Staff Papers* 14 (1967).

Rose, Richard. "The Variability of Party Government." *Political Studies* 17 (1969).

Scase, Richard. "Industrial Man: A Reassessment with English and Swedish Data." *British Journal of Sociology* 23 (1972).

Simey, T. S. "Social Investigations: Past Achievements and Present Difficulties." *British Journal of Sociology* 8 (1957).

Sköld, Lar, and Halvarson, Arne. "Riksdagens sociala sammansättning under hundra är." In *Samhalle och Riksdag*, Vol. 1, edited by Arthur Thomson. Uppsala: Almquist and Wicksell, 1966.

Socialdemokratiska Arbetareparti. *Arbetslöshetsförsäkringen, jämte andra sociala försäkringar.* Stockholm: Cooperative förbundet, 1926.

———. *Jämlikhet, Första Rapport från SAP-LO's Arbetsgrupp för Jämlikhetsfrågor* Stockholm: AB Grafisk Press, 1969.

———. *Protokolle.* Stockholm: reproduced, 1932.

———. *Vad vi Vilja, en Socialdemokratisk appell till väljarna.* Stockholm: Cooperative förbundet, 1924.

Svenska Försäkringsbolags Riksförbund. *Sweden, Its Private Insurance.* Stockholm: Försäkringsbolags Riksförbund, 1963.

Taira, Koji, and Kilby, Peter. "Differences in Social Security Development in Selected Countries." *International Social Security Review* 2 (1969).

Townsend, Peter, and Wedderbern, Dorothy. *The Aged in the Welfare State.* Occasional Papers in Social Administration. London: London School of Economics, 1960.

Wigforss, Ernst. "Arbetslöner, kristid, och kapitalbildning." *Tiden* 16 (1924).

———. "Demokratiska problem." *Tiden* 12 (1920).

———. "Oening Sakkunskap." *Tiden* 20 (1929).

———. "Professor Cassel och socialismen." *Tiden* 21 (1929).

———. "Spararen slösaren, och den arbetslose." *Tiden* 20 (1928).

Index

348 INDEX

Yale Studies in Political Science